ONE WEEK L

Retributivism Has a Past

STUDIES IN PENAL THEORY AND PHILOSOPHY

R. A. Duff and Michael Tonry, General Editors

Retributivism Has a Past
Has It a Future?
Edited by Michael Tonry

RETRIBUTIVISM HAS A PAST

Has It a Future?

Edited by Michael Tonry

OXFORD
UNIVERSITY PRESS

OXFORD
UNIVERSITY PRESS

Oxford University Press, Inc., publishes works that further
Oxford University's objective of excellence
in research, scholarship, and education.

Oxford New York
Auckland   Cape Town   Dar es Salaam   Hong Kong   Karachi
Kuala Lumpur   Madrid   Melbourne   Mexico City   Nairobi
New Delhi   Shanghai   Taipei   Toronto

With offices in
Argentina   Austria   Brazil   Chile   Czech Republic   France   Greece
Guatemala   Hungary   Italy   Japan   Poland   Portugal   Singapore
South Korea   Switzerland   Thailand   Turkey   Ukraine   Vietnam

Published by Oxford University Press, Inc.
198 Madison Avenue, New York, New York 10016

www.oup.com

Oxford is a registered trademark of Oxford University Press

Library of Congress Cataloging-in-Publication Data
Retributivism has a past : has it a future? / edited by Michael Tonry.
    p.   cm. — (Studies in penal theory and philosophy)
Includes bibliographical references and index.
ISBN 978-0-19-979827-8 (cloth : alk. paper) 1. Punishment—Philosophy. 2. Retribution. I. Tonry, Michael H.
K5101.R48   2011
364.601—dc22   2011010275

1 3 5 7 9 8 6 4 2

Printed in the United States of America
on acid-free paper

CONTENTS

Preface   *vii*
Contributors   *xi*

1. Can Twenty-first Century Punishment Policies Be Justified in Principle?   3
   Michael Tonry

2. Is Twenty-first Century Punishment Post-desert?   30
   Matt Matravers

3. What Does Wrongdoing Deserve?   46
   John Kleinig

4. Responsibility, Restoration, and Retribution   63
   R. A. Duff

5. Punishment and Desert-adjusted Utilitarianism   86
   Jesper Ryberg

6. The Future of State Punishment: The Role of Public Opinion in
   Sentencing   101
   Julian V. Roberts

7. A Political Theory of Imprisonment for Public Protection   130
   Peter Ramsay

8. Terror as a Theory of Punishment   155
   Alice Ristroph

9. Can Above-desert Penalties Be Justified by Competing Deontological
   Theories?   169
   Richard S. Frase

10. Never Mind the Pain, It's a Measure! Justifying Measures as Part of the Dutch
    Bifurcated System of Sanctions   188
    Jan W. de Keijser

11. Retributivism, Proportionality, and the Challenge of the Drug Court
    Movement   214
    Douglas Husak

12. Drug Treatment Courts as Communicative Punishment   *234*
    Michael M. O'Hear

13. Punishment Futures: The Desert-model Debate and
    the Importance of the Criminal Law Context   *256*
    Andreas von Hirsch

Index   275

PREFACE

For most of the past two centuries, normative theories about punishment bore close relation to punishment in practice. Most practitioners and theorists believed that crime prevention is the primary purpose of punishment, that rehabilitation, incapacitation, and deterrence are the paramount aims of sentencing, and that pursuit of those aims required that sentencing be highly individualized.

In the mid-1970s, things changed. Rehabilitative ideas and individualized sentencing fell from favor. Most theorists emphasized retribution, "just deserts," or proportionality. Sentencing systems in the United States, and a bit later in England and Wales, were changed to deemphasize or reject rehabilitation and crime prevention as primary aims and to apportion punishments to offenders' culpability and the gravity of their offenses. Retributivist ideas appeared to have taken over, and it appeared possible they would reign unchallenged for many years.

That did not happen. American policy makers and practitioners, after a decade of experimentation with statutory sentencing systems and sentencing guidelines premised on ideas about consistency and proportionality, soon rejected those ideas in substance. Some policy entrepreneurs used retributive-sounding language—"Do the time, do the crime" or "Adult time for adult crime"—but they did not typically mean that punishments should be apportioned in a consistent way to the gravity of offenses and the culpability of offenders. Instead, they meant that offenders should receive whatever punishments policy makers specified, whether or not those sentences respected retributive principles or ideas about proportionality, and whether those policies were adopted for substantive reasons or to demonstrate that politicians were tough on crime. Mandatory minimum sentences, three-strikes-and-you're-out laws, "dangerous offender" and "sexual predator" laws, "truth in sentencing," and life without the possibility of parole were the results.

Other policy makers and many practitioners moved to bring back individualized approaches. Some, taking note of research findings on the effectiveness of drug and correctional treatment programs, established drug courts, new treatment programs, and prisoner reentry programs. Others were influenced by the restorative justice movement and communitarianism; they established programs that sought to heal broken relationships, solve problems, and strengthen communities.

Unlike policy makers and practitioners, people engaged in theorizing about punishment remained focused on retributivism. Few writers tried seriously to engage with new policies and practices. Few efforts were made to develop systematic critiques of new approaches and ideas or to develop principled justifications for them. That is a pity. If philosophers and academic criminal lawyers don't do it, it is unlikely that anyone will. Judges, practicing lawyers, and policy makers have other things to do and seldom moonlight in the theory business.

Life will go on whether or not theorists, policy makers, and practitioners subscribe to common normative beliefs, or actively explore their differences, but the quality of moral and policy discourse will suffer. So will the quality of punishment policies and practices. And so will the relevance of punishment theory and theorists. Many theorists now say of incapacitative or rehabilitative policies, of three-strikes laws and drug courts, simply that they are unjust or unprincipled. Many say that restorative justice initiatives are acceptable in principle only if the dispositions they produce in individual cases are ones a retributivist would approve. Those dismissive reactions do not win friends, catalyze discussion, or enrich understanding. Nor do they illuminate principles on which policies and practices rest or facilitate examination of the normative cases their proponents do or might make for them.

This book is an effort to engage theorists with contemporary policies and practices. It is based on successive versions of papers produced for two conferences convened in the Netherlands in 2008 and 2009 under the auspices of and with funding from the Netherlands Institute for the Study of Crime and Law Enforcement and the Institute on Crime and Public Policy of the University of Minnesota Law School. The writers of the essays in this book and other participants in the meetings include many of the most influential writers on punishment philosophy and theory in the English-speaking countries over the past 40 years, as well as up-and-coming young American, British, Danish, and Netherlands scholars. The aim was neither to condemn nor to justify, but to take new policies and practices seriously and examine them closely. Some writers were asked to argue against belief in an effort to develop principled arguments for innovations with which they disagree.

Inevitably, alas, this book, like most on legal subjects, is parochial, attending, despite the involvement of people from continental Europe, primarily to issues that are prominent in the English-speaking countries. Legal issues tend to be time and place specific. There are significant differences in legal systems and legal cultures among the English-speaking countries. Differences between them and continental Europe are larger. European criminal law in the past 40 years has been much less politicized than in the United States, England and Wales, New Zealand, and parts of Australia and Canada. Laws that challenge traditional normative ideas about punishment—three strikes, life without the possibility of parole, mandatory minimum sentences measured in decades and lifetimes—were not adopted in Europe. Nor were consequentialist ideas as influential before 1970 as they were in the English-speaking countries. They had some influence, but nowhere displaced traditional views about retributive punishment and proportionality in relation to adult offenders. As a result, most countries did not experience dramatic shifts between consequentialist and retributive ideas in the 1970s, and thus have not experienced a strong shift back toward consequentialism. Changes have been evolutionary. Many of the issues discussed in this book are less salient outside the English-speaking countries. That, however, makes them no less important, universal in their implications, or deserving of closer consideration.

Books like this require lots of work. The conferences were attended by the writers and also by Andrew Ashworth, Gerben Bruinsma, Henk Elffers, Jean-Louis van Gelder, Nicole Haas, Nicola Lacey, Erik Luna, and Sandra Marshall. The people just named did not write papers, but through their participation they enriched those that were written. Adepeju Solarin and Ariena van Poppel organized the conferences. Su Smallen oversaw production of this volume. She, 'Peju, and Nick Wunder prepared the manuscripts for publication. John Kleinig a bit cheekily suggested the title; I grabbed it. I am grateful to them all. Readers will decide for themselves whether the final product justifies the effort.

Michael Tonry

CONTRIBUTORS

R. A. Duff is professor of law at the University of Minnesota and professor emeritus in the Department of Philosophy, University of Stirling.

Richard S. Frase is Benjamin N. Berger Professor of Criminal Law at the University of Minnesota.

Douglas Husak is professor of philosophy at Rutgers University.

Jan de Keijser is associate professor of criminology at Leiden University, Institute for Criminal Law and Criminology.

John Kleinig is professor of philosophy in the Department of Criminal Justice at John Jay College of Criminal Justice and professorial fellow in criminal justice ethics, Centre for Applied Philosophy and Public Ethics, Charles Sturt University.

Matt Matravers is professor of political philosophy and director of the Morrell Centre for Toleration and of the School of Politics, Economics, and Philosophy at the University of York.

Michael M. O'Hear is associate dean for research and professor of law at Marquette University Law School.

Peter Ramsay is lecturer in law in the Department of Law at the London School of Economics.

Alice Ristroph is professor of law at Seton Hall University.

Julian V. Roberts is professor of criminology at Oxford University.

Jesper Ryberg is professor of ethics and philosophy of law in the Department of Philosophy and Science Studies at Roskilde University.

Michael Tonry is professor of law and public policy at the University of Minnesota and senior fellow at the Netherlands Institute for the Study of Crime and Law Enforcement, Amsterdam.

Andreas von Hirsch is an honorary professor, law faculty, at the University of Frankfurt, emeritus honorary professor of penal theory and penal law at the University of Cambridge, and honorary fellow at Wolfson College, Cambridge.

Retributivism Has a Past

Can Twenty-first Century Punishment Policies Be Justified in Principle?

MICHAEL TONRY

Retributivism no doubt has a future. The question is whether it will be as a specialized topic in moral and political philosophy, of interest primarily to academic theorists, and principally concerned with institutional justification of punishment, as it was for 150 years before 1970, or as a generally accepted normative framework for understanding, talking, and arguing about punishment policies and practices. For a time, in the 1970s and 1980s, it appeared that retributivism might replace the consequentialist framework that long shaped policies and practices in the English-speaking countries.

That did not happen. By the mid-1990s incapacitative policies such as "dangerous offender" and "sexual predator" laws, deterrent policies such as mandatory minimum sentence and three-strikes laws, and rehabilitative policies such as drug courts and correctional treatment programs had proliferated. Restorative and community justice programs that celebrated case-by-case problem-solving were established in many countries. None of these initiatives was predicated on the retributive premise that responses to crime—if they are to be just—must take account of concerns about horizontal (treat like cases alike) and vertical (treat different cases differently) equity.

Proponents of retributive theories have made little effort to address proportionality-busting policies or expressed much interest in trying to do so. Here is an illustration: "In principle, retributivism can lay out the outer limits for punishment. . . . But beyond this, a retributive conception of proportionality need not have much in the way of precision to say about the particular details of punishment's implementation" (Markel 2010, p. 950).

Nor have proponents of consequentialist theories made much effort, except concerning restorative justice. In any case, consequentialist theories necessarily encompass what Bentham called parsimony—the proposition that no punishment is justifiable if more severe than is necessary to achieve the sought-after consequence. Parsimony for Bentham encompassed two conceptions of proportionality (Frase 2009). Both are predicated on the belief that causing suffering, including to offenders in the name of punishment, is an evil to be avoided. The alternative means test requires that there be no less costly way to achieve the sought-after goal. No punishment may properly be imposed if some approach other than punishment would do as well. The ends-benefits test requires that the pain to victims to be avoided by punishment be greater than the pain the offender would suffer. If not, punishment cannot be justified. Few modern American sentencing initiatives pass either test.

Philosophers and other theorists mostly talk retributivism. In any case, policy makers and practitioners are not listening. That's a pity. In theory, theory ought to matter. What to do?

Two strategies are available. The first is to measure new policies with traditional normative calipers and, if they don't measure up, declare them unprincipled and morally unjustifiable. Having called spades spades, let them fall. The harshest laws—three strikes, lengthy mandatory minimums, life without the possibility of parole (LWOPs), "sexual predator" laws—commonly prescribe prison sentences measured in decades and lifetimes. Drug laws often mandate sentences far longer than many that are imposed on violent and sexual offenders. Some three-strikes laws call for sentences of 25 years to life for property crimes. None of that can be squared with concerns for proportionality or parsimony. The belief is widespread within the theory class that these laws are per se unconscionable and unprincipled, the product not of normative considerations or ethical analysis, but of emotion, cynicism, and political posturing. That may explain why they are seldom the subjects of sustained analysis.

Restorative justice and some treatment programs, notably drug courts, have been discussed by retributive theorists. Typically they are criticized for failing to comport with proportionality requirements, and the proposed way forward is to approve of them (only) to the extent that dispositions in individual cases are consistent with conventional ideas about retributive proportionality (e.g., Robinson 2003 [restorative justice]; Husak 2008, 2011 [drug courts]). That will be a difficult challenge to meet. Restorative justice and treatment programs presuppose that outcomes and dispositions must be individualized to be effective. Restorative and rehabilitative programs will continue, however, whether or not theorists approve of them.

The other way forward is to engage new policies and practices on the merits, identifying their express or implicit normative rationales, assessing them on their own terms, and considering when and whether they can be reconciled with traditional retributive and consequentialist ideas. This is worth doing in its own right. Antony Duff (2001, 2011) has for a decade been showing the way by attempting to reconcile retributive, restorative, and communitarian ideas.

That kind of engagement is not easy. Most of the available theorizing has been around for a long time. Little of it attempts systematically to explore normative arguments for initiatives that appear to be facially incompatible with traditional theories. Arguments, in any case, are easier to carry out when they have at least two sides. Shadowboxing is the alternative. Shadows are not challenging opponents. They don't hit back.

Nineteenth-century theorists had an easier time. Bentham made his disdain for Kant's analyses clear.[1] Kant, and later Hegel, returned the favor.[2] They could disagree publicly because each set out his views in detail in writing. There were two sides to the argument. In our time, it is not easy to find theoretical writing that offers well-developed, principled justifications for new initiatives.

No one offers sustained, normative justifications for three-strikes laws, mandatory minimums, LWOPs, drug courts, or "dangerous offender" laws. People offer political arguments, such as the public wants or is reassured by harsh sentencing laws, or is sympathetic toward drug-dependent offenders, or supports electoral candidates who are tough on crime, and programs should be adopted for those reasons. People offer policy arguments, such as crime will be prevented through the deterrent or incapacitative effects of harsh punishments, or successful treatment will diminish drug abuse and related criminality. Some analysts observe that criminal justice policies are often adopted as much or more for expressive reasons—to reassure a frightened public, to acknowledge public anger or hatred, to demonstrate that *something* is being done—rather than because policy makers believe they will have any effects on crime (e.g., Garland 2001; Freiberg 2007).

England's New Labour government under Prime Minister Tony Blair, for example, made it clear that a major aim of its criminal justice policies was to "restore public confidence" by "rebalancing the system in favour of the victim." Many policies were meant to circumvent traditional procedural and evidentiary protections in order to make it easier to convict offenders and punish them more severely (Tonry 2004, 2010). Promoting the new policies, Blair made his distaste for the values that underlay the justice system clear: "All of these measures . . . have one thing in common: they bypass the traditional way the criminal justice system used to work . . . the rules of the game have changed" (quoted in Morgan 2006, p. 97). He complained: "We are trying to fight twenty-first century crime—antisocial behaviour, drug dealing, binge-drinking, organized crime—with nineteenth-century methods, as if we lived in the time of Dickens" (quoted in Morgan 2006, p. 110). Objections to proposed policies on grounds of procedural fairness, proportionality, or parsimony received short polemical shrift.[3]

Presumably principled arguments can be made for three-strikes laws, LWOPs, New Labour's crime policies, and drug courts. Such arguments would explain why their aims are legitimate for governments to pursue and when, why, and to what extent the interests and autonomy of individual offenders may appropriately be limited or disregarded in order to achieve them. There may be plausible principled arguments for why some shoplifters are imprisoned for decades under three-strikes laws, or why many drug dealers are punished more severely than rapists, but so far they have not been offered. The U.S. Supreme Court has upheld the constitutionality of the application of three-strikes laws to property offenders and the continued confinement of "dangerous offenders" after their prison sentences have expired. The explanations at their root, however, have been nothing more than assertions that legislatures possess constitutional authority to enact such laws.[4] That is a legal, not a normative conclusion, and demonstrates the truism that being legally allowable is not the same thing as being morally justifiable.

Normative analyses of less punitive new initiatives are little richer. Drug and other problem-solving courts and correctional treatment programs raise issues that were well ventilated a generation or two ago, but have largely disappeared from public and scholarly discussion. C. S. Lewis (1949/2011) and Anthony Burgess (1962), for example, challenged the morality of efforts coercively to change offenders in the interest of crime prevention or public protection. Frank Allen (1959, 1964), Kenneth Culp Davis (1969), and Norval Morris (1974) cautioned about the dangers that administrators would misuse their broad powers to individualize treatment. Others warned of the dangers of idiosyncratic and racially biased decision making (e.g., American Friends Service Committee 1971). Few such arguments have been made in our time. The principal issues discussed are instrumental: How good is the evidence about the effectiveness of treatment? How well tailored are programs to offenders' risks and needs? How well are they implemented? Concerns about the morality of their use, and about risks of abuse, are seldom expressed.

It has to be a Good Thing to explore whether and how recent innovations in punishment policies and practices can be justified in principle, in general, and in their application to individual cases. Legislators, judges, and prosecutors have not done that, but that is not the business they are in.

Even if policy makers and practitioners pay little or no attention in the here and now to what theorists argue or conclude, it is better that legal institutions and practices be deconstructed and dissected and the results displayed. Prevailing attitudes change. Policies and practices change. Arguments and analyses that are not influential in one time often become so in another.[5] Changing attitudes concerning racial discrimination and homosexuality provide familiar examples. Patterns of discriminatory and differential treatment that were commonplace a half century ago, and were widely justified, are almost unthinkable now. After attitudes changed, policies that were formerly unthinkable, such as domestic partner and gay marriage laws, were widely adopted. The propositions that black people can be forbidden to eat in restaurants, sleep in hotels, or ride at the front of a bus are unimaginable to people under 40. Examination of policies and practices that damage individuals' lives may demonstrate that they are not worth having. In the longer term, that demonstration may prove influential, even if in the short term blind eyes cannot see or deaf ears hear.

This essay canvasses a wide range of punishment policies and issues that need examination. No doubt the roster of issues is incomplete; it is not easy to survey the subject matter of a literature that scarcely exists. The first section, to set the stage, discusses the evolution and influence of punishment theories over the past two centuries.[6] The second section surveys recent policy initiatives that have been insufficiently examined and identifies issues they raise that deserve scrutiny. The third section identifies subjects theorists might explore if they want more fruitfully to address issues raised by contemporary punishment policies and practices.

I. FROM CONSEQUENTIALISM TO RETRIBUTIVISM AND BACK AGAIN

From early in the nineteenth century until the 1970s, punishment theories, institutions, policies, and practices in the English-speaking countries were based largely on consequentialist ideas.[7] The academic and real worlds lined up nicely. Practitioners and policy makers may not have read Cesare Beccaria (1764), Jeremy Bentham (1830/2008), or Enrico Ferri (1921), or known who they were, but they were in broad agreement with them that the primary purpose of punishment is to minimize harms associated with crime and state responses to it. Most of the institutions that comprise contemporary criminal justice systems—penitentiaries, training schools, reformatories, juvenile courts, probation, parole—were invented in the nineteenth century and premised on the pursuit of that purpose. So were individualized and indeterminate sentencing systems for dealing with adult offenders and the *parens patrie* rationale that underlies the juvenile court (Platt 1969; Rothman 1971; Mennel 1983).

Near the end of that 150-year period, the *Model Penal Code* (1962) laid out a blueprint for the mother of all consequentialist punishment systems.[8] Offenses were defined broadly and were categorized only into misdemeanors and three levels of felonies. Precise delineation of the seriousness of crimes was considered unimportant and unnecessary. The only important question was whether the defendant was guilty. Once that was determined, the judge was given broad discretion to decide what sentence to impose. Probation was available for any offense, including murder. If the judge believed that the sentences authorized for a crime were too severe, he or she could sentence the offender as if he had been convicted of something less serious. If a prison sentence was ordered, the parole board decided when the prisoner was released. The prison authorities could award and withdraw time off for good behavior. Consistent with the utilitarian principle of parsimony, presumptions were created to ensure that offenders were not punished more severely than was necessary: judges were directed not to send people to prison, and parole boards were directed to release inmates when first they became eligible, unless specified conditions existed to justify some other decision. Allusions to retributive ideas appear only three times, and faintly. Nonincarcerative penalties should not be imposed or inmates released on parole if doing so would "unduly depreciate the seriousness of the offense." One of the overall purposes of the code was to ensure that disproportionately severe punishments were not imposed.

Stop for a minute and think about that: Retributive ideas were almost absent from the most influential American criminal law document of the twentieth century. The code was developed under the aegis of the American Law Institute, then and now the most prestigious law reform organization in the United States. Lawyers then could not, and now cannot, simply join the institute. They must be nominated by current members and approved by a membership committee; membership is widely considered a great honor, the capstone of a successful career, and limited to people of great accomplishment. The code was developed over a 13-year period by a group of influential practitioners, including judges, prison commissioners, prosecutors, parole board heads, and defense lawyers. Work was directed by Herbert Wechsler, the century's leading academic criminal lawyer. Draft versions of sections were successively considered—and provisionally and then finally approved—at annual meetings of the American Law Institute. The voters were not primarily criminal lawyers or academics, but mostly commercial and business lawyers and federal and state judges. The *Model Penal Code* was drafted and approved by people who were neither radicals nor woolly-headed intellectuals. They were the most establishmentarian lawyers midcentury America had to offer, together with a group of leading criminal justice practitioners, and they did not believe that retributivism and proportionality should be central considerations in sentencing.

In our time, in contrast, retributive ideas seem an inherent part of thinking about crime and punishment, even if they have had little recent influence on policy except in the vindictive sense that policy makers have generally preferred harsher punishments to milder ones. Social and experimental psychologists instruct that human beings are hardwired to react punitively to crime (Darley 2010). Evolutionary psychologists explain that natural selection has favored human beings with that hard wiring. Individuals with clear senses of right and wrong and a willingness to act on them, it is said, are better community members, fostering cohesion, increasing the odds of community survival, and perpetuating the gene pool that predisposed people to be retributive (Robinson, Kurzban, and Jones 2007). Some influential philosophers of criminal law argue that those punitive intuitions justify retributive punishment theories (e.g., Moore 1993).

If retributive ideas and instincts are so common, how can it be that they had so little influence on the *Model Penal Code*? The answer is that right-thinking people in the 1950s and 1960s believed that retributivism was atavistic. Conventional wisdom and intuition can be morally or ethically wrong, as widely held beliefs about racial inferiority, homosexuality, and gender roles in earlier times demonstrate. That is what our midcentury predecessors believed about retributive instincts. They were wrong. Herbert Wechsler and his mentor Jerome Michael observed that retribution may represent "the unstudied belief of most men" but concluded, "no legal provision can be justified merely because it calls for the punishment of the morally guilty by penalties proportioned to their guilt, or criticized merely because it fails to do so" (Michael and Wechsler 1940, pp. 7, 11). A few years earlier Jerome Michael and University of Chicago philosophy professor Mortimer Adler explained that there are two incompatible theories of punishment: the "punitive" (retributive) and the "non-punitive" (consequentialist) and that "it can be shown that the punitive theory is a fallacious analysis and that the non-punitive theory is correct.... The infliction of pain is never justified merely on the ground that it visits retributive punishment upon the offender. Punitive retribution is never justifiable in itself" (Michael and Adler 1933, pp. 341, 344). The conventional ways of thinking, the zeitgeist, the prevailing sensibilities, rejected retribution and favored rehabilitation and, to a lesser extent, its consequentialist siblings deterrence and incapacitation.

Sensibilities, however, were changing. The American Law Institute's timing in releasing the code in 1962 could not have been worse. Harbingers of discontent with penal consequentialism had already begun to appear (e.g., Lewis [1949/2011]; Allen 1959) and recurred with increasing frequency (e.g., Burgess 1962; Allen 1964; Davis 1969). By the mid-1970s, dissatisfaction was widespread. Policy makers rejected many features of indeterminate sentencing and favored new approaches based on retributive ideas. Individualized, indeterminate sentencing was out. Retributive, determinate sentencing was in.

Whatever it was that changed policy makers' and practitioners' minds also influenced theorists. Consequentialism lost ground and influence. Retributivism came into vogue. In the 1950s, Norval Morris (1953), John Rawls (1955), and H. L. A. Hart (1959) attempted to reconcile general utilitarian rationales for punishment as an institution with resort to retributive considerations in individual cases. Herbert Morris (1966) and Jeffrie Murphy (1973) offered benefits-and-burdens theories, which, a bit obscurely, argued that the gravamen of crime is obtaining unfair benefit from others' law-abidingness and that punishment should balance things out. John Kleinig (1973), in the first book about punishment with "desert" in its title, assessed the relevance of desert considerations to the justificatory questions surrounding punishment. Joel Feinberg (1970) and Jean

Hampton (1984) argued in different ways for expressive theories and Herbert Morris (1981) and Antony Duff (1986) for communicative ones. Michael Moore (1993) offered an intuitionist account of punishment. Among the criminal lawyers, Norval Morris (1974) elaborated his theory of limiting retributivism, Alan Dershowitz (1976) his of "fair and certain punishment," and Andrew von Hirsch (1976) his of "just deserts."

University of Chicago law professor Albert Alschuler bewilderedly described the sea change: "That I and many other academics adhered in large part to [a] reformative viewpoint only a decade or so ago seems almost incredible to most of us today" (Alschuler 1978, p. 552). By the early 1980s, it was not unreasonable to believe that a corner had been turned and that policy makers, practitioners, and theorists would long march to the beat of distant retributive drums.

That did not happen, except for a few years. In the late 1970s and the early 1980s some legislatures enacted statutes meant to encourage proportionate sentences and abolished parole release in order to ensure that offenders served the proportionate sentences they received. Sentencing commissions adopted guidelines based on retributive premises. The rhetoric of deserved punishment and desert entered the political lexicon in the United States, and shortly thereafter in Australia, Canada, and England and Wales.[9]

The retributive moment quickly passed. Except in lip service, proportionality largely disappeared as a policy goal. Many of the sentencing laws enacted in the United States in the 1980s and 1990s, including mandatory minimum, three strikes, truth in sentencing, and LWOP laws, paid no heed to proportionality. Drug laws mandated sentences for street-level dealers longer than those typically received by people convicted of serious assaults, robberies, rapes, and many homicides. Three-strikes laws mandated lengthy and life sentences for repeat property and drug offenders. LWOP laws allowed lifetime sentences for a wide range of crimes, and not only for the murderers on whom, in the minds of many LWOP proponents, they were to be imposed in lieu of capital punishment. If principled rationales were implied by developments such as these, the principles were consequentialist—deterrence by means of threats of harsh punishment, incapacitation by means of lengthy periods of confinement, and moral education by means of the messages severe punishments ostensibly convey about right and wrong.[10]

New, less overtly punitive initiatives also paid little heed to proportionality. Drug courts and other problem-solving courts targeting mentally ill offenders, domestic violence, and gun crimes began in the early 1990s. By 2010 they numbered in the thousands (Mitchell 2011). Drug courts are predicated on the beliefs that drug treatment can work, that drug dependence is causally related to offending, and that coerced treatment backed up by firm judicial monitoring can break drug dependence. Other problem-solving courts are based on parallel logic. Proponents of problem-solving courts regularly announce that they are influenced by ideas about therapeutic jurisprudence, a school of thought that urges incorporation of therapeutic ideas into legal doctrines and processes (Wexler 1995, 2008a, 2008b; Winick 1997, 2005; Wexler and Winick 2003).

A vast new literature on correctional treatment asserts that many kinds of programs— sex offender treatment, anger management, cognitive skills training, vocational training, and drug abuse treatment—can reduce offending.[11] Correctional managers in many countries, including the United States, are paying attention and incorporating treatment ideas and programs into probationary sentences, prison regimes, and prisoner reentry policies.

In most developed countries, restorative justice programs are proliferating, sometimes as alternatives to the criminal justice system, sometimes as complements, and sometimes as integral components. The governing logic is not treatment effectiveness, but reconceptualization of crime and responses to it (e.g., Braithwaite 2001, 2002). If crime is seen not only as wrongful behavior by an offender that harms a victim, but also as a problem to be solved, or a rupture in relations among offender, victim, and community, or a sign of social or community breakdown, the best solution cannot simply be to punish and stigmatize the offender. It should instead be to solve the problem, restore good relations, or rebuild civic institutions and community solidarity while acknowledging the offender's wrongdoing and the victim's needs.

The rationales of drug courts, correctional treatment programs, and restorative justice are not the same, and they are not the same as the rationales for mandatory minimum sentences, three-strikes laws, and LWOPs. What all these programs and policies share, however, is that they do not give much weight to proportionality in deciding what should be done in individual cases, that is, to a search for a punishment appropriately calibrated to the gravity of the offender's wrongdoing.

II. UNDEREXAMINED POLICIES

Except concerning restorative justice (e.g., Braithwaite and Pettit 1990, 2001), I have found few efforts to justify proportionality-defying punishments on the merits. Philosophers and other theorists have paid mostly denunciatory attention to severe proportionality-defying punishments such as three-strikes and lengthy mandatory minimum sentence laws.

Half-hearted attempts have been made to explain why concerns about proportionality have not influenced such policies. Nigel Walker (1991) offered an outlaw argument: recidivists, through their obliviousness to community behavioral norms, forfeit any claim to have their liberty interests taken into account. People who have been law-abiding enjoy an immunity from disproportionate sentencing because of a presumption of harmlessness, but "someone who has harmed or tried to harm another person can hardly claim a right to the presumption of harmlessness: he has forfeited that right, and given society the right to interfere in his life. . . . The justification [of the right to interfere] is not a duty based on retribution but the offender's forfeiture of an immunity" (Walker 1996, p. 7).[12]

Arie Freiberg has, as devil's advocate, offered a social contract argument: "massive loss of liberty" following a third or subsequent offense "no longer has to be justified on the basis of the gravity of the precipitating offense . . . but can be justified simply on the basis that the implicit social contract has been fundamentally breached by the offender, thus bringing the contract to an end" (Freiberg 2001, p. 41; cf. Freiberg 2007).

Walker's and Freiberg's forfeiture arguments, however, are declamations, not theories.[13] They do not explain whether proportionality is or is not an important consideration in punishing first offenders, whether loss of immunity or contractor status makes proportionality concerns completely irrelevant, or whether any limits exist concerning the punishment of repeat offenders generally. Capital punishment or LWOPs for jaywalking, shoplifting, and possession of marijuana are presumably excessive, even for recidivists.

More fundamentally, the outlaw theories implicitly make consideration of all offenders' interests contingent. If prior convictions or especially serious crimes justify disregarding the interests of repeat offenders, presumably other circumstances could allow disregarding them even for first offenders. Many mandatory minimum sentence laws for drug crimes do exactly that; they require much longer minimum sentences for first offenders than are imposed on other offenders convicted of more serious crimes, including violent and sexual crimes. A series of examples follows of issues raised by recent policy initiatives that ought to be explored.

A. Three-strikes, Mandatory Minimums, and LWOPs

Laws of these types nearly always defy conventional ideas about proportionality. Theorists tend simply to denounce them. Even assuming that cases for such laws can sometimes be made on consequentialist grounds, analysis need not stop there. Distinctions need to be made. Washington State's pioneering three-strikes law, for example, was narrowly drawn by people who worried about the dangers of overbreadth. California's was not. As a result, Washington's law is potentially applicable only to a handful of offenders each year, while California's is applicable to tens of thousands. Accordingly, normative analyses of three-strikes laws should consider first whether such laws can ever be justified and, if so, for what kinds of offenses and under what circumstances, and what lengths of sentences they may justly specify under different circumstances. Analyses should address not only those issues, but also whether there are some categories of offenders who should be contingently or always exempt from their coverage. Examples might include mentally handicapped offenders, offenders younger than specified ages, offenders whose convictions were based on accessorial guilt, offenders whose involvement in a crime was minor, and offenders whose cases raised excusing defenses such as diminished capacity, self-defense, necessity, or duress for which there was some credible basis but which was or would have been unsuccessful at trial. Similar analyses are needed for mandatory minimum and LWOPs laws.

The recently developing literature on empirical desert, which argues that criminal law doctrine and punishment policies should take account of widely held intuitions and beliefs, may be germane (e.g., Robinson 2008). Several public opinion studies have shown that representative samples of the public opposed the federal 100-to-1 law for crack and powder cocaine offenses when they learned that crack and powder cocaine are pharmacologically indistinguishable, that most crack dealers are black, and as a result that black dealers typically receive much longer prison sentences than white dealers (Bobo and Thompson 2006, 2010). Similar widely held beliefs of ordinary people are likely to disapprove of punishing drug dealers more severely than rapists, robbers, assaulters, and burglars.

The problems of horizontal and vertical equity are especially acute for LWOP laws. Many were enacted with support from death penalty opponents on the supposition that they would serve as alternative punishments for people who might otherwise be sentenced to death. As enacted, however, many are applicable to other offenses. In 2008 more than 40,000 people were serving LWOPs, many following convictions for offenses other than murder (Nellis and King 2009). Even offenses committed by young offenders who cannot constitutionally be sentenced to death have resulted in LWOPs.

Three-strikes, LWOP, and mandatory minimum laws can be narrowly or broadly drawn and present greater or lesser problems of vertical equity when compared with laws governing sentences for other offenses. Unless they are subjected to normative scrutiny, all of these differences will continue to pass unnoticed and unjustified.

B. "Sexual Predator" and "Dangerous Offender" Laws

Every legal system has mechanisms for incapacitating people who are judged to be unacceptably dangerous to others. The most intellectually honest is to employ civil commitment procedures that authorize confinement of people who are determined, on the basis of clinical evidence, to be dangerous to themselves or others. Perforce such a commitment carries with it the possibility that committed individuals may later petition for release on the basis of clinical evidence that they are no longer dangerous.

Policy makers often are unwilling to have many violent and sexual offenders dealt with by mental health authorities. Approaches vary. The Netherlands and other European legal systems distinguish between punishments and measures. Both are called "sanctions." Imposition of a punishment should be guided by considerations of proportionality. "Measures," in contrast, are subject to no such constraint. Their use is primarily based on incapacitative considerations. People confined under measures can receive disproportionate and, sometimes, indeterminate placements and are released when deemed no longer to need confinement (de Keijser [2011] and von Hirsch [2011] discuss the Netherlands approach in detail). In England, indeterminate sentences for dangerous offenders include the possibility of lifetime confinement. American jurisdictions use "dangerous offender" and "sexual predator" laws, which authorize extended confinement even after a prison sentence has expired (Frase [2011] explores various possible theoretical justifications; Ashworth and Baker [2010] and Ramsay [2011] examine the English law).

Both approaches raise numerous normative issues. Why criminal law approaches rather than civil commitments? May any offense serve as the basis for such a disposition? In the Netherlands, repetitive property offenders and drug-dependent offenders sometimes are confined for a disproportionately long period of two years. Under England's habitual offender law in the first half of the twentieth century, most of those indeterminately confined were chronic property offenders (Morris 1951). If the basis of confinement or continued confinement is a prediction that the offender will commit future crimes, not a conviction for past ones, must individuals affected be held in more congenial conditions than offenders serving sentences? Argument can be made that, like people quarantined because they have infectious diseases, people quarantined because they are believed to be unacceptably dangerous should be held in normal, comfortable living conditions, subject only to controls on their movement.

Dangerous offender laws can operate like scalpels or like bludgeons. California's dangerous offender law is a bludgeon, potentially applying to thousands of offenders each year. England's dangerous offender law is comparably broad (Jacobsen and Hough 2010). Washington State's sexual predator law, in contrast, was a scalpel, carefully drafted, in light of civil liberties concerns and dangers of overuse, to apply only to a small category of offenders (Boerner 1992). Finland's dangerous offender law affects only a few cases a year; the number of people held under it can be counted on the fingers of two hands (Lappi-Seppälä 2001).

A generation or two ago there was a robust literature on ethical issues posed by incapacitative sentencing policies (e.g., Morris 1974; von Hirsch 1985; Tonry 1987). The issues, seldom discussed in recent decades, have not disappeared. They have been ignored. Only one of them—concerning whether previous convictions justify increased sentences for later offenses (the "recidivist premium")—has received recent attention (e.g., Roberts and von Hirsch 2010). Roberts (2011) discusses the issues. Other issues that need revisiting include the problem of false positives (most prediction instruments for serious crimes have false positive rates of at least two-in-three, meaning that most people held for incapacitative reasons would not have reoffended if they had been released), the use of ethically suspect prediction factors (race, gender, age, marital status, and class and race-linked social variables such as education, employment record, and residential stability),[14] whether increased punishment on the basis of past crimes (a major factor in most prediction instruments) violates the ethical principles underlying the "double jeopardy" doctrine, and whether incapacitative punishments for many offenders constitute—in effect—punishments for crimes that will never be committed.

C. Drug Courts and Other Rehabilitative Programs

Many rehabilitative programs fail both retributive and consequentialist tests. Offenders receive neither proportionate nor parsimonious handling. The issues requiring ventilation were familiar a generation ago (e.g., Allen 1959, 1981; Morris 1974). Can efforts to alter the personalities of offenders ever be justified? Can they be justified for some kinds of offenders but not others? Can they be justified in relation to some kinds of problems, needs, or deficits, but not others? C. S. Lewis was especially worried about psychiatric interventions: "To undergo all those assaults on my personality which modern psychotherapy knows how to deliver; to be re-made after some pattern of 'normality' hatched in a Viennese laboratory . . . —who cares whether this is called Punishment or not?" (Lewis 1949/2011, p. 93). Lewis was worried about preoccupations of his time; in our time, possibilities of chemical and electronic behavioral controls are even more worrying. The same worries extend to many kinds of changes contemplated by treatment programs. May participation be coerced overtly or by means of offers too good to be refused ("Otherwise, it's off to prison for you")? How can we protect against overzealous, bigoted, or idiosyncratic exercises of the treaters' powers over the treated? How should concerns about misuse of power be balanced with treatment or crime-preventive aims? Must the burdens imposed by treatment programs satisfy proportionality or parsimony concerns? O'Hear (2011) and Husak (2011) examine some of these issues.

D. Restorative Justice

Restorative justice has received much more attention from punishment theorists than have rehabilitative programs or punitive sanctions for at least three reasons. First, it is largely a bottom-up development promoted by grassroots activists and largely operates outside or parallel to the criminal justice system. A large, multinational, and introspective community promotes restorative justice, writes about it, and argues about it. Second, it springs from socially positive human instincts concerned, as the standard rhetoric proclaims, with rebuilding relationships among offenders, victims, and communities. One of its formative texts, John Braithwaite's *Crime, Shame, and Reintegration* (1989), argues that the criminal justice system is ineffective and that its destructive shaming should be replaced by an emphasis on reintegration of offenders into communities, on solving problems that give rise to offending, and on empowering victims. This stands in stark contrast to policy and political arguments for punitive sanctions that reify offenders into nameless, faceless stereotypes. Third, its proponents have generated a body of theoretical writing to which others can respond (e.g., Braithwaite and Pettit 1990, 2001; Walgrave 2008).

Not surprisingly, a sizable literature explores normative dimensions of restorative justice programs and explores differences between retributive and restorative approaches (e.g., Duff 2002, 2011; von Hirsch et al. 2003). Much of it has consisted of attempts to reconcile restorative processes with proportionality concerns. Other recurring issues concern whether restorative processes should be independent of the justice system or incorporated within it, whether programs should be available for all offenses or only for some, and how to ensure that offenders do not suffer unduly from the absence of procedural and evidentiary protections afforded by the justice system (Walgrave 2008). Other issues, some of which are mentioned below, might be pursued.

III. NORMATIVE PATHS NOT YET TAKEN

Theorists may be able to devise new normative accounts that explain, justify, and criticize contemporary punishment policies and practices. The most radical efforts look for positive justifications for laws that liberal observers dismiss as repressive and fundamentally unjustifiable. No doubt some policy makers who enacted and supported harsh contemporary punishment policies were not acting cynically or disingenuously but believed in what they were doing. Tony Blair and other leaders of New Labour, for example, were they theorists, might have tried to offer principled justifications for illiberal and repressive policies. They might have looked back to eighteenth-century ideas about the state and, invoking them, argued that a major function of government is to provide conditions of personal security that allow people to plan and carry out their lives as they wish. They might then have argued that citizens are obligated to respect one another's expectations of security and that the state can act to ensure that those expectations are honored. The focus would not, as retributivists and most liberal theorists would have it, be on when, under what circumstances, and how much the state may intrude into offenders' or prospective offenders' personal autonomy, but whether offenders have acted in ways that undermine others' sense of security and whether devices can be created to lessen the likelihood that they will do so in the future. From this starting point, arguments might be derived that attempt to justify New Labour's antisocial behavior policies and its approach to indeterminate sentencing of "dangerous" offenders.[15] Peter Ramsey (2011), Alice Ristroph (2011), and Andrew von Hirsch (2011) pursue some of the ways such theories might be developed, and some of their limitations. Others should try. In the end, retributivists and other liberal theorists might not be persuaded by theories that do not respect offenders' autonomy interests. The arguments and the differences between them would, however, become clearer than they are now.

A common theme animates many underexamined issues: analytical answers often conflict with emotional ones, and the conflict is not easy to resolve. The criminal law of attempts provides an example. A would-be assailant who has taken the last possible step in attacking a victim, but through bad eyesight, defective weaponry, or the victim's fortuitous last-minute movement caused no injury, is no less morally culpable than if he had succeeded. Nonetheless, most Common Law jurisdictions treat attempted crimes as less serious than completed ones, and punish them less severely. Criminal lawyers (Ashworth 1988) and philosophers (Nagel 1979, pp. 24–38; Williams 1981, pp. 20–39) have discussed these issues subtly and at length, sometimes characterizing the problem as one of "moral luck." Some conclude that traditional approaches for dealing with attempts are justifiable; others disagree.

The same problem, in reverse, commonly arises in vehicular homicide cases. Probably no one disagrees with the proposition that an inebriated driver should be criminally liable when harm occurs that is causally attributable to his inebriation. Sometimes, however, it may be an inebriated driver's sheer bad luck that an accident happens in which his condition played no causal role; many people and, more importantly, many judges believe nonetheless that the driver may properly be criminally prosecuted and punished as if intoxication had contributed causally to the accident. No one seriously proposes that the other, say, 999 of 1000 impaired drivers who arrived home safely that night should be prosecuted for attempted vehicular homicide. Yet their culpability is the same.

Norval Morris tried to explain the different results by distinguishing between guilt and blame. Guilt, for him, was culpable blameworthiness. Blame was social reaction, and it influences how most people think and what the legal system does: "The criminal law is a dependent system, very reliant on culture, morals, values, custom, and the texture of all the interwoven rules of law. If you are compromised morally and chance to violate any of those rules, and the dice roll against you, then you may lose badly" (Morris 1992, p. 152). That explanation may accurately describe conventional reactions but, like the moral luck analysis of attempts, does not provide a normative solution to the conflict between intuition and principled logic.

Conflicts between the literal application of conventional moral ideas and widely held intuitions recur frequently. In retributive principle at least, a punishment once performed should clear the ledger. For benefits-and-burdens (e.g., Murphy 1973) and penance theories (e.g., Duff 2001, 2011) this seems self-evident: punishment should have restored equilibrium; penance should have been performed; the price for wrongdoing should have been paid. Nonetheless, most people share an intuition that previous convictions justify a harsher punishment for a subsequent offense (Roberts 2008). Most systems authorize a recidivist premium, but no convincing moral explanation has yet been offered for why (Roberts and von Hirsch 2010). Sentencing policy issues raise similar problems: women typically receive less severe punishments than men,[16] and defendants in urban courts less severe punishments than defendants in rural courts. Policy makers, however, usually feel unable explicitly to authorize harsher punishments for male[17] and rural offenders, so they do not, knowing that the harsher punishments will be imposed in any event. The intuition that the sentencing outcomes are justifiable is widely shared, but theorists have not convincingly explained why it should be acted upon.

My aim in this essay is not to solve any of these dilemmas or to answer other analytical issues described. It is more modest than that. I suspect there are ways in which theorists can engage many punishment policies and problems more fruitfully than they do now. Four sets of problems whose solutions might help are sketched below.

A. Justice by Geography

A primary objection made by retributivist theorists to restorative justice programs is that they insufficiently respect the adjuration that like cases be treated alike. A hypothetical illustrates the problem. Many restorative justice programs include conferences in which offenders, victims, meaningful people in the lives of both, sometimes police or probation officers, and sometimes community representatives come together to discuss a crime and what should be done about it. The goals are usually to achieve unanimous agreement and then for the offender to do what has been agreed.

Two closely similar cases dealt with in adjoining conference rooms could easily result in substantially different outcomes. In one case, for example, the agreed disposition may be for the offender to apologize, perform modest service for the victim, and enter into an educational program. In the second, the agreed disposition may be for the offender to serve an 18-month prison sentence and, following release, compensate the victim for his or her loss or injury, participate in applicable treatment programs, and perform community service. From a traditional retributive perspective, those substantially different sentences for comparably culpable offenders are unjust—a violation of horizontal equity—even if both offenders consented to them and even if all observers agree that the consents were informed and voluntary.

There are at least three ways the inequality objection might be addressed. The first is to point out that there are many geographical differences in dispositions of closely comparable cases that are almost universally accepted as legitimate; it is not obvious why different outcomes in restorative justice proceedings should not be also. Examples include when they occur in different countries ("Americans are more punitive than Swedes," an observer might note) or in different states ("Texans are more punitive than Minnesotans"). Anyone who has worked with empirical data on sentencing knows, in addition, that there are often stark differences in sentencing severity within a state (urban versus rural courts) or a county (suburban versus inner-city courts). These intrastate differences are well known and accepted by many people as legitimate ("Differences in local culture, you know"), even if the normative case that punishments should vary depending on where an offender is sentenced is difficult to make, and is seldom, if ever, attempted. Restorative justice advocates would argue that the different outcomes in my hypothetical raise exactly the same issue and are justifiable on the same intuitive grounds.

The second is to focus on the unanimity requirement in restorative justice processes. As a factual matter, it may sometimes be difficult to be certain that an offender's acquiescence is informed and voluntary, but often it is, and for purposes of analysis I assume that often it is. If each of the differently sentenced offenders has consented to his disposition, in a process in which others concerned for his or her well-being participated, it is awkwardly paternalistic for outsiders to suggest that the offender did not know what he or she was doing and therefore should be unable to agree to a disposition he or she considers appropriate. In criminal court proceedings, many defendants agree after plea negotiations to particular sentences, and arguments are seldom offered that they should not be allowed to do so. Particularly for retributive theories premised on notions of respecting citizens' autonomy, it would be ironic to argue that the autonomy of people who participate in restorative justice proceedings should not be respected. It is difficult to imagine a coherent argument that criminal court defendants should be allowed to agree to dispositions but restorative justice participants should not.

The third is to reconsider how to define the relevant community by reference to which decisions about justice are to be made. This is the real justification for geographical differences in sentencing practices. The most circumstantially relevant community may consist of the people who are most directly affected by a crime and its consequences. For interpersonal crimes of violence and property, the offender, the victim, those closest to both of them, and representatives of the local community are the persons most affected and likely to have the greatest interest. As circles of interest expand—other neighborhoods in a town, other towns in a county, towns in other counties, counties in other states, other countries—the connections to the event become increasingly diluted and distant. This is probably why few principled objections are made to sentencing differences between countries or states and why vocal objections to differences between counties and between urban and rural areas are seldom very strident. If the most local community is the most relevant frame of reference for thinking about what is just in an individual case, a restorative justice conference appears to draw upon it.

B. Justice by Consistency in Process

Patterned geographical differences in sentencing severity may not receive much attention from theorists or policy makers, but seemingly ad hoc differences in the handling of comparable cases within a single jurisdiction do. One way to begin to think about possible principled justifications for such differences is to focus on the fairness of the processes involved. Proponents of restorative justice and rehabilitative programs, for example, might argue that justice requires consistency of process, not consistency of outcomes: "Consistency can be recognised through like cases resulting in like outcomes.... A better approach is to seek consistent application of explicit principles and standards, recognizing that these may result in justifiably disparate outcomes. The goal is consistency of approach, not uniformity of outcomes. This makes consistency difficult to monitor, but not impossible" (Halliday 2001, p. 16). This is one argument that can be made for why similarly situated offenders in criminal courts are allowed to agree after negotiations to plead guilty to different offenses or to agree to different sentences.

A consistency-in-process argument is easier to make concerning seemingly disparate dispositions resulting from restorative justice conferences than from plea negotiations. Defendants in conferences are usually supported by family members and are to some extent protected by unanimity requirements. Most defendants in criminal courts are dealt with in assembly-line fashion and are represented by poorly paid defense lawyers who cannot afford to invest much time or effort in routine cases. The negotiated guilty plea resulting from a few whispering minutes in the back of a courtroom is not only not a myth, it is common.

Punishment processes that respect consistency-in-process values might offer collateral benefits. Research on procedural justice and legitimacy repeatedly finds that people are more willing to accept, and accept the appropriateness of, criminal justice system outcomes if they perceive the process as legitimate (Tyler 2006). In other words, the process was seen as fair, the fact finder was seen as impartial, and the defendant or suspect was treated respectfully and given a chance to say his or her piece. These attributes are more likely to characterize restorative than criminal court processes.

Proponents of restorative justice programs, drug and other problem-solving courts, and many treatment programs would argue that their programs satisfy consistency-of-process criteria and that many or most offenders accept the outcomes or dispositions they receive. This is backed up by the consistent findings of restorative justice program evaluations that offenders (and victims) are more satisfied by the processes they experience than are comparable offenders (and victims) whose cases are dealt with in the criminal courts (e.g., Kurki 2000; Braithwaite 2001).

C. The Recidivist Premium

Partly because we are all parochial, and few people look across national boundaries, punishment theorists overlook fundamental questions. One concerns the questions of whether and to what extent offenders should be punished more severely because they have offended before. To Americans, it is obvious that they should be, and a lot (Reitz 2010). To Scandinavians, it is obvious that prior offenses are ordinarily irrelevant and when they are relevant they should not count for much (Asp 2010; Lappi-Seppälä 2011). To English folk and Australians, it is obvious that they should count some, but subject to tight limits (Lovegrove 1988, 1997; Ashworth and Baker 2010).

In American sentencing law and guidelines, prior convictions can make an enormous difference in punishment severity. Three-strikes laws offer an extreme example. Sentencing guidelines offer examples that are less widely recognized, but little less extreme. Under many sentencing guidelines systems, prior convictions can result in the imposition of prison sentences two, three, or four times longer than would be imposed for a first offense (Reitz 2010).

The widely divergent self-evident significance of prior convictions in the United States, the Scandinavian countries, England and Wales, and Australia shows that the subject is not self-evident at all. In the English-speaking countries, at least, we know that almost everyone—judges, probation officers, ordinary citizens, offenders—shares an intuition that previous convictions justify imposition of a harsher punishment (Roberts 2008). There have been a few attempts to justify the recidivist premium in retributivist terms (Bennett 2010; Lee 2010), but in the end they collapse into arguments that the additional punishment is predicated on either the offender's bad character or his or her defiance or disrespect of the court. Neither is easily reconciled with traditional liberal ideas. Bad character and rude behavior are not the bases for punishment of nonoffenders; it is hard to see why they become punishable when they characterize previous offenders. Andrew von Hirsch (2010) and others have argued that the premium is not a premium at all, but a "progressive loss of mitigation" granted to first or sometimes second or third offenders because their wrongdoing may have been out of character. These arguments collapse into little more than a rationalization for an intuition that cannot otherwise be justified, and say nothing about harsher punishments imposed on more prolific offenders. Consequentialists have a much easier, incapacitative, case to make: repeat offending is a well-established predictor of future offending.

The recidivist premium raises issues not unlike those presented by gender and geographical differences in sentencing—hard to justify, but ubiquitous and seemingly widely supported (or they would not be commonplace). From an equal treatment perspective, all seem difficult to justify: everyone convicted of a particular kind of robbery should be punished in the same or an equivalent way, irrespective of prior convictions; everyone convicted of a particular offense in a state (at least) should be punished in the same or an equivalent way, irrespective of whether they are women or men and irrespective of where in the state a court is located.

D. Subjectivity

Contemporary efforts to apply retributive ideas to punishment policies often argue, or assume, that proportionate punishments justly may, or must, be based on generic categorizations of offenses and generic depictions of punishments. Both are facially implausible. Robberies range from schoolyard takings of basketballs and pizza slices to gangland assaults on banks. A year's imprisonment can range from a stay in home confinement to time in a supermaximum security (supermax) prison under conditions approaching sensory deprivation. The proposition that a first robbery conviction should be punished by x year's imprisonment glosses over objective differences that in other contexts most people would think important. Objectively considered, a crime's characteristics are inherently important to assessment of a particular offender's blameworthiness. Objectively considered, the difference between a year's house arrest and a year in a supermax prison is inherently important to understanding the punishment an offender suffers.

But that is only the beginning of the problem of objective understanding of punishments. An objectively standard punishment—for example, one year's confinement in a particular medium security prison—may be experienced by different individuals in fundamentally different ways. A year in prison for a 19-year-old street gang member may be a rite of passage, a status enhancer, and a prerequisite to gang leadership. To a professional burglar, it may be a cost of doing business. To an effeminate and diffident young man it may be terrorizing. To a 40-year-old head of household, it may break up a family and fundamentally alter its future. To a terminally ill 70-year-old, it may be a life sentence.

Similar observations have recently been emphatically asserted by Adam Kolber to make the point that it is in the nature of retributive punishment theories that these kinds of differences should matter. He illustrates this by use of farfetched hypotheticals, including a sentence of "truncation:"

> People sentenced to truncation are forced to stand upright while the sharp end of a blade speeds horizontally toward them at a height of precisely six feet above the ground. Those shorter than six feet merely feel the passing breeze of a blade above their heads. Those about six feet tall receive a very imprecise haircut. Those much above six feet tall are decapitated. Each person sentenced to truncation receives the same punishment in name: They are all "truncated." Yet, in the most important ways, truncation punishments differ in severity, and they differ based on an arbitrary characteristic, namely the offender's height. (Kolber 2009, p. 188)

From this and similar examples he concludes that punishments must be subjectively considered in light of the diverse effects of seemingly standard punishments on different individuals. More realistic examples are more powerful. Few people would disagree that an individual's claustrophobia should be considered in deciding whether he or she may be placed in an unlighted windowless room as a form of administrative segregation following a violation of prison rules.

Kolber's claim was self-evident to Kant and Bentham. For Bentham, penalties should be set so that the expected burden of punishment is greater than the benefits of crime. In determining the amount of punishment required, the offender's situation has to be considered. The offender's "sensibilities," by which in modern vocabulary he meant sensitivities, must be taken into account. People have different sensitivities and are affected in different ways by the same experience, including experiences of punishment. Accordingly, "that the quantity actually inflicted on an individual offender may correspond to the quantity intended for similar offenders in general, the several circumstances influencing sensibility ought always to be taken into account" (Bentham 1970, p. 169).

Bentham, however, is the archetypal consequentialist, so he may not count as an authority in an era in which retributive views are predominant. Kant should. Kant's "principle of equality" can be misinterpreted, and has been, as requiring that punishments perfectly correspond to crimes in an objective way, as in a sense execution can to murder.[18] This might be interpreted as implying that punishments should be objectively calculated to "equal" the crime. Kant, however, approvingly gives examples of punishments that vary with the characteristics of the offender. For "verbal injuries," for example, a fine might ordinarily suffice, but not for a wealthy person; the "humiliation" of a public apology and kissing the hand of a lower social status victim would better serve for a wealthy person as the subjective equivalent of a poor man's fine. He gives another example. When a high-status person assaults a social inferior, he must apologize, but might also be condemned to "solitary and painful confinement, because by this means, in addition to the discomfort suffered, the pride of the offender will be painfully affected" (Kant 1798/1965, pp. 101–2).

I don't believe Kolber's challenge can be adequately answered by people who understand retributivism as a matter of imposing deserved suffering.[19] Dan Markel, who argues that retributivism does not require subjective assessments of punishment on individuals, has tried. His argument, however, reduces to a definitional stop: retributivism properly considered, he argues, is a theory about the justification of the institution of punishment and has only the most general implications for punishments in individual cases:

> One question is: What might justify the state's creation of legal institutions of punishment? This is what we call the "justification" question. The second question is: Once the state has determined someone's liability for a crime, how much and what kind of punishment should the state mete out in response? This is the "sentencing" question. That a retributivist theorist gives a retributive (or, specifically, communicative) answer to the justification question does not require her to offer a precise answer for each sentencing question. . . . A retributive conception of proportionality need not have much in the way of precision to say about the particular details of punishment's implementation, consistent with its greater concern with justifying the institution of punishment within and by the liberal state. (Markel 2010, pp. 950–51)

For Markel, the only important question is how the institution of punishment is to be justified. Questions of what happens to individual offenders are not especially important unless, objectively considered, the punishment is so excessively lenient or severe that it fails adequately to convey the wrongfulness of the offender's behavior. This is, in effect, to define away the problem. If only the justification question is an issue, however, as Hart (1959, 1968) long ago pointed out, a separate question of justice in the distribution of punishments remains.

Once it is recognized that individuals' subjective experiences of possible punishments raise important questions, openings are created for justifying punishments and programs such as restorative justice, drug courts, and rehabilitative programs that attempt to individualize dispositions to the circumstances of individual cases.

IV. Imagining the Future

No one knows what prevailing attitudes toward punishment will be like in 2025. In 2010 American sentencing laws and practices were extraordinarily severe compared with those in other countries. The imprisonment rate was nearly 800 per 100,000 population. That is eight times higher than the average rate of 100 per 100,000 for other developed countries, including Canada. It is more than 10 times higher than the 75 per 100,000 rate of the Scandinavian countries. No other Western country retains or uses capital punishment. No other developed country has broad-based, frequently used laws equivalent to American three-strikes, LWOP, or mandatory minimum sentence laws for drug offenses. In no other country are sentences measured in decades and lifetimes routinely imposed (Tonry 2009).

Whether retributivism, or punishment theories more generally, will have a role to play in 2025 outside common rooms and classrooms remains to be seen (Matravers 2011). Philosophers and other theorists of punishment have remarkably little useful or illuminating to say about contemporary American sentencing laws and practices, the proliferation of restorative and community justice programs, or the widespread revival of coercive correctional treatment programs. They should. If the time comes, as no doubt it will, when policy makers reconsider contemporary approaches and attempt to devise new ones, some will look for and want to find theoretical critiques of the recent past and justifications for possible futures. It will be a pity if the work has not been done to help them.

NOTES

1. Unlike Kant and Hegel, Bentham insisted that punishment theory had nothing to do with ideas about individual rights or respect for the moral autonomy of individuals. Commenting on the French Revolution, and the Declaration of the Rights of Man to which it gave rise, he acerbically observed that the idea of "natural rights is simple nonsense: natural and imprescriptible rights, rhetorical nonsense, nonsense upon stilts" (quoted in Harrison 1995).

2. Kant stressed the difference between his ideas and Bentham's: "The law concerning punishment is a categorical imperative, and woe to him who rummages around in the winding paths of a theory of happiness looking for some advantage to be gained by releasing the criminal from punishment or by reducing the amount of it" (Kant 1798/1965, p. 100).

   Hegel was as adamant: "This superficial [characterization of crime] as an *evil* is the primary assumption in the various theories of punishment as prevention, as a deterrent, a corrective, etc., and conversely what is supposed to result from it is just as superficially defined as a good. . . . As a result of these superficial points of view, however, the objective consideration of *justice*, which is the primary and substantial point of view in relation to crime, is set aside" (Hegel 1991, p. 125).

3. A *Guardian* story captures the Blair government's views of people who opposed expressive policy making: "Tony Blair said last summer's five-year crime plan would herald 'the end of the 1960s liberal consensus on law and order' and David Blunkett, Mr. [Charles] Clarke's predecessor [as Home Secretary], was known for his attacks on 'Hampstead liberals.' The north London neighbourhood was also the subject of attack from Jack Straw, Mr. Blair's first home secretary, who said only 'woolly-minded lawyers and Hampstead liberals' were opposed to his plan to curtail the right to trial by jury" (Jeffery 2005).

4. *Kansas v. Hendricks*, 521 U.S. 346 (1997), upheld the constitutionality of indeterminate confinement of "sexual predators" following expiration of prison sentences imposed for specific offenses. *Ewing v. California*, 538 U.S. 11 (2003), upheld the constitutionality of a 25-years-to-life sentence for theft of three golf clubs. *Lockyer v. Andrade*, 538 U.S. 63 (2003), upheld the constitutionality of a 25-years-to-life sentence for theft from a K-Mart store of nine video games with a retail value of $150.

5. This is equally true of empirical research on punishment practices. For nearly two decades research findings accumulated, and went unnoticed in policy circles, that correctional boot camps for young offenders were ineffective at reducing later offending or achieving lasting improvements to offenders' self-esteem or social functioning (Wilson, MacKenzie, and Mitchell 2008). The times changed. Notorious deaths of young people pushed too hard were publicized. Support for boot camps crumbled. The negative research findings were then often cited by policy makers as a reason to end the programs. The same pattern

underlies contemporary belief in the effectiveness of drug abuse treatment. The research findings—drug abuse is a chronic relapsing condition, most treated drug users relapse, the best predictor of treatment success is time in treatment, even if coerced—did not change (e.g., Anglin and Hser 1990). What changed, and led to the drug court movement, was policy makers' decision to shift focus away from "most relapse" and toward "relapsing condition . . . time in treatment" (President's Commission on Model State Drug Laws 1993).

6. Ryberg (2011) and Kleinig (2011) offer contemporary reexaminations of, respectively, consequentialist and retributive accounts of punishment.

7. Why penal consequentialism had comparatively little influence on continental European criminal justice systems is an important and, to my knowledge, unexamined question. Rehabilitative ideas had influence and rehabilitative programs were established, but retributive ideas about proportionality were nowhere abandoned. Nothing like the California and Washington systems, in which offenders were sentenced to the maximum possible prison term and parole boards determined whether and when they were released, was established or, probably, imaginable. The most likely explanations would probably emphasize the influence of the classical ideas of Beccaria about proportionality, the influence of German idealism, and the influence of Natural Law ideas on European jurisprudence.

8. The American Law Institute's deliberations and the *Model Penal Code* provisions described in this paragraph are described in considerable detail in Tonry (2004, chap. 7).

9. Minnesota's sentencing guidelines commission, for example, explicitly debated the choice between "just deserts" and "modified just deserts" as the rationale for the guidelines it promulgated in 1980 (this example and others are discussed in von Hirsch, Knapp, and Tonry [1987]). The Australian Law Reform Commission (1980), the Canadian Sentencing Commission (1987), and the Home Office (1991) of England and Wales each endorsed "just deserts" as a guide to policy making.

10. Scandinavian punishment theorists would point out that moral educative messages must respect proportionality concerns, otherwise the moral messages about what is more serious than what gets muddled, which undermines rather than reinforces basic norms about right and wrong (e.g., Lappi-Seppälä 2011).

11. The National Academy of Sciences recently summarized much of the evidence: "Contrary to the commonly quoted conclusion that 'nothing works,' the evidence shows that some approaches work for some offenders and that other approaches show promise. Post-release interventions that have shown measurable effects include treatment for substance abuse, especially when combined with frequent testing for drug abuse, and cognitive behavioral therapy. Comprehensive, multiservice employment and training programs and mentoring programs hold promise but require rigorous evaluation" (National Research Council 2007, p. 2).

12. Walker, throughout his career, offered a consequentialist account of punishment, so it is fair enough that he does not worry greatly about proportionality. The forfeiture/immunity argument, however, on its face assumes that normative justification relating to severe treatment of the individual recidivist offender is required. That implicitly acknowledges that without the special justification, such punishments would be unjust.

13. Philosophers for nearly a century have discussed forfeiture theories as explanations of punishment, but have invariably related the degree of forfeiture to the gravity of wrongdoing—forfeiture subject to proportionality constraints (e.g., Ross 1930; Goldman 1982; Lippke 2001). I have found no one who has offered a sustained argument for an outlaw theory of forfeiture of all rights.

14. This is not merely a theoretical question. Virginia's sentencing guidelines direct judges to consider gender, age, and marital status in deciding whom to sentence to imprisonment (Virginia Criminal Sentencing Commission 2010). Gender, age, and marital status are strongly correlated with race, which means that they result in systematically more severe punishments of minority offenders. In the 1970s and 1980s this was commonly seen as a

prima facie reason not to include them in sentencing or parole release criteria, or more generally as factors in prediction instruments (Gottfredson, Wilkins, and Hoffman 1978).

15. Antisocial behavior orders (ASBOs) could be issued for a vaguely defined category of actions (any action that "caused or was likely to cause harassment, alarm, or distress"), some criminal and some not, that government officials found disturbing. Civil court proceedings could be initiated, which if successful resulted in issuance of a court order not to repeat the behavior. Violation of the order was a criminal offense (Tonry 2010). Under the dangerous offender legislation, anyone convicted of any of dozens of offenses could be sentenced to an indeterminate sentence; release depends on a finding that he or she is no longer dangerous (Jacobsen and Hough 2010).

16. Part, but only part, of the explanation for gender differences is that judges take account of the effects of sentences on dependent children, and women more often than men are the primary care providers (Daly 1987, 1989).

17. The Virginia Criminal Sentencing Commission (2010) policy described in note 14 is a conspicuous exception.

18. The *ius talionis* "is obviously not capable of being extended. Crime and punishment are different things. Can they really be equated? What penalty equals the crime of forgery, perjury or kidnapping? For the state to exercise the same amount of fraud or brutality on the criminal that the criminal exercised on his victim would be demoralizing to any community" (Cohen 1940, p. 1010).

19. Proponents of communicative theories of retributive punishment probably have more persuasive responses to offer to Kolber's subjectivist challenge (e.g., Duff 2001, 2011).

ACKNOWLEDGMENTS

Helpful comments on an earlier draft were provided by Jan de Keijser, Antony Duff, Douglas Husak, and Matt Matravers. They were greatly appreciated.

REFERENCES

Allen, Francis A. 1959. "Legal Values and the Rehabilitative Ideal." *Journal of Criminal Law, Criminology, and Police Science* 50:226–32.

———. 1964. "Legal Values and the Rehabilitative Ideal." *The Borderland of Criminal Justice: Essays in Law and Criminology.* Chicago: University of Chicago Press.

———. 1981. *The Decline of the Rehabilitative Ideal: Penal Policy and Social Purpose.* New Haven, CT: Yale University Press.

Alschuler, Albert. 1978. "Sentencing Reform and Prosecutorial Power." *University of Pennsylvania Law Review* 126:550–77.

American Friends Service Committee. 1971. *Struggle for Justice.* New York: Hill and Wang.

American Law Institute. 1962. *Model Penal Code. Proposed Official Draft.* Philadelphia: American Law Institute.

Anglin, M. Douglas, and Yih-Ing Hser. 1990. "Treatment of Drug Abuse." In *Crime and Justice: A Review of Research,* vol. 13, *Drugs and Crime,* edited by Michael Tonry and James Q. Wilson. Chicago: University of Chicago Press.

Ashworth, Andrew. 1988. "Criminal Attempts and the Role of Resulting Harm under the Code, and in the Common Law." *Rutgers Law Review* 19:725–72.

Ashworth, Andrew, and Estella Baker. 2010. "The Role of Previous Convictions in England and Wales." In *Previous Convictions at Sentencing: Theoretical and Applied Perspectives,* ed. Julian V. Roberts and Andrew von Hirsch. Oxford: Hart.

Asp, Petter. 2010. "Previous Convictions and Proportionate Sentences under Swedish Law." In *Previous Convictions at Sentencing: Theoretical and Applied Perspectives*, ed. Julian V. Roberts and Andrew von Hirsch. Oxford: Hart.

Australia Law Reform Commission. 1980. *Sentencing of Federal Offenders*. Canberra: Australian Government Publishing Service.

Beccaria, Cesare. 1764. *Dei delitti e delle pene [On Crimes and Punishments]*, trans. Aaron Thomas and Jeremy Parzen. Toronto: University of Toronto Press.

Bennett, Christopher. 2010. "'More to Apologize For': Can a Basis for the Recidivist Premium Be Found within a Communicative Theory of Punishment?" In *Previous Convictions at Sentencing: Theoretical and Applied Perspectives*, ed. Julian V. Roberts and Andrew von Hirsch. Oxford: Hart.

Bentham, Jeremy. 1970. "The Utilitarian Theory of Punishment." In Jeremy Bentham, J. H. Burns, and H. L. A. Hart, *An Introduction to Principles of Morals and Legislation*. London: Athlone.

———. 1830/2008. *The Rationale of Punishment*. Amherst, NY: Kessinger.

Bobo, Lawrence D., and Victor Thompson. 2006. "Unfair by Design: The War on Drugs, Race, and the Legitimacy of the Criminal Justice System." *Social Research* 73(2):445–70.

———. 2010. "Racialized Mass Incarceration: Poverty, Prejudice, and Punishment." In *Doing Race: 21 Essays for the 21st Century*, ed. Hazel Rose Markus and Paula M. L. Moya. New York: Norton.

Boerner, David. 1992. "Confronting Violence: In the Act and in the World." *University of Puget Sound Law Review* 15:525–77.

Braithwaite, John. 1989. *Crime, Shame, and Reintegration*. Cambridge: Cambridge University Press.

———. 2001. *Restorative Justice and Responsive Regulation*. New York: Oxford University Press.

———. 2002. "In Search of Restorative Jurisprudence." In *Restorative Justice and the Law*, ed. Lode Walgrave. Cullompton, Devon, UK: Willan.

Braithwaite, John, and Philip Pettit. 1990. *Not Just Deserts: A Republican Theory of Criminal Justice*. New York: Oxford University Press.

———. 2001. "Republicanism and Restorative Justice: An Explanatory and Normative Connection." In *Restorative Justice: Philosophy to Practice*, ed. John Braithwaite and Heather Strang. Burlington, VT: Ashgate.

Burgess, Anthony. 1962. *A Clockwork Orange*. London: Heinemann.

Canadian Sentencing Commission. 1987. *Sentencing Reform: A Canadian Approach*. Ottawa: Canadian Government Publishing Centre.

Cohen, Morris R. 1940. "Moral Aspects of the Criminal Law." *Yale Law Journal* 49:987–1026.

Daly, Kathleen. 1987. "Structure and Practice of Familial-Based Justice in a Criminal Court." *Law and Society Review* 21(2):267–90.

———. 1989. "Neither Conflict nor Labeling nor Paternalism Will Suffice: Intersections of Race, Ethnicity, Gender, and Family in Criminal Court Decisions." *Crime and Delinquency* 35(1):136–68.

Darley, John M. 2010. "Citizens' Assignments of Punishments for Moral Transgressions: A Case Study in the Psychology of Punishment." *Ohio State Journal of Criminal Law* 8:101–17.

Davis, Kenneth Culp. 1969. *Discretionary Justice: A Preliminary Inquiry*. Baton Rouge: Louisiana State University Press.

de Keijser, Jan. 2011. "Never Mind the Pain; It's a Measure! Justifying Measures as Part of the Dutch Bifurcated System of Sanctions." In *Retributivism Has a Past. Has It a Future?*, ed. Michael Tonry. New York: Oxford University Press.

Dershowitz, Alan. 1976. *Fair and Certain Punishment*. New York: Twentieth Century Fund.

Duff, R. A. 1986. *Trials and Punishments*. Cambridge: Cambridge University Press.

———. 2001. *Punishment, Communication, and Community*. New York: Oxford University Press.

————. 2002. "Restorative Punishment and Punitive Restoration." In *Restorative Justice and the Law*, ed. Lode Walgrave. Cullompton, Devon, UK: Willan.

————. 2011. "Responsibility, Restoration, and Retribution." In *Retributivism Has a Past. Has It a Future?*, ed. Michael Tonry. New York: Oxford University Press.

Feinberg, Joel. 1970. "The Expressive Function of Punishment." *Doing and Deserving: Essays in the Theory of Responsibility*. Princeton, NJ: Princeton University Press.

Ferri, Enrico. 1921. *Relazione sul Progetto Preliminare di Codice Penale Italiano*. Milan.

Frase, Richard. 2009. "Limiting Excessive Prison Sentencing." *University of Pennsylvania Journal of Constitutional Law* 11(1):43–46.

————. 2011. "Can Above-desert Penalties Be Justified by Competing Deontological Theories?" In *Retributivism Has a Past. Has It a Future?*, ed. Michael Tonry. New York: Oxford University Press.

Freiberg, Arie. 2001. "Three Strikes and You're Out—It's Not Cricket: Colonization and Resistance in Australian Sentencing." In *Sentencing and Sanctions in Western Countries*, ed. Michael Tonry and Richard S. Frase. New York: Oxford University Press.

————. 2007. "Jurisprudential Miscegenation: Strict Liability and the Ambiguity of Crime." In *Governance and Regulation in Social Life: Essays in Honour of WG Carson*, ed. A. Brannigan and G. Pavlich. Oxford: Routledge-Cavendish.

Garland, David. 2001. *The Culture of Control*. Chicago: University of Chicago Press.

Goldman, Alan. H. 1982. "Toward a New Theory of Punishment." *Land and Philosophy* 1(1):57–76.

Gottfredson, Don M., Leslie T. Wilkins, and Peter B. Hoffman. 1978. *Guidelines for Sentencing and Parole*. Lexington, MA: Heath.

Halliday, John. 2001. *Making Punishments Work: A Review of the Sentencing Framework for England and Wales*. London: HM Stationery Office.

Hampton, Jean. 1984. "The Moral Education Theory of Punishment." *Philosophy and Public Affairs* 13(3):208–38.

Harrison, Ross. 1995. "Jeremy Bentham." In *The Oxford Companion to Philosophy*, ed. Ted Honderich. Oxford: Oxford University Press.

Hart, H. L. A. 1959. "Prolegomenon to the Principles of Punishment." *Proceedings of the Aristotelian Society, New Series* 60:1–26.

————. 1968. *Punishment and Responsibility: Essays in the Philosophy of Law*. Oxford: Oxford University Press.

Hegel, G. W. F. 1991. "Wrong [Das Unrecht]." In *Elements of the Philosophy of Right*, ed. by Allen W. Wood, trans. H. B. Nisbet. Cambridge: Cambridge University Press.

Home Office. 1991. *Crime, Justice, and Protecting the Public*. Cm 965. London: HM Stationery Office.

Husak, Douglas. 2008. *Overcriminalization: The Limits of the Criminal Law*. New York: Oxford University Press.

————. 2011. "Retributivism, Proportionality, and the Challenge of the Drug Court Movement." In *Retributivism Has a Past. Has It a Future?*, ed. Michael Tonry. New York: Oxford University Press.

Jacobson, J., and M. Hough. 2010. *Unjust Deserts: Imprisonment for Public Protection*. London: Prison Reform Trust.

Jeffery, Simon. 2005. "Liberal? No, not me . . . " *The Guardian* (January 19).

Kant, Immanuel. 1798/1965. "The Penal Law and the Law of Pardon." In *The Metaphysical Elements of Justice*, trans. John Ladd. Indianapolis, IN: Liberal Arts Press/Bobbs-Merrill.

Kleinig, John. 1973. *Punishment and Desert*. New York: Springer.

————. 2011. "What Does Wrongdoing Deserve?" In *Retributivism Has a Past. Has It a Future?*, ed. Michael Tonry. New York: Oxford University Press.

Kolber, Adam. 2009. "The Subjective Experience of Punishment." *Columbia Law Review* 109:182–236.

Kurki, Leena. 2000. "Restorative and Community Justice in the United States." In *Crime and Justice: A Review of Research*, vol. 27, edited by Michael Tonry. Chicago: University of Chicago Press.

Lappi-Seppälä, Tapio. 2001. In *Sentencing and Sanctions in Western Countries*, ed. Michael Tonry and Richard S. Frase. New York: Oxford University Press.

———. 2011. "Sentencing and Punishment in Finland: The Decline of the Repressive Ideal." In *Why Punish? How Much?*, ed. Michael Tonry. New York: Oxford University Press.

Lee, Jungjae. 2010. "Repeat Offenders and the Question of Desert." In *Previous Convictions at Sentencing: Theoretical and Applied Perspectives*, ed. Julian V. Roberts and Andrew von Hirsch. Oxford: Hart.

Lewis, C. S. 1949/2011. "The Humanitarian Theory of Punishment." In *Why Punish? How Much?*, ed. Michael Tonry. New York: Oxford University Press. Originally published in 1949 in *20th Century: An Australian Quarterly Review* 3(3):5–12.

Lippke, Richard L. 2001. "Criminal Offenders and Rights Forfeiture." *Journal of Social Philosophy* 32(1):78–89.

Lovegrove, Austin. 1988. *Judicial Decision-making.* New York: Springer-Verlag.

———. 1997. *The Framework of Judicial Sentencing: A Study in Legal Decision Making.* Cambridge: Cambridge University Press.

Markel, Dan. 2010. "Bentham on Stilts: The Bare Relevance of Subjectivity to Retributive Justice." *California Law Review* 98:907–87.

Matravers, Matt. 2011. "Is Twenty-first Century Punishment Post-Desert?" In *Retributivism Has a Past. Has It a Future?*, ed. Michael Tonry. New York: Oxford University Press.

Mennel, Robert M. 1983. *Thorns and Thistles: Juvenile Delinquents in the United States, 1825–1940.* Hanover: University of New Hampshire Press.

Michael, Jerome, and Mortimer Adler. 1933. *Crime, Law, and Social Science.* New York: Harcourt Brace.

Michael, Jerome, and Herbert Wechsler. 1940. *Criminal Law and Its Administration.* Chicago: Foundation Press.

Mitchell, Ohmarrh. 2011. "Drug and Other Problem-solving Courts." In *The Oxford Handbook of Crime and Criminal Justice*, ed. Michael Tonry. New York: Oxford University Press.

Moore, Michael S. 1993. "Justifying Retributivism." *Israeli Law Review* 27:15–36.

Morgan, R. 2006. "With Respect to Order, the Rules of the Game Have Changed: New Labour's Dominance of the 'Law and Order' Agenda." In *The Politics of Crime Control: Essays in Honour of David Downes*, ed. Tim Newburn and Paul Rock. Oxford: Oxford University Press.

Morris, Herbert. 1966. "Persons and Punishment." *Monist* 52:475–501.

———. 1981. "A Paternalist Theory of Punishment." *American Philosophical Quarterly* 18:263–71.

Morris, Norval. 1951. *The Habitual Criminal.* London: Longmans.

———. 1953. "Sentencing Convicted Criminals." *Australian Law Review* 27:186–208.

———. 1974. *The Future of Imprisonment.* Chicago: University of Chicago Press.

———. 1992. *The Brothel Boy and Other Parables of the Law.* Oxford: Oxford University Press.

Murphy, Jeffrie. 1973. "Marxism and Retribution." *Philosophy and Public Affairs* 2:217–43.

Nagel, Thomas. 1979. *Mortal Questions.* Cambridge: Cambridge University Press.

National Research Council. 2007. *Parole, Desistance from Crime, and Community Integration.* Committee on Community Supervision and Desistance from Crime. Washington, DC: National Academies Press.

Nellis, Ashley, and Ryan S. King. 2009. *No Exit: The Expanding Use of Life Sentences in America.* Washington, DC: The Sentencing Project.

O'Hear, Michael M. 2011. "Drug Treatment Courts as Communicative Punishment." In *Retributivism Has a Past. Has It a Future?*, ed. Michael Tonry. New York: Oxford University Press.

Platt, Anthony M. 1969. *The Child Savers; the Invention of Delinquency.* Chicago: University of Chicago Press.

President's Commission on Model State Drug Laws. 1993. *Final Report*. Washington, DC: U.S. Government Printing Office.

Ramsay, Peter. 2011. "A Political Theory of Imprisonment for Public Protection." In *Retributivism Has a Past. Has It a Future?*, ed. Michael Tonry. New York: Oxford University Press.

Rawls, John. 1955. "Two Concepts of Rules." *Philosophical Review* 44:3–13.

Reitz, Kevin. 2010. "The Illusion of Proportionality: Desert and Repeat Offenders." In *Previous Convictions at Sentencing: Theoretical and Applied Perspectives*, ed. Julian V. Roberts and Andrew von Hirsch. Oxford: Hart.

Ristroph, Alice. 2011. "Terror as a Theory of Punishment." In *Retributivism Has a Past. Has It a Future?*, ed. Michael Tonry. New York: Oxford University Press.

Roberts, Julian V. 2008. *Punishing Persistent Offenders: Exploring Community and Offender Perspectives*. Oxford: Oxford University Press.

———. 2011. "The Future of State Punishment: The Role of Public Opinion in Sentencing." In *Retributivism Has a Past. Has It a Future?*, ed. Michael Tonry. New York: Oxford University Press.

Roberts, Julian V., and Andrew von Hirsch, eds. 2010. *Previous Convictions at Sentencing: Theoretical and Applied Perspectives*. Oxford: Hart.

Robinson, Paul. 2003. "The Virtues of Restorative Processes, the Vices of 'Restorative Justice.'" *Utah Law Review* 2003:375–88.

———. 2008. *Distributive Principles of Criminal Law*. New York: Oxford University Press.

Robinson, Paul H., Robert Kurzban, and Owen D. Jones. 2007. "The Origins of Shared Intuitions of Justice." *Vanderbilt Law Review* 60:1633–88.

Ross, W. D. 1930. *The Right and the Good*. London: Clarendon.

Rothman, David J. 1971. *The Discovery of the Asylum: Social Order and Disorder in the New Republic*. Boston: Little, Brown.

Ryberg, Jesper. 2011. "Punishment and Desert-adjusted Utilitariansim." In *Retributivism Has a Past. Has It a Future?*, ed. Michael Tonry. New York: Oxford University Press.

Tonry, Michael. 1987. "Prediction and Classification: Legal and Ethical Issues." In *Crime and Justice: A Review of Research*, vol. 9, *Prediction and Classification in Criminal Justice Decision Making*, edited by Don M. Gottfredson and Michael Tonry. Chicago: University of Chicago Press.

———. 2004. *Thinking about Crime: Sense and Sensibility in American Penal Culture*. New York: Oxford University Press.

———. 2009. "Emerging Explanations of American Punishment Policies: A Natural History." *Punishment and Society* 11:377–94.

———. 2010. "The Costly Consequences of Populist Posturing: ASBOs, Victims, 'Rebalancing,' and Diminution of Support for Civil Liberties." *Punishment and Society* 12(4):387–413.

Tyler, Tom R. 2006. *Why People Obey the Law*, rev. ed. Princeton, NJ: Princeton University Press.

Virginia Criminal Sentencing Commission. 2010. *Manual*, 13th ed. Richmond: Virginia Criminal Sentencing Commission.

von Hirsch, Andrew. 1976. *Doing Justice*. New York: Hill and Wang.

———. 1985. *Past and Future Crimes: Deservedness and Dangerousness in Sentencing Criminals*. New Brunswick, NJ: Rutgers University Press.

———. 2010. "Previous Convictions and the Progressive Loss of Mitigation: Some Further Reflections." In *Previous Convictions at Sentencing: Theoretical and Applied Perspectives*, ed. Julian V. Roberts and Andrew von Hirsch. Oxford: Hart.

———. 2011. "Reflections on Punishment Futures: The Desert-Model Debate and the Importance of the Criminal Law Context." In *Retributivism Has a Past. Has It a Future?*, ed. Michael Tonry. New York: Oxford University Press.

von Hirsch, Andrew, Kay Knapp, and Michael Tonry. 1987. *Sentencing Commissions and their Guidelines*. Boston: Northeastern University Press.

von Hirsch, Andrew, Julian Roberts, Anthony E. Bottoms, Kent Roach, and Mara Schiff, eds. 2003. *Restorative Justice and Criminal Justice: Competing or Reconcilable Paradigms?* Oxford: Hart.

Walgrave, Lode. 2008. *Restorative Justice, Self-interest and Responsible Citizenship*. Cullompton, Devon, UK: Willan.

Walker, Nigel. 1991. *Why Punish?* Oxford: Oxford University Press.

———, ed. 1996. *Dangerous People*. London: Blackstone.

Wexler, David. 1995. "Reflections on the Scope of Therapeutic Jurisprudence." *Psychology, Public Policy, and Law* 1(1):230–36.

———. 2008a. *Rehabilitating Lawyers: Principles of Therapeutic Jurisprudence for Criminal Law Practice*. Durham, NC: Carolina Academic Press.

———. 2008b. "Two Decades of Therapeutic Jurisprudence." *Touro Law Review* 24:7–29.

Wexler, David B., and Bruce Winick, eds. 2003. *Judging in a Therapeutic Key: Therapeutic Jurisprudence and the Courts*. Durham, NC: Carolina Academic Press.

Williams, Bernard. 1981. *Moral Luck*. Cambridge: Cambridge University Press.

Wilson, David B., Doris L. MacKenzie, and Fawn Ngo Mitchell. 2008. Effects of Correctional Boot Camps on Offending. *Campbell Systematic Reviews*, 2003, no. 1 (first published January 8, 2003; updated February 12, 2008). http://www.campbellcollaboration.org/library.php.

Winick, Bruce J. 1997. "The Jurisprudence of Therapeutic Jurisprudence." *Psychology, Public Policy, and Law* 3(1):184–206.

———. 2005. *Civil Commitment: A Therapeutic Jurisprudence Model*. Durham, NC: Carolina Academic Press.

2

Is Twenty-first Century Punishment Post-desert?

MATT MATRAVERS

There are grave dangers in looking forward and making predictions about the way in which political theory and practice may develop. The obvious danger is simply that one might be mistaken. Less obvious, but still damaging, is to give in to the temptation to see the past and present as punctuated by decisive periodic breaks with a present fissure heralding a new era. The world is a complicated place and things are seldom predictable or describable in neat periods. Nevertheless, these dangers should not mean that we ignore broad shifts in emphasis or that we should be willfully blind to the evidence that things have changed, or are changing. Theories and policies do change, and the capacity of theory to respond to practice often depends on its ability to sense those changes and to think them through in advance of the policies getting too tight a grip on the way we act. With this in mind, there is good reason to consider the past and future of penal theory and practice.

Looking back, there is a now well-established story in penal philosophy that has it that the broadly consequentialist consensus of the postwar period was overturned in the 1970s by a retributivist revival. Although, as Michael Tonry makes clear in his introductory essay (Tonry 2011a), penal practice was much more complicated, the story does have some plausibility when applied to the theoretical literature. In 1969 a survey of justifications of punishment found that "there are no defenders [of traditional retributive theory] writing in the usual places" (Honderich 1969, p. 148). Ten years later one would have been able to say exactly the same about defenders of traditional consequentialism, while retributivists—in no fewer than nine varieties (Cottingham 1979)—were commonplace. However, the decline in consequentialism and the revival of retributivism does not map easily on to a story about desert. To see this, it is necessary to unpack the conventional story.

I. DESERT

There is little doubt that the retributive revival in penal theory was accompanied by, and could be thought to be part of, a general anticonsequentialism in the philosophical literature and a resurgence in the politics of desert. The decline of consequentialist moral thinking can be overemphasized, but the publication of John Rawls's *A Theory of Justice* (1971), which provided a systematic alternative to utilitarianism, was undoubtedly the dominant philosophical event of the period. Politically, in the United Kingdom and United States, the end of the decade brought electoral success to right-of-center parties led by Margaret Thatcher and Ronald Reagan. These leaders emphasized individual desert and responsibility, and their success can be measured in part by the fact that even when the political winds changed, their left-of-center successors went to extraordinary lengths to include these notions packaged as a "third way" that synthesized "rights and responsibilities" and insisted, for example, that welfare was "a hand up, not a hand out" (Matravers 2007, pp. 5–11).

Thus there seems to be a neat, almost overdetermined, story that leads from a consequentialist, welfarist heyday, dominant throughout the century until the 1970s, to a revolution that encompassed penal theory (Kleinig 1973; von Hirsch and Committee for the Study of Incarceration 1976); penal policy; legal, political, and moral theory (Hart 1968; Rawls 1971); and political practice. There is indeed much to this story, and many aspects of it are masterfully described in David Garland's *The Culture of Control* (2001). However, it is a mistake to think that there is a single story in which consequentialism's decline was accompanied, or caused, by a resurgence of the notion of desert.

The mistake is an easy one to make—particularly for penal theorists—since, as we have seen, over a relatively short period consequentialist penal theories (and some practices) declined, as did consequentialist theorizing more broadly (in the face of the Rawls-led neo-Kantian revival), retributive theories increased, and the rhetoric of desert became critical in political practice. Yet, this is not one story. To see this, consider just how odd it would be to claim that *desert* is critical to the criticisms of consequentialism and to the alternative neo-Kantian theory offered in Rawls's *A Theory of Justice*.

Rawls explicitly denies that the notion of moral desert has any part to play in a theory of distributive justice. "The principles of justice that regulate the basic structure," he writes, "do not mention moral desert, and there is no tendency for distributive shares to correspond to it" (Rawls 1971, p. 311). Given this, it is clear that Rawlsian theory should be included only in the "decline of consequentialism" part of the story and not in the narrative of the rise of desert. However, my claim is that this is true of the majority of retributive penal theories as well, and that these theories can, at best, only underwrite something that looks much more akin to Rawls than to traditional desert-based retributivisms. To see this, consider first Rawls's approach. Rawls's aversion to desert is well known, although I think sometimes misunderstood. One account has it that Rawls argues that we are all equally nondeserving (or, for that matter, deserving) because by declaring "morally arbitrary" everything that might differentiate us one from another, Rawls leaves nothing—natural talent, willingness to make an effort, social status, etc.—that could play the role of a desert basis and so legitimate anything other than equality of outcome (at least initially). A better account, I think, has it that Rawls thinks desert *irrelevant* to distributive justice. It is rejected as the foundation for justice because there is no sensible way of conceiving of a relevant, legitimate desert basis and then translating that into distributive shares. In cruder terms, one reading has it that no features of human beings can be attributed to them in a way that would legitimate treating one such being different from any other (we are not responsible for all those things—our heights, talents, intelligence, etc.—that enable us to achieve different things, so we do not deserve any differential reward or penalty for those achievements). The other, more plausible reading is that whether or not we are responsible for our talents, etc., there is no legitimate way of translating natural differences into distributive outcomes. Either way, the conclusion is, as Rawls puts it, that the common-sense tendency "to suppose that income and wealth, and the good things in life generally, should be distributed according to moral desert" is rejected (1971, p. 310).[1]

So the idea of a resurgent "desert theory" in theories of distributive justice—indeed, I think, in moral theory generally—is not sustainable. The Kantianism that forced out, and took the place of, the dominant consequentialist paradigm is one without Kant's metaphysics and one that has no place for a strong notion of desert. My claim, considered in the next section, is that the same is true of (most of) the penal theories that displaced their consequentialist counterparts.

II. WAS IT EVER ABOUT "JUST DESERTS"?

Tim Scanlon characterizes what he calls "the Desert Thesis" as follows: "the idea that when a person has done something that is morally wrong it is morally better that he or she should suffer some loss in consequence" (1998, p. 274).[2] Narrowed to the field of punishment, I take it that the relevant thesis is that a person who has committed a (legitimate) criminal wrong deserves to suffer some loss, and it is the function of the system of punishment to impose that loss for the wrong done. That is, the—or, at least, a— function of the system of punishment is to ensure that the suffering that is (prejusticially) deserved by a given offender for a given act is imposed on the offender.

Once desert is characterized in this way, it is not at all clear that there are many genuine desert theorists among those who would identify themselves, or be identified by others, as such. Of course, retributivists come in a variety of forms and the role of desert may be subtly different in each. However, our interest here is not in narrow differences between retributive arguments, but is rather in the place of desert in the overall approach. Thus it is possible to restrict the analysis to fewer, broader, and more abstract forms of the argument.[3] The retributive accounts briefly considered below are Michael Moore's intuitionist theory and so-called fair play theories. After that, the essay takes a longer look at communicative accounts and at mixed theories. The conclusion is that where desert has an independent and important role in the argument, the retributive theory is either implausible (Moore) or incomplete (communicative theories). In cases where the retributive theory fares better, desert is not central.

A. Michael Moore's Intuitionist Account

According to Moore, the retributive theory that he defends "is the view that we ought to punish offenders because, and only because, they deserve to be punished. Punishment is justified, for a retributivist, solely by the fact that those receiving it deserve it" (Moore 1987, 1993, p. 15; see also Moore 1997, chap. 2–3). Clearly this is a desert-based view. Since my main concern in this essay is not to evaluate retributive theories, but to establish that the retributive revival was not primarily a revival in desert thinking, Moore stands as a counterexample. However, for all the sophistication of his account, Moore's theory has not established itself in the mainstream. This is because it depends on a combination of a very demanding, if idiosyncratic, moral realism, and a thesis that our moral intuitions offer a good guide to the moral truth that offenders deserve to suffer (for Moore's moral realism, see Moore 1982, 1992). For reasons given elsewhere, I find this account implausible (Matravers 2000, pp. 81–86), but whether it is or not, it has played only a very minor role in the revival of retributive punishment theory (perhaps because of the metaphysical theory on which it relies).

B. Fair Play Theory

Fair play—or benefit and burden—theories enjoyed a brief period of popularity in the retributive revival of the 1960s and 1970s. The core of the argument is that, given a just initial distribution of benefits and burdens in society, a criminal offense disturbs this equilibrium and needs to be rectified. It does so because the criminal free rides on the willingness of others to constrain the pursuit of their interests in accordance with the law (Morris 1968; Murphy 1973). Again, the purpose here is not to consider the merits or otherwise of the account. That being said, taken as a complete account of punishment, few have found it compelling, and its critics include some of its early proponents. The problem, as Tonry puts it, is that "gaining an unfair advantage" by free riding is not "an adequate or even plausible characterization of the wrongfulness of many offenses" (Tonry 2011b, p. 109; for criticisms of fair play theory, see von Hirsch 1985, 1990; Duff 1986, 2001; Dolinko 1991; Matravers 2000; for a defense, see Dagger 1993). Putting that to one side, what of desert? Of course, in some sense the free rider "deserves" punishment. However, the kind of desert being invoked here is not the prejusticial desert of the desert thesis. There is not some appropriate level of suffering deserved by the offender that it is the job of the system of punishment to ensure that he gets. Rather, what the offender deserves is whatever loss (or suffering) is dictated by the system of justice that will restore the balance of benefits and burdens. Desert here is determined by the overall account of the balance of benefits and burdens; in Rawlsian terms (further discussed below), the offender and the wider society of which he has taken advantage have legitimate expectations, not desert claims, that need to be met.

C. Punishment as Communication[4]

Perhaps the most important and long-lasting of the retributive theories that emerged in the last third of the twentieth century was the communicative account of punishment. In its most sophisticated form, punishment aims, and is justified by the need, to convey censure. Moral wrongdoing deserves censure, and where a society has declared some behavior to be wrong, then censure is "owed" to the offender as "an honest response to his crime," to his victims "as an expression of concern for their wronged status," and to "the whole society, whose values the law claims to embody" (Duff 1998, p. 50).

There is a clear desert claim here: moral wrongdoing deserves censure (and its legal extension is that, following criminal wrongdoing, it is the job of punishment to inflict the deserved censure on the offender). Moreover—and perhaps one reason for the account's attractiveness and longevity—this claim does not seem to rely on any odd metaphysics or other mysterious ingredient. As Duff puts it, "whatever puzzles there might be about the general idea that crimes 'deserve' punishment . . . there is surely nothing puzzling about the idea that wrongdoing deserves censure" (1998, p. 50). However, this is not the desert thesis, which is about the deserved nature of an imposed *loss*. In short, the desert thesis as applied to punishment needs to accommodate deserved hard treatment. As Duff notes, while censure can be conveyed by hard treatment, it need not be. Thus the censure theory faces the "familiar task . . . to explain and justify the role of hard treatment" (Duff 1998, p. 51).

Although Duff believes that hard treatment can be intrinsically linked to censure, few others are persuaded. Of course, being censured might itself be unpleasant, but there is no reason to believe that it has to be so. Thus some additional argument is needed. According to Duff, hard treatment is intrinsic to the account because censure needs to be forcefully expressed; because sometimes words are insufficient to express remorse or repentance; and because the offender needs to undertake some form of suffering to show to her community that she is serious, and thus to achieve reconciliation. Discussion of these claims would take us beyond the purpose of the argument here (for criticisms, see Matravers 2011a). In relation to the argument here, the point is that, while censure may be deserved, hard treatment (at best) merely provides the vehicle of transmission for the censure and the offender's response to that censure. More plausibly, censure is deserved, but hard treatment must find some other justification. This—that censure is only one element of a complete account of punishment—is the argument that has had the most purchase in the literature, which means that unless the theoretical resources upon which a revised account draws are also desert-based, then the censure theory cannot be said to underpin a revival in the centrality of desert-based theorizing.

D. Mixed Theories

The mixed theory on which I want to concentrate is one that does indeed aim to supplement the censure-based account with an independent justification of hard treatment. However, it is worth adding a brief word about H. L. A. Hart's account, both because it remains influential and because Hart is sometimes cited in the orthodox story of the decline of consequentialism and the rise of desert.

Hart's work certainly fits the period. *Punishment and Responsibility* was published in 1968 and offers a broadly liberal account of the subject matter (on occasions in explicit opposition to the consequentialism of the English penal theorist Barbara Wootton) (see Hart 1968, chap. 7, 8). Yet, of course, Hart believed the overall purpose—the general justifying aim—of punishment to be consequentialist (Hart 1968, chap. 1). And while it is true that once the system is in place its operation is limited by desert side constraints, these are not expressions of the desert thesis.[5] Rather, these side constraints capture a liberal model of the proper relation between the state and its citizens. As a citizen, it should be up to me whether I put myself in the realm of punishment, and having done so, I should be treated as a "person" and not as something "alterable, predictable, curable or manipulable" (Hart 1968, p. 183). Hart, then, cannot be invoked in defense of the desert thesis, although his work (like Rawls's) was undoubtedly important in setting the tone of the post-consequentialist era.

Hart's is probably the most famous mixed theory among justifications of punishment. However, like most philosophical theories, its claim to have directly influenced policy is at best moot. That is not true of the mixed theory on which I want to focus in the rest of this section. For more than a quarter of a century, Andrew von Hirsch has championed "proportionality" in sentencing with considerable success in terms of both theory and practice. A bumper sticker for the account is that "the punishment must fit the crime," which can be understood in at least two ways. Confusion between these is probably the single most likely source of what I argue is the conflation of the rise of retributivism with the rise of desert.

In one interpretation, there is a desert thesis account of the idea that the punishment must fit the crime. This is that there is some preestablished quantum of suffering that is appropriate, that "fits" the crime, and that it is the job of the system of punishment to inflict on the offender. However, that is not what is meant by proportionality as championed by von Hirsch (and others). Proportionality in sentencing is primarily a matter of the relations within a scheme of penalties, not of the anchoring of that scheme. It requires two things. Ordinal proportionality requires that similarly culpable "persons convicted of crimes of comparable gravity should receive punishments of comparable severity." Cardinal proportionality concerns "the overall magnitude and anchoring points of a penalty scale" (von Hirsch 1990).

It is the proportionality interpretation of the punishment fitting the crime that has been championed by retributivists like von Hirsch and Andrew Ashworth, so the question arises whether proportionality is an expression of the desert thesis. The requirement of ordinal proportionality has nothing to do with the desert thesis. It merely requires that if offender A commits an offense O with no mitigating or aggravating circumstances and receives a punishment of severity P, then offender B, who commits a similar offense in similar circumstances should also receive a punishment of severity P. Similarly, offender C, who culpably commits an offense that is twice as serious as that committed by offenders A and B, should receive a punishment that is twice as severe as that handed out to A and B. Note how easy it is to describe this in terms of "desert." If, once the scheme is established, A and B are punished by P, it makes sense to say that C deserves 2P. But the desert claim here is relative to the scheme, not to some ideal of suffering that needs to be imposed in response to the offense. It is, in Rawlsian terms, an "entitlement." C is "entitled" or has a "legitimate expectation" to receive 2P, given the scheme and the treatment of A and B. C's punishment "fits the crime" in accordance with the scheme, as, of course, does A's and B's, and again, according to the scheme, these punishments are what is deserved, but none of this has the slightest thing to do with the desert thesis.

The overall magnitude and anchoring points of the scale, its cardinal status, could of course be fixed by considerations drawn from the desert thesis. If it is given—or can be intuited as a moral fact in Moore's sense—that the suffering appropriate for the least serious crime on the scale is a nominal monetary fine and that appropriate for the most serious is, say, death, then the scale would be most appropriately constructed in accordance with these requirements (ordinal proportionality would only be required if the moral truth about deserved suffering turned out to meet that condition). However, this is not the position that von Hirsch takes in any of his writing.

Rather, von Hirsch has contemplated a number of ways of fixing the penalty scale, derived from asking questions such as "what is available?" and "what is conventional?" (see, e.g., von Hirsch 1985, p. 159). More recently, in particular in his work with Andrew Ashworth (von Hirsch and Ashworth 2005), he has pursued a mixed theory in which censure plays a leading retributive role and hard treatment acts as a prudential supplement aimed to aid citizens—who are neither fully saints nor fully sinners—in their resisting the temptation to commit crime. In this case, then, one might say that censure is deserved (in response to some offense) and it is the job of the criminal justice system to deliver that censure. Hard treatment is deserved, too, but only in an "entitlement" sense. The offender may expect hard treatment both as a means of expressing censure and to deter him and others, but the degree of hard treatment is dependent on a scheme of penalties that has the reduction of future crime at its core.

E. Retributivism

In short, with the notable exception of Michael Moore, the mainstream revival in retributivism since the 1970s has not been a revival in the desert thesis. The slogan "the punishment must fit the crime" is part of contemporary retributivism, but its association with traditional notions of desert is inappropriate. Retributivists, of course, may welcome this conclusion. They may do so for two reasons. First, the traditional desert thesis is defensible only by invoking some pretty robust metaphysical commitments (such as can be found in Kant, Hegel, and Moore), and such commitments are not only out of fashion philosophically, but are widely regarded by liberals as an inappropriate basis on which to ground public policy in pluralistic societies (see Rawls 1999; famously, John Rawls described his theory as "Political not Metaphysical"). Second, it is often taken to be a cruel irony that what began for many as a liberal, left-of-center call for fairness in sentencing and an end to arbitrary punishments was hijacked by right-of-center politicians pushing for harsher punishments. If what I have said is correct, then there was no such capture of the "just deserts" movement, because that movement was only about proportional justice, not about desert. Reagan, Thatcher, and the theorists who followed them corrupted, rather than hijacked, the retributive revival. One example will suffice: California legislators may believe that those who commit three felony offenses deserve indefinite detention under the "three-strikes" law, but this clearly has nothing to do with retributivism understood as proportionality.

It may be thought that the argument has reached a dead end. This essay has relied on a particular, traditional, understanding of deserved punishment—the desert thesis—that, it turns out, few other theorists or theories share, and few would wish to share. Retributivists are broadly about the communication of censure and the proportional use of hard treatment; but that is what they said they were about, so what gains are made by pointing it out (other than clarifying why politically motivated rhetoric about desert has little to do with retributivism)? The gains, I think, lie in clarifying what needs to be done when confronted by recent and not so recent developments in penal practice. By that I do not mean that we are able to respond to the corrupt version of retributivism that has given us severe mandatory sentences for many crimes and three-strikes legislation, but also that if we are to respond to the challenge of thinking about recent therapeutic or restorative practices, we need to know what the issue is. If the above argument is correct, then the issue is *not* one of reconciling those practices to desert, or conceptualizing a post-desert world, but rather, or so I will argue below, it is one of thinking about the requirements of liberal justice as a whole.

III. PROPORTIONALITY

For most retributivists, then, the justification of systems of penal hard treatment is not that they exist in order to give an earthly form to some kind of "celestial mechanics" in which wrong actions deserve "an equal and opposite reaction" in the form of imposed suffering (Cohen 1939, p. 279). Rather, they are a mechanism of social order needed because living together on shared territory in conditions of moderate scarcity is difficult and throws up all manner of coordination problems.[6] However, not just any means to social order are acceptable. For retributivists (at least for those considered for the rest of this essay), the principle of proportionality stands independently and thus dictates at least a significant part of the system of punishment.

It is important to be clear: proportionality does not provide the ultimate rationale for having a system of punishment (as against not having one). It is not that there is some proportionate suffering that must be imposed on wrongdoers so that a system of punishment is required to fulfill this demand. It is that in designing or critiquing a system of punishment—one that is to be or has been created for some other reason—the demands of proportionality must be respected. Although not the desert thesis, this would still be a substantive demand, and one that could underpin criticism of much recent penal practice (disproportionate sentencing, therapeutic justice, etc.).

Although I have a great deal of sympathy with the proportionality thesis, for reasons given in the next section, I believe it should not be used too quickly. It is not at all obvious that proportionality is an independent principle that should automatically be deployed as a trump to defeat other approaches to crime management and reduction.

A. Proportionality and Fairness

The attractions of proportionality to those who consider fairness a value, and to liberals more generally, ought to be clear. Once the system of justice is in place, people are entitled to certain things, to be treated in certain ways. Penal hard treatment must respect those entitlements. Proportional sentencing—the claim that "the penal sanction should fairly reflect the . . . harmfulness and culpability of the actor's conduct" (von Hirsch and Ashworth 2005, p. 4)—treats people fairly both in the narrow sense of treating like cases alike (and unlike cases differently) and, its proponents claim, in the sense of treating people as agents who are entitled to a certain kind of respect.

The first of those claims looks to be uncontroversial: similarly harmful and culpable offenders will receive similar punishments and those whose harmfulness or culpability is different will receive different punishments. The second is not quite so apparent, but rests on the belief that citizens are entitled to a certain form of equal respect. This not only means that they are entitled to be treated alike (when relevantly alike), but also that they should not, in Hart's words (1968, p. 183), be treated as if "alterable, predictable, curable or manipulable." In short, the state should appeal to our capacities as reasoning agents, and not merely threaten or manipulate. Thus proponents of proportionality claim the anchoring points of the scale of penalties have to be such as to respect citizens as persons. To threaten citizens with death for a minor traffic offense might reduce violations of traffic laws, but it would hardly be to treat citizen drivers as agents.

Although attractive, I am not convinced that these arguments are sufficient to establish proportionality as an independent side constraint on permissible systems of punishment. Consider them in reverse order.

The second argument is that respect for persons as agents requires an overall anchoring of the penalty scheme such that threatened hard treatment is not so severe as to fail to recognize our status as reasoning beings. This means that were a penalty scheme to be proposed that was very severe—perhaps in response to some consequentialist argument that, for example, conviction rates are so low that general deterrence can only be achieved by increased penalties—the principle of proportionality would rule it out. The argument that is deployed in support of this position is the "drowning out" objection. That is, if the sentencing scheme is very severe, the moral appeal of the law will be lost and citizens will think only in prudential terms. This is to control citizens by threats rather than to offer them moral reasons for action (von Hirsch 1990; Duff 1998; von Hirsch and Ashworth 2005).

The problem with this is that it just does not seem very plausible once one considers the ways in which citizens actually reason. Consider someone considering parking illegally. Presumably many people park illegally for short periods without thinking too much about the moral wrong that may be involved. Now, consider what would happen if the state imposed a severe penalty for this offense (say, the confiscation of one's car). In such circumstances, presumably most people would pause and think the risk was not worth it. Should they then feel that they have been treated as less than an agent? That seems wildly overdramatic. All that has happened is that the state has changed the outcome of one's prudential reasoning.

For more serious offenses, the situation is difficult, but no less damaging for the drowning out thesis. Imagine the penalty for murdering one's spouse is to be choked and then burnt at the stake. Would that make most married citizens think any less about the moral reasons not to murder their husbands or wives? Surely not, since most people, most of the time, do not think about the reasons they have not to commit murder. For most people, the reasons not to do so are inert, since there is never an occasion in which they need to figure in their mental life.

What of those people who are sorely tempted to murder their spouses? In such cases it does not seem to me at all plausible that the *absence* of overwhelming prudential reasons not to do so would help them to focus on the moral reasons not to do so. That point has passed. In short, for the core criminal offenses, we are not—in Andrew von Hirsch's terms—neither saints nor sinners, but something in between (von Hirsch 1990). We are actually saints or sinners (in the relevant senses) for whom the threat is either inert or (we hope) sufficient.

Thus there is no independent principle of cardinal proportionality linked to a notion of the respect we are owed as persons that can limit the system of punishment or speak in favor of a reduction in sentencing levels. Of course, there are many other reasons why we should limit punishments. For example, the risk of wrongly falling foul of the law and the need to respect Bentham's (1970, p. 168) injunction that penalties should not encourage wrongdoers to greater wrongdoing, but these are not arguments that can underpin proportionality as an independent principle.

What of the first, seemingly more powerful argument that ordinal proportionality ensures equality; that like cases are treated alike? This has great appeal to liberals, for whom equality is a foundational value. Thus, clearly a system of penalties that distinguishes between persons on the basis of skin color and imposes greater penalties on black-skinned offenders than on white-skinned ones would be a paradigm instance of injustice. By extension, a system that penalizes the kinds of drug use associated with one community more severely than similarly harmful kinds of drug use associated with another is unjust.

However, the argument becomes more complicated once one considers other, less arbitrary rationales for different treatment (i.e., we need to be sure that the problem with the above examples is that they fail to respect ordinal proportionality rather than that they are based on arbitrary—and offensive—distinctions).

Assume that there are good public policy reasons for the state to wish to crack down on a particular kind of offense; say, the state is very worried about the influx of a certain gang culture and decides to issue sentencing guidelines that make gang-related crime automatically subject to an extra tariff. Thus two offenders who are equally culpable and have committed offenses involving equal harm may receive different penalties as a result of one being in a gang and the other not. Is this a violation of one's status as an equal?

I think that is at least arguable. Of course, their treatment *is* unequal, but the respect we are owed as citizens is, as Dworkin (1978) has usefully phrased it, not a matter of equal treatment, but of "treatment as an equal." Dworkin famously argued that it might be the case that the state has an interest in developing African American professionals (doctors and lawyers) and thus quotas for graduate school places in those disciplines could be compatible with treatment as an equal (since the reason for differentiating between applicants was not their skin color, but their ability to develop into socially useful role models). Similarly, to treat gang members differently from otherwise identical offenders seems less like treating blacks differently from whites and more like treating trainee brain surgeons differently from equally hard-working trainee beauticians. The brain surgeon is entitled to expect greater rewards not because social policy aims to reward the clever, but because rewarding the clever in this case serves a useful social policy.

The point of this section is not to deny that proportionality has an important role in our thinking about punishment. It does and will continue to do so. However, it is not an independent principle. Rather, it is one of many considerations that must be taken into account when we devise a system of criminal justice and punishment. It may often be one of the most important considerations, and violations of proportionality will require special justification, but it is not a liberal trump card that can be played without further need for justification in proposing or criticizing a penal system.

IV. PUNISHMENT IN THEORY

I have argued that neither the desert thesis nor the demands of proportionality necessarily dictate the shape of a legitimate and just criminal justice system. However, I have not said very much that is positive, that is, about how we might think about such a system. This is critical if we are to be able to respond—as I indicated we should—to developments in penal practice.

Of course, it is not possible here to offer a complete argument in defense of a system of criminal justice. Rather, I want to say something general about how we should go about constructing such an argument and something more particular about how it might inform our responses to at least some recent changes in the penal landscape.

Underlying the argument so far has been the Rawlsian thought that the only relevant notion of deserved hard treatment (but not deserved censure) is one that "presupposes the existence of the cooperation scheme" (Rawls 1971, p. 103). That is, once a just scheme is in place, it gives rise to legitimate expectations (e.g., if one does not break the law, then one will not be subject to punishment). In thinking about penal hard treatment, then, we have to think about the overall just scheme and the legitimate expectations it creates. That is best done, I believe (but cannot defend that belief here), by considering what agents would agree to in some suitably constructed hypothetical choosing situation (see Matravers 2000; for a more Rawlsian take on the social contract and its application to punishment, see Matravers 2011b, 2011c).

The task of giving an adequate account of punishment is, of course, familiar, and such accounts are invariably controversial. This is not the place to try to develop another. Rather, I want to say something about how we might evaluate some recent examples of penal practice and how, in doing so, we might better prepare for whatever is next as we enter the second decade of the new century.

A. Coercive Treatment

Consider the example of coercive treatment; say, the order that an offender undertake anger management therapy on pain of some further penalty. Coercive treatment was, of course, one of the targets in the revival of retributivism, and for some retributivists, the recent advance of so-called therapeutic jurisprudence (as championed by Wexler 1995, 2008; Winick 1997) represents a return to the dark days before the revolution.

Can coercive treatments of this kind be given a rationale that accords with the demands of liberal egalitarian justice? On the face of it, things are not promising. The coercive nature of directed treatments speaks against compatibility with freedom, the treatment element against autonomy, and the fact that different offenders may receive different punishment against proportionality. However, appearances may be deceptive.

Consider persons located in a suitably modified Rawlsian original position choosing principles of penal justice. They do not know, of course, whether they will be disposed to aggression in the "real world," but they will know general facts about that world, such as that there is a need for social order, assurance, and so on. They must then choose to respond to aggression, but there is reason for them to argue that the response can be moderated by the needs of social policy. There is no independent standard of entitlements that the people in the original position must translate into their principles of justice. Rather, what citizens will be entitled to is itself determined by the principles of justice. Thus they may be able to endorse coercive treatment models by reasoning over each of the potential problems.

Take treatment first. The clearest case would presumably be something akin (although not identical) to quarantine, but quarantine potentially avoids autonomy problems by conceiving of the agent as a mere "carrier." It is the virus (or whatever) that is quarantined; the agent's being coerced is merely an unfortunate by-product. A better analogy might come from distributive justice. It is held by some that an agent with unchosen expensive tastes should be compensated for the loss of welfare that results from these tastes unless, for example, he would choose to keep those tastes even were he able to take an otherwise harmless pill that would rid him of them. Or, imagine someone who needs very expensive treatment for depression. We may think, other things being equal, that she is entitled to such treatment at public expense, but not if we discover that there is an easy, harmless cure for her type of depression that she refuses to take.

Putting to one side issues of identification, false positives, and so on, an agent with anger management problems who (possibly as a result of those problems) regularly falls afoul of the law might be thought to be in a similar situation. It is compatible with his freedom for others to offer treatment, with the clear understanding that if he refuses that treatment he must then pick up the full costs of his behavior (which may in this case mean something like a severe penalty the next time he breaks the law). Establishing exactly what that means is difficult to determine without a full account of the theory of punishment a given contract would generate, but nevertheless the reasoning here is neither unusual nor incompatible with the liberal requirement to treat people as equals. The intuition is a standard one: Why should anyone else bear the costs of his behavior if he refuses to do what he can to change that behavior?

Of course, this example immediately raises autonomy worries, since I am speaking of the offender as being in need of treatment—as ill or defective—rather than as an autonomous chooser. I am less worried about this in theory, although how much we have to worry in practice depends on the proposed intervention (there is a significant difference between courses to teach information technology skills, cognitive behavioral therapy (CBT), and an intervention such as chemical castration). Many forms of intervention can make our lives better and better enable us to cope with the world and others. Recognizing that, and responding with offers to help, seems to me unproblematic. Except in very extreme cases, I think the offer must be one that can be refused. But as indicated above, in many instances it is a liberal principle that one should not be able to refuse while passing the continuing costs of the problem on to others.

Finally, what of the fairness (or proportionality) worry? Could those participating in the social contract endorse different punishments for the same offenses depending on, say, the potential dangerousness of the offender? One way around this might be to separate the punishment tariff from the dangerousness tariff and argue that in some circumstances it would be rational for the contractors to agree, in effect, to quarantine the dangerous. In circumstances (which are far from obtaining) in which we could identify the dangerous, there would not seem to be anything to bar this move.

V. PUNISHMENT IN PRACTICE

The above offers a very brief introduction to how one might think about penal policies in the abstract. Having rejected the desert thesis, I have argued that "an entitlement to proportionality in sentencing" is *not* an independent principle, but is—as with all "entitlements"—determined by the wider theory of justice. For this reason, policy proposals have to be thought through; they cannot simply be rejected as incompatible with desert or proportionality. The result, of course, cannot be known in advance. It may be that therapy, mandatory sentences, sentencing guidelines that are not strictly proportional, and so on are all incompatible with a liberal theory of punishment. I doubt it, but my case here does not rest on whether they are or are not. Rather, it rests on whether these things can be dismissed on the basis of being incompatible with retributivism understood in terms of the desert thesis or proportionality (they cannot). In thinking about the future of punishment, we must not be complacent. The revival of retributivism swept away many terrible practices, but it did not leave us with a coherent theory of punishment with which to judge future policies.

Finally, what has been said above relates to how we might, as penal philosophers, think about policy proposals. However, in responding to such policies we must be prepared to accept contingent facts that may play no part in ideal theory. That is, even if it were true that a form of preventive detention or a mandatory minimum sentence for some offense were compatible with the liberal requirement to treat citizens as equals, that does not mean that such policies are justified, all things considered. It may well be that the background conditions of distributive injustice, or the capricious nature of those who police (in the widest sense) the criminal justice system, mean that greater injustice would be done by departing from proportionality than by sticking with it.

In short, and to answer the question posed in the title, twenty-first century punishment will be post-desert, but that is not a recent change. Our best theories of punishment (and much else) are post-desert, and have been since long before the retributive revival at the end of the twentieth century. That revival was not about desert, but was about sweeping away many practices that resulted in actual injustices. It has left us with a principle of proportionality that is important, but insufficient. The actual injustices that occur as a result of our penal systems are still many, and in many places are increasing. What is needed in the future is not only to think through what are the legitimate entitlements and expectations of liberal citizens in relation to their criminal justice system, but also to confront the problems that arise in the nonideal world in which we live. That is probably best done by considering distributive and retributive justice together in the hope that the resulting thoughts will influence those who make and apply the law.

NOTES

1. Nevertheless, the difference between the readings is important because the former would seem to generalize to retributive justice (if, because we are not responsible for our natural starting points, we do not deserve different treatment on the basis of those differences, then that would seem to apply to all questions of desert), whereas the latter does not (since it may be that there are differences between distributive and retributive justice that mean natural inequalities can be legitimately translated into inequalities in outcome in the one but not the other). It is worth pausing to note just how radical is Rawls's rejection of desert (on this, and on why it may explain the difficulty Rawlsians confronted in addressing political questions at the end of the twentieth century, see Scheffler [2001, chap. 1] and Matravers [2004]). For a general discussion of the relationship of distributive and retributive justice in Rawls's theory, see Scheffler (2001) and Matravers (2011b, 2011c).
2. It is worth noting that Scanlon—a significant moral philosopher in the Rawlsian, neo-Kantian mold—regards the desert thesis as "morally indefensible," which is yet further evidence that the assault on consequentialism in the philosophical literature was not led by theorists committed to restoring desert to a central place in moral thinking.
3. As noted above, Cottingham identified nine forms of retributive thinking. Further distinctions can be found in Walker (1999) and Tonry (2011b, pp. 108–9) (see also Cottingham 1979).
4. This subsection draws extensively from Matravers (2011a).
5. As John Gardner puts it, "the only Hart-approved reason in favour of punishing the guilty (or anyone else) is the reason given by punishment's general justifying aim, viz. that future wrongdoing is thereby reduced" (2008, p. xxv).
6. The exceptions are Moore and Duff, who believe that the system of punishment gives form to the need for moral criticism in response to wrongdoing.

REFERENCES

Bentham, Jeremy. 1970. "An Introduction to the Principles of Morals and Legislation." In *The Collected Works of Jeremy Bentham*, ed. Fred Rosen and Philip Schofield. Oxford: Oxford University Press.

Cohen, Morris R. 1939. "A Critique of Kant's Philosophy of Law." In *The Heritage of Kant*, ed. G. T. Whitney and D. F. Bowers. Princeton, NJ: Princeton University Press.

Cottingham, John. 1979. "Varieties of Retribution." *Philosophical Quarterly* 29:238–46.

Dagger, Richard. 1993. "Playing Fair with Punishment." *Ethics* 103:473–88.

Dolinko, David. 1991. "Some Thoughts About Retributivism." *Ethics* 101(3):537–59.

Duff, R. A. 1986. *Trials & Punishments*. Cambridge Studies in Philosophy. Cambridge: Cambridge University Press.

———. 1998. "Punishment, Communication, and Community." In *Punishment and Political Theory*, ed. Matt Matravers. Oxford: Hart.

———. 2001. *Punishment, Communication, and Community*. Studies in Crime and Public Policy. New York: Oxford University Press.

Dworkin, Ronald. 1978. *Taking Rights Seriously: With a Reply to Critics*. London: Duckworth.

Gardner, John. 2008. "Introduction." In H. L. A. Hart, *Punishment and Responsibility: Essays in the Philosophy of Law*, 2nd ed. Oxford: Oxford University Press.

Garland, David. 2001. *The Culture of Control: Crime and Social Order in Contemporary Society*. Oxford: Oxford University Press.

Hart, H. L. A. 1968. *Punishment and Responsibility: Essays in the Philosophy of Law*. Oxford: Oxford University Press.

Honderich, Ted. 1969. *Punishment: The Supposed Justifications*. London: Hutchinson.

Kleinig, John. 1973. *Punishment and Desert*. The Hague: Martinus Nijhoff.

Matravers, Matt. 2000. *Justice and Punishment: The Rationale of Coercion*. Oxford: Oxford University Press.

———. 2004. "Philosophy as Politics: Some Guesses as to the Future of Political Philosophy." In *What Philosophy Is*, ed. Havi Carel and David Gamez. London: Continuum.

———. 2007. *Responsibility and Justice*. Cambridge: Polity Press.

———. 2011a. "Duff on Hard Treatment." In *Crime, Punishment, and Responsibility: The Jurisprudence of Antony Duff*, ed. Rowan Cruft, Matthew H. Kramer, and Mark R. Reiff. Oxford: Oxford University Press.

———. 2011b. "Mad, Bad, or Faulty? Desert in Distributive and Retributive Justice." In *Responsibility and Distributive Justice*, ed. Carl Knight and Zofia Stemplowska. Oxford: Oxford University Press.

———. 2011c. "Political Theory and the Criminal Law." In *Philosophical Foundations of the Criminal Law*, ed. R. Antony Duff and Stuart Green. New York: Oxford University Press.

Moore, Michael. 1982. "Moral Reality." *Wisconsin Law Review* 1982:1061–156.

———. 1987. "The Moral Worth of Retribution." In *Responsibility, Character and the Emotions*, ed. Ferdinand Schoemann. New York: Cambridge University Press.

———. 1992. "Moral Reality Revisited." *Michigan Law Review* 90:2424–533.

———. 1993. "Justifying Retributivism." *Israel Law Review* 27:15–49.

———. 1997. *Placing Blame: A General Theory of the Criminal Law*. Oxford: Oxford University Press.

Morris, Herbert. 1968. "Persons and Punishment." *Monist* 52:475–501.

Murphy, Jeffrie. 1973. "Marxism and Retribution." *Philosophy and Public Affairs* 2:217–43.

Rawls, John. 1971. *A Theory of Justice*. Cambridge, MA: Harvard University Press.

———. 1999. "Justice as Fairness: Political not Metaphysical." In *Collected Papers*, ed. John Rawls and Samuel Richard Freeman. Cambridge, MA: Harvard University Press.

Scanlon, Thomas M. 1998. *What We Owe to Each Other*. Cambridge, MA: Harvard University Press.

Scheffler, Samuel. 2001. *Boundaries and Allegiances: Problems of Justice and Responsibility in Liberal Thought*. Oxford: Oxford University Press.

Tonry, Michael. 2011a. "Can Twenty-first Century Punishment Policies Be Justified in Principle?" In *Retributivism Has a Past. Has It a Future?*, ed. Michael Tonry. New York: Oxford University Press.

———, ed. 2011b. *Why Punish? How Much?: A Reader on Punishment*. New York: Oxford University Press.

von Hirsch, Andrew. 1985. *Past or Future Crimes: Deservedness and Dangerousness in the Sentencing of Criminals*. Crime, Law, and Deviance Series. New Brunswick, NJ: Rutgers University Press.

———. 1990. "Proportionality in the Philosophy of Punishment: From 'Why Punish?' to 'How Much?'" *Criminal Law Forum* 1:259–90.

von Hirsch, Andrew. 1976. *Doing Justice: The Choice of Punishments: Report of the Committee for the Study of Incarceration*. New York: Hill and Wang.

von Hirsch, Andrew, and Andrew Ashworth. 2005. *Proportionate Sentencing: Exploring the Principles*. Oxford Monographs on Criminal Law and Justice. New York: Oxford University Press.

Walker, Nigel. 1999. *Aggravation, Mitigation, and Mercy in English Criminal Justice*. London: Blackstone.

Wexler, David B. 1995. "Reflections on the Scope of Therapeutic Jurisprudence." *Psychology, Public Policy, and Law* 1(1):230–36.

———. 2008. *Rehabilitating Lawyers: Principles of Therapeutic Jurisprudence for Criminal Law Practice*. Durham, NC: Carolina Academic Press.

Winick, Bruce. 1997. "The Jurisprudence of Therapeutic Jurisprudence." *Psychology, Public Policy, and Law* 3(1):184–206.

3

What Does Wrongdoing Deserve?

JOHN KLEINIG

T he question may seem dated or its answer obvious.[1] In any case, it has a well-worn
response, namely, that wrongdoing deserves punishment.[2] For reasons that I will
endeavor to make clear, I want to stay with the question—and, ultimately, the answer. I
propose, however, to consider the possibility of an alternative answer that accommo-
dates recent interest in ideas associated with restorative justice.

There are many and diverse reasons for considering the initial question to be dated,
though this essay attempts to address only a few of them. For one thing, the very idea of
moral wrongdoing may seem to have lost its place in scientific anthropology. Talk of
wrongdoing is suffused with implications of responsibility or—perish the thought—
free will and, it is said, these notions have been or soon will be rendered obsolete by advances in neuroscience and evolutionary biology (Greene and Cohen 2004). Along with
the demise of freewill and moral responsibility, even among those for whom the idea of
moral wrongdoing still has some resonance, will go appeals to desert. Desert, at least
moral desert, is often seen as a holdover from emotive and intuitive—even magical—
ways of thinking, its invocation now to be viewed as no more than a primitive or atavistic
reactive response to transgression. A response, moreover, that even among those who
continue to hew to the idea of moral wrongdoing, is ill-suited to the rational, constructive, and future-oriented ways of thinking appropriate to the twenty-first century. Even
the traditional response to the question of what wrongdoing deserves—punishment—
is said to be so corrupted and stained by the barbarism of incarceration that it no longer
represents an enlightened response to wrongdoing, however conceived, and needs to be
replaced by more humane, civilized, and communitarian practices, such as (though not
necessarily limited to) those represented by what are commonly characterized as restorative approaches to justice.[3]

As I noted, reactions such as the foregoing reflect diverse and, it might be added, to
some extent incompatible ways of thinking, but they come together by urging us to dispense with the idea that wrongdoing deserves punishment. I do not use the present

opportunity to discuss some of the more radical of these responses to the initial question—such as those that would seek to replace our traditional notion of wrong-doing with supposedly more scientific conceptualizations of human behavior and its control. I assume that it makes good sense to hold onto a notion of moral wrongdoing and that, when confronted by it, we are justified in asking what kind of response to it is appropriate. What I do explore is whether the language of desert can be given a credible place in our thinking about the appropriateness of a response to wrongdoing and, if so, what that deserved response might be. Does it follow seamlessly from the question of what wrongdoing deserves that punishment is the best or only appropriate answer? In section I, I briefly review the vicissitudes of desert before considering in sections II and III—also briefly—a range of other possible responses to wrongdoing that highlight the distinctive character of the response that is sought when the language of desert is invoked. In section IV I revisit the grammar of desert, before focusing on preinstitutional deserts and their implications for our response to wrongdoing in section V. In section VI, I take a brief look at the ill-desert–hard-treatment nexus before applying this, in section VII, to the demands of restorative justice.

I. THE VICISSITUDES OF DESERT

A review of the philosophical literature from 50 years ago and before leaves the strong impression that an earlier generation and its forebears had already consigned the notion of desert, along with its punitive expression, retribution, to the dustbin of history. Indeed, for much of the previous two centuries, various forms of "forward-looking" con-sequentialism had gained the ascendancy in English-language moral theory and, at least in relation to punishment, the "backward-looking" idea of desert was often asserted to express a gut reaction to wrongdoing, no more than a primitive response to serious inter-personal and social wrongdoing. It was considered more akin to payback or revenge than to rehabilitation, deterrence, or the various socially useful responses for whose fulfill-ment punishment was thought to be more appropriately directed.[4] The impressive eight-volume *Encyclopedia of Philosophy*, edited by Paul Edwards in the 1960s, had no article on (or index reference to) desert, and even in his excellent entry on punishment, Stanley Benn allowed to desert only the limited analytic role of signaling that punishment must be of the guilty. It could serve no justificatory function.[5]

During the 1960s and 1970s, however, desert underwent something of an academic revival, as various liberal theorists sought to disentangle it from its emotivist associations and to articulate its connections with important dimensions of justice (Feinberg 1970; Kleinig 1973; von Hirsch 1976; Sher 1987). *Doing Justice*—a 1976 report of the Com-mittee for the Study of Incarceration—began to influence criminal justice policy as "just deserts" theory. In addition, George Sher even devoted a monograph to desert as part of a prestigious Princeton University Press series. But despite this flowering of interest,[6] and several influential attempts to articulate the foundations of its often intuitive appeal, desert began to sink again into liberal desuetude. Those who had advanced desert as an appropriate and morally critical "gauge" for penal justice had trouble shaking it loose from powerful populist expressions of revenge or a retaliatory "getting back and getting even." Even when desert's connections to proportionality were acknowledged, its practical determinations were often beholden to conservative tough-on-crime policies.[7] Its seemingly "self-evident" connection with punishment ("wrongdoing deserves punishment") did not help matters.[8] A good number of liberally inclined writers, appalled by the punitiveness of—especially—American culture and by the criminal justice system's general failure to address the broken situations of both offenders and victims, gradually migrated back to rehabilitative approaches[9] or in the direction of more restorative responses to victimization and serious interpersonal and social transgression. Added to this was John Rawls's (1971) quintessentially liberal critique of desert as a distributive principle for social benefits.[10] In the end, efforts to revive its moral and philosophical fortunes have not done well.

And yet desert has refused to go away quietly, even for some liberal thinkers. In a moral and institutional environment whose theorizing has been largely governed by consequentialist thinking—whether the goal has been one of mere incapacitation or, now in revival, of rehabilitation, reform, treatment, and even the restoration of fractured relationships—desert's grounding in identifiable characteristics and acts with its implicit proportionality constraints has seemed to provide an important check on the potential for an oppressive open-endedness associated with results-oriented thinking. Moreover, it has, along with the language of merit, constituted an important (if not the only) principle of just social distribution. The critical question for desert is whether appeals to it can be rescued from their use to undermine the humaneness that liberal social responses to wrongdoing have generally sought to achieve.

II. WRONGDOING AND OUR VARIED RESPONSES TO IT

I do not want to suggest that "what does wrongdoing deserve?" represents the only, or main, or even always an appropriate question when wrongdoing—understood here as the violation of important socially sanctioned norms—occurs. Desert may simply be one factor to take into account in deciding how best to respond to wrongdoing. Moreover, given that our socially sanctioned norms are a mixed bag, the criteria we use to determine their violation are also a mixed bag. Therefore, any simple inference from "violation of a social rule" to "deserves X" is likely to beg important questions. U.S. drug laws, for example, represent a highly questionable articulation of the transition from "wrongdoing" (as it is socially and legally defined[11]) to "deserves punishment." Whatever we may want to say about the use of certain psychotropic substances, the question "What does their use deserve?" seems increasingly inappropriate.

Let me start then with a brief comment on how, in advance of a slightly more detailed discussion, I want to construe (moral) wrongdoing. I am working with a widely shared and intuitively plausible notion of wrongdoing that is centrally—though perhaps not exclusively—concerned with human conduct that violates shared basic expectations or norms about how people may appropriately engage with each other (where that engagement may be direct or mediated by roles and institutions). I come back to this, but it is sufficient to set up my next set of reflections. When what we deem to be wrongdoing occurs, our response to it will be an inherently negative one. Not to respond negatively is to fail to understand the idea of a norm violation. Even so, that negative response may tap into a variety of interests and only one of the various questions that may come to mind is likely to concern what the wrongdoing *deserves*.[12]

We may be interested in some explanation of how the wrongdoing came about, and that question may itself be differentiated into several sets of causal subsidiaries, some of which will be directed to what we might call quasi-scientific concerns (i.e., an understanding of the underlying mechanisms involved), some of which may focus on the issue of fault or blame (on whether, for example, the wrongdoer should be held responsible for what was done), and some of which may be directed to what we can characterize as our interest in controlling the social environment in which we live so that, for example, such untoward events may be prevented in the future (Feinberg 1970). Our interest in the first set of issues may involve us in questions of social environment, genetic predisposition, chemical reactions, and so forth. The second set of issues will have us interested in where the burden for wrongdoing should lie, with what and how great that burden should be, and the form that it should take. Finally, when it comes to the third, we will be looking at prevention by various means—deterrence, incapacitation, rehabilitation, moral education, social engineering, reconciliation, and the like.

Although it is in connection with the second set of issues that questions of desert are likely to arise, the response that we make to any of these three issues is likely to have implications for the others. Answering one of the quasi-scientific questions in a particular way may have important implications for the issue of control and for attributions of fault. However, this is not the place to track these and other connections. This essay is intended to focus narrowly on the question of what wrongdoing deserves, albeit in recognition that the response to this question will be embedded in assumptions about how a large number of other questions have been addressed.

III. CHIPPING AWAY AT THE WRONGDOING–PUNISHMENT NEXUS

As I mentioned at the beginning, the well-established response to the question "What does wrongdoing deserve?" is "punishment." Even though this response is well established, it has not been either universal or historically uniform. Some, for example, have wanted to argue that wrongdoing *as such* deserves only rebuke, criticism, censure, or condemnation.[13] One may respond negatively to moral wrongdoing, but more is not authentically required. On such an account, punishment as a response is to be seen as an institutional overlay, for example, the response we might make to wrongdoing that is socially constituted as "crime." Here the point of punishment may be viewed in consequentialist terms—"to ensure that acts of certain kinds are not done."

Even the history of "redress" is not monolithic. In his *Second Treatise Of Civil Government*, John Locke—echoing the ancient doctrine of *lex talionis*—asserts that in a state of nature, those who are wronged or aggressed against have a natural "right of retaliation."[14] Leaving aside the subtleties that may be implicit in the language of retaliation, the allusion is interesting. David Daube, in his insightful discussion of the ancient doctrine of *lex talionis*, argues that many Old Testament penalties for wrongdoing were compensatory or restitutive in form and that *lex talionis* did not originally constitute a principle of retribution so much as a proportionality constraint on the compensations to be exacted or restitutions made for certain kinds of wrongs (Exodus 21:23–27; Daube 1947).

But even when punishment has been considered the appropriate and deserved response to wrongdoing—that is, as an intentional imposition responsive to and defeasibly justified by wrongdoing—it has been thought about in different ways. The impositions that constitute punishment may be of various kinds and our sense of what may be appropriately called for as punishment has been subject to important normative shifts.[15] Many traditional definitions of punishment use the language of imposed "pain" or "suffering" when referring to such impositions. In post-Enlightenment thought, however, the language of "deprivation" or "loss" has become more common. Enlightenment perspectives have encouraged us to revalue the body (i.e., not to see it simply as the prison house of a soul that could be redeemed through flagellation) and, moreover, to see much bodily mortification as dehumanizing rather than liberating.[16] We have turned instead to penitential deprivations and losses that (supposedly) are more appropriately imposed on beings who possess rights by virtue of their personhood. Unlike inflictions of pain, it has been thought that such deprivations not only avoided the problem of dehumanization, but also possessed shaming and reformative potential. The key deprivation became deprivation of the Enlightenment's core humanistic values—liberty and property—and for much of the nineteenth and twentieth century severe legal punishment became almost synonymous with imprisonment.[17]

There is, of course, nothing to prevent us from rethinking our currently favored responses and—in much the same way as the Enlightenment, when it encouraged the shift from impositions on the body to deprivations of liberties or rights—looking to other ways of responding to wrongdoing.[18] Even, perhaps, ways that we would not as readily characterize as punishment.[19] Indeed, the failures associated with one of our key Enlightenment strategies (imprisonment), along with a growing dissatisfaction with the highly formalized processes associated with institutional responses to crime, have prompted alternative approaches such as those involved in restorative justice. To such I will soon return.

Our concern with imprisonment is heightened by recent studies suggesting that people have very different reactions to the immediate experience of imprisonment, that the length of imprisonment is not strongly correlated with experienced notions of proportionality, and that almost any imprisonment has long-term aftereffects that dwarf the occurrent experience (Bronsteen, Buccafusco, and Masur 2009; Kolber 2009).

IV. KINDS OF DESERT

To prepare the ground for a possible rethinking of our traditional response, let me go back to desert, and from there to some questions about the common intuition that what wrongdoing deserves is punishment.

In his seminal essay, "Justice and Personal Desert," Joel Feinberg (1970, p. 56) characterized personal desert as "a 'natural' moral notion (that is, one which is not tied to institutions, practices, and rules)."[20] Part of Feinberg's purpose in making this claim was to distinguish personal deserts from entitlements/liabilities. To say "S deserves X in virtue of F" is to say that X is a warranted response, to ground X in considerations of worthiness/unworthiness (F), and to distinguish these from conditions of institutional eligibility. A person who satisfies conditions of institutional eligibility may be entitled (or have a formal right) to some benefit (or be liable to some burden), but that entitlement (or liability) is distinguishable from and might even be in tension with what is deserved. Appropriate desert bases, Feinberg suggested, must be characteristics or activities of the deserving subject. Not any worthwhile (or otherwise) characteristics or activities will do, however. S does not deserve entrance to Harvard on the basis of kindness to strangers, though kindness to strangers may be deserving of some other reward or benefit. There must be some match between F and X.

Some years later than Feinberg, I distinguished, less elegantly, between what I called "raw" and "institutionalized" desert claims or, as they are distinguished in some subsequent writing, between preinstitutional and institutional desert claims (Kleinig 1971). This was not the same distinction as Feinberg's, though I too wanted to draw a firm distinction between deserts and entitlements.

What I distinguished as raw or preinstitutional desert claims included the following:

> You deserve a good time.
> You've worked so hard to prepare for the outdoor party, you deserve good weather.
> He deserved to have the gun blow up in his face.
> He deserves to suffer (prelegal) punishment.

There are no dispensing institutions to inform these desert claims. They refer simply to benefits or burdens that are deemed to be in some sense "naturally fitting" to activities by or characteristics of the deserving subject. Whether we are *justified* in making such particularized desert claims is a question that requires separate treatment, though considerations of proportionality will no doubt be critical to the determinations we make.

Institutionalized desert claims included the following:

> He deserved to win the art competition.
> His scholarship was well deserved.
> He deserved his 20-year sentence.

In each of these cases what is said to be deserved presumes the existence of certain social institutions—art competitions, scholarships to institutions of learning, and imprisonment or legal punishment. Whether or not we see the making of such claims as *justified* depends in part—though, as I will soon suggest, only in part—on the purposes of the institutions in question and on the criteria appropriate to their satisfying those purposes.[21]

In addition, as already noted, like Feinberg, I also distinguished deserts from entitlements (and liabilities), such as the following:

> He is entitled to the prize.
> Although he was entitled to go to Harvard, he did not deserve entry.
> Because he broke the rule, he was liable to a penalty.

These refer not to deserts, but to the satisfaction of formally mandated criteria for distributing benefits and burdens. Entitlements may contrast with deserts, and deserts may not be matched by entitlements.

I did not use the distinction between raw and institutionalized desert claims to make out the distinction between desert and entitlement. To make out the latter, the distinction I drew was between institutionalized desert claims and entitlements. In other words, in the context of various social practices and institutions, one might be able to distinguish those who deserve certain benefits or burdens dispensed via those institutional arrangements from those who are simply entitled to them.

In my view, then, we have (in the present context) three forms of dispensation/allocation/distribution. We have dispensations on the basis of raw or preinstitutional desert, dispensations on the basis of institutionalized desert, and dispensations on the basis of entitlement/liability.

I believe that the notion of desert is more basic than that of entitlement, and raw deserts are more basic than institutionalized ones. That is part of what Feinberg is getting at when he refers to desert as a natural moral notion. We often judge institutional entitlements by reference to deserts, complaining that entitlement criteria (or at least the ways in which they are applied) fall short of allocating benefits and burdens according to the deserts of those to whom the allocations are made. Although entitlement criteria/rules are often intended to reflect/capture desert (or merit), they tend to do so only roughly. Because they are institutionalized, such entitlement criteria tend not to be as finely nuanced as desert criteria, and our institutions and the criteria they use for distributing benefits and burdens may be designed to do more than allocate deserts. Even in cases in which institutions are committed to distributions based on deserts, there may be good and even overriding institutional reasons why we should dispense benefits and burdens only to those who are entitled or liable to them—why it is that although S deserved X, she was not and should not have been entitled to it because of some factor (such as illness) that got in the way of her getting what she deserved. The reasons are not unlike those that favor law over morality as a basis for social allocations.

But institutionalized desert claims, even when justified by reference to the purposes of the institution in question *and* the criteria for satisfying those purposes, may still be thought to lack justification because the institution in question is itself considered to lack justification. Consider the Miss Universe contest. One might say, for example, that whereas Zuleyka Rivera deserved to be Miss Universe 2006, Justine Pasek did not deserve the crown in 2002, even though the rules entitled her to it.[22] One might say this—maintaining the desert/entitlement distinction—while thinking that the institution in question (a beauty contest) ought to be abandoned. In other words, one might say that, *given* the institution in question, S deserved what it dispensed rather than T because S more adequately satisfied the purposes it served. One may do this while drawing a legitimate distinction between entitlements and institutionalized deserts. At the same time, one might think that, in a generally sexist culture, physical beauty ought not to be made the primary focus of a competition or other institutional rewards.

But there is a further way in which such claims can go wrong: Even if the general institution is thought to be justified, the kinds of institutional responses deemed to be deserved may be thought inappropriate to its ends. In other words, although we may develop legitimate institutions, our conventions within them regarding the allocations that are said to be deserved may be called into question. Consider, for example, certain kinds of education-oriented institutions—those designed to foster appropriate learning. Some would argue that meritorious students should be awarded education vouchers that give them access to a certain range of educational institutions. Others, however, might wish to argue that vouchers fail to provide an appropriate reward to those who are educationally meritorious. Linking this with our topic, we might consider the possibility of a system of laws for whose breach responses other than punishment (narrowly conceived, or in its current form) might be seen as deserved (or even more appropriate than our present desert conventions dictate).

V. PREINSTITUTIONAL DESERTS AND WRONGDOING

There is a certain indeterminateness to preinstitutional (noninstitutionalized, or raw) desert claims. If, for example, a person who has worked hard and selflessly all her life has a windfall—say, an unknown benefactor gives her a large sum of money—we may see that person as deserving of her good fortune. Or, if a person who has worked hard during the year gets wonderful weather for her holidays, we might say she deserved it (not that that would constitute a limit on what may have been deserved). These are intelligible claims and, insofar as they embody what we can conceive to be a reasonable, albeit imprecise proportionality, we might consider the upshot involved as acceptable. In cases of poetic justice, for example, we might see outcomes of certain acts as peculiarly fitting. We can see how disproportionality occurs if we consider the case of the person whose smoking leads to lung cancer: although we may appreciate the risks that smoking carries, we are likely to think (most of us do) that lung cancer is a disproportionately horrible outcome and therefore not deserved.[23]

Let us now go to wrongdoing—not crime, at least not yet. If interhuman engagements (and perhaps some others) are to work out in ways that will be conducive, or at least not detrimental, to our flourishing, they will require that we observe certain norms or standards in our interactions.[24] These norms or standards will embody not only forms of conduct, but also—especially as they are partially constitutive of the conduct—attitudes, dispositions, or reasons of certain kinds. We can think of these norms or standards as basic *moral* expectations—expectations whose observance or fulfillment it is reasonable to require of every appropriately placed human being capable of a certain level of self-reflection.[25]

Suppose, now, that S intentionally violates one of these basic moral expectations with respect to V. S has done wrong to V. It would not do simply to ignore it. Non-response would evince a failure to appreciate the wrong committed by S (Kleinig 1991). To the extent that we characterize what S does to V as a violation of practical norms or standards, we already accord it a practical disvalue, and where some opportunity exists, some kind of practical response is called for. Just as there would be something very odd about saying "F would be wrong, but that is no reason for not doing it," there would be something odd about saying "It was wrong of S to do F, but this gives one no reason to do anything about it." Nevertheless, responses to S's doing F may vary.

We could look to its not happening again and think about ways of preventing its recurrence (by means of general and specific deterrence, incapacitation, situational crime prevention, and so forth). That would be a purely consequentialist response, and if our response amounted to no more than that it would almost certainly be inadequate. For V has some claim on S. On the one hand, it would leave V's plight unattended to: matters are not "made right" for V. There needs to be some acknowledgement that V's personal standing has been compromised or undercut. On the other hand, it may lead to S being treated instrumentally rather than as a moral agent whose agency is taken into account.

Alternatively, to the extent that the breach occurred within the context of some institution, there may be ways in which that institution has already defined the breach and mandated a response. Depending on the institution, the wrongdoing may lead to shunning, to expulsion, or to penalization of some kind. Here, a lot would depend on the institution and the provisions that it made for such breaches. This is the realm of liabilities (or penalties). For the purposes of desert, it would be important to develop a penalty structure that supports a proportional response.[26]

But let us think a bit more radically and imaginatively, and try to strip away what we can of the somewhat particularized institutional frameworks within which much of our responsive thinking takes place, and then situate our response within the fairly bare framework of unencumbered human sociality and the conditions for our flourishing.[27] When S has intentionally violated a basic moral expectation with respect to V, what response is appropriate?

One thing I think we can say is that because of what S has done, he deserves X, where X refers to some burden that should be imposed on or befall S. Not to think that some burden should—deservedly—befall S is to fail to appreciate the fact that S has burdened V (either some individual or collective V).[28] Judgments of ill or good desert are the natural response to conduct that is deemed to fall short of or exceed the moral expectations that we have of each other. We would make them of ourselves were we to fall short or exceed in these ways.[29] The nature of this deserved X, though, is rather less clear. Assuming that what S did to V represented a culpable violation and not a mere transgression of norms,[30] blame is an obvious candidate, certainly in the minimal sense of holding S morally responsible for what was done to V. However, blame in the sense of holding S responsible for what was done does not go far enough. One can do that privately, without confronting S at all. Perhaps, though, a different kind of blame—blaming behavior—in which blame constitutes a form of censure, rebuke, or condemnation, might seem more appropriate, insofar as S will now be confronted with his wrongdoing. Will that do? No doubt it is part of what is called for—there is an expressive and communicative dimension to what wrongdoing deserves. Such expressions may even be somewhat burdening. Generally, though, it has been argued that even more than this is deserved. For though such expressions of blame constitute some kind of practical response to wrongdoing, they fail to "embody" it. That is why desert defeasibly requires not merely a response, but a proportionate one. One cannot separate out the "blame" from something more. To think otherwise is to make the same mistake as would be involved were someone to take the view that appropriate responses of gratitude to benefaction could always consist of sincere expressions of thanks (McConnell 1993). But what more might wrongdoing deserve?

VI. DESERT AND HARD TREATMENT

The usual response is that wrongdoing warrants some kind of "hard treatment."[31] This is then *automatically* assumed to be punishment. It may be punishment; in fact, I believe it to be, but need it be? Feinberg links "hard treatment" to what he calls the expressive function of punishment. That is, the appropriateness of expressing "resentment, disapproval, condemnation or reprobation" in the face of wrongdoing finds its symbolic enactment in punishment (rather than mere penalties, which may function only as a deterrent to certain kinds of behavior). But is hard treatment essential to this expressiveness, or might various kinds of blaming behavior such as "denunciation, castigation, reproach, censure, remonstra[tion], chastisement, degradation, humiliation, abasement, [and] shaming" be equally expressive, as Bedau (2002, p. 117) argues? I suspect that the latter are not—that hard treatment constitutes not only a more emphatic, but also a more proportionate expression than merely blaming behavior, even though the latter is expressive in its own way. It is not simply that punishment is expressive, but that hard treatment is proportionately expressive in a way that mere denunciation is not. Like the wrongdoing that "calls for" it, hard treatment has a sharp edge to it that mere censure lacks. It demands something *of the perpetrator* that denunciation and blaming do not.

The something that hard treatment demands of the perpetrator is not simply—even if ideally—a recognition on the perpetrator's part that what she did was wrong for her to do. Important as it is that the response to wrongdoing connect with a wrongdoer's conscience, the connection goes deeper than that. There ought to be a recognition on the part of the wrongdoer that a burden is appropriately borne—that one has no grounds for complaint about being burdened as a result of what one has done. It would be very odd for a wrongdoer to acknowledge her wrongdoing and yet say, "But I do not deserve to suffer some imposition as a result."[32]

Nevertheless, need the hard treatment take the form of punishment? Certainly hard treatment refers to some significant imposition on another. It imposes a substantial cost. The wrongdoer is made to *pay* in some way. But might it be argued that costs need not be punitive (or at least be merely punitive)? If we think of desert as a "natural 'moral' notion," then why should what is deserved by wrongdoing not (sometimes? often?) be the kind of hard treatment associated with required restitution or compensation or other facets of restorative processes (including apology) rather than the punishment that is usually said to be deserved? Making restitution to or compensating V will also constitute a sizable cost to S. It will ordinarily constitute a form of hard treatment imposed on S, even if it is one that S agrees to have imposed on him.[33]

What I am contemplating as a possibility, then, is that whether the burden deserved by wrongdoing takes the form of conventional (legal) punishment as against some other imposition (that might be more closely identified with elements within the restorative process) might be largely a function of the institutions we have in place, institutions that have no special sacrosanctity. If that suggestion has some plausibility, then it might allow for a rapprochement between retributivist punishment theorists (whose views have probably been too closely identified with the case for imprisonment) and restorative justice theorists (who are sometimes characterized as wimpy).

Before offering a response, let me add one further consideration. The very nature of wrongdoing may reasonably prompt us to look more closely at restorative possibilities. If, as I have suggested, wrongdoing is centrally, even if not exclusively, a matter of breaching the social norms that govern the ability of humans to flourish in their varied ways, it should not seem odd to suggest that the form taken by deserved hard treatment also serves—if not primarily, then to the extent possible—to heal the breach constituted by the wrongdoing in question. It might be claimed that one of the distortions encouraged by our common focus on *crime* as a breach of not only microinterpersonal relations, but also of macropublic norms has been to focus so exclusively on the societal or public dimension of wrongdoing that its interpersonal aspects have been marginalized.

What restorative approaches seek to accomplish—to speak very generally—is a recognition of the extent to which wrongdoing represents a breach not simply of impersonal social rules or norms, but rather a fracturing of the basic relations that ought to hold among human beings.[34] Moral violations—at their heart, even if not so obviously at their periphery[35]—are relational violations, violations of the terms that are appropriate to the interaction of humans as social beings who possess a particular conception of their flourishing. Our flourishing has a communal dimension and requisites: it does not occur in social isolation. When John Stuart Mill speaks of humans as "progressive beings" whose chief works are self-perfection and self-beautification, the social conditions for this achievement are acknowledged. Moral violations interfere with the conditions for such flourishing, however we might reasonably characterize it.[36]

Might we, then, argue that insofar as wrongdoing constitutes a breach of the norms appropriate to human interaction—not simply through some injury or harm, but also through the erosion of basic trust—it deserves a response that not only constitutes an imposition (albeit one that might be consented to), but also goes toward restitution or compensation and the repair of breached relations (or, more generally, the basic trust required by human sociality)? This might appear to make sense just because, in implementing the three standard elements of restorative justice—recognition, restitution, and reintegration—the offender will be burdened by confronting his actions, repenting of them, and by the expectation (as far as possible) of making good what has been damaged.

However, as attractive as aspects of a restorative justice approach may be,[37] I doubt whether we can advance it via the language of *desert*. To the extent that restorative justice incorporates hard treatment, it is still best to see that hard treatment as punishment, and then to argue that punishment may sometimes serve or be integrated into restorative goals. It is not the restorative aspect of restorative justice that is deserved, but at best its character as hard treatment. What it envisages as hard treatment—restitution or compensation—is not deserved for wrongdoing, but at best for doing harm.[38] It is what we would consider deserved compensation in tort law that characterizes the "making good" of restorative justice. What intentional wrongdoing deserves is a hard treatment that expresses condemnation, and that is punishment. Required restitutive or compensatory activity might, no doubt, become a vehicle for censure rather than constituting a form of imposition separate from punishment, but in such cases it would be roughly analogous to the "punitive damages" of tort law.

Note, though, that I am not arguing for punishment as against restorative justice. We may well argue for both, and even for restorative justice as primary. For what we may argue is that although wrongdoing deserves punishment, what we ought ultimately to seek is a restoration of fractured relationships. Although desert defeasibly warrants punishment, what we ought to do in a particular case may be to design the punishment in a way that serves restorative goals. Some writers have wished to argue that any morally viable restorative program must be built upon the premise of wrongdoing deserving punishment—and on the expectation that punishment will sometimes, if not always, be imposed (Duff 2003). On that view, restorative and retributive approaches to wrongdoing need not be seen as opposed so much as complementary. The appropriate language in such cases will not be that wrongdoing deserves some restorative imposition, but rather that restorative concerns will incorporate retributive concerns. That is, moral restoration requires the recognition that punishment is deserved.

Admittedly, this will not satisfy some defenders of restorative approaches to criminal wrongdoing who see punishment as fundamentally opposed to restorative aims. Although I do not believe that is a defensible position to take—even if it represents a telling commentary on our institutionalized punishment practices—it might be more defensibly expressed by saying that although wrongdoing deserves punishment, what is deserved does not exhaust what may be relevant to our overall decision making concerning wrongdoing. For the "ought" that is implied by desert is not "ought, all things considered," but "ought, other things being equal." We may sometimes think it better not to give others what they deserve. So although desert may provide a defeasibly sufficient reason for punishing wrongdoing, its defeasibility may allow for other considerations to prevail. In some cases, we may wish to restore broken relations as well as—perhaps even more than—penalizing their breach.

VIII. CONCLUDING NOTE

I began writing this essay as a serious attempt to rethink the implications of desert theory. It might have involved a more radical project—one that called the whole enterprise of desert attributions into question—but I remain convinced that desert is too closely related to our judgments about (certain forms of) justice to be dispensed with just yet. Rethinking the wrongdoing–punishment nexus, however, seemed to have something more to be said for it, especially in light of our egregious social practices of punishment. Much of the critique of those practices that we find represented in the literature of restorative justice strikes me as important and on target, and so it seemed plausible to consider the possibility that whatever the wrongdoing deserved, it should not be construed as punishment. Might the hard treatment perhaps take the form of restorative impositions? I have suggested that they do not qualify unless those impositions themselves can double as punishments.

However, because desert is not the only consideration that we may want to take into account in determining what we ought to do, we might couple a recognition that wrongdoing deserves punishment with the morally relevant considerations that restorative justice advocates identify as being ignored or underemphasized by our current practices, and develop responses to wrongdoing and crime that will, as the U.S. Supreme Court put it in another context, better reflect "the evolving standards of decency that mark the progress of a maturing society" (*Trop v. Dulles*, 356 U.S. 86 [1958]).

ACKNOWLEDGMENT

I wish to thank members of the Leiden Workshop for their probing questioning of earlier versions of this essay, and especially Antony Duff, Doug Husak, and Jesper Ryberg for their written comments. I have endeavored to address their concerns; whether I have adequately done so is for others to say.

NOTES

1. It is, moreover, not the *only* question one might and ought to ask here. What do *wrongdoers* deserve? What do *criminals* deserve? What do *victims* deserve? And, perhaps more importantly, what is an appropriate response to wrongdoing? Except for returning to the last of these questions at the end, I shall largely leave to one side what differences it might make to use one formulation rather than another. My primary concern, though, is with moral wrongdoing (as the more fundamental) rather than criminal wrongdoing, which (I am inclined to argue) refers to a narrower set of moral wrongdoings, those in which violation of some significant public or social standards is involved. But this is a large and complex question (see Feinberg 1986; Kleinig 1986).

2. I understand this in its most primitive sense—as referring to moral wrongdoing and not particularly to legal punishment. Criminal wrongdoing and legal punishment are more complex notions.

3. In a recent book, David Boonin (2008) argues that no (legal) punishment can be justified, and opts instead for restitution. His account of restitution, however, bears many similarities to punishment. Although Boonin does not argue for a restorative justice approach, most restorative accounts have some place in them for restitution.

4. Henry Sidgwick (1901, p. 281) captures the spirit of much of this thinking when he writes of retributive desert: "Personally I am so far from holding this view that I have an instinctive and strong moral aversion to it; and I hesitate to attribute it to Common Sense, since I think that it is gradually passing away from the moral consciousness of educated persons in the most advanced communities: but I think it is still perhaps the more ordinary view." I have cataloged similar sentiments (Kleinig 1968, pp. 98–101).

5. That was also true of the massive 13-volume *Encyclopaedia of Religion and Ethics*, edited by James Hastings (1908), though it did have an entry on the related idea of "Merit." Significantly, reflecting latter day interest, the *Routledge Encyclopedia of Philosophy* (Craig 1998) has an entry, as does the *Stanford Encyclopedia of Philosophy* (Zalta 2011) and the successor to Hastings, Mircea Eliade's 16-volume *Encyclopedia of Religion* (1987).

6. Assisted by growing skepticism concerning the instrumental value of conventional punishment—for example, Martinson's (1974) review of treatment programs, supposedly showing that "nothing works."

7. There is no doubt that this was and is aggravated by the difficulty of constructing a desert-based penalty scale.

8. Even though there were formidable attempts to get beyond the appeal of self-evidence. Prominent among those was the effort by Herbert Morris (1968) and others to articulate punitive desert as the rectification of wrongful disadvantage. See also Wojciech Sadurski (1985) for a defense of Morris against some of his early critics. For a later variant, see Sher (1987).

9. Even Martinson (1979), so influential in undermining rehabilitative ambitions for state punishment, came to have doubts about "nothing works."

10. Although his position has been vigorously attacked (see, e.g., Sher 1987), Rawls's main complaint about desert concerns the impracticability—for distributive purposes—of trying to separate out what our endowment and opportunities have contributed to our effort and achievement as against factors for which we can be held responsible.

11. One might well wonder whether any moral wrongdoing is involved in drug use. That it is socially considered to involve moral wrongdoing is not determinative, and points to the deeper problem of providing defensible criteria for wrongdoing.

12. This is not, of course, to deny that other questions that may come to mind—such as how we might appropriately respond to wrongdoing—might have their answers structured, or at least influenced, by considerations of what the wrongdoing deserves.

13. That is H. L. A. Hart's view.

14. Locke also speaks of the "right to punish" as a natural right (Simmons 1991).

15. Once again I emphasize that I am operating first and foremost with what I would see as a conventional rather than legal understanding of punishment. Many of those who write about punishment (Hart, Benn, Flew, Feinberg, Rawls) tend to take institutional (in particular, legal) punishment as paradigmatic. That is, to use Hart's (1968, p. 5) formulation, punishment must (a) involve pain or other consequences normally considered unpleasant; (b) be for an offense against legal rules; (c) be of an actual or supposed offender for his offense; (d) be intentionally administered by human beings other than the offender; and (e) be imposed and administered by an authority constituted by a legal system against which the offense is administered. To the extent that legal punishment is viewed as paradigmatic, the wrongdoing-punishment nexus is more problematic than I later suggest—if for no other reason than that what the law deems to be wrongdoing may not be deserving of punitive burdens.

16. Not all would agree (Neuman 1995).

17. The foregoing paragraph is not intended as a serious endorsement of such developments so much as a schematic representation of historical change. It is, of course, also a bit too swift. Hard labor was frequently involved as well (though that was also seen as reformative). Although the deprivation of property rights through fines remains more ubiquitous, fines tend to occupy the more lenient end of institutional punishments.

18. We might equally and at the same time want to rethink what we categorize as wrongdoing, especially in relation to drug use, one of the projects of "therapeutic jurisprudence."

19. If every imposition for wrongdoing counted as punishment, that could settle the issue. But some reparative and compensatory impositions of the kind likely to be contemplated in restorative contexts might be better described in other terms. The most immediate issue, though, is not whether there might be more appropriate ways of responding to wrongdoing, but whether they could be said to be deserved by it.

20. Although I understand why Feinberg sees personal desert as a moral notion rather than a more broadly normative notion, I doubt whether it needs to be cast as narrowly.

21. Not every institution or the desert claims that might be considered internal to its purposes will be justified. A winner of the Ku Klux Klansman of the Year Award may deserve the award, given the purposes of the institution, but would not be morally justified in being awarded it. On the other hand, even if the institution itself can be justified (say, a school), it may sometimes be morally justifiable to give a place to someone who does not meet the desert criteria for entry (desert criteria not being absolutely determinative of what ought to be done). In some contexts, it is important to keep distinct the two claims: "S does not deserve X" and "S deserves not to get X."

22. The title had originally been awarded to Oxana Fedorova—a popular winner—but it was later withdrawn and bestowed on Pasek, the runner up, reputedly because Fedorova failed to fulfill certain of the contractual responsibilities associated with the title.

23. It should be clear from such cases that for someone to deserve something there does not have to be a dispenser of deserts. It may be a matter of luck, and not divine benefaction, that someone gets good weather for her holidays. Cosmic and poetic justice point to proportionalities rather than to intentional distributions of benefits or burdens. Nevertheless, some raw desert claims do assume desert dispensers. Without there being any social institutions to dispense them, Mother Teresa would have deserved social recognition and support for what she did.

24. Not simply instrumentally, but as integral to that flourishing. Our capacity for and disposition to engage in moral discrimination is central to our dignity.

25. No doubt statements as to what those basic expectations are will be contestable and variously articulable. In addition, we may want to distinguish morality from the moral theories (metaethics) that undergird it. Or we may want to distinguish between conventional and critical morality (as do Hart and Dworkin). Or we may want to distinguish morality from ethics (as its role-governed or institutionalized expression). Or we may variously characterize it in relation to other normatively based forms of action guiding, such as etiquette, mores, politics, economics, and religion. All these large issues may be set aside for now.

26. Here Kolber (2009) argues that retributivists do badly. He argues that proportionality must have regard for the experience of punishment and that different offenders will react very differently to a particular punishment. Although I think much of the power of Kolber's argument derives from the parlous state of U.S. prisons, and fails to take adequate account of the complications introduced by differential "victim impact," he offers a plausible case for a less mechanical approach to sentencing. To some extent his argument is undercut by Bronsteen, Buccafusco, and Masur's (2009, p. 1038) equally empirical claim that "adjusting the size of a fine or the length of a prison sentence does not meaningfully adjust the amount of unhappiness that is ultimately experienced by the offender."

27. That is a difficult—and maybe impossible—demand, even if it has precursors in the Lockeian state of nature and Rawlsian original position. Even so, we can imaginatively divest ourselves of much of our institutional baggage, which is probably enough.

28. If that seems implausible, consider the situation of a person, T, who goes beyond what might be seen as basic moral expectations. Here, too, we are inclined to think it appropriate to say of T that she deserves Y, where Y refers to a benefiting of T in some way— certainly by means of praise, but often we might think that some reward would be appropriate (whether or not we think it our place to ensure it). The failure to think so would be to underestimate the significance of what T has done.

29. What would it say about us were we not to?

30. Which might reasonably lead to deserved compensation/restitution.

31. I think Feinberg was the first to use this phrase in 1965 (see "The Expressive Function of Punishment" in *Doing and Deserving* [1970]). It refers to burdensome rather than harsh treatment, and is not exclusive to legal punishment. Parents may impose hard treatment on their children, and even friends may have occasion to do the same to each other. For those who deserve well, we might speak of "agreeable treatment." But why hard treatment is warranted in the event of wrongdoing rather than something that does not burden is something about which there is a good deal of disagreement. Some argue that considerations of proportionality (which may itself be variously understood) mandate something more "substantial" than blaming-type behavior. Others focus on what might be called anthropological factors—hard treatment, as needed, if the wrongness of wrongdoing is to register appropriately with people as we find them.

32. Of course, it might be reasonable to argue that although one deserves to suffer an imposition as a result of one's wrongdoing, one ought not to have it imposed upon one or that a particular imposition is not deserved.

33. We should not ignore the fact that those who acknowledge their guilt often deem their conduct to be worthy of a punitive response.

34. I appreciate that this is something of a stretch when connected with violations of tax or pollution laws, where the impact on individual others is achieved only cumulatively. Although I think a case can be made for the legitimacy of criminalizing such conduct, it is easier if, for present purposes, we stay with direct harms to others.

35. What I mean by this is that we have extended the scope of our moral expectations to cover such matters as our treatment of animals, self-regarding conduct, environmental responsibility, and so on.

36. More needs to be said. We would need, for example, to rule out conceptions of human flourishing that were predatory. Moreover, we would need to confront those for whom the idea of human flourishing appears too "humanistic," although I take it that those with religious sensibilities who are more inclined to see the glory of God as the end of man might still be accommodated. Such conceptions of human purpose are generally embedded in theologies that consider human perfection to be realizable in divine devotion. On the complexities of and problems associated with appeals to human flourishing, see Harman (1983), Wong (1988), Foot (2001), and the special issue of *Social Philosophy & Policy* 16, no. 1 (Winter 1999), especially the essays by Thomas Hurka and Richard Arneson.

37. It is not my intention here to downplay the problematic aspects of many restorative justice initiatives, especially those connected with its potential for circumventing due process and consistency (see Delgado 2000).

38. It might be argued that restitution and compensation are implausibly seen as punishment because they do not accommodate the non-material costs of wrongdoing. That may be true of much that passes as restitution. However, I can envisage forms of restitution that would go beyond the material effects of wrongdoing. Admittedly, it becomes much more difficult to determine what would restore or compensate when we go beyond material harms.

REFERENCES

Arneson, Richard J. 1999. "Human Flourishing Versus Desire Satisfaction." *Social Philosophy & Policy* 16(1):113–42.

Bedau, Hugo Adam. 2002. "Feinberg's Liberal Theory of Punishment." *Buffalo Criminal Law Review* 5:103–44.

Boonin, David. 2008. *The Problem of Punishment*. Cambridge: Cambridge University Press.

Bronsteen, John, Christopher Buccafusco, and Jonathan Masur. 2009. "Happiness and Punishment." *University of Chicago Law Review* 76(3):1037–81.

Craig, Edward, ed. 1998. *Routledge Encyclopedia of Philosophy*. 10 vols. London: Routledge.

Daube, David. 1947. *Studies in Biblical Law*. Cambridge: Cambridge University Press.

Delgado, Richard. 2000. "Prosecuting Violence: A Colloquy on Race, Community, and Justice—Goodbye to Hammurabi: Analyzing the Atavistic Appeal of Restorative Justice." *Stanford Law Review* 52:751–75.

Duff, R. A. 2003. "Restoration and Retribution." In *Restorative Justice and Criminal Justice: Competing or Reconcilable Paradigms?*, ed. A. von Hirsch et al. Oxford: Hart Publishing.

Eliade, Mircea. 1987. *Encyclopedia of Religion*. New York: Macmillan.

Feinberg, Joel. 1970. *Doing and Deserving*. Princeton, NJ: Princeton University Press.

———. 1986. "Harm to Others: A Rejoinder." *Criminal Justice Ethics* 5(1):16–29.

Foot, Philippa. 2001. *Natural Goodness*. Oxford: Oxford University Press.

Greene, Joshua D., and Jonathan D. Cohen. 2004. "For the Law, Neuroscience Changes Nothing and Everything." *Philosophical Transactions of the Royal Society of London B (Special Issue on Law and the Brain)* 359:1775–85.

Harman, Gilbert. 1983. "Human Flourishing, Ethics, and Liberty." *Philosophy and Public Affairs* 12(4):307–22.

Hart, H. L. A. 1968. *Punishment and Responsibility*. Oxford: Oxford University Press.

Hastings, James. 1908. *Encyclopaedia of Religion and Ethics*. 13 vols. Edinburgh: T&T Clark.

Hurka, Thomas. 1999. "The Three Faces of Flourishing." *Social Philosophy & Policy* 16(1):44–71.

Kleinig, John. 1968. "Desert and Punishment." PhD dissertation, Australian National University.

———. 1971. "The Concept of Desert." *American Philosophical Quarterly* 8(1):71–78.

———. 1973. *Punishment and Desert*. The Hague: Martinus Nijhoff.

———. 1986. "Criminally Harming Others." *Criminal Justice Ethics* 5(1):3–10.

———. 1991. "Punishment and Moral Seriousness." *Israel Law Review* 25(3–4):401–21.

Kolber, Adam. 2009. "The Subjective Experience of Punishment." *Columbia Law Review* 109(1):182–236.

Martinson, Robert. 1974. "What Works? Questions and Answers about Prison Reform." *Public Interest* 35:22–54.

———. 1979. "New Findings, New Views: A Note of Caution Regarding Sentencing Reform." *Hofstra Law Review* 7:243–58.

McConnell, Terrance. 1993. *Gratitude*. Philadelphia: Temple University Press.

Morris, Herbert. 1968. "Persons and Punishment." *The Monist* 52:475–501.

Neuman, Graeme. 1995. *Just and Painful: A Case for the Corporal Punishment of Criminals*, 2nd ed. Monsey, NY: Criminal Justice Press.

Rawls, John. 1971. *A Theory of Justice*. Cambridge, MA: Belknap/Harvard University Press.

Sadurski, Wojciech. 1985. *Giving Desert Its Due: Social Justice and Legal Theory*. Dordrecht: Reidel.

Sher, George. 1987. *Desert*. Princeton, NJ: Princeton University Press.

Sidgwick, Henry. 1901. *The Methods of Ethics*, 6th ed. London: Macmillan.

Simmons, A. John. 1991. "Locke and the Right to Punish." *Philosophy and Public Affairs* 19:311–49.

von Hirsch, Andrew. 1976. *Doing Justice: The Choice of Punishments*. New York: Hill and Wang.

Wong, David B. 1988. "On Flourishing and Finding One's Identity in Community." *Midwest Studies in Philosophy* 13:83–96.

Zalta, Edward N. 2011. *Stanford Encyclopedia of Philosophy*. Stanford, CA: Metaphysics Research Lab. http://plato.stanford.edu/.

4

Responsibility, Restoration, and Retribution

R. A. DUFF

Retributivism, the idea that what justifies criminal punishment is that it is deserved for past criminal wrongdoing, famously (or notoriously) underwent a revival in the 1970s—a revival whose influence is still evident both in penal philosophy and in penal policy. With the benefit of hindsight, we can now more clearly identify a number of problems with that revival: what we must then ask is whether those problems are fatal. Can a robust version of retributivism (I comment later on what makes for a robust version) be rendered plausible in our contemporary penal and philosophical climate, or is it time to move on beyond retributivism to some quite different kind of penal philosophy?

I will argue that penal philosophy and policy should retain a central place for a suitably understood idea of retribution. This argument involves paying closer attention than penal theorists often pay to the criminal process that precedes punishment and to the conception of responsible citizenship that should structure such a process. It will also involve showing how a practice of appropriately retributive punishments can meet some of the main concerns of advocates of "restorative justice" by providing a better account than they often provide of what needs to be restored in the aftermath of crime, and how it can be restored. These tasks will occupy sections III and IV, preceded (in section II) by a discussion of the idea of crime as that to which punishment is a response. First, however, we should attend briefly to the problems that impaired the retributivist revival.

I. PROBLEMS FOR RETRIBUTIVISM

We should not underplay the importance of the retributivist revival of the 1970s, but we must also recognize its weaknesses. One weakness was that it was more forceful as a negative critique of the consequentialist attitudes that had dominated penal thinking in the preceding decades than as advocacy for a robust or "positive" retributivism that takes the aim of punishment to be the imposition of an offender's penal deserts. That negative critique could trade, in part, on the perceived failure of consequentialist policies of crime prevention to achieve their overambitious aims, but that failure was relative rather than total. The cry that "Nothing works" (Martinson 1974) proved to be as much an exaggeration as the extravagant claims about what would work to which it was responding: a more modest attention to specific kinds of program focused on specific kinds of offense or offender, guided by a more realistic conception of what should count as working, showed that some kinds of penal provision can be modestly effective in reducing some kinds of crime by some kinds of offender. But the retributivist critique did not really depend on the efficiency or otherwise of consequentialist programs, since its real target was the moral inadequacy of a purely consequentialist perspective. The most salient inadequacy was the failure of any such perspective to do justice to the rights of the (relatively) innocent: the right of those who have committed no crime not to be subjected to the coercive attentions of the penal system; the right of those who have committed crimes not to be punished unduly harshly. But even if strict consequentialism is open to such objections, this does not force us to abandon primarily consequentialist penal thinking: all it requires is the adoption of the kind of "side-constrained" model that became popular in subsequent years. We are to pursue the consequential ends that give punishment its "general justifying aim," but we may not do so by means that violate the nonconsequentialist demands of justice or fairness. Nor indeed does this require us to accept even a negative form of retributivism, which tells us that we may not punish the innocent, or punish the guilty more harshly than they deserve: at least the first of these constraints may be explained, as Hart explained it, by appeal not to retributive desert, but to the importance of choice. Citizens should, as far as possible, be subject to the coercive penal attention of the law only when they have chosen to act in a way that they were warned would make them liable to such attention (Hart 1968, chaps. 1–2).[1]

Some retributivist revivalists also, and more pertinently, raised objections to the ways in which consequentialist approaches portrayed and treated not the innocent, but the guilty. If, for instance, the aim of penal treatment was supposed to be to reform offenders so that they would become law-abiding citizens, the objection was that this would (or might) treat them not as responsible agents, but as objects to be manipulated or reconditioned (Lewis 1953; Morris 1968). If the aim was to deter potential offenders, the objection was that this would treat offenders as means to some social end, in breach of the Kantian injunction to respect each other as ends. If such objections as these are sound, they undermine not only purely consequentialist accounts of punishment, but also side-constrained accounts that preserve a consequentialist justifying aim, since it is the very pursuit of that aim that is argued to violate the demands of respect for responsible agency. However, this kind of objection was not developed in enough plausible detail to persuade those who were not yet anticonsequentialist. Reformative or rehabilitative programs were admittedly often advocated (even if they were not operated) in ways that did not portray those subjected to them as responsible agents—and some of their advocates would argue that this was wholly appropriate, either because the idea of responsible agency was a myth that we should now abandon, or because, even if responsible agency was still a reality, offenders were not responsible agents (Menninger 1968; Skinner 1972). But not every kind of reformative program had this character; and if to be a responsible agent is to be one whose conduct can be guided by a grasp of reasons for action, deterrent punishment can be said to treat those against whom it is threatened as responsible agents, since it offers reasons for refraining from crime. It is, of course, still true that those who are punished are used as means to deter others (assuming that any plausible deterrent theory must appeal to general and not merely to special deterrence). But apart from the obscurity of just what the Kantian proscription means, what it formally proscribes is treating others *merely* as means; to which deterrent theorists can respond that if punishment is conditional on the voluntary commission of a crime, it does not treat the person punished *merely* as a means (Kant 1785).

However, even if critics of consequentialism can render normatively implausible not only a pure, but even a side-constrained consequentialism, this does not yet deliver retributivism. It could appear to do so only if, first, we assume that these two types of account exhaust the possible justifications of criminal punishment—that if it is to be justified, its justification must be either consequentialist or retributivist; and, second, we beg the institution by assuming that punishment must be justified—that the task for normative penal theory is to ask not whether, but precisely how, punishment is justified. The first assumption is at best arguable, though if we use "retributivism" (unhelpfully) to cover any and every nonconsequentialist justification of punishment it becomes a truism. The second assumption is clearly wrong, though the lack of proper attention to abolitionist ideas among penal theorists for so many years suggests that it was often implicitly made.[2] A full-scale retributivist revival required not merely a critique (however powerful) of consequentialism, but a normatively plausible account of punishment as retribution; which brings us to the second major weakness in the retributive revival of the 1970s.

The intuition that the guilty deserve to suffer may be widely and deeply felt, as becomes evident, at least in Britain and the United States, in the aftermath of any horrific crime. But intuitions, however deeply felt and widely shared, cannot simply be accepted: they must be critically analyzed and appraised. In particular, in the context of punishment, we need to ask precisely *what* criminal wrongdoers deserve to suffer; *why* they deserve to suffer it (how it is that crime makes such suffering appropriate); and why it should be the business of the state to create and maintain an institution whose purpose is to impose that deserved suffering.

Retributive revivalists did try to answer these questions, but their answers were not, on the whole, persuasive, which meant that positive retributivism still looked too much like an intuition in search of a theory. One popular answer, for instance, which did at least address the questions noted above, was that in committing a crime, the criminal took unfair advantage of the law-abiding self-restraint of those who refrained from crime, thus gaining for himself an unjust benefit. Punishment, as the imposition of a burden that matched that benefit, served to remove his unfair advantage and restore the balance of benefits and burdens that the crime disturbed; this was a proper task for the state, since it was a matter of doing justice to and between citizens. Such a view still has its supporters, who have worked hard to render it more plausible—with some success (Dagger 1993, 2008); but it still seems to its critics to fail to capture either the reasons why we should criminalize such wrongs as murder and rape, or the point or focus of convicting and punishing those who perpetrate them. I cannot discuss other retributivist answers here, but simply note that this challenge, to make plausible normative sense of the idea that punishment is justified as retribution for past wrongdoing, is one that retributivist revivalists struggled to meet.

Their task was made harder by two limitations on their approach. First, punishment was too often portrayed simply as some (unspecified) kind of burden or suffering to be imposed by the state on a passive recipient—which makes all too tempting the abolitionist's portrayal of punishment as a matter of "delivering pain" (Christie 1981), and all too reasonable the consequent thought that delivering pain cannot be a proper task or ambition for a liberal state, or for a polity that aspires to be humane. If we are to make plausible sense of the idea of retribution, we need to attend more carefully to the character and meaning of the suffering that punishment is meant to involve, and to the kind of response that it must aim to evoke in those who are punished. It is indeed a defining feature of punishment that it is intended to be burdensome, or in some sense painful, but that is not to say that the immediate aim of punishment must be understood simply as the imposition of a burden or the delivery of pain. Retributivists would do better to begin by offering a richer characterization of an appropriate formal response to wrongdoing and then show how that response must be burdensome or in some appropriate sense painful if it is to have the meaning it requires. I will return to this point in section IV.

The second limitation on many retributivist accounts (indeed, on many accounts, whether retributivist or nonretributivist) of criminal punishment is that they tend to treat punishment in isolation from its institutional context, and in particular from the criminal process by which it is preceded. This reflects a general failure by philosophical theorists to take the criminal process, and in particular the criminal trial, seriously enough, as if that process serves simply to connect crime to punishment by identifying those who are eligible for punishment and by determining the punishment for which they are eligible. We will understand punishment better if we see it as part of a larger process through which we respond, as a polity, to criminal wrongdoing—and if we pay more attention to the role that defendants play in that larger process.

Retributivist theorizing about punishment has moved on since the 1970s; more recent theorists have tried to meet the challenges faced by the earlier revivalists. This is not the place for a survey of recent retributivist thinking (Duff 1996, 2008). Instead, I will briefly note some new challenges that retributivist thought faces, before going on to show how both the old and the new challenges can be met. One striking point is that retributivism is now challenged in both its positive and negative guises. For a long time it seemed that even if ambitiously positive forms of retributivism could not be made normatively plausible, a negative retributivism (or, at least, the constraints that it implies) was an important part of any acceptable penal theory or practice: that is, whatever aims punishment should be used to serve, we should not punish those whom we know to be innocent, or punish the guilty more harshly than they deserve.[3] It might not be clear whether such principles are best explained by appeals to retributive desert, or to a nonretributive idea of fairness (Hart 1968),[4] or to a sophisticated form of consequentialism (Braithwaite and Pettit 1990), but it was very widely agreed that a justifiable system of criminal punishment must respect them. Hence the attractions of "mixed" theories, including "limiting retributivism" (Morris 1974; Morris and Tonry 1990), which seemed to do justice both to the retributivist thought that punishment must be warranted by past criminal wrongdoing and to the consequentialist concern that any such practice can be justified only if it secures consequential goods sufficient to outweigh its manifest costs. However, even such a modest retributivism faces at least three new (or renewed) kinds of challenge.

The first comes most vividly from proponents of "therapeutic justice," discussed by Doug Husak (2011), and reflects a renewed confidence that some things do work—that, for instance, specialist courts advised by sensible experts, with access to adequate resources, and with appropriately modest ambitions, can impose sentences that will achieve real successes in crime reduction and the rehabilitation of offenders. This movement challenges retributivist ideas not merely because it is consequentialist in spirit, since the same is true of the familiar kinds of side-constrained consequentialism, but because, like many therapeutic movements, it is impatient with the insistence on a backward-looking proportionality (at least one that does relative justice as between different offenders) that characterizes any retributivism. What must matter, from this perspective, is what is needed to achieve the desired results (results that will, of course, benefit the offender as much as others); although the costs and burdens must be proportionate to that benefit, it would be absurd, for instance, to scale back the program that an offender is required to undertake simply on the grounds that it is disproportionately burdensome relative to the offense that brought him before the court and to the sentences that others who committed similar offenses have received.

A second challenge comes from "preventive" justice—from the increasing tendency for governments concerned with "security," and the efficient prevention of crime and other kinds of harm, to adopt measures that aim to preempt criminal conduct rather than just to respond to it. Some such measures are imposed on convicted offenders by way of extra or indefinite terms of detention for reasons of public safety or protection; others involve what are formally civil rather than criminal orders that impose restrictions on people who have not as yet been convicted of any offense in order to prevent the crimes that, it is feared, they or others might commit (Zedner 2007; Zedner and Ashworth 2008; Ashworth and Zedner 2011). Such provisions are familiar in the context of offenses related to terrorism, and might be seen as posing a threat not so much to retributive conceptions of punishment as to the very idea of punishment as a response to past wrongdoing. That threat appears most dramatically when it is suggested, explicitly or implicitly, that those who commit terrorist attacks should be treated not as defendants or offenders within the framework, and so under the protection, of the criminal law, but as enemies, outlaws, or "unlawful combatants;"[5] but it is not far from the surface whenever politicians and policy makers are swept up by the idea of a "war" against crime—or against certain kinds of crime.

A third challenge comes from the by now multifarious forms of "restorative justice," itself the offspring of older abolitionist ideas. This challenge, too, is not merely to retributivism as a particular penal philosophy (although the contrast is often drawn between "restorative" and "retributive" justice), but to the very practice of punishment—and indeed to the very idea of criminal law. More precisely, that is the challenge that comes from some radical advocates of "restorative justice." Some programs or practices that are called "restorative" figure as part of or complements to the traditional criminal justice processes of trial, conviction, and punishment. They might, for instance, take place during (though not formally as part of) the offender's sentence,[6] or they might take place between conviction and sentencing, and affect the sentencing decision, while the sentence might itself include participation in a restorative program (Gabbay 2006; Luna and Poulson 2006; O'Hear 2009). It is important to think about what the aims of such processes should be and how those aims relate to the traditional aims of punishment. The following discussion bears on these questions. However, my main focus will be on restorative justice processes that are seen not as aspects of or complements to the criminal justice process, but as alternatives to it, since they raise more sharply the questions I want to consider about the proper role of retribution in penal theory. Rather than being prosecuted, convicted, and sentenced, the offender agrees to enter a restorative process, which typically involves a meeting with the victim and other interested parties, and (it is hoped) an agreement on some kind of reparative action (Braithwaite 1999; Johnstone 2002; von Hirsch et al. 2003; Johnstone and van Ness 2006). Even here there are, of course, more and less radical approaches. The less radical approach portrays restorative justice programs as modes of diversion from the criminal process—a kind of diversion that is, it is claimed, appropriate for certain kinds of offense or offender (notably for relatively minor victimizing offenses and for young offenders), but that would not, it is implicitly admitted, be appropriate for all kinds of offense and offender. The more radical approach portrays restorative justice not merely as an alternative to, but as a replacement for, criminal justice: we should (as far and as soon as is practicable) abandon the entire apparatus of criminal law, criminal process, and criminal punishment in favor of more "civil," informal practices that aim to repair harm and restore relationships rather than to condemn wrongs and punish their perpetrators. It is this conception of restorative justice that carries forward the ambitions of abolitionist theorists who similarly sought to abolish not merely this or that kind of especially oppressive or destructive punishment, nor indeed (though this is ambitious enough) criminal punishment as such, but all of criminal law, in favor of processes very like those now urged by radical advocates of restorative justice.[7]

According to such radical critics of criminal law, we should talk and think not of crimes that must be condemned and punished, but of "conflicts" or "troubles" that need to be resolved or repaired. We should focus not on wrongs whose perpetrators must be prosecuted by the formal force of the law and subjected to the pains of criminal punishment, but on harms that need to be repaired and relationships that need to be restored. In response to such conflicts or troubles we should not focus on "the offender" as the person whom we must condemn and punish, but on all those with an interest in the matter. Instead of criminal courts that subject lone defendants to the accusing, condemnatory attention of the criminal law, "steal" conflicts from those to whom they properly belong, and inhibit any productive engagement with those conflicts by their abstractions and their professionalism, we need informal fora in which those involved in the affair, either directly or as concerned fellow members of the local community, can come together to work out what to do. Instead of imposing punishments that aim simply to deliver pain, we need to help the interested parties come to agree on reparative measures that will mend the harm and restore the relationships that have been damaged.

I do not suggest that this kind of radical abolitionism is common among advocates of restorative justice, or that they typically share all its concerns and attitudes. However,

I do think that we can make progress toward a better understanding of the need for punishment as retribution, and of the role that ideas of repair and restoration can properly play in a system of criminal law and punishment, by starting with radical abolitionism and seeing where and why it goes wrong. We will then also be able to appraise less radical types of restorative justice—and, I will argue, to see that the kind of restoration that crime makes necessary is, properly understood, compatible with retributive punishment (once *that* idea is properly understood).

It is this abolitionist challenge that provides the focus for this essay (other challenges are discussed in other essays). Part of what motivates the challenge, and gives it its moral force, is the manifest destructiveness and inhumanity of so much of what now passes for punishment in our existing institutions of criminal justice; another part lies in the rather crude brutalism of some retributivist thought, with its emphasis on making offenders suffer—on imposing a kind of pain that is purely backward-looking and that lacks any redemptive or constructive character. It must, of course, remain a defining feature of any penal theory that is to be recognizably retributive that what it justifies is precisely the imposition of something burdensome or unwelcome, and of any theory that is to count as robustly retributivist that what it justifies is precisely the intention or attempt to impose such burdens; but we will see in what follows that such intentions and attempts may not be best described simply as the intention or attempt "to make the guilty suffer."

There is another kind of abolitionism that I cannot discuss here—one that does not reject the very idea of the criminal law, but does reject or seek to undermine the idea of responsible agency on which criminal punishment depends, arguing that we should be looking instead for efficient kinds of treatment that will prevent further criminal conduct (though one question is whether the idea of crime can survive the removal of that conception of responsible criminal agency). A simple version of this kind of abolitionism is found in psychiatrists who portray crime as a (symptom of) mental disorder (Menninger 1968); another is found in Wootton's (1963) argument that we should cease to attend to *mens rea* as a condition of guilt, or to try to distinguish the culpably responsible from the excusably disordered.[8] This species of abolitionism offers a salutary reminder that criminal punishment can be less oppressively coercive, and can be subject to more stringent principled constraints, than some of the alternatives to it;[9] but what matters for present purposes is that it denies or sidesteps the idea of personal responsibility, whereas advocates both of restorative justice and of retributive punishment insist on the importance of personal responsibility—although they differ sharply in their understandings of what such responsibility brings with it.

II. CRIMES, WRONGS, AND HARMS

Before we can talk usefully about criminal punishment, we must talk about crime itself: while it might not be a necessary truth that crime entails punishment, since we could retain a kind of criminal law while doing away with punishment, criminal punishment presupposes crime, as that for which it is imposed. Furthermore, as I noted above, the most radical kind of penal abolitionism argues not that we should respond to crime in nonpunitive ways, but that we should cease to use the concept of crime at all—that we should see our social world through a different conceptual lens.

The criminal law deals in wrongdoing: in its substantive mode, it defines certain kinds of conduct as (criminally) wrongful; in its adjudicative mode, it provides the procedures through which accusations of the commission of such wrongs can be dealt with; in its punitive mode, it provides for the punishments (or other disposals) that are to be imposed on the perpetrators of such wrongs. To understand its punitive mode, we must understand its substantive mode (the topic of this section) and its adjudicative mode (the topic of section III).

To say that the criminal law deals in wrongdoing is, of course, not yet to say that it deals in *moral* wrongdoing: a system of law could define as "legal wrongs" conduct that violates its rules without implying that such conduct is morally wrong. Indeed, to insist that the criminal law does and should deal in moral wrongdoing might be understood to imply a type of legal moralism, according to which the proper aim of criminal law is to condemn and punish moral wickedness, that many contemporary liberals reject. Now, I do think that legal moralism rests on an important truth about the nature of criminal law as a distinctive type of legal regulation: what is defined as criminal must be so defined because it is believed to be morally wrong.[10] The point is not just that, as even staunch opponents of legal moralism might agree (Feinberg 1984), moral wrongfulness should be a necessary condition of criminalization: it is, more ambitiously, that the criminal law's focus should be on the moral wrongfulness of the criminalized conduct—that that is the proper object of criminalization (Duff 2007, chaps. 4, 6). I do not mean by this that we have reason to criminalize every kind of moral wrongdoing (Moore 1997, chaps. 1, 6): a sensible legal moralism will incorporate the familiar liberal view that some kinds of moral wrongdoing are, "in brief and crude terms, not the law's business"—not even in principle the criminal law's business (Wolfenden 1957). Crimes are "public" wrongs, which is to say that they are wrongs that properly concern "the public"—all citizens, simply by virtue of their shared membership of the polity. We must look to political theory—a theory of the proper aims and functions of the state, and an accompanying account of the nature of the civic enterprise of living together as a polity—if we are to work out what kinds of wrongs are in that sense public (Marshall and Duff 1998, 2010).

The key claim for present purposes concerns not the precise contours of such a theory (of the state, of political community, of the role of criminal law in a political community, and thus ultimately of criminalization), but that it will have a place for criminal law as a practice focused on wrongdoing. I take it that it does not need arguing that our extralegal, social lives have an essential moral dimension. Though there are various conceptual lenses through which we see our own and others' actions (whether we are in deliberative or evaluative mode), and though that of morality might not be omnipresent or even always the most important, it is nonetheless one essential lens. The moral character of what we and others do is significant, and both our deliberation and our judgment should sometimes focus on it. Nor indeed need abolitionists deny (although some seem inclined to) that this is true of our extralegal lives. What concerns them is the question of whether and how the law should view us through that lens. To see why it should, and why we therefore need a criminal law that takes wrongdoing seriously, we can begin simply, with a limited, shallow description of a kind of occurrence to which advocates and critics of criminal law might respond rather differently. It is established, let us suppose, that A deliberately broke a window of B's house (knowing that it was not his own house) in order to get in and take whatever items of salable value he could find; that he took B's laptop and some money (without B's consent), intending to sell the laptop to make some money; and that he caused various kinds of damage in his search for valuables.

That is a description on whose truth we should be able to agree, whatever our view of the criminal law and of punishment—partly, of course, because it is a very limited description. It is limited in the "thickness" of the concepts it applies: it does not talk of theft, or dishonesty, or of a violation of B's home.[11] It is limited in its scope: it tells us nothing about either A's or B's background, condition, or social or financial status; nothing about the social and political conditions under which they live; nothing about any past dealings or acquaintanceship between A and B. It is limited in its depth: it tells us nothing about A's motives, beyond his concern to obtain money, or about the life and character from which this action emerged, and nothing about the psychological impact on B. Nor indeed does it tell us who "we" are in relation to the affair: whether we are neighbors of A or B, or both; or friends or family; or residents of the same village, city, or country; or observers who just read about it from afar.

On the face of it, this occurrence involves both harm and wrong. B suffers material harm to his house, he loses some of his possessions, and a fuller description might show that he has also suffered psychological distress and longer-term harm (anxiety, fear, insecurity). As so far described, the occurrence involves no harm to A, but a fuller description might reveal that he too has suffered various kinds of harm—the poverty or drug use that led him to see this as the best or only way to obtain money; the fear of detection; perhaps the remorse at what he did to B. Now the harms that B suffers, as so far described (at least if we leave out the details of what he felt or feels), can be identified and understood as harms without reference to the actions that caused them:[12] they could, in principle, have resulted from natural causes. At first glance, however, we should also say that A has wronged B: only at first glance, since it could turn out, on closer inquiry, that no wrong was done (one can imagine various accounts that would have this implication); but at least at first glance, since as so far described, it looks as if A has wrongfully invaded B's house, stolen his possessions, and damaged his property; and perhaps also presumptively, since the facts as so far stated seem to warrant an inference of wrongdoing absent some countervailing explanation.

One question that I cannot pursue here concerns the relationship between the harm that B has undoubtedly suffered and the wrong that A has presumptively done to B. It is at the least arguable that if A has wronged B, this does not merely add a wrong to that harm, but changes the character of the harm itself. We cannot separate what B has suffered into a set of harms plus a set of wrongs, but should rather see being burgled, suffering theft, and willful damage to one's property as a harmful wrong or a wrongful harm that cannot be analyzed into two distinct constituents (Duff 2007, chap. 6 sect. 2). If that is right, it poses a serious problem for abolitionists who urge us to focus on harms rather than on wrongs (Walgrave 2003), since an adequate understanding of the harms, one that does justice to what those who suffer them have suffered, will need to include reference to the wrongfulness of those harms. Even apart from that possibility, however, we must ask whether the polity's public conception of this affair between A and B, as determined by its formal, legal institutions, should focus solely on the harm that was caused (and on who is to pay for it, and on how that question should be determined), or should also take formal notice of the wrong that B has presumptively suffered. Surely the obvious answer is that it should, and we collectively should, take such formal notice. We owe this, we might say, to victims of such wrongs: as fellow citizens, we owe it to them to notice and to care about what they have suffered—and what they have suffered includes the wrong. We owe it, we might also say, to ourselves collectively, as members of a polity that defines itself by a shared commitment to certain values, including those at stake in this affair: for to be committed to a value is to be committed to taking note of its violation. But we also owe it, we might add, to A (to all those who commit such wrongs). To take each other seriously as citizens is, in part, to take proper notice of our "public" conduct, including our commissions of public wrongs.

More generally, an essential part of what makes a society a political community (rather than a mere collection of unassociated strangers) is some shared understanding of the values that define their civic life. Central to those values will be a conception of how people should behave toward each other, of the (perhaps fairly minimal) constraints they should observe in their dealings with each other. The more significant of those values and constraints require some public, formal expression, and this is the first function of criminal law as a distinctive type of law: it constitutes a public declaration and definition of those wrongs of which, as violations of its core defining values, the polity should take formal note. There is, of course, much more to be said about how those values and the correlative wrongs are to be identified, and about the proper scope of such a criminal law;[13] nor have I yet said anything about how we should collectively and formally respond to the commission of such wrongs. All I have suggested so far is that we do, as a polity, need a formal institution with this central feature of the criminal law: an institution that defines, and by implication condemns, a range of public wrongs. The question then is this: How should a polity respond to the (actual or suspected) commission of such wrongs?

III. RESPONSIBILITY AND CALLING TO ACCOUNT

A polity that takes its self-defining values seriously, and that takes its members seriously (a polity, that is, whose members take each other seriously) as citizens who are both bound and protected by those values, cannot ignore violations of those values or the wrongs that citizens do to each other.[14] One way in which it takes note of such wrongs is by publicly defining and declaring them as wrongs: this is, I suggested in the previous section, an initial function of criminal law. But what should it do after the event?

Part of what it should do, part of what we should do as citizens, concerns the victims of such wrongs: we owe them a recognition of what they have suffered, and help in coping with it (though it will not always be clear what kind of "coping" is possible). In part, of course, that recognition and help will focus on whatever harms they have suffered, as sympathy for that suffering and assistance in trying to repair the harm (in so far as it is reparable). However, they have suffered not just harm, but wrong, and our collective response must address that dimension as well. Now, for two reasons, we can most appropriately address that dimension by tackling, or trying to tackle, the person(s) who wronged them.

First, it is plausible to think that part of what we owe to the victims is to seek to call those who wronged them to account for those wrongs—and that this is also something we owe to ourselves collectively in so far as we share those wrongs as their victims' fellow citizens.[15] This is a common complaint by victims when the police do not investigate "their" crime with what they take to be sufficient commitment, or when prosecutors do not bring charges against "their" offender: that "their" crimes have not been taken seriously enough. It is also a common motivation for civil suits in cases of allegedly negligent killing: those who lost loved ones in a train crash, or in a workplace accident, or in a hospital, and who suspect that this was due to negligence by the rail company or the employer, or doctors, might bring a case whose formal aim must be compensation, but whose real aim (they argue) is to call to account those whose negligence caused their loss. What they properly seek is not (just) compensation for whatever independently identifiable harm they have suffered, but an accounting for the wrong.

Second, once we see what is properly involved in "tackling" the wrongdoer, we can also see that this is something that we collectively owe to those who commit as well as to those who suffer such wrongs. Granted, on one familiar but crude kind of retributive view, what victims properly demand is that those who wronged them be made to suffer: this goes with the idea that what wrongdoers deserve is to suffer, and that the polity's first or primary responsibility is to make sure that they suffer. Such a demand for suffering is admittedly one aspect both of public opinion and of many victims' responses to their crimes, and if we focus on that demand, it is indeed hard to see its satisfaction as something that we owe to those who are to be made to suffer: if that is what punishment is, the idea of a right to be punished is as absurd as its critics claim. However, this is not the only salient demand, nor, I think, is it the demand on which we should initially focus.[16] We should instead focus on the demand that the wrongdoer be called or held to account for what he has done—that he answer for it. This is, I suspect, as powerfully felt a demand as the demand that he be made to suffer, as is perhaps evidenced most clearly in the case of international criminal trials: what matters, to many people, is not so much that those who have perpetrated "crimes against humanity" be punished (what punishment, we might ask, could fit such wrongs?), but that they be called to public account for what they have done. But to call someone to account is to treat and address him as a responsible agent, and as a fellow member of a relevant normative community. I can be called to account only if I am a responsible agent who can be expected to answer for what he has done, and only by fellows who are themselves committed to the values for an alleged violation of which I am now called to account, and who participate in the particular form of life within which I am thus called. To call someone to account for an alleged wrong, however condemnatory that calling is, is therefore also to show him a certain kind of respect, or even concern, as a fellow who is, along with us, both bound and protected by the values to which that calling appeals.

Advocates of restorative justice often also make the idea of responsibility salient in their accounts of how we should collectively respond to (what we now see as) crime. What is important, they argue, is to develop structures and procedures through which responsibility can be discussed, negotiated, accepted, and discharged—through which people can come to take responsibility for what they have done, and work out how to discharge that responsibility through reparative actions. They differ, however, over just what those structures and procedures should be, and sometimes fail to appreciate the significance of the distinctive kind of calling to account that (I will argue) the criminal law can provide.

One important point that should have emerged from the previous section is that we must attend not just to harms, but to wrongs. It is not just a matter of determining (or negotiating) responsibility for a harm that was caused, but of determining responsibility for wrongdoing. The former kind of responsibility would be standardly discharged by repairing or paying for the harm. We need to ask how the latter can be discharged, and what goes with accepting it, but the point to note here is that a process that is to do justice to victims and to what they have suffered must aim not merely to call a harm-causer to account, or bring him to recognize his responsibility for that harm, but to call a wrong-doer to account for the wrong he has done.

Further important issues are raised by the emphasis that advocates of restorative justice often place on informal negotiation between the parties most directly involved in the affair rather than a formal determination by a court. What matters, they argue, is that people should be able to discuss their concerns, explain their actions and reactions, freely and openly. They should be able to come to accept their own responsibilities, and to recognize that the responsibility for a harm might well not be properly allocated to just one person—that often it may be shared in complex and nuanced ways that cannot be captured in the formal process of a criminal trial, which is focused on just one person, the defendant. These are certainly valuable features of the ways in which we can conduct our social lives, and it might well be that, even when a "conflict" in which we find ourselves involves criminal conduct, we would do better to try to resolve our problems through such an informal process rather than by appealing to the formal (and coercive) apparatus of the criminal law. But such informal processes will not always be adequate.

First, they privatize the conflict: but some kinds of wrong should be treated as public matters that concern us all as citizens. That is why, as argued in the previous section, we need a criminal law, which defines a category of public wrongs that are our collective business; and a public wrong requires a public response.

Second, the wrongs that we should treat as public are typically wrongs that require categorical recognition and condemnation rather than (or at least before) the kind of nuanced negotiation (and compromise) that a "conflict"-oriented process is likely to involve. No doubt we should sometimes (perhaps more often than we are inclined to) ask versions of Christie's (1977, p. 8) question, "How wrong was the thief, how right was the victim?" No doubt we will sometimes come to see that, having initially portrayed ourselves as innocent victims, we should accept some responsibility for what happened in a way that thereby reduces the responsibility of the person we portrayed as the perpetrator. Sometimes, however, that is inappropriate. One reason for this is that sometimes it is simply not plausible to argue that the victim was in any immediate way even partly responsible for the crime. And although it is true that if we delved more deeply into the conditions from which the crime emerged, we might see reason to share a deeper kind of responsibility more broadly,[17] it is also important to our conception of ourselves and each other as agents that we take full responsibility for our actions. But another reason is that while, when what is at stake is who should pay to repair some harm that has been caused, a victim who is partly responsible for the harm should bear part of the cost, so that responsibility that is shared is thereby reduced for each person, this is not how responsibility is properly allocated for wrongs. It might be true, for instance, that the victim of a rape behaved negligently in exposing herself to a risk of being attacked; it might be appropriate for her to criticize herself or for a friend to criticize her for her imprudence. But while "contributory negligence" plays a proper role in civil cases, since it warrants the conclusion that responsibility, and thus the cost of the harm, should be shared between plaintiff and defendant, no such conclusion is warranted in a criminal case. It would be insulting for a criminal court to ask, "How wrong was the rapist, how right was the victim?" in such a case. The defendant cannot be allowed to argue, by way of mitigation, that the victim's negligence was a contributory factor in the crime; her negligence does nothing to reduce the attacker's culpable responsibility. In this context, unlike that of liability to pay for harm, responsibility that is shared is not thereby reduced for each of those who shares it, and it would be misleading to talk of the rapist and his victim sharing responsibility: his attack constitutes, in moral terms, an utterly *novus actus interveniens*, for which he alone is criminally responsible. The attacks that constitute paradigmatically criminal *mala in se* are wrongs from which every citizen should be able to expect to be, as it were, categorically safe, and which are therefore to be categorically condemned rather than negotiated.[18] That is why, for instance, it is right to prosecute domestic violence as a criminal offense rather than simply seeing it as a private matter to be negotiated between the people directly involved. Such violence must be marked, categorically, as wrong, and it is a kind of wrong in which we should, collectively, take an active interest as fellow citizens of both victim and perpetrator.[19]

One further aspect of informal procedures is worth noting: that it is harder to set limits on what is raised for critical discussion. What begins as a conflict between neighbors over a precise, limited issue can easily spread out, once discussion begins, to bring in other aspects of their lives. If the aim is to restore their relationship, anything about the relationship that is problematic can be brought up. This is, of course, sometimes just what is needed, especially in a close-knit community, but it is worrying for those who are committed to an idea(l) of liberal political community that respects the boundaries of our personal lives. In such a polity we are related to, and deal with, the majority of fellow citizens not, admittedly, as complete strangers (we recognize them as fellows), but as people with whom our bonds are limited and relatively shallow. We share a civic life with them, but that life is only one dimension of our lives, and we should be able to keep much about the other dimensions of our lives private—shared only with members of those smaller groups with whom we choose to share or with whom we find ourselves living in greater intimacy. When we commit wrongs that count as "public," we must be willing to answer for them publicly, but even then the realm of private life and thought should be protected. The fact that I committed a wrong against a fellow citizen should not give my fellows the right to discuss every aspect of my life that bothers them. But that is just what can happen in an informal, unconstrained discussion of our "conflict."

I have suggested so far that a polity that takes wrongdoing as seriously as it should (i.e., as something neither reducible to nor unimportant as compared to harm), and whose members aspire to treat each other with appropriate respect and concern as responsible citizens, should make provision for those who commit public wrongs to be called to account for them (and, as well, for those accused of committing such wrongs to be called to answer those accusations), but that it should also protect alleged and actual wrongdoers against responses that intrude into what should still be the private realms of their lives. I have also suggested that the kinds of processes favored by advocates of restorative justice might not be of this proper kind. But we do have an institution that, in the aspiration that its forms and rhetoric imply, even if sadly all too infrequently in its actual operations, is of that kind: the criminal trial.

Philosophers who write about criminal law have tended to focus on substantive criminal law, and on the punishments that those who commit crimes may incur. But the process that connects crime to punishment is also important to a normative understanding of criminal law; indeed, the formal and public aspects of that process are central to the criminal law's purpose. That process includes the investigation of crime and the treatment of suspected offenders (Ashworth and Redmayne 2005; Sanders and Young 2006; Kleinig 2008), but we can focus here on the criminal trial as the formal culmination of the criminal process.

It might be tempting to see the criminal trial in purely instrumental terms, as a method of establishing who is to be subjected to the punishments (or other kinds of coercive measures) that give the trial its point; but this does not do justice to important aspects of criminal trials or their role in a democratic system of law. Rather, we should see the criminal trial as a formal process through which an alleged wrongdoer is called to answer to his fellow citizens by the court that speaks in their name. He is called, initially, to answer to the charge of wrongdoing—either by pleading "guilty," thus admitting his culpable commission of the wrong, or by pleading "not guilty," thus challenging the prosecution to prove his guilt. If the prosecution does prove that he committed the offense, he must then answer for that commission, either by offering a defense—a justification or excuse showing that he should not be condemned for committing the offense—or by submitting himself to the court's formal condemnation and to the sentence it imposes. The criminal trial is thus a formal analogue of the informal moral processes through which we call each other to account for wrongs that we have committed. It addresses the defendant not simply as someone who is the subject of a formal inquiry, but as a citizen who is to participate in the process, and who is expected to answer to his fellows for his alleged violation of the values that define their polity.[20]

The criminal trial, as thus understood, provides an appropriate response to what the law defines as crimes. It constitutes the kind of calling to account that, I have suggested, criminal wrongdoing requires—a calling that takes the wrongdoing seriously and addresses its agent as a responsible citizen. It is precisely focused on the wrongdoing, not just on the harm that might also have been caused, and focuses on that wrongdoing as a public rather than a private matter: the polity as a whole calls the alleged perpetrator to account for a wrong that concerns all citizens. However, that calling to account respects the boundaries of private life. What is at issue is whether the defendant is guilty of the particular wrong specified in the indictment, and only matters bearing directly on that issue are to figure in the trial.

If the prosecution proves that the defendant committed the crime charged, and disproves any exculpatory defense that he offers, he is convicted of the crime. A conviction is not just a formal finding that he did commit the crime, and is therefore eligible for punishment: it also condemns his criminal action, and censures him as its agent.[21] That, we can say, is one thing that a criminal wrongdoer deserves, and one thing that we owe to his victim: a formal, public condemnation of his crime. That is also a kind of punishment, since condemnation by one's fellow citizens is intended to be painfully burdensome as a justified response to one's wrongdoing. It could indeed be seen as a particularly pure kind of punishment, since (leaving aside for the moment the further consequences that may attend a conviction) it is burdensome or painful only in virtue of its meaning as a condemnation, whereas the "hard treatment" that postconviction punishments typically involve is burdensome independently of any meaning that it might have.[22]

However, conviction is not typically the end of the matter for the offender; nor indeed is it typically thought to constitute an adequate response to his crime. It is time to turn, finally, to the material punishments that normally follow a conviction.

IV. THE MEANING AND PURPOSE OF PUNISHMENT

Although I promised at the start of this essay to defend a robust retributivism, I have not yet said anything, retributivist or otherwise, about the role of punishment in the kind of criminal law sketched in the previous two sections. By a "robust" retributivism, I mean one that takes the past wrongdoing for which a person is punished to be not merely a necessary condition of punishment, or a source of limits on the severity of punishment, but the (or a) primary focus of punishment: punishment is to be justified as an appropriate response to that wrongdoing. It might now seem, however, that I have made it harder rather than easier to justify punishment at all, let alone retributive punishment. For I have been emphasizing the respect and concern that citizens owe each other as fellow members of the polity, a respect and concern that is due to offenders as well as to victims. But how can the deliberate infliction of penal hardship be consistent with, let alone expressive of, that concern and respect? Should we not rather follow an abolitionist route and look for nonpunitive provisions and procedures that could restore and repair the civic relationships that crime has damaged?

It is certainly true that the kind of criminal law and criminal process I have sketched does not make punishment necessary. We could, in principle, do nothing more to or with offenders after their convictions: the polity formally censures them, and that is all. If we find this quite unacceptable, we need to ask why. Is it, for instance, because a criminal process that did not culminate in punishment would be unacceptably ineffective in preventing crime; or because it would not inflict the suffering that wrongdoers deserve; or because such a process would not take crime seriously enough? But even if we must do something more than convict, and thus censure, criminal wrongdoers, it is not yet clear that or why that "more" must be punishment. We could, for instance, subject the convicted offender to whatever "measures" might seem to be necessary and potentially effective in preventing future offending (Wootton 1963; de Keijser 2011; Matravers 2011). But this would hardly be to treat or respect them as responsible citizens. Or we could require them to make some appropriate kind of reparation or restitution, or to pay compensation for what they have done. This brings us closer to the territory of restorative justice (Golash 2005; Boonin 2008), but we have to ask what could count as reparation or compensation not just for whatever harm was caused, but for the wrong that was done.

Both the reform of future conduct and reparation for past wrongdoing are important purposes for the criminal process. My suggestion is, however, that if we are to pursue those aims in a way that is consistent with the respect that we owe each other as citizens, and in a way that does justice to the wrongs that crimes involve (and to those who suffer and those who perpetrate such wrongs), we should do so through a system of retributive punishment—a system that will also serve the reconciliatory aims urged by advocates of restorative justice in a manner appropriate to a liberal polity. What follows is a necessarily bare sketch of this suggestion.[23]

We can begin with the by now familiar idea that punishment serves a communicative purpose: it communicates (directly to the offender, but also to all citizens) the censure that the crime deserves.[24] It is in that sense retributive: it is justified as a response to the wrong for which it is imposed and must be appropriate in its character and severity to that wrong. But such communication is not purely backward-looking: for to censure someone for their past conduct is also to say both that they should take care to reform their future conduct to avoid such wrongdoing, and that they should make some suitable reparation to those whom they wronged. The question then is, how can penal "hard treatment," the imposition of something that is burdensome independently of its censorial meaning, serve such aims of a communicative process? One familiar, and by itself not wholly persuasive, answer is that the hard treatment makes the communication more effective by making it harder to ignore (Kleinig 1991). But we can say something more than that by looking more carefully at each dimension of the two-way communicative process that punishment should ideally be or become.

First, punishment communicates censure from the polity to the offender. The aim should be not just to ensure that he hears the censure, but to persuade him to attend to it, in the hope that he will be persuaded by it to repent his crime (and thus also to see the need to reform his future conduct). But merely verbal censure, as conveyed by a conviction, or purely symbolic punishments, are likely to be inadequate, since they are all too easily ignored or forgotten. It is all too easy, and too tempting, for us to distract ourselves from giving our wrongdoing the remorseful attention it deserves. One function of burdensome punishment, then, is to make it harder for the offender to ignore the message that punishment communicates. It is a way of helping to keep his attention focused on his wrongdoing and its implications, with a view to inducing and strengthening a properly repentant understanding of what he has done.[25] Such an understanding will include a recognition of the need to reform his future conduct (unless the crime was a genuine aberration), and although such reform must ultimately be something that he achieves for himself as a responsible agent, punishment can help in that endeavor. This is one of the central aims of probation, and of the kinds of programs that may be offered to offenders to help them confront and deal with the sources of their crimes. If the program is so focused on the crime itself and its immediate causes that we can say that an offender who refused to undertake the program would be refusing to take his crime seriously, undertaking the program could be required as part of the punishment.[26]

Second, something must also be communicated from the offender to the polity, and to the victim (when there is a victim). He has committed a wrong against the victim, and against the polity's values, and he must "make up" for that wrong by making some reparation to them. The criminal law is, as we have seen, focused on wrongs rather than on harms. What matters, therefore, is not (just) reparation for whatever harm was caused, but moral reparation for the wrong that was done. It is this aspect of the reparation that crime makes necessary that is missing from accounts of restorative justice that urge us to focus on repairing or making good the harm that was caused. But what could constitute reparation for a wrong? Central to such moral reparation is apology. If I recognize that I have wronged you, I must recognize that I owe you an apology. Apology expresses my repentant recognition of the wrong I did. It owns the wrong as mine, but disowns it as something that I now repudiate. It implies a sincere commitment to avoid doing wrong in future, and it expresses my desire to seek forgiveness from and reconciliation with the person I wronged.

A verbal apology is often sufficient reparation: nothing more is, or should be, expected. Sometimes, however, when the wrong is more serious, or when the victim and the wrongdoer do not stand in the kind of relationship in which words can carry sufficient moral weight, words are not enough, since words can be too cheap and too easy. If the apology is to address the wrong adequately, if it is to show the victim that the wrong is taken seriously, and if it is to focus the wrongdoer's attention on the wrong as it should be focused, it must take a more than merely verbal form. That "more than merely verbal form" will involve something burdensome that the wrongdoer undertakes—some task that he undertakes for the benefit of the victim or the wider community, some penitential suffering that he undergoes, perhaps some burdensome program aimed at dealing with the root of his wrongdoing. The key point to notice here is that it must be burdensome to him if it is to serve its apologetic purpose. Something that was not burdensome, something that cost no more than mere words, would be no more adequate an apology than mere words; if I am to give material form to my repentant recognition of the burden of guilt that I now carry, that form must itself be something burdensome.

The second communicative aspect of punishment, then, is the communication of apology from the offender to those whom he wronged—the direct victim, and the wider community. The burdensome punishment gives material form, and so greater moral force, to that apology. Of course, we know that many offenders who undergo punishment are not truly apologetic; in undergoing their punishment they are not expressing a genuinely repentant recognition of the wrong they have done. Criminal punishment is, on this account, a species of required apology: the offender is required to go through the motions of apology, even if he does not mean it.

It might now be objected that such required apologies lack real value, and that to require people to apologize is inconsistent with a due respect for them as responsible moral agents.[27] But we can still see value even in required apologies whose sincerity is unknown or doubtful: they make clear to the offender what he ought to do (apologize sincerely) and to the victim that the community recognizes and takes seriously the wrong he has suffered. As to respect, what punishment requires of the offender is not actual repentance, but that he undergo the ritual of apology and moral reparation. It is still up to him to make, or refuse to make, that apology a genuine one (Garvey 1999; Tudor 2001; Bennett 2008).[28] By requiring him to undergo the burdensome sanction that would constitute appropriate reparation for his wrong, we hope that he will come to recognize the need for that reparation himself, and to make it his own, but that is up to him.

To say that punishment has these two communicative dimensions is not to suggest that it should be divided into two parts. The burdensome punishment that is imposed on or required of an offender in order to bring him to confront and recognize his crime should also be a burden that would constitute moral reparation for his crime. It is precisely by requiring him to undertake or undergo such a burden as reparation for his crime that we hope to bring him to a clearer, repentant understanding of that crime. Punishment is, on this view, a kind of secular penance.

This communicative enterprise—the communication of censure to the offender and the ritual of apology that he is required to undertake or undergo—also serves a reconciliatory aim. It is not, admittedly, well suited to restore the kinds of personal relationship on which those who advocate restorative justice sometimes focus: it is not apt to reconcile spouses, family members, partners, friends, or neighbors, if reconciliation is understood as the restoration of those bonds of affection and close mutual concern by which such relationships are structured. But that kind of reconciliation of those kinds of relationship is not the criminal law's business, or indeed the business of the liberal state, beyond perhaps offering mediation services that citizens can use if they so wish. The criminal law's proper concern is with our relationship as fellow citizens, a relationship that is, as far as the law is concerned, somewhat distant and formal. It is that relationship that crime, as a breach of our civic values, damages. It is that relationship that can repaired by the punishment that the offender undertakes or undergoes, *if* his fellow citizens play their proper part in the ritual. They will play that part if they accept the completion of the ritual as adequate moral reparation for the wrong without inquiring into the sincerity of the apology that is thus offered. For while, in our more intimate relationships, apologies, and the rituals through which they may be expressed, are only of value if they are sincere, in the civic life of a liberal polity that takes privacy seriously, what matters is that the ritual is undertaken.[29]

On this account, criminal punishment is robustly retributive, since it is focused on and justified by the crime for which it is imposed. It is justified as an appropriate response to that crime, a response that marks the character and seriousness of the crime and constitutes an appropriate, public, and formal reparation for it. It is not, however, merely retributive, since it also looks to the future: to the offender's (self-) reform, and to the restoration of the bonds of citizenship that the crime damaged. Nor is it opposed, as advocates of restorative justice often take it to be opposed, to ideas of restoration and reparation. It is something that citizens can properly impose on each other, and accept for themselves, as the appropriate way in which the distinctive damage wrought by crime can be repaired and civic relationships restored.

I have offered only the barest sketch of this conception of punishment. Much more needs to be said (but not here) about the details of this conception, about its implications for the operations of a criminal justice system (in particular, for sentencing), and about how we should respond to the gaping chasm between this ideal of what criminal punishment ought to be and our existing penal practices (but see Duff 2001). I hope, however, that I have said enough to show how we can hope to meet the challenges faced by retributivism and remedy the weaknesses that, I have argued, undermined the retributivist revival of the 1970s—in part by getting a clearer view of just what kind of burden punishment should be intended to impose (what it is that offenders can be said to deserve), and by setting punishment in the context of criminal law as a whole. That was why I spent so long, in sections II and III, on the idea of criminal law and on the criminal trial. We can best make sense of criminal punishment by seeing it as an aspect of the way in which a polity can properly deal with public wrongdoing—wrongdoing that is defined as public by the criminal law, and whose perpetrators are called to account in the criminal trial.

ACKNOWLEDGMENT

Thanks to participants in two workshops in Leiden at which earlier sketches of this essay were presented, and especially to Peter Ramsay for his detailed comments, and to Erik Luna and Michael O'Hear for advice on American restorative justice programs.

NOTES

1. It is less clear whether the second constraint, on the excessive punishment of the guilty, could be explained without recourse to retributive ideas of desert (see Feinberg 1988, pp. 144–55).
2. Philosophers of punishment have recently begun to take more seriously the idea that we should seek to abolish punishment rather than justify it (e.g., Golash 2005; Boonin 2008). There is still, however, a striking lack of engagement with the rich literature of abolitionism.
3. Though there has been persistent controversy over whether "upward departures" from desert constraints could be justified for offenders reliably identified as "dangerous" (see, recently, von Hirsch and Ashworth 2005, chap. 4; Robinson 2008, chap. 6).
4. See note 1 above, and accompanying text.
5. Compare Jakobs's notorious distinction between "*Bürgerstrafrecht*" and "*Feindstrafrecht*," on which see Gomez-Jara Díez (2008).
6. See, e.g., the Wisconsin prison program of meetings between offenders and victims organized by Janine Geske, a former Wisconsin Supreme Court justice (Umbreit et al. 2005, p. 265).
7. For some central examples of this kind of abolitionism, see Christie (1977, 1981); Hulsman (1986, 1991); Bianchi (1994).
8. Discussed in Matravers (2011). Also compare the use of supposedly nonpunitive "measures," discussed by de Keijser (2011).
9. Compare also Bianchi's (1994) support for compulsory "sanctuary."
10. Only "because it is believed," since legislators can of course criminalize what they mistakenly believe to be morally wrong (Tadros and Tierney 2004).
11. On "thick" concepts, see Williams (1985, chap. 8); on their significance for criminal law, see Duff (1998).
12. Something that Feinberg (1984, pp. 31–6) makes central to his account of harm.
13. It might seem that such a criminal law could deal with "*mala in se*," wrongs that can be identified as wrongs independently of law, but not with "*mala prohibita*," whose wrongness cannot be identified independently of the law. For a response to this objection, see Duff (2007, chap. 4, sect. 4, and chap. 7, sect. 3).
14. I focus here on the domestic criminal law of a national polity and on wrongs committed against each other by its citizens. Further accounts must be given of international criminal law and of how domestic criminal law also binds and protects noncitizens, but these will be further accounts. Domestic criminal law is still the familiar paradigm of criminal law, and the law's primary addressees are the polity's citizens.

15. On sharing wrongs, see Marshall and Duff (1998). The point is not that the harm or wrong is done to us collectively rather than (just) to the victim; it is that we share in his wrong as his fellows.
16. Compare Kleinig's (2011) comments on the meaning and proper role of the question "what does wrongdoing deserve?"
17. Compare Norrie (2000, pp. 220–21) on a "relational theory of blame," according to which responsibility "lies with individuals *and* with societies of which they are a part, so that, neither individualized nor denied, it is shared."
18. Contrast Bergelson (2009), arguing that in criminal law a defendant's responsibility can be reduced by the victim's own share of responsibility for the crime. But her argument is undermined by a failure to take seriously enough the fact that while, in a civil case, responsibility shared is responsibility reduced, in a criminal case that is not (always or necessarily) so.
19. Compare Dobash and Dobash (1992, chap. 7) and Dempsey (2009).
20. For further explanation and defense of this conception of the criminal trial, see Duff et al. (2007). It should be clear that this is an account of what trials should be, not of what they actually are in our existing courts.
21. That is why jury nullification (Abramson 2000, chap. 2) plays an important role in a democratic polity: it marks a citizens' judgment that the defendant does not deserve condemnation.
22. On "hard treatment," see Feinberg (1970) and Duff (1996, p. 34).
23. It is also in part a response to the final parts of Kleinig (2011).
24. See Feinberg (1970) on punishment as expressive, von Hirsch (1993), Duff (2001), and Markel (2005, 2009).
25. I talk of "burdensome punishment" rather than of "hard treatment" to avoid suggesting that the main aim is to hurt. Community service orders and probation are paradigm examples of communicative punishments: they are intended to be burdensome, but it might be misleading to describe them as "hard treatment."
26. See, e.g., the CHANGE program for domestically violent men (Dobash and Dobash 1992). One worry about "therapeutic" justice is that it ignores this requirement that what we require an offender to undertake must be something focused on and justifiable as a response to his crime.
27. See, e.g., von Hirsch and Ashworth (2005) for this and other criticisms.
28. For some insightful criticism, see Tasioulas (2006).
29. We should recognize, however, that "*if* his fellow citizens play their proper part in the ritual" marks a vital condition on the legitimacy of criminal punishment—a condition that, like so many other of the conditions that a just system of punishment must satisfy, is all too often and obviously not satisfied at the moment.

REFERENCES

Abramson, J. 2000. *We, the Jury: The Jury System and the Ideal of Democracy.* Cambridge, MA: Harvard University Press.

Ashworth, A. J., and M. Redmayne. 2005. *The Criminal Process*, 3rd ed. Oxford: Oxford University Press.

Ashworth, A. J., and L. Zedner. 2011. "Preventive Orders: A Problem of Under-Criminalization?" In *The Boundaries of the Criminal Law*, ed. R. A. Duff, L. Farmer, S. E. Marshall, M. Renzo, and V. Tadros. Oxford: Oxford University Press.

Bennett, C. 2008. *The Apology Ritual: A Philosophical Theory of Punishment.* Cambridge: Cambridge University Press.

Bergelson, V. 2009. *Victims' Rights and Victims' Wrongs; Comparative Liability In Criminal Law.* Stanford, CA: Stanford University Press.

Bianchi, H. 1994. *Justice as Sanctuary: Toward a New System of Crime Control* Bloomington: Indiana University Press.

Boonin, D. 2008. *The Problem of Punishment.* Cambridge: Cambridge University Press.

Braithwaite, J. 1999. "Restorative Justice: Assessing Optimistic and Pessimistic Accounts." In *Crime and Justice: A Review of Research,* vol. 25, ed. Michael Tonry. Chicago: University of Chicago Press.

Braithwaite, J., and P. Pettit. 1990. *Not Just Deserts: A Republican Theory of Criminal Justice.* Oxford: Oxford University Press.

Christie, N. 1977. "Conflicts as Property." *British Journal of Criminology* 17:1–15.

———. 1981. *Limits to Pain.* London: Martin Robertson.

Dagger, R. 1993. "Playing Fair with Punishment." *Ethics* 103:473–88.

Dagger, R. 2008. "Punishment as Fair Play." *Res Publica* 14:259–75.

de Keijser, J. 2011. "Never Mind the Pain; It's a Measure! Justifying Measures as Part of the Dutch Bifurcated System of Sanctions." In *Retributivism Has a Past. Has It a Future?,* ed. Michael Tonry. New York: Oxford University Press.

Dempsey, M. M. 2009. *Prosecuting Domestic Violence.* Oxford: Oxford University Press.

Dobash, R. E., and R. P. Dobash. 1992. *Women, Violence and Social Change.* London: Routledge.

Duff, R. A. 1996. "Penal Communications: Recent Work in Recent Work in the Philosophy of Punishment." In *Crime and Justice: A Review of Research,* vol. 20, ed. Michael Tonry. Chicago: University of Chicago Press.

———. 1998. "Law, Language and Community." *Oxford Journal of Legal Studies* 18:189–206.

———. 2001. *Punishment, Communication, and Community.* New York: Oxford University Press.

———. 2007. *Answering for Crime.* Oxford: Hart.

Duff, R. A. 2008. "Legal Punishment." *Stanford Encyclopedia of Philosophy (Fall 2008 Edition),* edited by E N Zalta. http://plato.stanford.edu/archives/fall2008/entries/legal-punishment/.

Duff, R. A., L. Farmer, S. E. Marshall, and V. Tadros. 2007. *The Trial on Trial (3): Towards a Normative Theory of the Criminal Trial.* Oxford: Hart.

Feinberg, J. 1970. *Doing and Deserving.* Princeton, NJ: Princeton University Press.

———. 1984. *Harm to Others.* New York: Oxford University Press.

———. 1988. *Harmless Wrongdoing.* New York: Oxford University Press.

Gabbay, Z. 2006. "Holding Restorative Justice Accountable." *Cardozo Journal of Conflict Resolution* 8:85–141.

Garvey, S. 1999. "Punishment as Atonement." *UCLA Law Review* 47:1801–58.

Golash, D. 2005. *The Case Against Punishment.* New York: New York University Press.

Gomez-Jara Díez, C. 2008. "Enemy Combatants Versus Enemy Criminal Law." *New Criminal Law Review* 11:529–62.

Hart, H. L. A. 1968. *Punishment and Responsibility.* Oxford: Oxford University Press.

Hulsman, L. 1986. "Critical Criminology and the Concept of Crime." *Crime, Law, and Social Change* 10:63–80.

———. 1991. "The Abolitionist Case: Alternative Crime Policies." *Israel Law Review* 25:681–709.

Husak, D. 2011. "Retributivism, Proportionality, and the Challenge of the Drug Court Movement." In *Retributivism Has a Past. Has It a Future?,* ed. Michael Tonry. New York: Oxford University Press.

Johnstone, G. 2002. *Restorative Justice: Ideas, Values, Debates.* Cullompton, Devon, UK: Willan.

Johnstone, G., and D. van Ness, eds. 2006. *Handbook of Restorative Justice Reader.* Cullompton, Devon, UK: Willan.

Kant, I. 1785. *Groundwork of the Metaphysic of Morals,* trans. H. Paton, 1948, as *The Moral Law.* London: Hutchinson.

Kleinig, J. 1991. "Punishment and Moral Seriousness." *Israel Law Review* 25:401–21.

———. 2008. *Ethics and Criminal Justice: An Introduction.* Cambridge: Cambridge University Press.

————. 2011. "What Does Wrongdoing Deserve?" In *Retributivism Has a Past. Has It a Future?*, ed. Michael Tonry. New York: Oxford University Press.

Lewis, C. S. 1953. "The Humanitarian Theory of Punishment." *Res Judicatae* 6:231–37. (Reprinted in 1970, *Readings in Ethical Theory*, 2nd ed., ed. W. Sellars and J. Hospers. New York: Appleton-Century-Crofts.

Luna, E., and B. Poulson. 2006. "Restorative Justice in Federal Sentencing: An Unexpected Benefit of Booker?" *McGeorge Law Review* 37:787–818.

Markel, D. 2005. "State, Be Not Proud: A Retributivist Defense of the Commutation of Death Row and the Abolition of the Death Penalty." *Harvard Civil Rights-Civil Liberties Law Review* 40:407–80.

————. 2009. "Executing Retributivism: Panetti and the Future of the Eighth Amendment." *Northwestern Law Review* 103:1163–222.

Marshall, S. E., and R. A. Duff. 1998. "Criminalization and Sharing Wrongs." *Canadian Journal of Law and Jurisprudence* 11:7–22.

————. 2010. "Public and Private Wrongs." In *Essays in Criminal Law in Honour of Sir Gerald Gordon*, ed. J. Chalmers, F. Leverick, and L. Farmer. Edinburgh: Edinburgh University Press.

Martinson, R. 1974. "What works? Questions and Answers about Prison Reform" *Public Interest* 10:22–54.

Matravers, M. 2011. "Is Twenty-first Century Punishment Post-desert?" In *Retributivism Has a Past. Has It a Future?*, ed. Michael Tonry. New York: Oxford University Press.

Menninger, K. 1968. *The Crime of Punishment*. New York: Viking Press.

Moore, M. S. 1997. *Placing Blame: A General Theory of the Criminal Law*. Oxford: Oxford University Press.

Morris, H. 1968. "Persons and Punishment." *The Monist* 52:475–79.

Morris, N. 1974. *The Future of Imprisonment*. Chicago: University of Chicago Press.

Morris, N., and M. Tonry. 1990. *Between Prison and Probation: Intermediate Punishments in a Rational Sentencing System*. New York: Oxford University Press.

Norrie, A. W. 2000. *Punishment, Responsibility, and Justice*. Oxford: Oxford University Press.

O'Hear, M. 2009. "Rethinking Drug Courts: Restorative Justice as a Response to Racial Injustice." *Stanford Law and Policy Review* 20:463–500.

Robinson, P. H. 2008. *Distributive Principles of Criminal Law: Who Should be Punished How Much?* New York: Oxford University Press.

Sanders, A., and R. Young. 2006. *Criminal Justice*, 3rd ed. Oxford: Oxford University Press.

Skinner, B. F. 1972. *Beyond Freedom and Dignity*. New York: Bantam.

Tadros, V., and S. Tierney. 2004. "The Presumption of Innocence and the Human Rights Act." *Modern Law Review* 67:402–34.

Tasioulas, J. 2006. "Punishment and Repentance." *Philosophy* 81:279–322.

Tudor, S. K. 2001. "Accepting One's Punishment as Meaningful Suffering." *Law and Philosophy* 20:581–604.

Umbreit, M., B. Vos, R. B. Coates, and E. Lightfoot. 2005. "Restorative Justice in the Twenty-First Century: A Social Movement Full of Opportunities and Pitfalls." *Marquette Law Review* 89:251–304.

von Hirsch, A. 1993. *Censure and Sanctions*. Oxford: Oxford University Press.

von Hirsch, A., and A. J. Ashworth. 2005. *Proportionate Sentencing: Exploring the Principles*. Oxford: Oxford University Press.

von Hirsch, A., J. Roberts, A. E. Bottoms, K. Roach, and M. Schiff, eds. 2003. *Restorative Justice and Criminal Justice*. Oxford: Hart.

Walgrave, L. 2003. "Imposing Restoration Instead of Inflicting Pain." In *Restorative Justice and Criminal Justice: Competing or Reconcilable Paradigms?*, ed. A. von Hirsch, J. Roberts, A. E. Bottoms, K. Roach, and M. Schiff. Oxford: Hart.

Williams, B. 1985. *Ethics and the Limits of Philosophy*. London: Fontana.

Wolfenden, J. 1957. *Report of the Committee on Homosexual Offences and Prostitution* (The Wolfenden Report). London: HM Stationery Office.

Wootton, B. 1963. *Crime and the Criminal Law*. London: Stevens & Sons.

Zedner, L. 2007. "Preventive Justice or Pre-punishment? The Case of Control Orders." *Current Legal Problems* 60:174–203.

Zedner, L., and A. J. Ashworth. 2008. "Defending the Criminal Law: Reflections on the Changing Character of Crime, Procedure, and Sanctions." *Criminal Law and Philosophy* 2:21–51.

5

Punishment and Desert-adjusted Utilitarianism

JESPER RYBERG

T he dominance of retributivist thinking that has characterized the penal theoretical field over the last three or four decades, and the corresponding decline of the consequentialist approach that dominated it in earlier periods of the last century, is well described in the modern penal theoretical literature (see, e.g., Duff and Garland 1994, "Introduction"; Ryberg 2004, "Introduction"). As is often emphasized, one of the things that catalyzed this striking theoretical reorientation was acknowledgment of the failure of consequentialist strategies to achieve their declared crime-preventive goals. The belief that one could build a cost-effective crime-preventive punishment system was replaced by a widespread pessimistic attitude encapsulated in the "nothing works" mantra. However, today, this pessimism is no longer upheld with the same force. Even though it is generally acknowledged that the optimism related to early consequentialist penal theory was not well founded—in fact, it was based on several empirically false assumptions—it is also the case that there is an increasing tendency to regard "nothing works" as an overreaction. Once more realistic goals are formulated, certain things do work. However, if this is the case—that is, if the earlier prevailing atmosphere of disillusionment is displaced by a moderate but increasing optimism—is it conceivable that this will lead to reassessments at the penal theoretical level? Are we here faced with the seeds of a postretributivist forward-looking theoretical reorientation?

Posing this question immediately gives rise to two comments. First, in the same way that it is an obvious fallacy to jump from the premise that "nothing works" to the conclusion that consequentialism is mistaken—clearly, all that follows is that the consequentialist should not subscribe to any penal strategies if they do not work—it is also a fallacy to conclude, on the grounds of the premise that certain things do work, that retributivism is mistaken. Second, and more importantly, even if some theorists are nevertheless inspired to engage in penal theoretical reconsiderations, they will immediately be confronted by the question, in which direction should they look? Could one possibly exclude the concept of desert from a plausible theory of punishment? And if this is not the case, are there any genuine alternatives to retributivism that allow for the possibility of letting in forward-looking considerations, thereby accounting for what actually works?

The purpose of this essay is not to depict the entire field of theoretical options, but rather to focus on one theoretical alternative to retributivism. What characterizes this theory is that it has been developed within the broader discussion of ethical theory as an attempt to reconcile respects to consequences and justice. Now, it is well known that several penal theories have been developed that seek to take into account both forward-looking and backward-looking considerations (see, e.g., Primoratz 1989; von Hirsch 1993; Ryberg 2004). One possibility is *negative retributivism*, which opens for consequentialist considerations as long as the offender is not punished in a way that is disproportionately severe (e.g., Murphy and Hampton 1988). Another possibility is *limiting retributivism*, according to which there is, for a certain crime, an upper and lower limit of deserved punishment severity within which consequentialist considerations help in fixing the punishment to be imposed (e.g., Morris and Tonry 1990; Tonry 1993). A third possibility has been to advocate a theory allowing for *exceptional deviations from retributivist punishment* when there are sufficiently strong countervailing consequentialist reasons for doing so (e.g., Robinson 1988). However, what characterizes these hybrid models is that they are all relaxed retributivist theories; that is, they open for the possibility of letting consequentialist considerations operate within an overall desert-theoretical framework.[1] In contrast, the theory to be considered in the following has the opposite shape. It incorporates respects to desert within an overall consequentialist scheme.

As is well known, consequentialist theories can take various forms depending on, for instance, whether one advocates a monist or a pluralist theory of value.[2] However, what I shall do in the following is consider the version of desert-adjusted consequentialism that has been most thoroughly developed by its recent advocates, namely, desert-adjusted utilitarianism. In section I, the theory is presented and some of its implications with regard to the justification of punishment are outlined. The ensuing two sections are devoted to critical considerations. First, in section II, it is pointed out that in order for the theory to be operational—that is, in order to provide genuine action guidance with regard to how criminals should be punitively dealt with—there are several theoretical challenges that need to be met; challenges, however, that do not seem to allow for easy answers. Second, in section III, a moral objection against the theory is presented. The overall thinking behind this criticism is the simple assumption that the idea of a hybrid theory is to avoid the difficulties with which each of the involved theories in its pure form is confronted, while at the same time maintaining the insights of both. Or, somewhat more modestly, that such a theory must have a comparative advantage. Though, admittedly, while it is hard to compare the pros and cons of different theories, I end up suggesting that it is dubious that desert-adjusted utilitarianism in this respect constitutes a viable position. However, it is suggested that the fact that it is possible to let desert considerations operate within a consequentialist framework directs attention to a weakness in the way in which retributivism has been defended within the modern era of penal theory.

I. DESERT-ADJUSTED UTILITARIANISM AND PUNISHMENT

Even though there exist minor variations in the ways in which consequentialism is presented, the definitional nuances between different accounts of the position are not important here. Let us simply say that an act is morally right if and only if its outcome is at least as good, intrinsically, as the outcome of each alternative act. In order for consequentialism to have any substantial normative content, the principle must be combined with an axiology. That is, what is needed is a theory specifying what should be regarded as intrinsically good. The traditional answer within penal theory, as well as in normative ethics in general, is provided by hedonistic utilitarianism, according to which the amount of positive and negative intrinsic value is equated with the amount of pleasure and pain. Obviously hedonism is only one possible theory of well-being. Some utilitarians would advocate a different view of well-being, and thus what should be regarded as intrinsically valuable. However, let us, for reasons of ease in exposition—and in accordance with the way desert-adjusted utilitarianism has been advanced by its adherents—simply assume that the bearers of intrinsic value are episodes of pleasure and pain.

Now, what has been suggested by a number of theorists, including Fred Feldman, Shelly Kagan, and others, is that the hedonistic axiology could be modified in such a way that in addition to the value of well-being, it takes into account factors concerning people's desert. What this means is, as Feldman puts it, that "the intrinsic value of an episode of pleasure or pain is a function of two variables: (i) the amount of pleasure or pain the recipient receives in that episode, and (ii) the amount of pleasure or pain the recipient deserves in that episode" (Feldman 1997, p. 162; see also Kagan 1998, chap. 2). Now, it is well known that considerations on desert involve a backward-looking perspective. A person deserves something at a certain time on the grounds of how she has previously acted. However, this does not change the fact that the suggested theory is basically consequentialist. As long as the right act is the one that maximizes the amount of value, there is nothing in the definition of consequentialism that excludes the possibility that the goodness of a state of affairs can be determined partly by events prior to the state of affairs. Analogously, there is nothing that prevents a consequentialist from holding that one state of affairs is better than another because it contains fewer broken promises or violated contracts (see Hubin, n.d., p. 8). Thus there is no doubt that what we are faced with is a consequentialist theory. The obvious question is what is gained by adopting this somewhat complex axiology. In other words, what are the merits of desert-adjusted utilitarianism?

The motivation for proponents of this theory is simple, namely, to account for the justice objections that have been directed against traditional utilitarianism without giving up what is seen as its advantages (Feldman 1995, 1997). Consider first a situation involving a single individual. Suppose—to take one of Kleinig's examples—that a Nazi war criminal has escaped to an uninhabited island where he manages to carve out an idyllic existence for himself. Suppose further that he is discovered thirty years later, that he has no desire to leave or cause any trouble, and that it will have no future effects on any other persons as to whether or not he is held accountable for his terrible crimes. Should the Nazi criminal be punished for his misdeeds? The utilitarian answer is obvious: Punishing the offender would be wrong. As long as nothing is gained in terms of well-being by punishing the Nazi, it would, in Bentham's oft-quoted words, "be only adding one evil to another" (1838–43, p. 396). However, many (some?) would find this implication very hard to swallow. As Kleinig himself underlines, "the principle that the wrongdoer deserves to suffer seems to accord with our deepest intuitions concerning justice" (1973, p. 76). Now, what would desert-adjusted utilitarianism prescribe in this case? As we shall return to shortly, the theory can be interpreted in somewhat different ways. However, in one interpretation the suffering imposed on a person who deserves to suffer is intrinsically valuable. While suffering inflicted on someone who does not deserve anything (or who deserves pleasure) is intrinsically bad, the suffering imposed on someone who deserves to suffer—and is imposed to the extent matching this person's desert level—is intrinsically good. Thus, in contrast to traditional utilitarianism, the desert-adjusted theory apparently succeeds in capturing the positive retributivist intuition of justice in this case.

Let us next consider situations involving several individuals. Naturally it is typical in such cases—involving the weighing of the interests of several persons—that the utilitarian has been accused of failing to properly account for respects to justice. One frequently quoted and general way of formulating the justice objection is—as Rawls puts it—that "utilitarianism does not take seriously the distinction between persons" (1971, p. 26). For the utilitarian, persons function merely as vessels into which value may be poured. And all that matters is that that value is poured out in whatever way will yield the greatest total (Feldman 1995, p. 582). Consider the following case. Suppose one could deter Peter from committing a serious crime by punishing either Bob or Paul for a previous crime and that Bob and Paul will suffer equally from being punished. Now, suppose further that the only difference between Bob and Paul is that Bob is actually guilty of the crime for which he may be punished, while this is not the case with regard to Paul. Who should the state punish: Paul or Bob? In this case the answer seems obvious. Even people who may have their doubts as to whether the Nazi criminal should be punished in the former case will probably insist that Bob is the one who should be punished. However, this is not the answer that follows from a utilitarian outlook. In this hypothetical case, the utilitarian would be indifferent as to who should be punished. If the deterrent effect is the same, if Bob and Paul would be equally affected by being punished, and if there are no other differences with regard to the effects of the punishment on third parties, one might just as well punish Paul as Bob. This conclusion, however, does not follow if one alternatively turns to the desert-adjusted utilitarian position. Since Bob deserves to suffer, the value of punishing him may, as we have seen, be positive, while the value of punishing Paul, who due to his innocence does not deserve to suffer, would be negative. Thus in this way the latter approach seems to far better capture our justice intuition. Put in more general terms, the desert-adjusted position does not seem vulnerable to the objection that it does not take the distinction between persons seriously. Since the value of pleasure and pain depends upon whether it is justly or unjustly experienced, that is, on the recipient's level of desert, it does make a difference whether what is valuable is poured into one "vessel" or another.

Given these apparent attractions of the desert-adjusted utilitarian position, have we here found a principle constituting a viable option for someone who wishes to bring penal strategies "that work" into focus without giving up the concept of desert? As we shall see in the following, the answer is hardly in the affirmative. The principle faces a number of problems. I shall start by considering some more technical problems and subsequently turn to a more basic moral objection.

II. THE CONTENTS OF DESERT-ADJUSTED UTILITARIANISM

The first challenge to which we shall turn concerns the overall goal of engaging in penal theoretical considerations. The purpose of a penal theory—indeed, this view seems to be generally accepted by penal theorists across different theoretical positions—is to provide guidance as to how the state should deal with criminals. A theory that fails in this respect, fails as a penal theory. Or as the point is made by an influential theorist in the broader context of applied ethics: "ethics is not an ideal system that is noble in theory but no good in practice. The reverse of this is closer to the truth: an ethical judgement that is no good in practice must suffer from a theoretical defect as well, for the whole point of ethical judgments is to guide practice" (Singer 1993, p. 2). This point has sometimes formed the background of a criticism directed against the utilitarian approach to punishment. What has been underlined is that, with the lack of the requisite insight into the actual or probable consequences of setting penal levels at one place rather than at another, we simply cannot do what utilitarianism ideally tells us to do. As Davis emphatically puts it "the trouble with the utilitarian principle of setting penalties is not so much that it leads us astray as that it leads us not at all" (1983, p. 733). Whether this criticism is convincing is not something that I shall attempt to settle here. But it is obvious that if there is anything to the criticism, then this will equally well form an objection to a desert-adjusted version of utilitarianism. However, what is more important is that even if it is actually possible to make the sort of estimates on consequences that are required in order to make the utilitarian theory workable, this is still not sufficient to save the desert-adjusted model from the accusation that something is missing when it comes to the union of theory and practice. The reason is that it is simply not sufficient to estimate the consequences of alternative penal strategies. Even if these consequences were able to be roughly predicted, we would also have to know how they should be assessed. If it is not possible to specify the value of the alternative outcomes of our actions, then it will not be possible to carry out the comparison and weighing on the grounds of which action guidance is derived. However, once the traditional equation of the amount of positive and negative intrinsic value with the amount of pleasure and pain is abandoned in favor of a more complex axiology, this specification of value itself becomes much more complicated.

So far, all that has been said in the above presentation of the desert-adjusted utilitarian principle is that the intrinsic value of pleasure and pain varies with the desert level of the person who has the hedonic experience. As the discussion of this principle has revealed, this idea can be interpreted in different ways. One possibility is to hold that the value relates to the *degree of fit* between an individual's hedonic experiences and what this individual deserves (Carlson 1997). Another possibility is to ascribe different values to different levels of desert (Persson 1997). In the following, I shall not engage in a scrutiny of the details of these alternatives, but simply present a number of overall questions to which answers are required in order to provide us with an applicable theory of punishment.

The first obvious question that should be answered concerns the "charge" of the value of deserved suffering. If suffering befalls a person who does not deserve it (or who deserves pleasure), then obviously and plausibly this will count negatively. However, the answer is less obvious if the person, due to previous misdeeds, actually deserves to suffer. One possibility is to hold that if the person receives the amount of suffering she deserves, then this will count positively. This is what Feldman refers to as a case of "transvaluation of the evil of pain by negative desert" (1995, p. 579). Another possibility is to suggest that negative desert merely mitigates the intrinsic badness of pain. That is, in this view the suffering experienced by the one who deserves to suffer counts negatively, but it does so to a lesser extent than if the same amount of suffering befalls the undeserving. Whether one adopts one view or the other obviously makes a significant difference. While the former view, as illustrated above, implies that the desert-adjusted utilitarian should, everything else being equal, subscribe to the punishment of a criminal, the latter view implies that this punishment would be wrong. The former view would probably strike the Kantian-minded person as the most plausible, while the latter view would appear more plausible to the one who shares the intuitions of a Benthamite. But which view should one adopt?

In fact, the question about the charge of the value of suffering turns out to be more complicated than that. So far we have only considered the value of deserved suffering. But what if we consider a case where a person experiences an amount of suffering that does not fit the negative desert level of that person? Or to put the question in punitive terms, would it contribute positively or negatively to an outcome to impose a disproportionate punishment on a criminal? This question can be answered in different ways. One possibility is to suggest that below-desert and above-desert suffering contributes negatively to an outcome. In principle, this view could be held even if one subscribes to the idea that suffering fitting a person's level of desert counts positively.[3] Another possibility is to distinguish between above-desert and below-desert suffering by holding that below-desert suffering mitigates the disvalue of the suffering (compared to the suffering of the undeserving) or that it counts positively, while above-desert suffering counts negatively. This would reflect the intuition that there is a moral difference between inflicting too much rather than too little suffering on someone who deserves to suffer. Which answer is the more plausible is not something I shall pursue. The point here is simply to point out that the question about whether suffering counts positively or negatively to an outcome needs to be answered in order to make the desert-adjusted utilitarian principle applicable. However, this is only the first of the things that need to be settled.

The second question that an adherent of desert-adjusted utilitarianism would have to address concerns the size of the value ascribed to different states of affairs. Since we are considering a consequentialist theory, what is needed in order to achieve genuine action guidance is that we are able to compare and weigh the value of different possible outcomes. Suppose that one holds that deserved suffering counts positively. Than how much value do we gain from imposing the deserved suffering on a person? In order to be able to say something about how this should be weighed against the costs of this imposition (i.e., of having a punishment system), some sort of consideration of the size of the values involved are required. Suppose, alternatively, that deserved suffering mitigates the disvalue of suffering compared with undeserved suffering. Then, how large is this mitigation? Obviously something needs to be said at this point if the desert-adjusted utilitarian wishes to be able to weigh the costs of punishing a criminal with the possible gain in terms of preventing suffering befalling undeserving potential victims of crime. It is hardly an overstatement to contend that the abandonment of the traditional equation, of the amount of positive and negative intrinsic value with the amount of pleasure and pain, makes the comparison of outcomes—containing different distributions of pleasure and pain between individuals with different levels of desert—much more complicated.

The final question worth posing concerns the basic assumption behind the whole idea of adjusting the value of pleasure and pain to the desert of the receiver of these hedonic experiences, namely, that it is possible to specify how much pleasure or suffering a person deserves. But how should this be done? In penal terms, what we are asking is how severely does a criminal who has committed a crime of a certain degree of gravity deserve to be punished? Obviously, by asking this question we are moving into traditional retributivist territory. Even though there is no space here to consider this question in any detail, I shall nevertheless shortly outline some of the answers that have been presented.

The most simple answer to the question is provided by the Hegelian-inspired view, that one should impose the same amount of suffering on a criminal as the criminal inflicted on her victim by committing the crime. However, this view faces a number of problems. For instance, if it disregards respects to culpability, then this is hardly plausible from a retributivist point of view. If it, on the other hand, admits that the culpability is crucial in the determination of the deserved punishment, then it will no longer do to advocate the idea of harm equivalence. This principle does not provide an answer as to how a perpetrator who has caused a certain harm with a somewhat diminished degree of culpability should be punished. Thus, with a very few exceptions, no one in the modern retributivist era seems to be satisfied with the idea of harm-for-harm equivalence. However, once this simple way of linking crime and punishment is abandoned, the question as to how severely different crimes should be punished becomes more complicated. It is not sufficient to merely construct a scale of crime gravity and a scale of punishment severity. What is needed is some sort of rationale as to how these scales should be linked.

One way of dealing with this challenge has been to suggest that crime and punishment scales should be linked at certain anchor points. Here is how one recent advocate of this idea puts it: "The main idea of solving these problems is to consider a scale that includes all crime and a scale that includes the full range of acceptable punishments, and then anchor the scales to each other at two points. We anchor the most severe punishment to the most serious crime . . . and the least severe punishment for the least serious crime . . . with the other crimes falling in between" (Scheid 1997, p. 494; see also Kleinig 1973). However, this proposal faces several challenges. For instance, it is not clear how one should, in a nonarbitrary way, determine the most serious crime constituting the upper anchor point. After all, for any possible crime it is always possible to imagine another more harmful. Furthermore, it becomes no less complicated if we ask what is supposed to constitute the most severe punishment. There seems to be no obvious upper limit as to how severely a person could be punished. One answer that has been suggested, though, has been to draw on the concept of *human dignity*. That is, to contend that the upper anchor point is determined by the punishment that, if it was made one step more severe, would violate human dignity. However, it does not require much reflection to see that this is a somewhat vague proposal. We may well accept the idea that some types of punishment would violate the dignity of the perpetrator (say boiling her in oil, or gouging out her eyes, or the like) (see, e.g., Murphy 1979, p. 233). But this will not be of much help when it comes to drawing limits with regard to punishment severity. For instance, most modern retributivists seem to accept that incarceration can be used as a type of punishment. But if that is the case, then what is needed in order to make the suggested anchor theory work is that we are able to draw a line somewhere in the duration of a prison term. However, it is hardly unfair to say that the concept of human dignity has not been developed with anything close to the degree of precision that would justify the claim that twenty years of imprisonment is acceptable while twenty years and a month in prison is unacceptable because this violates a person's dignity. But it is precisely this sort of line that needs to be drawn in order to identify the upper punishment severity anchor point. Thus there are several challenges that have to be overcome in order to make this type of anchor theory workable.[4]

An alternative way of dealing with the anchor problem has been to draw on considerations of crime prevention and parsimony. Andrew von Hirsch has suggested that one should adopt a decremental strategy in the form of a pro rata reduction of the penalties. This progressive diminution of the punishment level should continue until one reaches a point determined on the grounds of crime prevention. However, what von Hirsch has in mind is not a traditional optimizing view of prevention. Such a view might imply that a person will be used as "a tool for promoting the most socially efficient system of prevention," in which case the person could rightly object that her "interests are being sacrificed to the social good" (von Hirsch 1993, p. 42). In von Hirsch's account, the hard treatment provides only an *extra* reason for compliance, that is, a reason that is supplementary to the fact that a person is being censured for her wrongdoing when she is punished. In short, then, the idea is that the progressive diminution of the punishment level should continue until the minimal point is reached at which the system still succeeds in providing a prudential incentive for compliance. Although this proposal has several advantages in comparison with the former anchor theory, there are still several things that need to be settled in order for the theory to applicable. For instance, what is the minimal degree of hard treatment that would still constitute a disincentive in relation to the crime placed at the lowest point of the crime scale? What if a scale anchored at this lower point does not succeed in providing a genuine disincentive with regard to other crimes on the scale (see Ryberg 2004, pp. 145–47)? And what if there exist interpersonal variations with regard to what constitutes the minimal prudential incentive for compliance? If the anchoring is based on the amount of hard treatment that would *typically* provide a person with a supplementary prudential reason for compliance, could not a person who needs less hard treatment—that is, less than what is typically required in order to constitute an extra incentive for compliance—rightly complain that a punishment system based on this solution to the anchor problem ends up punishing her more severely just because other people are more tempted than she and therefore require larger (minimal) incentives for compliance? Or, that this is inconsistent with the principle of parsimony on the grounds of which the decremental strategy is initiated in the first place? What these questions indicate, I believe, is that much still needs to be clarified in order to make the suggested solution to the anchor problem operational.

It is important to underline that I certainly do not wish to suggest that the above considerations of different retributivist approaches to the anchor problem are in any way exhaustive. I have dealt with them more thoroughly elsewhere, and obviously much more needs to be said in order to fairly evaluate these theories (see Ryberg 2004). However, the discussion here is only meant to indicate that the question as to what constitutes the deserved punishment for a certain crime, that is, what constitutes a person's level of desert, does not allow for a straightforward answer. Much still needs to be said in order to reach an answer with a sufficiently high degree of precision. Thus, when this conclusion is added to the foregoing considerations concerning the need for clarification when it comes to the question of the determination of the value of outcomes on the grounds of the desert-adjusted utilitarian principle, then it is clear that given the assumption that what we wish from a theory of punishment is genuine action guidance, much still needs to be said with regard to the content of the principle. In this respect, desert-adjusted utilitarianism seems to add to, rather than avoid or reduce, the challenges facing the combined theoretical positions in their pure forms. This being said, the time has now come to consider a more basic moral objection to the idea of desert-adjusted utilitarianism.

III. AN IMPLICATION OF DESERT-ADJUSTED UTILITARIANISM

The retributivist approach to punishment is sometimes presented as the view that a wrongdoer deserves to suffer. Both certain classical retributivists and a number of more recent adherents to retributivism have advocated a view along these lines. However, it is obvious that this way of presenting a retributivist theory is inaccurate. As we have seen, a consequentialist might subscribe to the same view. But clearly all retributivists agree— despite the fact that retributivism has been developed in many different versions—the theory they are defending is very much not a consequentialist theory. In addition, there is another aspect of the above formulation of retributivism that is controversial, namely, whether it is at all correct that the object of desert is suffering. One of the challenges facing this view—as long as no other qualifications are added—is that suffering may befall a wrongdoer in various ways. A wrongdoer may experience—for reasons that have nothing to do with her wrongdoing—that her husband wishes to divorce her; she may break a leg; or she may become the victim of a severe depression. However, that the suffering caused in these ways should constitute a way in which a wrongdoer can be seen to have paid her desert debt is a view to which a number of modern retributivists would not subscribe. There is nothing valuable in the fact that a burglar suffers from swine flu or other contingent calamities. This point has most clearly—and in my view plausibly— been underlined by modern expressionist versions of retributivism, according to which the purpose of punishing wrongdoers is not merely to ensure that suffering is inflicted, but rather that the wrongdoer is held accountable for her misdeed by being appropriately blamed for her action. The purpose here is not to pursue the question as to what constitutes the proper object of desert from a retributivist point of view. Rather, the point is that if there are problems related to the basic idea that what wrongdoers deserve is suffering, then these problems may well face the theory we are here considering. As we have seen, what desert-adjusted utilitarianism is concerned with precisely is deserved suffering. Furthermore, what will be argued in the following is that the fact that suffering may befall a person in various ways constitutes the core of a serious objection facing the desert-adjusted utilitarian principle.

What distinguishes desert-adjusted utilitarianism from traditional utilitarianism is that a certain amount of pain or pleasure does not have a constant intrinsic value. The value of certain units of pain varies with the desert level of the person on which the pain befalls. As we shall now see, this fact opens up the possibility of maximizing value in a way that seems very hard to accept. Let us start by assuming that we accept the version of the axiology, according to which the infliction of pain that fits a person's negative desert level has positive value. Now, suppose that Peter knows that he will suffer severely sometime in the future. For instance, he may have been told by his doctor that he suffers from a disease that will break out in one or two months and will cause him much suffering. If it is not possible to relieve this suffering through some sort of palliative treatment, then, from a traditional utilitarian point of view, there is just nothing we can do about it. However, if we adopt a desert-adjusted utilitarian outlook, then there is still one possibility open. If one could turn the suffering into *deserved* suffering, then this would significantly improve the value of the future state of affairs. But how could this be done? The answer is simple: Peter could commit a crime. If Peter commits a crime that leaves a desert level that corresponds to the amount of his expected future suffering, then what at first looked like a future state of affairs that would have negative value has suddenly turned into a state of affairs of positive value. Now, obviously, committing a crime would harm the victim(s) of Peter's crime. And the suffering that the crime causes to an undeserving victim would, of course, count negatively in the desert-adjusted utilitarian calculus. But what follows from the desert-adjusted utilitarian principle is that if the disvalue of the suffering of the crime victim subtracted from the positive value of Peter's desert-adjusted future suffering leaves more value than the state of affairs in which Peter does nothing and suffers from his disease, then Peter should commit the crime.

As we have seen, the axiology of the desert-adjusted utilitarian view need not imply that deserved suffering has positive value (i.e., one need not accept the idea of transvaluation). Suppose instead that one subscribes only to an axiology according to which deserved suffering carries less negative value than undeserved suffering. If this is so, it would probably be less likely that Peter could improve the future situation by carrying out a crime. But even in this case, it might still be possible that the disvalue of the suffering of the crime victim and the (reduced) disvalue of Peter's suffering would leave a state of affairs that is preferable to the one in which Peter does not commit the crime and simply goes through the suffering caused by his disease. Thus, in sum, what follows from desert-adjusted utilitarianism is that a person who faces unavoidable future suffering will sometimes have an obligation to commit a crime even though this does not in any way relieve the future suffering and even though it has no beneficial consequences on third parties. I shall refer to this as "the obligatory crime objection." And I suggest that most people will find this implication of desert-adjusted utilitarianism very hard to swallow.

Then, is there a way in which the desert-adjusted utilitarian could possibly block this objection? The only possibility I can think of is to contend that there will be no such cases in which a person facing future suffering will produce an overall preferable outcome by committing a crime. The reason for holding this view could be the following. Suppose that Peter commits a crime against (undeserving) John and that this crime causes a certain amount of suffering to John. Suppose, furthermore, that the suffering Peter thereby deserves to experience is somewhat or even much less than the suffering caused to John. In that case, it no longer seems possible that the fact that Peter's unavoidable future suffering changes value (is mitigated or transvalued) because it is now deserved is sufficient to outbalance the disvalue caused by committing the crime against John. Does this constitute an answer to which the desert-adjusted utilitarian might resort?

Whether this is so obviously depends on the question of how the desert level of a person who has committed a crime is set. If the suffering that Peter deserves from having committed the crime is less than the suffering caused to John by the crime, then it seems that there might be something to the outlined answer.[5] Whether this is so is a question that brings us back to the considerations of the previous section on what the desert-adjusted utilitarian principle more precisely amounts to. However, what the adherent to the principle could hold is that the desert level should not be determined by a principle like harm-for-harm equivalence. It is a fact that most of the prominent modern retributivists have certainly not defended a throw-away-the-key approach to punishment. On the contrary, what has been argued for is much more leniency in punishment compared with existing penal levels, which means that the deserved suffering of the offender could plausibly be held to be less than the suffering caused by the defender. Whether this really suffices to block the obligatory desert objection is a question that easily becomes a little technical and, at the end of the day, it obviously rests upon the shoulders of the desert-adjusted utilitarian to establish that this is the case. In the following, I shall not enter into a more thorough discussion of this question except to point out that even if we, for the sake of the argument, take the above assumptions for granted, the answer will still not succeed in saving the desert-adjusted utilitarian from a slightly modified version of the obligatory crime objection.

Suppose once again that Peter faces unavoidable future suffering, but also that he would not produce a preferable state of affairs by committing a crime against John because the suffering of undeserving John would weigh too heavily in the calculus. In that case there is still the possibility that Peter could find another victim that would make the crime obligatory if committed against that victim. More precisely, if Peter knows that Bob has committed a crime (for which he has not been punished), then making Bob suffer by committing a crime against him would count much less negatively than if the person were undeserving; in fact, if one accepts the idea of transvaluation, it would even count positively. And now it will no longer do merely to contend that the level of deserved suffering is lower than the suffering caused by the crime that generates the negative desert. Thus, once again, there will be a situation in which Peter, due to his disease, ends up with an obligation to commit a crime. Whether this example is as counterintuitive as the case involving the crime against innocent—and thus undeserving—John can, of course, be discussed (after all, Bob is not innocent), but I still believe that most people would, on reflection, hesitate to accept a moral principle implying that a person facing future unavoidable suffering might ceteris paribus have an obligation to commit a crime against someone—say a tax dodger, a jaywalker, or another criminal.

What the above examples have in common is that they involve cases where a person, as a way of increasing the value of a future state of affairs involving suffering, may be under an obligation to commit a crime. However, there is a final and slightly different version of the obligatory crime objection that is also worth pointing out. Suppose again that one accepts, firstly, the idea of transvaluation of suffering, that is, that deserved suffering has positive value; secondly, that a person will be punished if she commits a crime; and, finally, that there are cases where this positive value outweighs the disvalue caused by the crime. Given these assumptions, it follows that the person would have an obligation to commit a crime. Committing a crime and being punished for it would produce a state of affairs preferable to one in which no crime is committed.[6] This version of the obligatory crime objection also strikes me as being hard to accept. Moreover, what is particularly interesting to note is that, in contrast to the former versions of the objection, this version would remain intact even if one gives up the idea of desert-adjusted utilitarianism in favor of other desert-adjusted consequentialist theories designed to capture retributivist intuitions. Suppose, for instance, that one rejects that the proper object of desert is suffering, defending instead the idea that the object of criminal desert is a punitive reaction that manages to hold the criminal accountable in a way that mere suffering does not. That is, suppose one holds that what has positive value is deserved *punitive* suffering. The consequentialist theory with which we would then end up would still be vulnerable to the outlined version of the obligatory crime objection. Thus any desert-adjusted consequentialist theory that seeks to capture retributivist intuitions—such as the intuition that the earlier-mentioned Nazi war criminal should be punished—seems committed to the conclusion that there may be an obligation to commit crimes simply for the reason that one will thereby be punished. As mentioned, I believe that many would hesitate to accept this implication.

Summing up, what we have seen is that in order to account for the justice objections directed against traditional utilitarianism, the desert-adjusted utilitarian holds that the value of experienced pleasure or pain is dependant on the level of desert of the person who receives these experiences. As we have seen, this move makes it possible to capture some retributivist intuitions. However, as argued above, this view also has a noteworthy drawback: it implies that in some situations in which we face future unavoidable suffering we would have an obligation to commit crimes against other people, even though this would in no way change the fact that we will have to undergo suffering. Furthermore, it implies that the mere fact that one will be punished may itself place a person under an obligation to commit a crime. Neither of these implications constitutes a morally insignificant drawback.

IV. CONCLUDING REMARKS

That there might be a temptation to consider the possibility of developing a hybrid theory that attempts to combine considerations on desert and the future consequences of punishment is not hard to understand. Seen from a more practical point of view, one might hope that a hybrid theory could turn a punishment system that focuses both on desert and consequences, and that at the surface seems conspicuously incoherent—such as, for instance, different versions of dual-tracking sanction systems—into a coherent system. And from a more theoretical point of view, one might hope that such a theory would succeed in uniting some of the basic intuitions that are usually held to point in different theoretical directions. However, in order for a hybrid theory to be convincing it must have a comparative advantage, that is, as initially pointed out, it must be able to capture some of the advantages and resist some of the drawbacks of each of the combined theories in their pure forms. Whether desert-adjusted utilitarianism succeeds in this respect is, as the previous considerations indicate, dubious. For a theorist favoring a consequentialist approach to punishment, the theory might succeed in capturing some retributivist intuitions. However, though it is difficult to weigh pros and cons, it is clear that this is achieved only at the cost of facing the outlined obligatory crime objection. Moreover, the theory is faced with many more challenges than the traditional utilitarian approach when it comes to the deliverance of genuine action guidance. For a theorist favoring a deontological approach to punishment, the desert-adjusted utilitarian principle hardly constitutes an attractive theoretical option. As mentioned, some theorists would find it hard to accept that the object of desert merely consists of suffering. And more importantly, the theory is, qua its consequentialist nature, confronted with the punishment-of-the-innocent objections that have constituted the traditional retributivist attack against the utilitarian approach. Thus it does not seem unfair to hold that the theory does not succeed in capturing the pros and avoiding the cons of each of the combined theories in their pure forms.

Even though desert-adjusted utilitarianism may not constitute the most plausible attempt to develop a theory of punishment, there may, nevertheless, be a lesson to be learned from recognizing the theory as a theoretical option on the palette of possible penal theoretical positions. First, penal theory is sometimes discussed as if the basic theoretical division lies between desert and consequences. For instance, this is the case if it is pointed out that what the consequentialist ignores is the moral significance of treating criminals as persons—that is, as individuals responsible for their wrongdoing—which is precisely what is recognized by giving them what they deserve. However, as we have seen, this apparent conflict is not genuine: considerations of desert might be incorporated into a deontological as well as a consequentialist theoretical framework. Second, the fact that a consequentialist theory might include considerations of desert as part of the basic axiology means that the retributivist, in the advocacy of her theory, will have to place the main focus on the *deontological* nature of her theory, that is, on the plausibility of the existence of constraints. As mentioned, the traditional way in which this is done has been to point out the counterintuitive implications related to versions of punishment-of-the-innocent objections directed against consequentialist principles. As is well known in ethics in general, most ethical theories face some counterintuitive implications. However, retributivists almost never engage in comparative considerations of the counterintuitive implications that follow from a consequentialist and a deontological approach to punishment. Realization of the fact that the retributive point of view is not defended merely by emphasizing the significance of desert consideration, but that further arguments have to be presented in order to establish the deontological nature of the desert theory, might—at least it should—contribute to raising the sophistication of the discussion of penal theory. For instance, few modern retributivists have engaged in more thorough considerations of *why* it is wrong to punish one person disproportionately if this is the only way to avoid ten persons being disproportionately punished. In most discussions, this is simply taken for granted. And merely to appeal to the view that this would be unjust or that we would end up with a terrible world clearly does not succeed in bringing the discussion to what would constitute a desirable level of sophistication.[7]

If there are some theorists who, on the grounds of a rejection of the initially mentioned "nothing works" mantra, believe that penal theory is moving in a postretributivist direction, and who are inspired to engage in reconsiderations of versions of penal consequentialism, then this might constitute a strong incentive for the modern retributivist to engage in more thorough considerations on questions of the above type. This would strengthen the level of the existing discussion of punishment and perhaps bring us to an understanding of the limits of how far we can expect to move in the defense of one penal theory in favor of another. Obviously this, in itself, would constitute a significant insight.

NOTES

1. However, obviously some of these relaxed retributive theories might come close to being genuinely consequentialist. This would be the case, for instance, in a version of limiting retributivism that, for each type of crime, allows for a very wide range of deserved punishment within which the proper punishment can be fixed on the grounds of utilitarian considerations.
2. That is, whether the theory operates with one intrinsical value or several intrinsical values (see, e.g., Sinnott-Armstrong 2006).
3. However, it seems obvious that this will leave a somewhat complicated value function. For the possibility of combining what is sometimes referred to as "the fit model" and "the merit model," see Persson (1997).
4. For a more thorough discussion of this theory, see Ryberg (2004, chap. 4).
5. However, it should be noted that this answer faces the problem that if there are some crimes that do not cause suffering, then obviously the deserved suffering of the offender would be larger then the suffering caused by this type of crime.
6. This version of the obligatory crime objection could, of course, be blocked by rejecting the transvaluation assumption in favor of the view that deserved punitive suffering has less negative value than undeserved punitive suffering. However, as indicated, this would be tantamount to giving up the positive retributivist intuition that the earlier-mentioned Nazi war criminal should be punished.
7. With regard to the former claim, it would obviously also be unjust to let ten persons be unjustly punished. Sometimes penal theorists try to block this answer by referring to the doctrine of double effect or the doctrine of act and omission. However, the discussion rarely becomes more thorough, even though it is a well-known fact that there exists a comprehensive literature on these doctrines and that they both face several objections. As for the latter claim, this is something that might well constitute an indirect consequentialist reason for advocating retributivist principles.

REFERENCES

Bentham, J. 1838–43. "Principles of Penal Law." In *The Works of Jeremy Bentham*, ed. J. Bowring. Edinburgh: William Tait.

Carlson, E. 1997. "Consequentialism, Distribution, and Desert." *Utilitas* 9:307–18.

Davis, M. 1983. "How to Make the Punishment Fit the Crime." *Ethics* 93:726–52.

Duff, A., and D. Garland, eds. 1994. *A Reader on Punishment*. Oxford: Oxford University Press.

Feldman, F. 1995. "Adjusting Utility for Justice: A Consequentialist Reply to the Objection from Justice." *Philosophy and Phenomenological Research* 55(3):567–85.

———. 1997. *Utilitarianism, Hedonism, and Desert: Essays on Moral Philosophy*, Cambridge: Cambridge University Press.

Hubin, D. E. n.d. "Retributive Consequentialism." Unpublished manuscript. Ohio State University, Department of Philosophy. http://people.cohums.ohio-state.edu/hubin1/documents/Retributive%20Consequentialism.pdf.

Kagan, S. 1998. *Normative Ethics*. Boulder, CO: Westview Press.

Kleinig, J. 1973. *Punishment and Desert*. The Hague: Martinus Nijhoff.

Morris, N., and M. Tonry. 1990. *Between Prison and Probation*. New York: Oxford University Press.

Murphy, J. 1979. *Retribution, Justice and Therapy*. Dordrecht: Reidel.

Murphy, J., and J. Hampton. 1988. *Forgiveness and Mercy*. New York: Cambridge University Press.

Persson, I. 1997. "Ambiguities in Feldman's Desert-adjusted Values." *Utilitas* 9:319–27.

Primoratz, I. 1989. *Justifying Legal Punishment*. London: Humanities Press.

Rawls, J. 1971. *A Theory of Justice*. Cambridge: Harvard University Press.

Robinson, P. H. 1988. "Hybrid Principles for the Distribution of Criminal Sanctions." *Northwestern University Law Review* 82:19–24.

Ryberg, J. 2004. *The Ethics of Proportionate Punishment: A Critical Investigation*. Dordrecht: Kluwer Academic.

Scheid, D. E. 1997. "Constructing a Theory of Punishment, Desert, and the Distribution of Punishment." *Canadian Journal of Law and Jurisprudence* 10(2):441–506.

Singer, P. 1993. *Practical Ethics*. Cambridge: Cambridge University Press.

Sinnott-Armstrong, W. 2006. "Consequentialism." *Stanford Encyclopedia of Philosophy*. Stanford, CA: Center for the Study of Language and Information, Stanford University.

Tonry, M. 1993. "Proportionality, Interchangeability, and Intermediate Punishments." In *Penal Theory and Penal Practice*, ed. R. Dobash, R. A. Duff, and S. Marshall. Manchester: Manchester University Press.

von Hirsch, A. 1993. *Censure and Sanctions*. Oxford: Clarendon Press.

6

The Future of State Punishment

The Role of Public Opinion in Sentencing

JULIAN V. ROBERTS

W hat role, if any, should public opinion play in determining sentencing policy and practice? Penal policies in all jurisdictions have been influenced by appeals to public opinion. Politicians responsible for introducing punitive policies (such as mandatory sentencing legislation) often justify reforms by reference to the public (see Roberts et al. 2003; Pratt 2007), and research suggests that courts in several jurisdictions have become more punitive in response to perceptions of community views (Millie, Jacobson, and Hough 2005[1]). To the extent that public opinion has spawned punitive sentencing laws, the influence of the community has been perceived as negative. This may explain why scholars (and practitioners) have been skeptical about the utility of public opinion as a guide to sentencing policy or practice. It may also explain why there have been few systematic explorations of the role of public opinion at sentencing.[2] In contrast, empirical researchers have been active for more than a century.

As long ago as 1909, Sharp and Otto introduced the first empirical investigation by noting that "popular attitudes towards retribution as a ground of punishment by the state . . . is a matter about which the moralist and the student of political and social life need definite knowledge" (p. 341). In almost the same year, Roscoe Pound warned of creating a "permanent gulf between legal and popular thought" (1907, p. 611). Today, as a result of the accumulated research, we know a great deal about community views regarding legal punishment, including the principles that people perceive to be relevant to sentencing. It is unclear, however, whether the considerable literature on public opinion and sentencing has anything to add to the ongoing debate about sentencing theory. Most publications simply report empirical findings from an empirical project in which the views of the public are explored or contrasted with current practice—no attempt is made to define the relationship between the two.

I. PUBLIC ATTITUDES TO SENTENCING AND SENTENCERS

Opinion polls around the world have for years documented widespread public criticism of the courts coalescing around the issue of sentencing. Thus, although judges are generally seen as fair decision makers (MORI 2004), public confidence in the courts evaporates when people are asked about sentencing practices. Much of this criticism arises from perceptions of excessive leniency toward offenders. Thus, in 2008, three-quarters of the polled public in England and Wales expressed the view that sentencing was too lenient (British Crime Survey 2009). A decade earlier a similar percentage of the public held this view (Hough and Roberts 1998). In fact, more than 70 percent of the polled public has expressed this view on every administration of the survey. The perception of leniency also emerges from qualitative research such as focus groups (Hough 2006).

This attitude toward sentencing has been repeatedly replicated over time, using different methodologies and across disparate jurisdictions. For example, 85 percent of respondents in South Africa (Schonteich 1999) and 74 percent in Scotland (Justice 1 Committee 2002) expressed the view that sentences were too lenient. Comparable findings emerge from other countries, including Belgium (Parmentier et al. 2004) and Germany (Kury, Oberfell-Fuchs, and Smartt 2002). U.S. polls also reveal little variation over time in the percentage of respondents perceiving sentences to be too lenient, ranging from 79 percent in 1975 to 67 percent in 2002 (Sourcebook of Criminal Justice Statistics 2010). The same pattern emerges from Australian and Canadian polls over the same period (see Roberts, Crutcher, and Verbrugge 2007; Roberts and Indermaur 2009). However, the perception of leniency is only part of the story. Courts are seen to be out of touch with "what ordinary people think," with 82 percent holding this view of judges in England and Wales (Hough and Roberts 1998). Sentencers are also criticized for taking into account the "wrong" factors at sentencing—evidence of a lack of fit between judicial practice and community perceptions.

A. Tension between Retributive Theories and Public Opinion

A clear state of tension arises when sentencing practices depart from a sound theoretical model, and also exists when sentencing theories and practice differ markedly and continuously from community values. It is this difference between community opinion and judicial practice that will be explored in this essay. The focus is upon retributive theories because, as a number of writers have noted, there is little justification for consulting the public about sentencing practices if the goal of sentencing is rehabilitation or incapacitation[3] (e.g., Golash and Lynch 1995). Sentencing systems can respond in a number of ways to the long-standing public antipathy toward sentencing and sentencers. They may take the position that while this criticism is regrettable, it simply reflects a lack of information on the part of the public—arising from media-driven distortions of sentencing practice—and should therefore be ignored. On the other hand, it may seem desirable to accommodate community values in sentencing policies and practices.

Contemporary retributive theories and intuitive reactions to punishment are manifestly at odds. The use of previous convictions at sentencing represents an obvious example:

retributive theories either ignore prior convictions entirely (e.g., Fletcher 1982) or assign only a very limited role to them (e.g., von Hirsch 2010). On the other hand, members of the public see an offender's criminal record as being very relevant to sentencing decisions; public sentencing decisions increase in severity to reflect increments in the number of prior convictions.[4] The difference between retributive theories and the public usually involves a disagreement about the circumstances and factors relevant to sentencing. Retributive theorists place strict limits on the factors that determine an offender's level of culpability, and hence liability, for punishment. These limits exclude factors such as remorse or prior convictions on the grounds that they do not affect culpability for the offense or the harm occasioned by the crime. Community opinion embraces a more comprehensive list of relevant factors.[5] Most people see issues such as prior offending, and the offender's attitude—whether remorseful or not—to be relevant to establishing his blameworthiness. The critical questions are whether sentencing policy and practice should accommodate these public views, and if so, how?

In order to incorporate community views into the sentencing process, three elements are needed, and all will be discussed in the course of this essay:

- A justification for modifying sentencing purposes, principles, or practices to align them more closely with public opinion;
- Clear limits on the criminal justice decisions that will be subject to scrutiny and potential modification;
- An appropriate methodology for measuring public views

Systems of legal punishment do not exist in a vacuum; it is a truism to say that state responses to offending are culturally determined. Sentencing practices reflect the larger society within which they are embedded. This observation suggests the need for some kind of relationship between the sentencing practices of the courts and the communities in which punishment is imposed. Yet, to date, this relationship has not been adequately explored by researchers. Instead, a clear gulf has emerged between contemporary retributive writings and empirical sociolegal scholars. The former generally have ignored or overlooked community views, while the latter have systematically documented the topography of public reaction to sentencing. This essay attempts to determine what influence—if any—findings from the public opinion literature should have on sentencing practices. On what basis can we justify modifying sentencing guidelines in light of community opinion? The justification for considering public opinion at sentencing can only be found, as Ryberg (2011) notes "in a complicated theoretical field that does not allow for simple answers."[6] No simple answers will be offered here; rather, I attempt to find a place, albeit a limited one, for public input into sentencing practices.

B. Alternative Models

An *exclusionary* model of public opinion would result in a sentencing system in which community values play no role. For example, seriousness rankings would be determined objectively by harm-based analyses or some other measure of gravity. Under an exclusionary model, factors influencing the offender's level of culpability would be derived from moral philosophy. Any resulting system would have universal application—since it would be insensitive to local variation regarding the seriousness of specific offenses or the weight (and relevance) of various sentencing factors. In contrast, according to a *direct importation* model, community values would be directly imported into sentencing practice. This would surely lead to unacceptable results; one can easily imagine public sentiment turning against a particular category of offender or public hostility being aroused against a particular offense.[7] If public views were followed, the result would be severity premiums for a particular kind of offender or some specific offense—which could not be justified by any retributive principles. Golash and Lynch (1995) are surely correct when they affirm that "the opinions of the population cannot, by themselves, justify a particular measure of punishment" (p. 714; see also Bagaric 2001, p. 15). Neither the exclusionary nor the direct importation perspective therefore seems desirable or compelling.

Some link between community values and sentencing practice is therefore necessary. As Gwin (2010, p. 174) notes, "community sentiment must be an important part of any just system of sentencing." More specifically, from a utilitarian perspective it is important to maintain some level of public confidence in the sentencing process without which it would be harder for the justice system to function (see discussion in Robinson 2007, 2008). From a retributive perspective it makes little sense to overlook community values if they contain principles that may be relevant to proportional sentencing. Locating a place for the public requires finding some middle ground, where the community's views are considered, but with significant qualification.

C. Circumscribing Public Views

Which decisions taken in the criminal justice system should be influenced by public opinion? It is important to set aside a number of issues and circumscribe the domain of criminal justice in which public consultation is justified. Few would claim a role for public opinion at bail or parole hearings, since these stages of the criminal process involve a different set of determinations, such as whether the accused will appear for trial or whether the prisoner would benefit from release on parole. While there may be a case for asking the public whether they support a system of graduated release from prison, there would be little merit in asking people which kinds of factors should be considered by a parole authority. Releasing authorities are concerned about the risk of reoffending and the likelihood of rehabilitation (see discussion in Roberts 2009). There is no collective censure being expressed in a decision to grant bail or parole.

A more plausible claim for public input can be made for sentencing. However, public views need to be subject to careful scrutiny to determine whether they should be imported into the determination of sentencing. A model that directly imports public views throughout the criminal justice system would lead to undesirable outcomes. For example, most members of the public would probably oppose guilty plea discounts or mitigation for first offenders convicted of serious crimes.[8] If public views of these sentencing factors were blindly accepted, the result would be a loss of sound sentencing principles.

D. Overview of Essay

Section II describes and explores competing perspectives on the issue of community involvement in sentencing. The arguments against community involvement involve the limited public knowledge of sentencing, and the at times unprincipled nature of reactions to crime, as well as the dangers of punitive populism. The justifications for heeding public opinion are both consequentialist and retributive in nature. First, it is argued that public views need to be heard because this will produce greater compliance with the law—a consequentialist justification. Second, retributivists should recognize that the seriousness of an offense is determined in part by the societal reaction to the proscribed conduct. The seriousness of a crime—a primary determinant of sentence severity—is to a degree culturally determined and not invariant over time and across jurisdictions. In section III, I demonstrate that principled reactions to offending may be extracted from public opinion research, even if these principles have been ignored by retributivists. One of the central lessons of the empirical research—and an important message of this essay—is that public opinion is not always and everywhere an unprincipled torrent of punitiveness. Section IV addresses some practical issues and draws conclusions for the future of legal punishment.

Before exploring the way that public opinion might reasonably influence sentencing, it is important to clarify what is meant by public opinion and, in particular, the way in which public views are measured.

E. Measurement Issues

Letters to the editor or politicians, reader response surveys, internet polls, and the like all offer a version of public opinion, albeit one that is unscientific. For present purposes, the research I deem relevant to sentencing refers to scientific measures of public attitudes that fulfill certain criteria. They need to generate findings that are (i) potentially falsifiable, (ii) replicable, (iii) based on samples that permit generalization of findings to the populations from which the samples are drawn, and (iv) derive from a reasoned or deliberative environment. For example, a simple poll that asks people whether offenders have too many rights or whether sentencing is too harsh or too lenient may conform to the first three criteria, but fail on the last, as would so many public opinion polls in the field of sentencing.

Poorly constructed public opinion research has caused much mischief in the domain of sentencing policy. Members of the public have often been asked to make snap decisions about complex subjects such as mandatory sentencing, parole, or prison conditions. The consequence has been a systematic distortion of the nature of public attitudes, which are less punitive when people are provided with sufficient information about a case with which to make an informed decision (for specific examples and discussion, see Roberts et al. 2003). This is one of the most robust and often-replicated findings in the field. Demonstrations of the effect can be found in Knight (1965), Parker (1970), Doob and Roberts (1984), Hough and Roberts (1998), Roberts and Hough (2005a), and de Keijser, van Koppen, and Elffers (2007).[9]

Methodological tank traps abound and inadequate measures of public opinion will yield an inaccurate representation of community views. The most obvious pitfall involves the use of a simple question posed to people who, having not thought much about the issue, then provide a "top of the head reaction." If the question is given to a representative sample of the public, the result is defended on the basis of representativeness, yet the result is not representative of an informed public. The weaknesses of different methodological approaches are not random. The format of opinion polls privileges punitive public responses. For this reason researchers need to use more refined techniques to determine the true nature of public opinion with respect to relevant sentencing factors.

Community views should therefore only be considered when they are the views of an informed sample of the public—generally defined as those people who have been given some time and information to arrive at a decision (see Golash and Lynch [1995] for a discussion of the use of surveys in shaping sentencing policy, and Green [2006] for a discussion of methodologies). It would be no more reasonable to use a public opinion poll to determine a penal policy than to use this device to determine the outcome of a jury trial: in both cases we require a decision taken by a representative sample of the public with adequate time to consider relevant evidence.

The use of previous convictions at sentencing provides a good illustration of what I mean. Theories of sentencing offer competing, alternative accounts of whether and how previous convictions should affect sentencing practices. Some versions of desert theories exclude previous convictions entirely, some use prior misconduct in a very limited way, while others assign an important role to criminal antecedents at sentencing (see Roberts and von Hirsch [2010] for representative views). Where does the public stand on the issue? We now have a robust research record of public opinion studies exploring this issue. This literature derives from multiple jurisdictions and uses qualitative and quantitative methodologies, the essential findings from which have been replicated over time and across cultures (see Roberts 2008). In this sense we have a clear idea of where the public stands, and for what reasons. This kind of research cannot answer the question of *why* the public's view should be considered when determining sentencing policies involving offenders with prior convictions, but we can at least be confident of the nature of public opinion on the issue.

II. COMPETING PERSPECTIVES
A. Retributive Rejection of Public Input at Sentencing

As noted in the introduction, scholars have generally expressed deep misgivings about allowing community views to influence sentencing. Thus retributive theorists have ignored public reaction to sentencing principles or factors. Simons, for example, notes retributivism's "insensitivity . . . to popular preferences and social context" (2000, p. 639). Writers assume that there is strong public support for proportional sentencing[10] but have seen little utility in measuring community acceptance of other sentencing principles. Bagaric and Edney (2004) perceive no role for public opinion at sentencing, taking the view that sentencing is a matter best left to professional judges guided by principles derived from a coherent moral philosophy of punishment. These authors write that "seeking public views on sentencing is analogous to doctors basing treatment decisions on what the community thinks is appropriate or engineers building cars, not in accordance with the rules of physics, but on the basis of what lay members of the community 'reckon' seems about right" (Bagaric and Edney 2004, p. 129). Their image is striking, but wide of the mark; sentencing is not a technical matter governed by physical laws, but rather a cultural exercise (e.g., Garland 1991).

Some scholars would take issue with Bagaric and Edney's view and appear more sympathetic to community input. For example, Hutton (2008) argues that "there is nothing distinctively 'legal' about applying views about punishment . . . seriousness and blameworthiness to reach 'just' sentencing decisions. . . . there is therefore no reason why lay people should not be able to make sensible sentencing decisions" (p. 219). Morgan (2002) notes that "congruence [between community views and sentencing practice] is desirable," while some years earlier Ashworth (1987) observed that "since sentencing is a function performed in the public interest, it is clearly right that the public's view should be taken into account" (p. 6). However, these writers do not elaborate on how congruence between courts and community may be achieved.

A number of other writers, while not overtly hostile to public opinion, nevertheless appear untroubled by a divergence between community views and sentencing practices. R. A. Duff, for example, notes that the radical "lack of fit between normative theory and actual practice, between criminal punishment as the theory says it ought to be and criminal punishment as actually practiced does not constitute an objection to the theory" (2001, p. 175). While it is true that public opposition hardly undermines the integrity of a specific theory, it is surely worth questioning whether there is any utility to achieving a better fit between theory and opinion. Finally, von Hirsch (2010, pp. 4–5) observes that while desert judgments derive "some of their logic" from ordinary moral evaluations, principles cannot be extracted from ordinary moral assessments; the public are simply insufficiently knowledgeable about the issues. Von Hirsch (2010) uses the double jeopardy rule as an example of a sound principle that should not be abandoned if, say, it became clear that the public opposed restricting the state's ability to prosecute a defendant twice for the same allegation of misconduct.

B. The Case against Incorporating Public Views at Sentencing

There are four principal objections to community input into sentencing practices. They generally relate to the lack of expertise on the part of the public and the adverse impact that public opinion has had upon sentencing policies in recent years.

1. Public Ignorance of Sentencing.

First, the public know little about sentencing, and therefore cannot be relied upon to generate any principled approach to punishment (see, e.g., Durham 1985; discussion in Lovegrove 1998). Slobogin (1996) argues that even when there is a demonstrable and convincing consensus about a legal formulation, this should not carry weight as a normative matter because the consensus is based on a limited degree of knowledge. This representation of the public is to a large extent true. Research around the world has documented the limitations of public knowledge in the area of sentencing. Representative surveys of the public in the United States, United Kingdom, Canada, Australia, and other countries have demonstrated that people underestimate custody rates and custody lengths as well as the average amount of time served in custody. At the same time they overestimate parole grant rates, and have little understanding of sentencing principles such as those that regulate the use of custody or the application of maximum penalties (see Roberts and Hough 2005*b*; Butler and McFarlane 2009). Moreover, the public overestimates the deterrent effect of harsh sanctions, especially custody. This helps to explain the strong public support for custody as a sanction, as well as skepticism about community-based penalties. A wealth of research has by now demonstrated that the public views of sentencing reflect a faulty knowledge base derived from inadequate or incomplete media accounts of sentencing decisions. Moreover, people tend to be punitive, and to react to serious crime without much reflection. In light of these public misperceptions, so the argument runs, it would be foolhardy to introduce community values into the determination of punishments.

2. *Public Opinion as a Source of Punitiveness.*

The second objection turns upon the impact that public opinion has had on sentencing policy and practice in recent years. There is evidence that public views—or rather, views ascribed to the public—have fueled a more punitive response to offending.

For example, penal policies in England and Wales over the period 1997–2007 became tougher, in large measure because successive administrations cited the need to respond to public views. Thus the Conservative home secretary introduced proposals for tougher sentencing by noting they were necessary "if public confidence is to be maintained" (Howard, cited in *Law Gazette* 1995). The subsequent Labour government expressed a desire to align policies more closely with its perception that the public demanded more punitive responses to crime and antisocial behavior (see Ashworth and Hough 1996; Tonry 2003, pp. 5–6). And, as noted, research in several jurisdictions has identified sentencers' responsivity to community intolerance as a cause of harsher sentencing (Millie, Jacobson, and Hough 2005).

More recently, the Canadian government has introduced a series of punitive sentencing policies such as abolishing reviews of parole eligibility dates, creation of mandatory sentences, and the introduction of limits on the use of a form of community-based sentencing. These reforms were explicitly justified by reference to public opinion. For example, a government publication noted that "[the government] shares the 'common-sense belief of Canadians, that the punishment should fit the crime" and "our government *agrees with Canadians*: the justice system must not put the rights of criminals ahead of the rights of law-abiding citizens" (Department of Justice Canada 2010*a*, p. 1, 2010*b*). Similar developments have been witnessed in New Zealand (see Casey and Mohr 2005; Pratt 2007). Many punitive and ineffective sentencing policies of recent years such as "three-strikes" sentencing laws have been linked to public opinion. The historical record is therefore far from encouraging for advocates of greater public consultation. Seen from this perspective, the public represents a source of pressure toward more punitive sentencing.

3. *Unprincipled Attitudes to Punishment.*

A third objection to incorporating community views is that public reactions to sentencing issues are unprincipled, reflecting prejudice against a group in society—offenders—for whom most people have little sympathy. This implies that intuitive reactions to criminal wrongdoing are a very unreliable guide to principled sentencing. When confronted with misconduct, we tend to blame people whom we like less stringently than strangers, and strangers less harshly than people for whom we have developed some animosity. Distinctions of this kind are clearly invidious and unprincipled. We also tend to blame people more for transgressions that violate consensual standards of acceptable behavior, independent of the objective harm of the actions, and this may not be quite so indefensible a practice. The criminal law should not unquestioningly import the logic of interpersonal behavior when determining liability and allocating punishments, but it must bear some resemblance to community censuring practices.

4. *Volatility of Public Views.*

A final objection to increased public input into sentencing turns upon the observation that public views are manifestly volatile, and can change rapidly, usually in response to high-profile cases reported in the media. Examples abound, but include the hardening of public attitudes toward juvenile offenders in the United States and the United Kingdom after notorious cases such as the Bosket case in New York State and the murder of James Bulger in England (see Roberts 2004). If some institutionalization of public attitudes was implemented with respect to sentencing, the consequence would be an unwelcome degree of volatility in policies and practices.

The following brief responses may be made to these four critiques of public input. First, the admittedly low levels of public knowledge in the general population simply mean that community input should not be achieved through public opinion surveys or referenda, but rather by means of more careful methodologies involving informed samples of respondents (see the introduction).

Second, the pressure toward more punitive and exclusionary penal policies is a political phenomenon by which populist politicians have represented a distorted view of public opinion derived from an imperfect methodology—simple public opinion poll questions. Nor is it the case that punitive policies always or accurately reflect community views. A number of research projects have demonstrated that politicians and policy makers have misinterpreted public attitudes in the area of punishment. The misinterpretation is almost always in the direction of a more punitive reading of public opinion than is in fact the case (e.g., Riley and Rose 1980; Johnson and Huff 1987; Roberts 2003).

Third, there is now an abundance of empirical evidence to demonstrate that principles of punishment may be derived from the public. When deciding upon the allocation of punishments people make subtle and reasoned decisions based on a neoretributivist philosophy of punishment. This has been demonstrated in research in which people are asked to identify factors that should mitigate or aggravate sentence (see Lovegrove 2007; Roberts et al. 2008, 2009).

Finally, the undeniable volatility of public attitudes toward crime and offenders can be addressed by placing limits on the use of public opinion research. In this way the threat to principled sentencing posed by short-term waves of public emotion can be contained.

C. Justifications for Incorporating Public Views at Sentencing

Three principal justifications exist for considering public views at sentencing: (i) to enhance legitimacy and encourage compliance with the law; (ii) to amplify the censure conveyed by a legal sanction; and (iii) to reflect the social element of criminal wrongs.

First, if sentencing policy and practice completely ignores public opinion, the legitimacy of the sentencing system will be threatened. More than this, the legitimacy of a state that punishes individuals without considering the community will be called into question, with adverse consequences for the criminal justice system. This consequentialist argument is most closely associated with the writings of Paul Robinson and will be discussed at greater length below.

A related function of the sentencing process is to reinforce social norms and to mark, by the severity of the punishments imposed, the relative seriousness of proscribed conduct. The second justification for a link between community views and sentencing practice therefore relates to the communicative nature of sentencing. Here the argument is that the communication of blame must to some degree be linked to the community on whose behalf condemnation is expressed. Otherwise the censuring function will lose all force, and effective censure will be lost.

The third justification is unrelated to achieving demonstrable objectives such as perceived legitimacy, compliance, or effective censure. Rather, the argument is that punishment as a social exercise must consider community views. The penal value of specific conduct is in part determined by social consensus—hence the need to consider the views of the community. Concordance between sentencing and community opinion ensures that offenders will experience censure rather than mere punishment. Let us explore each of these justifications in turn.

1. Empirical Desert and the Legitimacy–Compliance Link.

A substantial body of literature suggests that the perceived legitimacy of the justice system is founded upon the extent to which members of the public consider the decisions taken to be fair and to reflect consensual values. In addition, compliance with the law is dependent upon the extent to which the community perceives the system to be legitimate.[11] It is clear that compliance with the law cannot be achieved by threats alone. Research by Tom Tyler and others has demonstrated the important role of perceived legitimacy in eliciting compliance with the law (see Tyler 2006). These twin, related arguments are essentially consequentialist in nature: ignoring the views of the community will undermine perceptions of legitimacy as well as levels of compliance with the law. Both arguments assert a benefit (legitimacy, and consequently compliance) that is contingent upon a degree of concordance between opinion and practice. Thus if the practice of the courts drifts too far from the views of the community, this dissociation will ultimately undermine the functioning of the system. The argument is straightforward—even simplistic—in the sense that clear benefits are associated with a system sensitive to public opinion. However, the matter is more complex.

The term "empirical desert" derives from the recent writings of Paul Robinson, John Darley, and their coauthors (e.g., Robinson and Darley 1995, 2007; Robinson 2007, 2008, 2009). These authors distinguish "deontological" from "empirical" desert. By the term "empirical desert," they refer to the responses of the community as measured by empirical research rather than positions derived from moral philosophy (deontological desert). Robinson and his colleagues advocate restructuring sentencing policies and practices to reflect the intuitions about punishment held by members of the public. Robinson argues that the credibility of the criminal law is essential to effective crime control and is enhanced if the sentencing process assigns punishment in a way that is consistent with "shared intuitions of justice."

Ultimately this perspective argues that a system that fails to track public opinion will result in a number of adverse effects, including the prospect of people resorting to vigilantism. "The resort to vigilantism is a dramatic reaction to the system's failure to do justice" (Robinson 2007, p. 13). In addition to promoting public confidence and perceptions of legitimacy, a policy of empirical rather than theoretical desert will achieve other goals, including changing the nature of public opinion. Robinson writes:

> By tracking a community's shared intuitions of justice, the criminal law can build its moral credibility and then use that influence in select situations such as drunk driving, domestic violence, and date rape, to help shape community norms (2007, p. 103).

Robinson (2009) does not argue that shared intuitions of justice must *always* be followed at sentencing; rather he warns that ignoring these intuitions will undermine crime control effectiveness. But community views remain the default position: the sentencing scheme would begin by aligning itself with empirical desert and only after this is established would it determine if deviations from this model are appropriate. As Taslitz pithily notes, "Robinson's presumption is in favor of ordinary folks" (2009, p. 56). Advocates of the empirical desert model are well aware that community perceptions and values may often be morally wrong—Robinson offers the compelling example of attitudes toward slavery. He concedes that "there might be any number of reasons that justify a deviation [from empirical desert]" (Robinson 2009, p. 38).

2. *Critiques of Empirical Desert.*

The concept of empirical desert and its practical implications have been addressed in several critiques (e.g., Denno 2000; Kolber 2009; Ryberg 2011; for brief rejoinders from a number of contributors and a response, see Robinson, Garvey, and Ferzan 2009), but some comments are in order. First, there are difficulties locating the justification for incorporating public views within a consequentialist model of crime control effectiveness—at least while the sentencing system retains a proportionalist orientation. Under the Robinson model the punishment of offenders represents a means to achieve better crime control: "the rationale for empirical desert is instrumental not deontological" (Robinson 2009, p. 62).

Second, it is unclear *how much* concordance is necessary to attain an acceptable level of public confidence in and compliance with the law. At what point is it justified to abandon an established principle because it deviates from empirical desert, or for that matter, to derogate from empirical desert? Third, there appears to be no qualification to the affirmed relationship between practice and opinion; the model assumes that the closer the links between the two the better. Yet, as the force of public opinion increases in influence, other problems may well arise. Community confidence in justice and public compliance are important, but can carry a cost. As Ryberg (2011) observes, the increased compliance that derives from a justice system sensitive to community views must be set against the very real possibility of unjust outcomes (see also Simons 2000). One can easily conceive of sentencing policies or practices that would have a salutary effect upon levels of public confidence and compliance with the law but which would be unjust.[12] Realigning sentencing arrangements in order to promote public compliance is therefore highly problematic.

3. *Ensuring Effective Censure.*

A related justification for public input at sentencing invokes the censuring function of the criminal sanction. As noted, regardless of their specific nature and severity, all punishment systems reflect and interact with the social context in which they are set. The nature and perceived severity of specific sanctions, the factors considered to aggravate or mitigate, and indeed the overall objectives and principles reflect, in large measure, the culture of the society. Moral blameworthiness—whether as a function of crime seriousness or culpability—also has a social component. Conceptions of what is blameworthy must to some degree be empirically derived from the community or no blame will be communicated to the offender.

Retributivism involves the collective censure for criminal wrongs. The phrase "collective censure" implies some social consensus about the kinds of conduct worthy of legal censure. Advocates of this perspective would argue that a sentencing framework derives its *coherence* from adhering to a theoretically sound model, but its *legitimacy* from its relationship to the community on whose behalf legal punishments are imposed. The degree of censure that we experience is affected by the legitimacy of the censuring power. Penalties imposed by forces or governments considered illegitimate may be harsh, and may be experienced as harsh punishments, but the individuals on whom they are imposed are unlikely to feel censured—just punished. For example, the penalties imposed by an occupying foreign power will be perceived as punishments, yet they lack all legitimacy—they are totally decoupled from the community to which the punished individual belongs.

If public opinion is jettisoned, the censuring function of a court-imposed sentence would be divorced from the community on whose behalf censure is expressed. A purely theoretical account of sentencing would ultimately drift away from community views and the result will be a failure in the censuring power of the sentencing process. Ewing (1929) observed almost a century ago that when the sentencing system fails to impose adequate punishment "the moral judgments of those who represent the State . . . will cease to be taken seriously" (p. 95). The expression of legal censure is different from the blame we assign in daily life for noncriminal transgressions, but there must be some relation between the two systems.[13]

To summarize, an exclusionary model would therefore result in a lack of legitimacy, compliance, and the ability to effectively censure offenders. The imposition of a sentence would impose a sanction, but convey little or no censure—sanction without censure.

4. *Analogizing Collective Censure.*

In his recent contribution to the debate about the role of public opinion at sentencing Ryberg (2011) describes an analogy involving a company that allocates bonuses to its employees. Annual bonuses are allocated to reward employees for their professional performance over the previous year. Large bonuses are bestowed upon the individuals who perform best according to a publicly declared set of criteria—amount of overtime, number of units produced, etc. These bonuses come from a fund to which all employees contribute and which is designed and promoted with the collectivity of employees in mind. In this sense the annual awards are an expression of public approbation on behalf of the collectivity, the way that penal sanctions are assigned to reflect collective *dis*approbation. The criteria for determining the magnitude of any given employee's bonus are analogous to the objective determinants of harm in a proportionality-based model of sentencing.

Imagine further that there are criteria that the employees themselves perceive to be relevant to any determination of an individual's contribution to the company (and hence the magnitude of his or her bonus) but which are unrelated to the company's productivity. Employees might, for example, value sociability in the workplace, or may consider a record of volunteering for company events as worthy of recognition by the company committee that determines bonuses.[14] If these employee-derived criteria were totally ignored, the bonuses would lose some of their collective value; they would be seen as conveying praise for exclusively managerial goals rather than for purposes more holistically related to the collective on whose behalf they are granted. The collective element would be lost.

These employee-derived criteria should not assume a fundamental importance, or bonuses would reflect an individual's popularity rather than their contribution to the company's productivity, the promotion of which is the fundamental purpose of the scheme. But these criteria cannot be ignored if the scheme is to retain its character as a collective enterprise. This loosening of strictly objective, performance-related criteria for determining bonuses is the equivalent of allowing cultural, community-derived factors to affect the determination of sentences. Therefore, any censure-based model of sentencing would ultimately lose its censuring power if links to community values were totally abandoned.

The censure-amplification argument is susceptible to some of the same critiques of empirical desert. Collective censure can easily become unprincipled—for example, if the majority expresses its greater disapproval of crime committed by minorities. For this reason, the public's position on any punishment-related issue should be subject to careful scrutiny rather than imported directly into the practice of sentencing and should be subject to strict limits. Increasing the censuring power of the criminal sanction cannot provide a direct justification for realigning sentencing practices, even though there are clear dangers of the system losing credibility and hence the ability to provide effective censure.

5. *Recognizing the Societal Element of Crime Seriousness.*

The final justification for introducing public views into sentencing invokes the social component of state punishment. The gravity of crimes, the legitimacy of legal defenses,[15] and many other components of criminal law are influenced by community values. With respect to the determination of punishment, this means that cultural factors cannot be overlooked in favor of some abstract or purely theoretical model. This justification for the introduction of community input is internal to a retributive rationale. Seriousness ratings and sentencing factors (for example) should reflect public opinion not for instrumental reasons—because the public will have more confidence in or respect for sentencing—but because community views constitute an inherent element of crime seriousness. Public input does not represent a corruption of proportionality, but a more contextual calibration of proportionality's components—seriousness and severity (see below).

To summarize, although incorporating public views may promote perceptions of legitimacy and, ultimately, compliance with the law, these are insufficient justifications for importing community values. On the other hand, there is a compelling argument that cultural factors should play a role in determining sentencing outcomes, albeit within limits.

At this point I turn, in section III, to exploring specific areas in which public opinion may reasonably play a role at sentencing.

III. INCORPORATING PUBLIC VIEWS INTO SENTENCING

The domain of legal punishment is vast, and there are many issues on which public attitudes are relevant, including the following: the scale and limits of criminal punishments, the severity rankings of criminal punishments, ratings of crime seriousness, and the

Retributivism Has a Past

nature of aggravating and mitigating factors at sentencing. In the discussion that follows I focus on rankings of crime seriousness and sentencing factors.

A. Rankings of Crime Seriousness and Ordinal Proportionality

Crime seriousness can be defined and measured in different ways. Von Hirsch and Jareborg (1991) have proposed a "living standards" analysis as a way of gauging criminal harm. According to this scheme, seriousness is a function of the degree to which the crime victim's living standard is infringed.

With respect to sentencing, it would make no sense to aggravate the severity of the sentence to reflect factors that the public believed did *not* affect crime seriousness or offender culpability. It would be equally odd to ignore circumstances the public *reasonably* believed made a crime more or less serious, or an offender more or less blameworthy. Crime seriousness rankings are derived in part from community evaluations of criminal acts. Consider domestic burglary—an offense once considered serious enough to warrant life imprisonment.[16] This offense now occupies a much lower rung on the ladder of crime seriousness, not because of any reduction in its objective harm or the extent to which it interferes with the victim's living standard in the von Hirsch and Jareborg sense, but rather because community perceptions have shifted. Domestic violence is an obvious example of the opposite tendency—public views of the seriousness of this crime have increased in recent generations. Offense definitions are also determined by cultural factors.

Determining the relative seriousness of crimes—with a view to developing rankings of seriousness within the framework of a guideline scheme—is one area where an argument for public consultation can clearly be made. Ordinal proportionality refers to the ranking of offenses according to their relative seriousness (von Hirsch 1993). Determining offense seriousness rankings is a natural activity for sentencing guidelines authorities, and in several jurisdictions the public have been "consulted" with respect to the central retributive concept of crime seriousness. Perceptions of crime seriousness have been the subject of criminological inquiry for decades, and some guidelines schemes have drawn upon public rankings of offenses or have derived rankings of offense seriousness from public ratings of the seriousness of different crimes.[17] Determining seriousness ratings for the purposes of establishing ordinal proportionality is a common exercise for sentencing guidelines authorities.

B. Defining Crime Seriousness: Moving beyond the Living Standard Analysis

Von Hirsch and Jareborg (1991) cite two reasons for rejecting the use of public opinion polls. First, the public may have inaccurate views about the true and relative seriousness of criminal acts, and second, because the criteria the public use for judging "have not been reflected on" (p. 6). Having initially excluded recourse to community values, von Hirsch and Jareborg (1991) ultimately accord these values some importance in the determination of crime seriousness, noting that "how harmful burglary is ... depends on its impact and that impact will vary across cultures" (p. 6). Surely this brings us back to empirical investigation to determine how much cultural variation exists. There may well be scope for public consultation on this issue, however.

The seriousness of any particular act is determined, to some degree, by the extent to which it offends community mores. Certain conduct constitutes an affront to community values independent of the degree to which a crime victim's living standards are affected. Hate-motivated crime represents a good example of this. Most western jurisdictions have made this circumstance a statutory aggravating factor, but the extent to which hate motivation should enhance the sentence is highly dependent upon the community in which the offense takes place. The ethnic composition may well affect the extent to which the offense is deemed more serious. "Flag burning" offers another example. Imagine two jurisdictions, both of which have created a criminal offense of desecrating the national flag. A determination of the seriousness of burning the national flag in a public place would require some community input. State A may be one in which the polity consider this act as being relatively serious, constituting a mild act of treason, while state B may take a more tolerant view of political dissent and regard the conduct as only barely worthy of criminalization.

Consider a second example involving the theft of a fishing boat in a small fishing village. Many small fishing communities ascribe a significance to their vessels beyond that which attaches to pleasure craft—the theft of the former is therefore reasonably considered more serious. The heightened seriousness comes not just from a living standard analysis—the loss of livelihood arising from the fishing vessel theft—but from the community perception. There is a social value to the offense that is derived from community perception—the context in which the offense takes place. A sentencing system needs to be sensitive to these distinctions, which derive from community reaction (Bottoms 1995; see discussion in Tonry 1995b).

However, difficulties also abound in terms of public consultation. Members of the public may have very inaccurate perceptions of the relative seriousness of different offenses and these misperceptions can distort any offense rankings based on public opinion—with adverse effects if these rankings are used to establish ordinal proportionality (see Ryberg 2011). For example, members of the public tend to overestimate the seriousness of assaults against the police—which are often merely scuffles involving a suspect resisting arrest rather than an intentional assault against a state representative. Similarly, laypersons fail to recognize the true consequences of some offenses against the administration of justice such as perjury. If these public misperceptions were used, they would distort ordinal rankings and undermine proportionality in sentencing. This potential source of bias needs to be addressed by the use of informed samples of the public. As with many issues then, public input should be carefully structured to ensure that participants have as veridical a perception of the offenses being ranked in terms of their relative seriousness.[18]

In practical terms, how might a sentencing guidelines authority incorporate public opinion? With respect to crime seriousness ratings, this involves a careful analysis of public seriousness rankings—and as noted in the introduction, there is significant academic literature on this subject. A similar exercise should be undertaken with respect to severity rankings of punishments: it makes little sense to infuse seriousness ratings with a sense of public opinion if the same exercise is not undertaken regarding punishment severity.[19] Of course, the public will be as likely to subscribe to misperceptions with respect to severity scales as seriousness rankings. People may well underestimate the severity of some community penalties such as curfews. This underscores again the need for a careful and informed calibration of community opinion.

C. Sentencing Factors

If public views play a role, albeit a limited one, in the determination of ordinal rankings of offenses, they should also affect consideration of factors that may aggravate or mitigate the sentence. Public views are relevant to the second branch of a proportional sanction—offender culpability. The extent to which we consider an offender blameworthy—and hence worthy of legal censure—is affected by many factors, some arising from objective criteria, such as the extent of harm. For example, we consider offenders more blameworthy if the crime involves clearly foreseeable harm. An offender convicted of speeding for a sustained period of time on a busy highway and who ignores appeals from other motorists to slow down is deemed more culpable than someone who speeds on an empty country road. But there is also a social component to blameworthiness that should not be overlooked.[20] We blame people for conduct that transgresses community standards, and accordingly it is necessary to consult the community to determine the nature of these standards.

D. The Influence of Culture

In a recent essay, Manson (2011) draws attention to the limitations on desert theory with respect to mitigation and aggravation. Although he does not discuss the issue directly, Manson's model clearly raises the question of community input into sentencing. He argues that culture plays a role in the evolution of attitudes toward criminal acts and their respective punishments, and discusses the concept of "legitimate sympathy." This term refers to culturally derived sources of sympathy that may justify mitigation at sentencing. Manson argues that neither sympathy for the offender nor a legitimacy defined by reference to sentencing goals is sufficient, and that only some combination of the two constitutes an adequate conceptualization of sentencing factors. In order to establish legitimate sympathy Manson asks first whether the culture creates sympathy, and if so, can sympathy (i.e., mitigation) be accommodated without undermining the essential legitimacy of state punishment that requires that like cases be treated in a similar fashion.

Sentencing factors provide a context where an examination of community reaction offers useful modification to a purely theoretical model of proportional sentencing. For each of the factors discussed below the public view contains a principled justification for a particular position—even if there is also an unprincipled, usually punitive response present at the same time. The other element that these factors have in common is that they pertain to the blameworthiness of the offender, not the gravity of the conduct, which is unaffected by whether the offender has committed offenses before or expressed remorse after committing the current crime. Retributivist theorists and the public disagree about the relevance of these factors; the purpose of this discussion is to demonstrate that a careful analysis of public opinion research reveals that some widely held sentencing intuitions reflect a principled foundation. These two factors illustrate the richness of public reactions to offending and offenders.

1. *Aggravating Factors:[21] Previous Convictions.*

Turning to the role of prior convictions at sentencing, the gap between public opinion and judicial practice on the one hand, and retributive theory on the other is so striking that it warrants further consideration. Yet between 1978, when Fletcher argued that repeat offenders could not be considered more blameworthy, and 2008, when papers appeared arguing against this view (e.g., Roberts 2008; Lee 2009), nothing was published on the subject. Retributivists noted the inconsistency between their models and sentencing practices around the world and appear to have assumed that the latter reflected misguided judges imposing sentences within flawed statutory frameworks. All these writers appear to assume a direct influence model, whereby public sentencing preferences are introduced into sentencing practice simply to ensure a better fit between courts and community. The growing literature arguing for previous convictions to be considered relevant to blameworthiness should encourage retributivists to revise their models, or provide the impetus to convince the skeptical community of the public and criminal justice professionals that they are wrong to consider prior offending at sentencing.

Should an offender's previous convictions affect the sentence imposed for a fresh offense? Scholars have debated this question for years now (see the discussion in von Hirsch 1976; Fletcher 1982; Roberts and von Hirsch 2010). There are two traditional retributivist accounts. According to one view, previous convictions have no role to play. The second perspective assigns mitigation to first offenders following the principle of the progressive loss of mitigation. Although the progressive loss of mitigation principle articulated by von Hirsch is incorporated in some retributive models, "tolerance for a lapse" (von Hirsch 2010) is not an inherently retributive concept. The truly retributive position is one that accords no role for previous convictions at sentencing (e.g., Fletcher 1982; Bagaric 2001; Robinson and Darley 2007).

The justification for this counterintuitive position is that prior convictions do not affect crime seriousness, nor, in the view of retributive theorists, do they affect the offender's level of culpability for the offense. Thus retributivists would not consider an offender convicted of rape for the fifth time to be any more blameworthy than the first-time rapist. This account is clearly at odds with community values, the views of criminal justice professionals, and sentencing practices around the world (see Roberts [2008] for a review of empirical research[22]). Research clearly shows that members of the public consider recidivists to be more blameworthy—but is their view in any way principled? The discrepancy between courts and community alone is insufficient to justify abandoning the retributive perspective. However, careful analysis of the community's position reveals a number of principled grounds for incorporating previous convictions into a retributive sentencing model. Several proposals have been advanced to justify a recidivist sentencing premium.

One argument in favor of such a position is that in everyday life we are sensitive to the previous conduct of those who transgress. In ascribing "liability" to quotidian, noncriminal transgressions we modulate our censure to reflect any prior misconduct. Should censure expressed by the criminal law abandon this for such a radically different approach? There is also a line of argument that repeat offenders are legitimately seen as being more culpable for having ignored an implicit legal admonition to desist. This perspective has been developed by Lee (2010), who argues that repeat offenders are more blameworthy for failing to take steps to correct their offending. The public may invest a sentence with the expectation that it will generate desistance—or at least attempts at desistance.[23] When the offender repeatedly reoffends, the public may wish to activate a greater prudential disincentive to reoffend.

2. *A Mitigating Factor: Remorse.*

For the second illustration of principled public reactions to offending I turn to a common sentencing factor, offender remorse. This is a mitigating factor for which most (but by no means all) retributivists have little sympathy.[24] Remorse cannot affect the seriousness of the offense or the offender's level of culpability for the offense. Yet sentencing research makes it clear that offenders who express remorse usually receive a mitigated punishment (e.g., Harrel 1981). In addition, members of the public favor more lenient treatment of offenders who express remorse (Kleinke, Wallis, and Stalder 1992; Robinson, Smith-Lovin, and Tsoudis 1994). As was the case with previous convictions and premeditation, there may be an unprincipled explanation for this public reaction. Thus people may simply infer good character from the remorseful reaction, in which case it is simply another instance of sentencing on character. Or they may apply some standard of personal morality ("I would be remorseful if I had done that . . .").

However, the public also probably wishes to recognize that the offender has taken a public stand against his own offense, and the community response is to consider him less culpable for his conduct and to allocate less blame, which then translates into a more lenient sentencing outcome. Here, as with the other examples discussed in this essay, the retributivist focus is, from the perspective of the public, restrictively narrow. It focuses on the offense, and factors affecting culpability for the offense. This analysis is therefore relevant only prior to or at the commission of the act and is at odds with community views and the practice of contemporary criminal justice.

IV. CONSEQUENCES FOR SENTENCING PRACTICES

Where does all this leave the "future of punishment" addressed throughout this volume?

A. Sentencing Theories

As noted in the introduction, public views are most often discussed in the context of retributive theories of punishment. Retributive theorists have generally ignored community views, citing the dangers of populism, the limitations on public knowledge of sentencing, and other reasons for excluding public opinion at sentencing. This perspective is a classic example of losing the baby with the bathwater. An exclusionary approach to considering the views of the public denies the sentencing process any status as a social exercise—it divests a system of collective censure of its collective nature. A neo-retributive model in which proportionality considerations are modified by reference to community-based or cultural factors offers a far more compelling alternative future for punishment. A superior approach involves considering public opinion at sentencing, but places clear limits upon this consideration. Returning to a practical level, how might a sentencing guidelines authority assimilate public opinion into its guidelines?

B. Incorporating Public Views: The Role of a Guidelines Authority

Sentencing guidelines authorities in a number of jurisdictions have so far made only very modest attempts to reflect community views in sentencing policy or practice.[25] For example, the Sentencing Advisory Panel in England and Wales[26] conducted several public opinion surveys to explore community views on sentencing.[27] This research has then been considered when the panel has (in conjunction with the Sentencing Guidelines Council) devised sentencing guidelines. The panel commissioned research on public perceptions of the relative seriousness of different forms of rape. The public's view that no distinction in seriousness should be made between rapes involving strangers and those involving relationships was adopted in the ultimate guideline (see Ashworth 2008). The panel also conducted public opinion research into community views of the sentencing of culpable driving offenses resulting in death in order to shape the guidelines for those crimes. Similarly, the U.S. Sentencing Commission conducted a comprehensive analysis of public opinion and sentencing (see Rossi and Berk 1997).

Guidelines authorities in other jurisdictions have undertaken only very limited public "consultations" or have reserved places for community members on the commission or council.[28] These consultations and their impacts are relatively modest or largely political in nature. The results have had little impact on guideline ranges or the sentencing factors identified in guidelines. In addition, these efforts appear atheoretical in the sense that no *principled* justification is offered to justify modifying guideline ranges in light of community views. There also appears to be an assumption that community opinion is inevitably unprincipled and capricious and as such constitutes an unreliable guide for sentencers.

The task of considering public opinion should clearly be undertaken by a sentencing guidelines authority and not by individual sentencers. A number of steps need to be followed. First, the authority would need to determine whether there is a strong consensus about the relevance of a sentencing factor such as remorse or prior offending. This would be established by means of an appropriate methodology and would offer evidence that the factor is culturally relevant. Second, the authority would need to establish whether there was a defensible principle underlying the public's view or whether the position reflected reflexive punitiveness or prejudice. Answering these two questions would require the kind of careful methodology described in the introduction to this essay. Third, if a principle was found that could distinguish, say, first offenders from recidivists, the guidelines authority would have to decide whether this distinction violated a more fundamental principle, such as consistency of treatment. Distinguishing first offenders from multiple recidivists would not violate equity of treatment, as the two categories of offenders are distinguishable on the grounds articulated in the previous section.

Once an analysis of this kind is completed, some factors favored by the public would be excluded from consideration and a number of others would be incorporated into formal sentencing guidelines. An obvious consequence of this more inclusionary approach to determining relevant sentencing factors would be an increase in the variability of sentencing outcomes—a natural consequence of taking more factors into account. This is not an adverse outcome; it merely ensures that a more consensual conception of proportionality is reflected in sentencing practices. This approach would enhance the legitimacy of the sentencing process, and possibly encourage compliance with the law, but these are ancillary benefits, not fundamental justifications for incorporating public opinion. There would be an expanded conceptualization of crime seriousness and offender culpability. A number of authors have decried the "oversimplified view of offenders' culpability, in which the only meaningful differences among offenders concern their crime and some consideration of their past criminal records" (Tonry 1995a, p. 194).

This expanded conceptualization would come about by considering factors that are linked to the culture in which sentencing takes place. Such a reform may also ultimately require us to accept that the sentencing system incorporates factors that are external to a retributive sentencing model, even if the overall architecture of the system is largely guided by proportionality. Examples of this more expansive model might include system-driven leniency—to defendants who assist the state in prosecuting other alleged offenders, and leniency related to social reaction—for example, the expression of remorse accompanied by an apology. In addition, there would be a dilution of a strict proportionality requirement in the allocation of punishments as a result of an increased use of sentencing factors *external* to a retributive model of sentencing.

According to this model, sentencing practices do not simply track public opinion— the consequence would be unprincipled sentencing. However, when a specific policy or practice is clearly at odds with community values, this inconsistency should at the very least provoke an inquiry into the nature of these views, and possible modification of sentencing practices.[29] If a principle cannot be found to justify the community position—because it reflects populist punitiveness or unprincipled prejudice—the criminal justice system should demonstrate why public opinion is mistaken and attempt to correct the public misperceptions. Many people believe in deterrence and think that exemplary sentencing serves to deter potential offenders. The consistent public demands for harsher sentencing are explained in part by faith in deterrence as a crime control mechanism. Systematic research has clearly demonstrated the ineffectiveness of such sentencing strategies.[30] One strategy might therefore involve communicating the findings from this body of research to the community. On the other hand, examination of community views may generate legitimate reasons to modify the theory and practice of sentencing.

C. The Need for Public Education as well as Public Consultation

The relationship between community values and sentencing practices should be dynamic and bidirectional. There is also a need to educate the public with respect to the sentencing process and the reasons why particular factors are considered (or excluded from consideration) at sentencing. Wherever and whenever possible, courts and sentencing guidelines authorities should attempt to explain the use of sentencing factors that, from the perspective of the public, are counterintuitive. For example, it would be useful for a court to explain why a mitigated punishment was imposed in a serious case of sexual violence to reflect the fact that the offender had no prior criminal history.[31] Similarly, the public may not immediately accept the position that offenders who plead guilty should receive a sentencing discount. For factors such as these, some engagement with the community is necessary.

D. Conclusion

To summarize, although multiple arguments have been offered to justify incorporating the views of the community in the sentencing process, the consequentialist accounts fail as justifications. It is true that a total disengagement between court and community would undermine perceptions of the legitimacy of the justice system, and ultimately compliance with the law. It is also true that a system of state censure that ignored the community on whose behalf censure is expressed would ultimately lose its condemnatory power. In this respect some concordance is clearly necessary both to secure and ensure compliance with the law and to ensure the censuring function of the sanction. However, these instrumentalist concerns cannot themselves justify realigning sentencing practices.

In contrast, public input is justified by reference to the social nature of a legal sanction. The seriousness of any offense is in part determined by the nature of social reaction to the proscribed conduct, and sentencing factors relevant to culpability should also reflect the context in which blameworthiness is established. Intuitive responses to offending often have a principled foundation and, as such, constitute a fertile source of guidance. There are both objective and culturally relative components to crime seriousness and sentence severity that need to be accommodated within any system of guidance for sentencers. As Garland (1991, p. 160) notes, "thinking of punishment as a social institution should change not only our mode of understanding penality, but also our normative thinking about it." The dangers of introducing community views into sentencing practices are apparent, but so too are the benefits.

ACKNOWLEDGMENTS

I am grateful to the participants of the seminars held at Leiden and to Michael Tonry, Jan de Keijser, and Mike Hough for comments on an earlier draft of this essay.

NOTES

1. After reviewing explanations for the increase in the English prison population, these authors identify public pressure for courts to "get tough" as a cause (Millie, Jacobson, and Hough 2005, pp. 102–5).
2. Much of the writing in the field merely asserts the importance of exploring public opinion without explaining why or how community views should be heeded. For example, Winick simply notes: "Knowledge of public opinion can be valuable to legislators and other policy makers: it provides the opportunity to trace changing public attitudes" (1983, p. 1333).
3. There is a link to deterrence: Public views of the relative seriousness of different penalties will determine their relative power as a deterrent. However, this question is not explored here.
4. Other examples of factors perceived to be relevant by the public—but not by retributive writings—abound. Thus the public—unlike most retributive theorists—regard remorse as worthy of mitigation.
5. The divergence between the public and retributive writers is not the only conflict in perspectives on sentencing. Victims represent another important constituency in the future of punishment, and their views also diverge from punishment theories. Crime victims emphasize the harm occasioned by the offense rather than the offender's level of culpability. Whether the offender foresaw, or could reasonably have foreseen, the harm caused is less important to victims, but primordial to theorists.
6. Simons (2000, p. 640) also describes the role of community views as "complex and uncertain."
7. Culpable driving offenses causing death are an example of a crime that the public punishes harshly because they focus on the harm caused—the fatality—at the exclusion of the culpability of the offender, which for many of these offenses tends to be relatively low.
8. Several explanations may be offered for these intuitive and punitive reactions. First, people may lose sight of the importance of culpability as a determinant of sentence, focusing instead upon the harm component. Second, they may adopt a victim-oriented perspective in which the impact of the crime trumps considerations relating to the offender's level of culpability.
9. The visual research design involves randomly assigning members of the public to assign a sentence for an offense under one of two conditions. Half the subjects receive just an offense description while the other half are provided with information approaching that which is available to a sentencing court. Subjects in the high information condition typically impose significantly less severe sentences.
10. For example, von Hirsch and Ashworth (2005) note: "Proportionalist sentencing. comports with common-sense notions of justice" (p. 4). The assumption is well founded: empirical studies in a number of jurisdictions have shown that when asked to impose punishments, the public generally conforms to proportionality considerations, although harm often outweighs offender culpability in a way that is at odds with retributivism (see Roberts and Hough [2005b] for a review). In addition, von Hirsch (1993) noted that the "potency of the idea of the proportionate sentence" could be explained because it is "ethically plausible. Most of us, as part of our everyday notions of justice think that penalties should reflect the degree of the blameworthiness the conduct involves" (p. 1).

11. Since researchers have not tested the effect of declining confidence in sentencing on public levels of compliance with the law, or cooperation with the criminal justice system, this appears to be a reasonable inference rather than an empirical finding.

12. Similarly, promoting public confidence cannot be a direct goal of sentencing: dispositions should not be constructed and imposed with the purpose of placating community values. Public confidence in sentencing should be a consequence, not a goal, of the sentencing system. This point was made by Lord Auld in his report on courts in England and Wales (see Auld 2001; for a discussion, see Roberts 2002).

13. Even if we agree to exclude the public and rely on theorists to determine the contours of legal punishment, we are left with the problem of what to do when these theorists disagree, for example, with respect to the role of prior convictions or offender remorse at sentencing. Both factors have generated considerable debate in recent years (see von Hirsch and Ashworth, 2005).

14. Pursuing the analogy reveals how this approach permits local variation. Different companies or divisions of the same company may have different additional criteria to import into the determination of the bonus. One division's employees may wish to reward individuals who decline to take any sick days, while another collective may see this as inappropriate.

15. For example, it is trite to note that the test of whether a reasonable person would have acted in a particular manner requires a consideration of the community standard of reasonableness.

16. Although it still carries a statutory maximum of life imprisonment in many nations, sentencing practices are far less severe.

17. For a recent empirical analysis of public attitudes toward crime seriousness, see Roberts et al. (2009).

18. Ryberg (2011) suggests another qualification on the use of public opinion in this manner. He argues that when the public rate crime X as being more serious than crime Y, it must be established that they are drawing upon an intuitive conception of desert, not extraneous considerations. This qualification can also be addressed by means of an adequate methodology.

19. Rossi and Berk (1997) provide an example of such an analysis, conducted for the U.S. Sentencing Commission. To my knowledge this kind of analysis has not been repeated in other jurisdictions.

20. Crime victims offer another perspective on the issue of culpability. Victims often attribute blame according to the consequences of the offender's actions, even when these consequences were adventitious or not foreseeable. Offenders convicted of careless driving causing death are regarded by victims as highly culpable because the consequences of their conduct are so serious. In an adversarial model of justice, however, the state must privilege community conceptions of culpability, or the sentencing process will lose its legitimacy (see the discussion in Gardner 1998).

21. Premeditation is another example of a sentencing factor that places courts and the community in opposition to retributive theorists, and for which a principle may be found within the views of the public. Members of the public regard premeditation as an important aggravating circumstance, favoring the punishing of offenders who plan their crimes more harshly than "spontaneous" offenders (e.g., Home Office 2001). Retributivists, however, generally see little justification for aggravating sentence severity on the grounds that the offender carefully planned his offense; scholars either offer examples of spontaneous offenders who are equally blameworthy, or they fail to discuss the issue at all. However, if the circumstances surrounding the offense and offender characteristics are held constant, the importance of premeditation becomes clearer. Imagine two cases of assault, with all elements comparable except that X spent considerable time planning the crime, while Y

spontaneously assaulted the victim. The fact that X had (and rejected) many opportunities to *not* commit the crime surely renders him more blameworthy than Y.

22. Research in a number of jurisdictions has demonstrated that members of the public favor sentencing repeat offenders more harshly than first offenders. In addition, when asked to identify important aggravating factors, people ascribe a high level of importance to previous convictions (see Roberts 2008, chap. 8).

23. When someone commits an "offense" against us in daily life, we are seldom, if ever, oblivious to the possibility that they may repeat the transgression. This is true regardless of the seriousness of the offense. If the offense is repeated, our reaction is likely to be more punitive on the second occasion. At the very least we will query whether the person took any steps to prevent a reoccurrence of what may have been represented as an accident or an unintentionally inflicted harm. It would be a strange legal punishment that carried no appeal, implicit or explicit, to the offender to desist. The fact that courts do not always or often explicitly enjoin the offender to abjure from further offending does not mean that the sentences they impose are uninterested in communicating such a message.

24. For example, Duff (2001, p. 120).

25. A number of reports are aspirational in tone with respect to engaging the public. For example, in its consultation document relating to proposed sentencing reforms, the New Zealand Law Commission (2006) noted that its recommendations were designed to "allow community perspectives to be brought to bear on the development of sentencing policy," but without specifying exactly how or why this constituted a salutary development.

26. The Sentencing Advisory Panel was, until 2010, one of two statutory guidelines authorities in this jurisdiction. There is now a single body, the Sentencing Council for England and Wales.

27. See, e.g., Roberts et al. (2008), as well as other public opinion research available on the Sentencing Council website (see www.sentencing-guidelines.gov.uk).

28. For example, the Sentencing Advisory Council in Victoria reserves two places for individuals with experience with community issues (see http://www.sentencingcouncil.vic.gov.au). The Sentencing Advisory Panel in England and Wales also had three lay members.

29. A point made by Bentham (1843).

30. For recent reviews of this literature, see Bottoms and von Hirsch (2010).

31. See Lovegrove (1998) for a proposal regarding the use of a policy and research group attached to the Court of Appeals for the purposes of community consultation and education.

REFERENCES

Ashworth, A. 1987. "Criminal Justice, Rights and Sentencing: A Review of Sentencing Policy and Problems." In *Sentencing in Australia—Issues, Policy and Reform*, ed. I. Potas. AIC Seminar Proceedings no. 13. Canberra: Australian Institute of Criminology.

———. 2008. "English Sentencing Guidelines in Their Public and Political Context." In *Penal Populism, Sentencing Councils and Sentencing Policy*, ed. A. Freiberg and K. Gelb. Cullompton, Devon, UK: Willan.

Ashworth, A., and M. Hough. 1996. "Sentencing and the Climate for Public Opinion." *Criminal Law Review* 1996:776–87.

Auld, L. 2001. *Review of the Criminal Courts of England and Wales*. London: HM Stationery Office.

Bagaric, M. 2001. *Punishment and Sentencing: A Rational Approach*. Sydney: Cavendish.

Bagaric, M., and R. Edney. 2004. "The Sentencing Advisory Commission and the Hope of Smarter Sentencing." *Current Issues in Criminal Justice* 16:125–39.

Bentham, J. 1843. *The Works of Jeremy Bentham*, vol. 1. Edinburgh: W. Tait.

Bottoms, A. 1995. "The Philosophy and Politics of Punishment and Sentencing." In *The Politics of Sentencing Reform*, ed. C. Clarkson and R. Morgan. Oxford: Clarendon Press.

Bottoms, A., and A. von Hirsch. 2010. "The Crime Preventive Impact of Penal Sanctions." In *The Oxford Handbook of Empirical Legal Research*, ed. Peter Cane and Herbert Kritzer. Oxford: Oxford University Press.

British Crime Survey. 2009. Data tables available from the author.

Butler, A., and K. McFarlane. 2009. *Public Confidence in the NSW Criminal Justice System*. http://www.lawlink.nsw.gov.au/lawlink/scouncil/ll_scouncil.nsf/vwFiles/monograph_2.pdf/$file/monograph_2.pdf.

Casey, S., and P. Mohr. 2005. "Law-and-Order Politics, Public Opinion Polls and the Media." *Psychiatry, Psychology and Law* 12:141–51.

de Keijser, J. W., P. J. van Koppen, and H. Elffers. 2007. "Bridging the Gap between Judges and the Public? A Multi-method Study." *Journal of Experimental Criminology* 3(2): 131–61.

Denno, D. 2000. "The Perils of Public Opinion." *Hofstra Law Review* 28:741–66.

Department of Justice Canada. 2010a. "Government Introduces Bill to Ensure Serious Time for Serious Crime." Press release, April 20, 2010.

———. 2010b. "Government Introduces Legislation to End House Arrest." Press release, April 22, 2010.

Doob, A., and J. V. Roberts. 1984. "Social Psychology, Social Attitudes and Attitudes toward Sentencing." *Canadian Journal of Behavioral Science* 16:269–80.

Duff, R. A. 2001. *Punishment, Communication, and Community*. Oxford: Oxford University Press.

Durham, A., III. 1985. "Weighting Punishments: a Commentary on Nevares-Muniz." *Journal of Criminal Law and Criminology* 76:201–7.

Ewing, A. C. 1929. *The Morality of Punishment*. London: K. Paul Trench.

Fletcher, G. 1982. "The Recidivist Premium." *Criminal Justice Ethics* 1:54–59.

Gardner, J. 1998. "Crime: In Proportion and In Perspective." In *Fundamentals of Sentencing Theory*, ed. A. Ashworth and M. Wasik. Oxford: Clarendon Press.

Garland, D. 1991. "Sociological Perspectives on Punishment." In *Crime and Justice. A Review of Research*, vol. 36, ed. Michael Tonry. Chicago: University of Chicago Press.

Golash, D., and J. Lynch. 1995. "Public Opinion, Crime Seriousness, and Sentencing Policy." *American Journal of Criminal Law* 22:703–32.

Green, D. 2006. "Public Opinion versus Public Judgment about Crime: Correcting the Comedy of Errors." *British Journal of Criminology* 46:131–54.

Gwin, J. 2010. "Juror Sentiment on Just Punishment: Do the Federal Sentencing Guidelines Reflect Community Values?" *Harvard Law and Policy Review* 4:173–200.

Harrel, W. 1981. "The Effects of Alcohol Use and Offender Remorsefulness on Sentencing Decisions." *Journal of Applied Social Psychology* 11:83–91.

Home Office. 2001. *Making Punishments Work. Report of the Sentencing Framework of England and Wales*. London: Home Office.

Hough, M. 2006. "People Talking about Punishment." *Howard Journal of Criminal Justice* 35:191–214.

Hough, M., and J. V. Roberts. 1998. *Attitudes to Punishment: Findings from the British Crime Survey*. Home Office Research Study no. 179. London: Home Office.

Hutton, N. 2008. "Institutional Mechanisms for Incorporating the Public." In *Penal Populism, Sentencing Councils and Sentencing Policy*, ed. A. Freiberg and K. Gelb. Cullompton, Devon, UK: Willan.

Johnson, B., and C. Huff. 1987. "Public Opinion and Criminal Justice Policy Formulation." *Criminal Justice Policy Review* 2:118–32.

Justice 1 Committee. 2002. *Public Attitudes towards Sentencing and Alternatives to Imprisonment.* http://www.scottish.parliament.uk/business/committees/historic/justice1/reports-02/j1r02-pats-01.htm.

Kleinke, C., R. Wallis, and K. Stalder. 1992. "Evaluations of a Rapist as a Function of Expressed Intent and Remorse." *Journal of Social Psychology* 132:525–37.

Knight, D. 1965. "Punishment Selection as a Function of Biographical Information." *Journal of Criminal Law, Criminology, and Police Science* 56:325–57.

Kolber, A. 2009. "How to Improve Empirical Desert." *Brooklyn Law Review* 75:429–57.

Kury, H., J. Oberfell-Fuchs, and U. Smartt. 2002. "The Evolution of Public Attitudes to Punishment in Western and Eastern Europe." In *Changing Attitudes to Punishment,* ed. J. Roberts and M. Hough. Cullompton, Devon, UK: Willan.

Law Gazette. 1995. "Howard on Sentencing Reforms." June 14.

Lee, Y. 2009. "Recidivism as Omission: A Relational Account." *Texas Law Review* 87:571–622.

————. 2010. "Repeat Offenders and the Question of Desert." In *The Role of Previous Convictions at Sentencing: Theoretical and Applied Perspectives,* ed. J. V. Roberts and A. von Hirsch. Oxford: Hart.

Lovegrove, A. 1998. "Judicial Sentencing Policy, Criminological Expertise and Public Opinion." *Australian and New Zealand Journal of Criminology* 31:287–313.

————. 2007. "Public Opinion, Sentencing and Lenience: An Empirical Study Involving Judges Consulting the Community." *Criminal Law Review* 2007:769–81.

Manson, A. 2011. "The Search for Principles of Mitigation and Aggravation: Integrating Systemic and Cultural Demands.: Unpublished manuscript, Queen's University, Kingston, Ontario, Canada.

Millie, A., J. Jacobson, and M. Hough. 2005. "Understanding the Growth in the Prison Population in England and Wales." In *The Persistent Prison,* ed. C. Emsley. London: Francis Boutle.

Morgan, R. 2002. "Privileging Public Attitudes to Sentencing?" In *Changing Attitudes to Punishment,* ed. J. V. Roberts and M. Hough. Cullompton, Devon, UK: Willan.

MORI. 2004. *Confidence in the Criminal Justice System.* Data tables on file with the author.

New Zealand Law Commission. 2006. *Reforms to the Sentencing and Parole Structure.* Wellington: New Zealand Law Commission.

Parker, H. 1970. "Juvenile Court Actions and Public Response." In *Becoming Delinquent: Young Offenders and the Correctional Process,* ed. P. Garabedian and D. Gibbons. Chicago: Aldine.

Parmentier, S., G. Vervaeke, R. Doutrelepont, and G. Kellens. 2004. *Public Opinion and the Administration of Justice: Popular Perceptions and Their Implications for Policy Making in Western Countries.* Brussels: Politeia.

Pound, R. 1907. "The Need for a Sociological Jurisprudence." *Green Bag* 19:607–15.

Pratt, J. 2007. *Penal Populism.* London: Taylor and Francis.

Riley, P., and V. Rose. 1980. "Public vs. Elite Opinion on Correctional Reform: Implications for Social Policy." *Journal of Criminal Justice* 8:345–56.

Roberts, J. V. 2002. "Public Opinion and Sentencing Policy." In *Reform and Punishment: the Future of Sentencing,* ed. S. Rex and M. Tonry. Cullompton, Devon, UK: Willan.

————. 2003. "Public Opinion and Mandatory Sentences of Imprisonment: A Review of International Findings." *Criminal Justice and Behavior* 20:1–26.

————. 2004. "Public Opinion and the Evolution of Juvenile Justice Policy in Western Nations." In *Crime and Justice: A Review of Research,* vol. 31, *Youth Crime and Youth Justice: Comparative and Cross-National Perspectives,* ed. M. Tonry and A. Doob. Chicago: University of Chicago Press.

————. 2008. *Punishing Persistent Offenders.* Oxford: Oxford University Press.

————. 2009. "Listening to the Crime Victim: Evaluating Victim Input at Sentencing and Parole." In *Crime and Justice: A Review of Research,* vol. 38, ed. Michael Tonry. Chicago: University of Chicago Press.

Roberts, J. V., N. Crutcher, and P. Verbrugge. 2007. "Public Attitudes to Sentencing in Canada: Exploring Recent Findings." *Canadian Journal of Criminology and Criminal Justice* 49:75–107.

Roberts, J. V., and M. Hough. 2005a. "Sentencing Young Offenders: Public Opinion in England and Wales." *Criminal Justice* 5:211–32.

———. 2005b. *Understanding Public Attitudes to Criminal Justice*. Maidenhead, Berkshire, UK: Open University Press.

Roberts, J. V., M. Hough, J. Jacobson, A. Bredee, and N. Moon. 2008. "Public Attitudes to Sentencing Offenders Convicted of Offences Involving Death by Driving." *Criminal Law Review* 2008(July):525–40.

Roberts, J. V., M. Hough, J. Jacobson, and N. Moon. 2009. "Public Attitudes to Sentencing Purposes and Sentencing Factors: An Empirical Analysis." *Criminal Law Review* 2009(November):771–82.

Roberts, J. V., L. S. Stalans, D. Indermaur, and M. Hough. 2003. *Penal Populism and Public Opinion. Lessons from Five Countries*. Oxford: Oxford University Press.

Roberts, J. V., and A. von Hirsch, eds. 2010. *The Role of Previous Convictions at Sentencing: Applied and Theoretical Perspectives*. Oxford: Hart.

Roberts, L., and D. Indermaur. 2009. *What Australians Think about Crime and Justice: Results from the 2007 Survey of Social Attitudes*. Australian Institute of Criminology. http://www.aic.gov.au/publications/current%20series/rpp/100-120/rpp101.aspx.

Robinson, P. 2007. *How Psychology is Changing the Punishment Theory Debate*. Public Law and Legal Theory Research Paper Series no. 07-01. Philadelphia: University of Pennsylvania Law School.

———. 2008. *Distributive Principles of Criminal Law*. Oxford: Oxford University Press.

———. 2009. "Empirical Desert." In *Criminal Law Conversations*, ed. P. Robinson, S. Garvey, and K. Ferzan. Oxford: Oxford University Press.

Robinson, P., and J. Darley. 1995. *Justice, Liability, and Blame. Community Views and the Criminal Law*. Boulder, CO: Westview Press.

———. 2007. "Intuitions of Justice: Implications for Criminal Law and Justice Policy." *Southern California Law Review* 81:1–49.

Robinson, P., S. Garvey, and K. Ferzan, eds. 2009. *Criminal Law Conversations*. Oxford: Oxford University Press.

Robinson, D. T., L. Smith-Lovin, and O. Tsoudis. 1994. "Heinous Crime or Unfortunate Accident? The Effects of Remorse on Responses to Mock Criminal Confessions." *Social Forces* 73:175–90.

Rossi, P. and R. Berk. 1997. *Just Punishments. Federal Guidelines and Public Views Compared*. New York: Aldine de Gruyter.

Ryberg, J. 2011. "Punishment and Public Opinion." In *Punishment and Ethics: New Perspectives*, ed. J. Ryberg and C. Tamburrini. Basingstoke, Hampshire, UK: Palgrave MacMillan.

Schonteich, M. 1999. *Sentencing in South Africa. Public Perception and Judicial Practice*. Occasional Paper 43. Cape Town, South Africa: Institute for Security Studies.

Sharp, F., and M. Otto. 1909. "A Study of the Popular Attitude Toward Retributive Punishment." *International Journal of Ethics* 20:341–57.

Simons, K. 2000. "The Relevance of Community Values to Just Deserts: Criminal Law, Punishment Rationales, and Democracy." *Hoftsra Law Review* 28:635–67.

Slobogin, C. 1996. "Is Justice Just Us: Using Social Science to Inform Substantive Criminal Law." *Journal of Criminal Law and Criminology* 87:315–33.

Sourcebook of Criminal Justice Statistics. 2010. "Table 2.47. Attitudes toward severity of courts in own area, by demographic characteristics, United States, selected years 1985–2002." http://www.albany.edu/sourcebook/pdf/t247.pdf.

Taslitz, A. 2009. "Empirical Desert: The Yin and Tang of Criminal Justice." In *Criminal Law Conversations*, ed. P. Robinson, S. Garvey, and K. Ferzan. Oxford: Oxford University Press.

Tonry, M. 1995a. *Malign Neglect*. New York: Oxford University Press.

———. 1995b. *Sentencing Reform Across National Boundaries*. In *The Politics of Sentencing Reform*, ed. C. Clarkson and R. Morgan. Oxford: Clarendon Press.

———. 2003. *Confronting Crime. Crime Control Policy Under New Labour*. Cullompton, Devon, UK: Willan.

Tyler, T. 2006. *Why People Obey the Law*. Princeton, NJ: Princeton University Press.

von Hirsch, A. 1976. *Doing Justice: The Choice of Punishments*. Boston: Northeastern University Press.

———. 1993. *Censure and Sanctions*. Oxford: Clarendon Press.

———. 2010. "Proportionality and Progressive Loss of Mitigation: Further Reflections." In *The Role of Previous Convictions at Sentencing: Theoretical and Applied Perspectives*, ed. J. V. Roberts and A. von Hirsch. Oxford: Hart.

von Hirsch, A., and A. Ashworth. 2005. *Proportionate Sentencing*. Oxford: Oxford University Press.

von Hirsch, A., and N. Jareborg. 1991. "Gauging Criminal Harm: A Living-Standard Analysis." *Oxford Journal of Legal Studies* 11:1–38.

Winick, C. 1983. "Public Opinion and Crime." In *Encyclopedia of Crime and Justice*, vol. 4, ed. S. Kadish. New York: Macmillan.

7

A Political Theory of Imprisonment for Public Protection

PETER RAMSAY

In April 2005 the UK government introduced a new regime of indeterminate sentences called imprisonment for public protection (IPP). A prisoner subject to such a sentence will serve a minimum sentence after which he or she will remain in prison until the parole board is satisfied that continued imprisonment is no longer necessary in order to protect the public. By March 2011, there were more than 6,000 IPP prisoners, comprising more than 5 percent of the total prison population.[1] The rapid growth in the number of prisoners on indeterminate sentences has caused considerable controversy on both normative and practical grounds (Jacobson and Hough 2010). But as Andrew Ashworth (2004, p. 522) has observed, the underlying emphasis on public protection is the "essential core of modern public policy." This essay addresses the values and interests that IPP seeks to protect.

Criminal justice theorists have sought to explain why the policy of public protection has come to enjoy its preponderant influence in recent years. Influential sociological theories have explained the wider "return of the prison" in terms of the triumph of neoliberalism over the old welfare state. The rise of neoliberalism is said to have unleashed both increased crime and insecurity, and this process has led to a "preventive turn" in criminal justice policy (Crawford 2009) and the emergence of a *Culture of Control* (Garland 2001). In the postwelfarist political culture, the emphasis in the provision of social *security* has shifted away from providing benefits to those disadvantaged by the market system (including offenders) and towards *Punishing the Poor* instead (Wacquant 2009b).[2] To put it mildly, neither the civil rights nor the social rights of those convicted or suspected of criminal offenses are high on the criminal justice agenda. Rather, it is the rights and security of victims and potential victims that have been at the heart of penal policy.

In these circumstances it is perhaps unsurprising that the figure of Leviathan has reappeared in the discussion. The agenda of public protection, with its extensive deployment of the state's penal power in the name of the security of the potential victim and with minimal concern for the rights of those who threaten that security, seems to raise the themes of Thomas Hobbes's (1968) account of an absolutist sovereignty inaugurated by an insecure population. For Loic Wacquant (2009a) "the return of the prison is part of an exercise in statecraft, it is part of the building of a neoliberal Leviathan."[3] For David Garland, "Hobbes is the thinker whose vision seems most relevant in situations where 'law and order' is perceived to be breaking down" (McCormick and Garland 1998).

Here I want to describe a theoretical justification for IPP that is different from and arguably more politically influential at present than traditional utilitarian justifications for selective incapacitation.[4] This justification puts into doubt the apparently obvious connection between the current turn towards the preventive control of the dangerous and Hobbes's political theory. Though Wacquant (2009a) is right that contemporary penal policy is evidence of "a transformation of the state," we should not assume that the old models of authoritarianism account for that transformation. When we think about "neoliberalism" we should pay as much attention to the "neo" as we do to the "liberalism," because the justification for the policy of public protection that I identify here is at odds with key assumptions of the liberal tradition.

In the first part of the essay I argue that the IPP regime of preventive detention can be justified in the terms of two theories that derive from traditions that, in the minds of their protagonists at least, are alternatives to liberalism in general and to Hobbes in particular. The two theories that I argue can do the justificatory work for IPP are the Third Way theory of Anthony Giddens and the republican penal theory of John Braithwaite and Philip Pettit. Both have been influential over the period during which the preventive turn has occurred. The Third Way is derived, according to Giddens (1998), from a mutualist strand in social democracy, and has been highly influential on the political imagination of the governing party that introduced IPP. The republican theory has been developed from the writings of early modern authors, and its adherents present its understanding of power and freedom as a "rival" to that of liberalism (Braithwaite and Pettit 1990, p. 47; Pettit 1997; Skinner 1998). Republicanism has enjoyed a revival in academic political theory in recent years. While the connection between the Third Way and IPP can be made quite simply and uncontroversially, the interpretation of the republican theory will go against the grain of its authors' own express preferences and hopes for it.

Having established that these theories can provide a normative justification for IPP, in the second part of the essay I then argue that these justifications are expressions of a wider ideology that is indeed a necessary counterpart of neoliberal economic and social policy. But I suggest that this ideology nevertheless constructs the relation of security and freedom in a way that is both inconsistent with the foundations of liberal thought and denies to the state the political authority that characterized Hobbes's Leviathan.

I. THE PROBLEM WITH INDETERMINATE SENTENCES

Under the provisions of the Criminal Justice Act (CJA) 2003 (as amended by the Criminal Justice and Immigration Act 2008), any offender who has been convicted of one of a specified range of violent or sexual offenses *and* is judged to represent "a significant risk to members of the public of serious harm occasioned by the commission by him of further specified offenses" is liable to a life sentence, "imprisonment for public protection," or an "extended sentence," depending on the precise nature of the offense. Extended sentences add periods of release on license to the normal sentence and are subject to upper limits. I do not consider them further here.[5]

A life sentence or a sentence of imprisonment for public protection may be imposed where an offender who is adjudged to represent a significant risk of serious harm has been convicted of an offense that carries a maximum penalty of 10 years or more. Where the maximum is life and "the court considers that the seriousness of the offense, or the offense and one or more offenses associated with it, is such as to justify the imposition of a sentence of imprisonment for life," then a life sentence must be imposed.[6] Where the maximum is less than life or the court does not consider the offense serious enough to justify a life sentence, an IPP sentence may be imposed.[7] However, an IPP sentence may only be imposed if, at the time the offense was committed, the offender had previously been convicted of one of a specified range of serious offenses or the notional minimum term of the IPP sentence is two years.[8] The IPP sentence itself consists of a minimum term specified by the sentencing court after which the offender remains in custody until the parole board is "satisfied that it is no longer necessary for the protection of the public that the prisoner should be confined."

At the time of writing, the Coalition government has published a consultation paper suggesting that the minimum sentence necessary before an IPP sentence can be imposed should be raised from two to five years (Ministry of Justice, 2010). This would have the effect of limiting the use of the sentence to prisoners who have committed more serious offenses. If enacted, the reform will alleviate some of the practical problems posed by the growth in prison numbers, but the normative issues would remain.

These sentences increase the period of incarceration over the minimum that is determined by what is proportional to the seriousness of the offense, and they make release from custody, and the actual time served, dependent upon the parole board's judgment of the persistence of the risk that the defendant is thought to represent. These sentences are available for more than sixty offenses, and with regard to life sentences and IPP, Ashworth (2005, p. 212) observes that "the rights of the offender are . . . chiefly rights to regular review of the need for continued detention."

These sentences do not appear to be justified on retributive grounds since their indeterminate element is, by definition, in excess of what is required by offense seriousness. Moreover, the evidence for any deterrent effect they may have in reducing future offending is weak or nonexistent, while their incapacitating effect is notoriously subject to the low accuracy of risk assessments in relation to future offending (Ashworth 2004, p. 520). With no reliable evidence of reduced offending as a consequence of such measures and no retributive justification, these offenses appear to lack any ethical justification.[9] Worse still, not only do they lack justification, they suffer from the distinct normative objection that the problem of false positives creates a risk of serious injustice being done without any certainty of consequential benefits.

Looking at the problem in this way is to interpret the phrase "public protection" in a particular way, taking it to mean protection from an unjustified invasion of the public's interests in the future. However, this is only one sense of public protection. As Ashworth (2004, p. 519) observes, "there are at least two distinct senses of public protection, the objective and the subjective. Both are problematic, and the relationship between them is unclear." This is because public protection is understood to be a question of achieving "security," and security is a quality that, in theory at least, can be thought of objectively or subjectively. So far we have only considered its objective sense by asking if IPP can be justified in terms of the probability of future criminal acts. This objective sense of security is a question of the future relations between subjects. However, the relations between subjects necessarily include the subjects' perception of that "objective" probability—a subjective sense of security. The position is complicated by the fact that in practice these two analytically distinct senses of security are impossible to disentangle because the subjective sense of security is an essential mediation of objective or "intersubjective" security. A person's objective security is in part a function of their own actions, and these will be in part a function of their subjective security, or, as Ian Loader and Neil Walker (2006, p. 157) put it, "the socially inflected experience of feeling or not feeling secure is itself internal to and partially constitutive of what we mean by insecurity." If indeterminate sentences are hard to justify on grounds of objective security, might they be easier to justify on grounds of subjective security? As Ashworth (2004, p. 531) observes:

> One conception of public protection, we must recall, is a subjective feeling of security. The Government might argue that its aim is to create such feelings in members of the public. But is it justifiable to pursue policies aimed at fostering such feelings or aimed at increasing "public confidence" (a nebulous notion, at best), when it is known that such policies are unlikely to have a significant effect on objective risk or protection?

II. A RIGHT TO SECURITY?

The problem of false positives provides a starting point for searching out a justification for IPP in terms of protecting interests in the subjective sense of security. These sentences trade off the probability that someone will be unjustly treated by a sentence longer than is proportional to the offense they committed against the probability of the injustice of a future offense that might be avoided. But the trade-off is undertaken in conditions of considerable uncertainty and ignorance about the probabilities in any particular case.

Jean Floud and Warren Young (1981, p. 49) formulated this unreliable trading off as a question of "moral choice between . . . alternative risks: the risk to potential victims or the risk of unnecessarily detaining offenders judged to be dangerous?" Ashworth paraphrases Floud and Young's approach to that choice to the effect that a presumption of good intentions applies to persons in general, but once someone has "manifested, by committing a serious crime, the capacity to entertain and to implement harmful intentions, that presumption no longer applies" (Ashworth2005, p. 216). Ashworth argues that the approach of the CJA 2003 is broadly similar. The language of presumption is useful here because it reflects the process through which the offender subject to the indeterminate sentence must go.

For the offender to be released, the parole board's assessment of the offender must overturn the assessment of the trial judge, or earlier parole hearings, that the offender poses a "significant risk of serious harm." Although the courts have insisted that there is no legal burden on the prisoner to prove that he is safe to release, the House of Lords ruled that the "default position . . . is that the prisoner is to remain detained unless the Board are satisfied he can be safely released" (*James, Lee and Wells v. Secretary of State for Justice* [2010] 1 AC 553, Lord Brown at 605). The benefit of any doubt is to be enjoyed by the public who are to be protected (*Lichniak and Pyrah* [2003] 1 AC 903). In other words, they have recognized that there is an effective onus on the prisoner to give the parole board some evidence that enough has changed to permit it to reverse the earlier judgment regarding dangerousness. In *Wells v. Parole Board*, Lord Justice Laws ruled that the secretary of state was in breach of his public duty by unreasonably failing to provide courses through which IPP offenders could provide any evidence that would permit the parole board to displace earlier assessments—in other words, through which the prisoners could reassure the board (*Nicholas Wells v. Parole Board* [2007] EWHC 1835 QB). Such courses are an intrinsic aspect of the sentence, and if they were not made available to an IPP prisoner for a period of years after the expiry of the tariff, then, in the opinion of Lord Brown in *Secretary of State for Justice v. James*, the imprisonment would become arbitrary and therefore unlawful (*Secretary of State for Justice v. James* [2009] UKHL 22 per Lord Brown at 51).

What the parole board is looking for is evidence that will reassure it that whatever risk the offender was thought to pose when he was sentenced has now diminished sufficiently or disappeared, and this requires the prisoner to provide some evidence to reassure the board on this point. Looked at in this way, a justification for the entire process might be found if it could be argued that the dangerous offender is, in some way, under an obligation to reassure the state. Such an obligation might exist if it could be said that the offender has no right to represent a "significant risk of serious harm," which is to say, if it is a criminal wrong to be dangerous.

A broad legal basis for such a wrong was articulated by Lord Steyn in the House of Lords, when he observed that "the aim of the criminal law is . . . to permit everyone to go about their daily lives *without fear* of harm to person or property" (*Attorney-General's Reference (No. 3 of 1999)* [2001] 2 WLR 56 at 63F, emphasis added).[10] If Lord Steyn is right, then the control of fear of crime, even its suppression, is a legitimate aim of the criminal law. Sentencing might well seek to serve that aim. If the aim of the criminal law is to create a social environment free of the fear of crime, then to cause the fear of crime could plausibly count as a punishable wrong. The law can be said to protect an interest in the subjective feeling of security. Those who have been proven to have "manifested, by committing a serious crime, the capacity to entertain and to implement harmful intentions," and who are assessed as a significant risk of future offending, are likely to cause fear of crime to those who are aware of it, and, the argument runs, knowledge that such people are at liberty would undermine public confidence in the safety of the social environment generally. In such cases, it would therefore not be wrong to withdraw the presumption of good intentions. On the contrary, from this standpoint, that would be right, and the offenders concerned would be under an obligation to reassure the authorities that they are not a significant risk.

But is Lord Steyn correct? Can it be a criminal wrong to cause fear of crime? Should our legally protected interests extend to a "right to security"? A positive answer to that question is suggested by Anthony Giddens, the theorist who has had the most influence over New Labour policy.

III. THE THIRD WAY TO POSITIVE OBLIGATION

For Giddens (2002, p. 17), "freedom from the fear of crime is a major citizenship right." This proposition is derived from the central preoccupations of his Third Way theory.

Giddens argues that, in the contemporary world, "self-fulfillment, the fulfillment of potential" are more than just "therapy-talk, or the self-indulgence of the affluent." Rather, they represent "a sea change in people's attitudes and aspirations" that has arisen with the decline of old ideological and social solidarities, and he describes this change as a "new individualism" (Giddens. 1998, p. 37). In his earlier work, he gives an account of this "therapeutic individualism" and the individual subjects it imagines. A precondition of the realization or fulfillment of the self and its potential is a secure sense of a self to be realized and the self-esteem to pursue the project of self-realization. This in turn is a question of what he calls "ontological security" (Giddens 1991, p. 40). This is the basic trust in the predictability of the ordinary life around them, without which individuals would be beset with an enervating anxiety in which the elaboration of any "self-identity," let alone actually achieving authentic self-knowledge, would be impossible.

Fear of crime has the capacity to undermine this ontological security by exposing the vulnerability of the self to the potential danger represented by others. Fear of crime is corrosive of the conditions that permit the maintenance of a secure sense of the self whose fulfillment is the purpose of the political community. From this standpoint, therefore, freedom from the fear of crime becomes "a major citizenship right." As a right of citizenship, its violation is a wrong against the whole community, engaging the interests of the state and an appropriate matter for punishment (Ramsay 2006, p. 29).

In the Third Way, individual autonomy is a question of self-fulfillment, and this autonomy is intrinsically vulnerable to others. It is the protection of this "vulnerable autonomy" that is the core normative proposition of the Third Way. One key means of protecting it is by upholding a right to freedom from fear of crime. Such a right imposes a degree of positive obligation on all citizens, for to avoid causing fear of crime, it is necessary, at a minimum, to maintain an awareness of what will cause fear. In circumstances where the grounds for fearing a particular citizen are particularly strong because of that citizen's own actions, this obligation might require positive acts of reassurance on her part. The Third Way embraces such positive obligations because it is very much a theory of active citizenship.

As the discussion of ontological security and fear of crime suggests, a key political question for Giddens is the maintenance of "social cohesion" between the diversity of selves seeking their self-fulfillment. This social cohesion can only be achieved by recognizing that "all of us have to live in a more ... reflective manner," and that "we need more actively to accept responsibilities for the consequences of what we do and the lifestyle habits we adopt" (Giddens 1998, p. 37). "We have to find a new balance between individual and collective responsibilities today," he writes (1998, p. 37). He presents the new balance in a slogan: "One might suggest as a prime motto for the new politics, no rights without responsibilities" (Giddens 1998, p. 65). In other words, rights can no longer be thought of as unconditional. One result is that "unemployment benefits, for example, should carry the obligation to look actively for work" (Giddens 1998, p. 65). *The Third Way's* discussion of rights is focused on the welfare rights of the old "social citizenship," but he is explicit that "the theorem that responsibilities go along with rights . . . should be seen as a general principle of citizenship, by no means confined to the welfare area" (Giddens 1998, p. 8). Moreover, the scope of the "welfare area," as it is conceived of by the Third Way, is massively expanded on that which formed the original concerns of the welfare state.

> Welfare is not in essence an economic concept, but a psychic one, concerning as it does well-being. . . . Not only is welfare generated by many contexts and influences other than the welfare state, but welfare institutions must be concerned with fostering psychological as well as economic benefits (Giddens 1998, p. 117).

Plainly, ontological security is a key element of those "psychological benefits." In its 1998 green paper *New Ambitions for Our Country: A New Contract for Welfare* (Department of Social Security 1998), New Labour expressed this Third Way thinking in the form of a contract between the individual and the state that specified a number of duties on each side. The list concluded with one duty that applies to both government and individual citizen, and which implies the huge conceptual expansion of welfare in government thinking:

> Duty of us all: To help all individuals and families to realise their full potential and live a dignified life, by promoting economic independence through work, by relieving poverty where it cannot be prevented and by building a strong and cohesive society where rights are matched by responsibilities (Department of Social Security 1998).

New Labour believed itself to be committed to building a "cohesive society" in which we all bear responsibilities to each other's psychic welfare, responsibilities that are the basis and condition of our enjoyment of rights. A key element of this psychic welfare is the protection of the vulnerable autonomy of the self. An important means of protecting vulnerable autonomy is by the enforcement of a responsibility not to cause fear of crime.

From this point of view, there is no right to be perceived as dangerous. On the contrary, in so far as it results in the fear of crime, to be perceived as dangerous is a wrong against others' citizenship rights, and this justifies control or punishment. This is a wrong against security interests that is independent of the criminal violation of someone else's protected interest that results in the minimum part of an IPP sentence. To avoid liability to punishment for this independent wrong the citizen must maintain an awareness of others' security needs, and reassure them where her own actions might give other citizens cause to fear. In this way, the law's subjects will fulfill their responsibility to ensure social cohesion and enjoy the rights of citizenship. The sentence for public protection persists as long as an offender fails to meet their obligation to reassure.

From the Third Way standpoint, instrumental effectiveness is not necessarily the issue, providing that government is seen to be upholding the rights of vulnerable citizens.

If the aim of the "positive welfare society" is "psychic welfare," then the subjective concept of security is the aim of criminal justice policy. In so far as improved objective security is a means to that end, it should be improved, but objective security is not the primary end. The pursuit of subjective security is justified in a language of rights, the rights of the vulnerable citizen. In so far as the government is able to claim that it is doing the right thing by offenders and the public, this normative structure tends to insulate these public protection measures from a critique based on the absence of evidence for their objective effects on ordinary offending.

A further interesting aspect of this penal theory is that it goes some way to achieve a union of forward and backward-looking rationales for punishment. The indeterminate part of a sentence achieves the incapacitation of many prisoners who would go on to commit further offenses, but also punishes all IPP prisoners for the continuing wrong of failing to reassure other citizens' of their good intentions. This wrong is neither a one-off event, nor does it lie in the future, but is, on the contrary, committed for as long as the prisoner continues to remain "dangerous." This apparent unity of rationales that are often thought to be incommensurate is interesting because it is claimed by a more established theory of punishment and on similar grounds.

IV. REPUBLICANISM AND VULNERABLE CITIZENSHIP

The theme of reassurance raised here is foreshadowed in normative penal theory in John Braithwaite and Phillip Pettit's (1990) republican theory of punishment. Braithwaite and Pettit nevertheless maintain an explicit commitment to parsimony in sentencing and are cautious about incapacitation. They claim that their theory creates an aim for punishment that is "satiable." But, as we shall see, to achieve this it seems to require that a particular empirical assumption holds true. Without this assumption, their theory seems potentially to justify IPP.

The aim of punishment in the republican theory is maximizing republican freedom, or to put the point more precisely, "minimizing the invasion of dominion" (Braithwaite and Pettit 1990, p. 69). For Braithwaite and Pettit, dominion is a *status* in which a citizen:

- enjoys "a prospect of [negative] liberty" that is equal with all others; and
- this status is reflexive (known to the citizen and all other citizens); and
- that it is the maximum prospect of liberty consistent with its equal distribution (1990, pp. 64–65).

They argue that their theory finds in dominion a category that unites both the backward-looking concern to respond to wrongs to victims and the forward-looking concern with maximizing a good, which is to say dominion itself. Although they oppose the retributivist theory that the *measure* of punishment should be determined by what an offender deserves, the republican theory is not purely consequential. A key aspect of the promotion of dominion through punishment is reprobation of the invasion of dominion (Braithwaite and Pettit 1990, pp. 88–90), with the consequence that a precondition of punishment in the republican theory is that the offender has done the wrong of invading another's dominion.

The reflexivity of dominion status in the second condition (the requirement that, to enjoy the status, the citizen must know that she enjoys dominion, that others know this, that she knows that they know this, and so on) makes dominion in part a question of subjective perceptions. For Braithwaite and Pettit, to cause a person to feel vulnerable to crime is to invade their dominion and is therefore a wrong. When comparing minimizing harm with maximizing dominion as aims of criminal justice, they comment: "If it be said that some conceptions of harm cast the causing of a feeling of vulnerability as harmful, we would reply that any such conception is congenial for it represents harm as something close to the invasion of dominion" (Braithwaite and Pettit 1990, p. 70, n. 7). They are clear that "dominion, unlike the liberal idea of freedom, can be reduced through psychological subversion" (Braithwaite and Pettit 1990, p. 77). The aims of punishment must therefore include both ensuring that the dominion of citizens is recognized and that actual citizens are reassured that they do in fact enjoy their dominion (Pettit and Braithwaite 1993, pp. 231–32).

With respect to those already victimized by offenders, Braithwaite and Pettit (1990, p. 77) comment, "someone who has been the victim of a crime almost certainly requires reassurance about her liberty-prospects, if she is to regain her old level of dominion." Without that reassurance, the requirement of equality of liberty prospects that is essential to the status of dominion would not be met. Moreover their theory emphasizes the threat to the liberty of every citizen from every crime: "Dominion is a good whose enjoyment is highly sensitive to evidence of its enjoyment by others" (Pettit and Braithwaite 1993, p. 230).

Since the aim of republican punishment is to minimize the invasion of dominion, the extent of the invasion of dominion caused by fear must be set against the invasion of dominion caused by the incarceration of those who do not reassure. In republican calculations concerning punishment, not only must the gain in ordinary citizens' dominion exceed that of the loss to the prisoner, but it must do so once it has been discounted by the uncertainty of that gain when set against the certainty of the prisoner's loss. In so far as the putative gains to dominion from IPP are the result of the actual prevention of future criminal offenses against other citizens' objective security interests, indefinite preventive detention will be difficult to justify owing to the high degree of uncertainty attaching to such gains. But if reassurance against fear and anxiety is a means to maximizing dominion, as their theory appears to allow, the gain to ordinary citizens from incarcerating the dangerous seems less uncertain. What could be more reassuring than the knowledge that any offender remains in prison for as long as he is assessed as dangerous? Braithwaite and Pettit doubt the value of imprisonment generally and cite the evidence that prison is criminogenic to dispute the point about reassurance (Pettit and Braithwaite 1993, pp. 234–35). However, the rigors of the IPP system would seem to provide an answer to this: the still dangerous prisoner does not get out. Even if this point were to be conceded, the republican might yet respond that the republican theory nevertheless takes the dominion of the offender seriously, and that the gains in reassurance of the ordinary citizen are rather too "nebulous" when set against the more definite losses to the offender's dominion.

How then might this calculation of gains and losses to dominion that is entailed by the reassuring imprisonment of the dangerous offender be made? The extent to which dominion would be diminished by fear of dangerous offenders who have been released, and anxiety at the knowledge that dangerous offenders are being released, will necessarily be a function of the degree of risk aversion that can be attributed to the citizenry. The dominion of a citizenry that is highly risk averse will be diminished more than a citizenry that is willing to bear more risk. IPP sentences might conceivably so enhance the dominion of millions of highly risk-averse citizens as to outweigh the cost in the loss of dominion endured by a few thousand prisoners. If this is right, then the republican theory may provide a target for punishment that is harder to satiate than Braithwaite and Pettit imagine.

Pettit and Braithwaite (1993, p. 226) deny that their theory permits such a "license to optimise" sentencing policy. But, as Andrew Ashworth and Andrew von Hirsch (1993) have pointed out, it is not clear how else invasions of dominion are to be minimized, and as a result, this reassurance element of republican penal theory does not provide adequate upper limits on penal severity because reassurance is as much a question of what makes citizens feel safer as it is of what makes them in fact safer. Braithwaite and Pettit sought to counter this by arguing that all citizens would be able to imagine themselves as potential offenders as much as potential victims, and the prospect of unlimited punishment would therefore reduce their dominion by leaving citizens in "a condition of utter vulnerability" to state coercion (Pettit and Braithwaite 1993, pp. 235–36). Leaving aside the empirical plausibility of their response in its own terms, it seems to discount the invasion of dominion that they themselves have asserted will result when feelings of vulnerability to crime are caused. Moreover, it overlooks the element of positive obligation that arises from the requirement to minimize such an invasion. Once these implications of their concept of dominion are recognized, it turns out that there is an upper limit to penal severity, at least in theory: it is the incapacitation necessary to render the offender no longer a threat. However, this "limit" is one that, according to Braithwaite and Pettit's own account, gives to the state a power that in turn menaces the dominion of citizens.

It seems that ensuring an equal dominion that is conceived of as being vulnerable to fear will tend toward a regime of preventive detention that is itself a threat to dominion, unless we can assume that the risk aversion of the population is sufficiently low that the cost to the dominion of offenders outweighs the losses due to the vulnerability of other citizens. Braithwaite and Pettit's own account of republican theory seems to rest on this empirical assumption concerning the citizenry's risk aversion. Certainly a republican might respond that their outlook's concern for dominion requires that less intrusive means are used "until the evidence is clear that more intrusive practices are required to increase dominion" (Braithwaite and Pettit 1990, p. 80). The question then becomes one of citizens' actual empirical risk aversion, and the extent to which the dangers posed by released criminals actually impinge on other citizens' dominion. This is a complex and reflexive issue since citizens' risk aversion is not a variable that is independent of political and social theories, which themselves have an influence on political actors, and therefore on the broad political culture in which citizens make judgments about risk and how to evaluate them.

Republicans who wish to avoid the potential support that the theory might give to indeterminate sentencing will have to do something. It might be possible to substantiate the empirical assumption and argue that citizens' are not in fact so risk averse that their dominion is reduced by fear and anxiety to anything like the extent necessary to justify IPP. Alternatively, perhaps it should be admitted that the republican theory of punishment is an ideal theory that is only coherent in a society that is consistently republican in all its practices,[11] and among the necessary civic virtues required of a republic's citizens is the courage of conviction in the force of republican norms.[12]

It is not clear just how essential the citizen's interest in subjective security is to republican freedom, but the connection may run deeper than Braithwaite and Pettit's penal theory. According to Pettit, for Niccolo Machiavelli the whole point of living in a "free state" was that it ensured to the citizen "the power of enjoying freely his possessions without any anxiety, of feeling no fear for the honor of his women and his children, of not being afraid for himself" (Pettit 1997, p. 28). This may be the underlying reason why the contemporary republican theory of punishment offers a justification of IPP, notwithstanding the subjective inclinations of that theory's authors.

V. IS IPP WHAT DANGEROUS OFFENDERS DESERVE?

The possibility that IPP is justified by republican or Third Way theory rests on the proposition that to be dangerous and cause fear in others is a public wrong and, therefore, *some* punishment is deserved. What is less clear is that the IPP sentence can be said to be proportional to the wrong, so that the IPP sentence is *no more than* the punishment that is deserved by a dangerous offender. Of course, for Braithwaite and Pettit, strict proportionality is not the issue, but it is worth clarifying what is at stake once IPP is thought of as, in some sense, deserved punishment.

It might be argued that for as long as the prisoner remains dangerous, his incarceration is exactly proportionate in amount and that, in so far as the wrong done is the causing of insecurity, the indeterminate character of the sentence is peculiarly appropriate as a type of punishment.[13] On the other hand, it might be argued that once he is incarcerated, the offender is no longer committing the wrong of being dangerous, as he is no longer in fact dangerous (at least not to people outside the prison). In response, it could be suggested that the sentence is nevertheless proportionate to the wrong of being dangerous that the prisoner *would* commit were he not incarcerated. This seems to be an incarceration that is proportionate to preventive necessity rather than penal desert. If the punishment that is deserved is whatever is proportionate to preventive necessity, then, paradoxically, what is deserved appears to be forfeiture of the right to proportionate punishment in the retributive sense.[14]

To deserve to forfeit the right to retributive punishment is to be treated as something other than an equal citizen or legal subject. It is to be treated as something closer to an outlaw or an enemy. By definition, enemies (at least until they have been in some way neutralized) deserve only to be regarded as threats, not as persons. Understood in this way, IPP seems broadly to share some of the characteristics of the concept of "enemy criminal law" proposed by Gunther Jakobs.[15] The enemy criminal law's subjection of the person of the offender to the calculus of necessity is also characteristic of emergency rule. I return to Jakobs and to emergency below. But to get a picture of the full significance of this forfeiture of the rights enjoyed by those subject to "citizen criminal law," I need first to take a wider view of the theories we have just considered that seem to justify this forfeiture.

VI. THE IDEOLOGY OF VULNERABLE AUTONOMY

The apparent openness of the republican theory to IPP, notwithstanding its authors' express commitment to parsimony, derives from their concept of dominion as a quality of intersubjective relations. In republican dominion, like the vulnerable autonomy at the heart of Giddens's theory, the individual's capacity for self-determination is dependent on others' attitudes and dispositions as well as on their actions. This places positive duties on all to avoid causing fear and anxiety to others, and these duties arguably provide a justification for the right to security protected by the IPP regime.

It may be that New Labour's penal policies enjoyed a remarkable legitimacy in practical politics because the vulnerable autonomy at the core of the Third Way is a concept that enjoys influence well beyond its position within the sociological theory of Anthony Giddens. I have argued elsewhere that this basic concept can be found in both the influential strand of "liberal communitarianism" represented by Amitai Etzioni and Michael Sandel (Ramsay 2009). Briefly Etzioni (1996, p. 21) argues that the autonomy of people who do not reflect upon and consciously assimilate the moral requirements of the community within which they live is vulnerable to social forces beyond their control or understanding, forces that have the capacity to determine their decisions. Etzioni explicitly derives his argument on the point from Sandel's notion of the "encumbered self." For Sandel (1982, p. 165), the self that is unencumbered with such moral bonds is vulnerable to the "heteronomous determination" of "purely preferential choice."

In the present context, it is probably more significant that the basic proposition of the vulnerability of autonomy can also be found at the heart of the social theory of F. A. Hayek, the inspiration of neoliberalism (Ramsay 2009). Hayek's theory was premised not on an absolute promotion of the free market as the producer of optimum or necessarily adequate welfare outcomes, but on its defense as a system that was better than the alternatives to it. In this relativist defense of the market, written in the wake of the Great Depression, Hayek (1944, p. 151) explicitly recognized the vulnerability of the individual to the unfathomable and unpredictable actions of the marketplace. While he was not much directly concerned with criminal justice, he did draw from his observation of this basic vulnerability the proposition that traditional moral and religious beliefs and institutions were essential to the maintenance of social order (Hayek 1979, p. 167), describing himself as an Old Whig and invoking Edmund Burke (Hayek 1960, p. 353).

The significance of this aspect of Hayek's theory is that while the broad spirit of Hayek's economic policy proposals appears to have triumphed across the mainstream political perspective, and to be entirely accepted by mainstream parties of the old left, traditional values have never regained a hold on social policy. Margaret Thatcher's "Victorian values" resulted in no practical reforms and John Major's "Back to basics" collapsed into farce within days. Traditional morality has not returned as a justification for policy since.[16] The twentieth-century faith in the state as a means of organizing production, distributing wealth, and solving social problems may have declined, but there has been no revival of the Protestant ethic, "family values," or even the nationalism that once provided alternative sources of moral order.[17] It is this experience of a market system shorn of its traditional sources of moral order that provides the context for Giddens's new individualism of the diverse subjects of the consumer society, who, from the Third Way standpoint, are free of the shackles of traditional solidarities to pursue their self-fulfillment, but free too of the reassurances that came with those solidarities.

In the absence of those traditional shackles, insecurity has been directly mobilized as a source for new concepts of right and wrong, concepts derived from the risks we are supposed to represent towards each other. In the absence of competitors, this new source of duties, and the right to security that comes with them, has influenced the entire political mainstream. It is doubtful that Hayek himself would have approved of the sort of positive obligations required by the Third Way. Nevertheless, Giddens is grappling with the same problem of moral order posed by unmediated market relations that Hayek recognized. But Giddens, like the contemporary politicians he has influenced, must seek solutions in the absence of the traditional sources that Hayek believed were essential.

Giddens calls the problem one of ensuring "social cohesion," and solves it by posing mutual responsibility for each other's psychic welfare. As he has put it: "We can't return to nature or tradition, but, individually and as a collective humanity, we can seek to remoralize our lives in the context of a positive acceptance of manufactured uncertainty" (Giddens 1994, p. 227). By "manufactured uncertainty," he means the uncertainties that are the reflexive product of modern social and technological development. While environmental uncertainties are uppermost in Giddens's mind, the potential for fear and anxiety about others' intentions, which he argues has arisen with contemporary society's loss of traditional certainties and solidarities, fits the bill just as well. By adjusting our rights and duties, so as to accept this "manufactured uncertainty," it is thought that the lack of social cohesion engendered by the atomistic neoliberal economic and social order might be ameliorated.[18]

The IPP regime is therefore backed by theories in which punishment for public protection is nevertheless deserved, because those punished have failed to reassure in a way that the positive acceptance of the uncertainty they represent requires of them. These theories of vulnerable autonomy are the ideology of the neoliberal order: the set of beliefs that make sense of that order, and without which policy makers and officials would be unable to motivate or justify the decisions and actions that are conducive to the continued survival of that order. The IPP regime in turn is one of the measures that institutionalizes the belief system of that order.

Understanding the influence of this ideology of vulnerable autonomy is essential to understanding penal phenomena such as IPP. Firstly, it can help to qualify significantly the explanatory account of the origins of the new politics of punishment in the rise of a neoliberal policy consensus. Secondly, it allows us to be more specific about the relationship of neoliberalism to earlier forms of liberalism and, in particular, its relationship to the foundations of liberalism in the oft-invoked theory of Thomas Hobbes. Thirdly, it shines some light on the fatal flaw at the heart of this penal regime. To each of these we now turn.

VII. IDEOLOGY AND POLITICAL CHOICE

David Garland's *Culture of Control* has been perhaps the most influential account of the rise of the new penality. It has been criticized, however, for tending to present the new order as a sociologically determined dystopia (Zedner 2002). One of the inevitable dangers of explaining changes to policy frameworks through the influence of structural socioeconomic changes is that it tends to overlook or downplay the fact that, as Tonry (2004, p. 70) points out, New Labour's response to recent social and economic change remains a question of political choice. There is more than one way to respond to structural change, and Tonry concludes that on the big criminal justice issues, "politics is the order of the day" (Tonry 2004, p. 146). He suggests that New Labour's preference for tough stances in penal policy was intended to "stalemate" the Tories on the issue, and Labour's commitment to extensive police powers and indeterminate sentencing was an endeavor to avoid the political blame should an outrage like the Bulger killing or the Dunblane massacre occur (Tonry 2003, p. 22).[19] These seem very plausible interpretations of what was going on in the defensive, tactical minds of contemporary politicians. Yet this only raises further questions: Why is it on the crime issue that the Tories needed to be stalemated? Why has it been public protection measures that achieved that stalemate? Why did the government feel the need to avoid the blame for failing to prevent rare and unpredictable outrages perpetrated by individuals at the margins of society?

What is needed is a mediating link between the broad sociological changes and the narrow day-to-day imperatives of political choice. Though virtually all commentators recognize the centrality of popular fears and anxieties, in tending to read people's fears and insecurities directly from changed material conditions, they also tend to neglect the mediating structure of beliefs about rights and wrongs. As Richard Garside observes of Tony Blair's casual equation of wrongful acquittals and wrongful convictions being comparable as miscarriages of justice: "That such an attempt to subvert the liberal notion of the miscarriage of justice has genuine purchase, rather than merely being dismissed as spurious and dangerous, is a sign of the changed ideological climate in which debates about law and order are now taking place" (Garside 2006). It is in a *changed ideological climate* that New Labour's public protection measures may find their justification and their political effectiveness: these measures invoke a shared ideology that tends to neutralize political opponents.

But in the piece cited, Garside, too, stops just short of identifying this new climate's ideological content. My argument here is that the content of the changed climate is the protection of vulnerable autonomy by the acceptance of the manufactured uncertainty that is others' subjective insecurities. This vulnerable autonomy can be found in theories like the Third Way, communitarianism, and as vulnerable citizenship, even in contemporary republicanism.

It is striking that theories that are able to have this influence in an environment of neoliberal economic policy are not themselves classically liberal theories. Commentators have been divided on how these theories should be characterized. Giddens claims the mantle of a mutualist social democracy for his Third Way, contemporary republicans draw attention to their differences with liberalism, while communitarians often contrast their theories to atomistic liberalism. Nevertheless, these theories remain normatively grounded in some conception of individual autonomy, allowing Nikolas Rose (1999) to describe communitarianism and the Third Way as "advanced liberal." On the other hand, this idea of autonomy is one saturated with a positive duty of awareness of others' insecurities, positive duties that are logically prior to individuals' rights. It is this logical priority of duties to others that allows these theories to justify measures such as IPP, measures that penal theorists working in the liberal tradition find difficult or impossible to justify. Others have seen this emphasis on prior duties as indicative of these theories' "post-liberalism" (Reece 2003). Either way, the ideology of vulnerable autonomy that seeks to secure social order in neoliberal societies is not itself straightforwardly liberal.

The "neo" in neoliberalism indicates, at the very least, that the normative aspects of this policy framework draw heavily on non-liberal and anti-liberal traditions. Explanatory theories that stop at the pejorative category "neoliberalism" may tend to give a distorted image of the problem. Moreover, in one fundamental sense the neoliberal penal regime is not consistent with the liberal political tradition at all.

VIII. BEYOND THE NORMALIZATION OF EMERGENCY

Gunther Jakobs has argued that some of contemporary criminal law should be characterized as "enemy criminal law," a legal form that he contrasts with "citizen criminal law" (Gomez-Jara Diez 2008; Dubber 2010; Ohana 2010). In the "enemy criminal law," punishment precedes actual harms, is disproportionate to any wrong actually done, and the defendant's procedural rights are suppressed. The reverse is true in "citizen criminal law." The reason is that those who appear to be dispositionally hostile to the norms of the criminal law are to be treated as a threat to be controlled rather than as a citizen whose basic loyalty to the law's norms can be presumed, and who must be punished proportionately so as to communicate the moral wrong they have done. Jakobs explicitly justifies enemy criminal law in terms of the citizens enjoying a "right to security" (Gomez-Jara Diez 2008; Dubber 2010; Ohana 2010).

Imprisonment for public protection plainly shares the characteristics of enemy criminal law. But the power's justification in terms of vulnerable autonomy (and the "deserved" forfeiture of the right to "deserved" punishment) spells out the normative implications of Jakobs's right to security and the normative relativity of enemy and citizen criminal law. Punishment for wrongs against vulnerable autonomy precedes only the harms recognized by citizen criminal law, it does not precede the harm of insecurity that is the object of the enemy criminal law itself; punishment is disproportionate only to the wrongs recognized by citizen criminal law; and it suppresses only the procedural rights of citizen criminal law.

The enemy criminal law's use of state coercion in general, and detention in particular, to anticipate and neutralize threats is also characteristic of the state of emergency. In the state of emergency, legal norms cease to apply and the state's agents are permitted to act for reasons of state, which is to say, on the grounds of what is necessary for the defense of the state against its enemies. In the state of emergency, necessity is the rationale of the state's coercive action. Enemy criminal laws, in so far as they are part of the permanent and ordinary legal regime, serve to normalize the emergency power (Krasmann 2007). In the IPP regime, the calculus of necessity is incorporated into the normal sentencing powers of the criminal courts. Notice that this normalization of emergency cuts both ways—the normal legal order does the work of emergency rule and emergency rule acquires some characteristics of legality. Just as preventive necessity establishes itself as the legal norm, so lawyers and judges may apply their rule-making (and exception-making) expertise to the preventive regime.

This normalization of emergency rule is far from an entirely new development. Since World War I, democratic regimes have maintained emergency powers in force long after the exigencies that brought them into being have passed (Scheppele 2004; Agamben 2005; Neocleous 2008, chap. 2). The emergence of enemy criminal laws, such as IPP, as part and parcel of the normal legal regime represents the obverse of the same process. Instead of explicit emergency powers being normalized, explicitly normal legal powers acquire the characteristics of emergency powers. This process represents a challenge to traditional liberalism, which, at least in theory, has tried to maintain the separation between the normal condition of the rule of law and the exceptional conditions of emergency. We can see this most clearly if we look at the way one of liberalism's critics on the security question presents the problem.

Mark Neocleous argues persuasively that many leading thinkers in the liberal tradition have recognized the ultimate priority of security over liberty, and from John Locke onward the rule of law has always ultimately depended upon the existence of the emergency power.[20] Neocleous (2008, p. 22) suggests that for liberalism the project of liberty has always been "wrapped in" the project of security. It is this underlying (and underplayed) commitment that explains the defenselessness of liberal societies in the face of the demands of security (Neocleous 2008, p. 32). Neocleous traces the steady transformation of the martial law of the nineteenth century into the emergency powers of the twentieth, powers that were to become an increasingly permanent feature of the legal regime of apparently liberal societies. However, as he points out, notwithstanding this real historical development, the presentation of the question by liberalism has always emphasized the exceptional character of emergency powers. Even if emergency powers have in fact long been the "norm", the idea of the rule of law remains essential to the liberal worldview. As a result, Neocleous (2008, p. 72) argues, "liberalism seeks to ideologically separate 'normal' constitutional order from emergency rule, thereby preserving the constitution in its pristine form while providing the executive with the power to act in an emergency."

But it is precisely this *appearance* of separation between the normal and exceptional, that for Neocleous is characteristic of liberalism, that is abandoned in the ideology of vulnerable autonomy. In the new ideology, the enforcement of what is necessary in the name of security is no longer the exceptional moment that "temporarily" overrides the norm, but is now the norm itself—the right to security. Neocleous (2008, p. 71) argues that to speak of the normalization of emergency is to set out from the ideological standpoint of norm and exception. But the ideology of vulnerable autonomy has already eliminated the liberal distinction from its premises. The new ideology drops any pretence of the exceptional character of what liberals might have called emergency power and instead presents the power's very permanence as the condition of freedom. The reflex of a citizen's "right to security" is the duty to reassure others of your good intentions.

This is not the place to address the question of what, if anything, is left of liberalism once the project of individual liberty is not just wrapped up in the project of security but entirely merged with it.[21] For the present, we can at least point out that something as apparently fundamental to the liberal ideology as the separation of normality and emergency is erased by the justification of measures like IPP in terms of vulnerable autonomy. Moreover, the disappearance of this distinction suggests that a still more fundamental category of the classical liberal political theory may be put in doubt by the ideology of vulnerable autonomy.

IX. HOLLOW SOVEREIGNTY

The purported right to security empowers state action rather than limits it. On the face of it, powers to deal with threats to the peace such as those taken by the state under the IPP regime seem to fit the model of sovereign action perfectly. Indeed, formally that is exactly what they are. It is tempting to reach for Hobbes and to find the hand of Leviathan in this power grab effected in the name of security. Yet, in so far as the IPP powers are justified by the protection of the *right to security*, enjoyed because of the citizenry's *vulnerable autonomy*, an assumption has been made that is radically at odds with Hobbes's account of Leviathan's regime.

Hobbes was unquestionably a theorist of mutual vulnerability. Natural equality between individuals was such that no "one man can thereupon claim to himselfe any benefit, to which another man may not pretend, as well as he," and, moreover, "the weakest has strength enough to kill the strongest" (Hobbes 1968, p. 183). The state of nature was therefore, and notoriously, a war of "every man against every man" (Hobbes 1968, p. 184). Of all the disastrous consequences of this condition "worst of all [is] continuall feare and danger of violent death" (Hobbes 1968, p. 186). It was this vulnerability that made it rational for all to contract with each other to exchange their natural liberties for the security offered by obedience to a sovereign—the mighty Leviathan, upon whom they "conferre all their power and strength" (Hobbes 1968, p. 227). This sovereign was authorized by the subjects to do what "he shall think expedient, for their Peace and Common Defence" (Hobbes 1968, p. 228). Since Hobbes's view of punishment was avowedly consequentialist (1968, p. 210),[22] it might seem that the security gains offered by IPP might well lead a Leviathan to countenance such a measure. However, as we shall see, to justify the ordinary penal law *by reference to the security benefits of the vulnerable* is an admission of defeat for Hobbes's sovereign.[23]

To be certain that the marginal security gains of millions from IPP outweigh both the loss of liberty to IPP prisoners and the coercion of everyone else arising from the possibility of being subjected to an indeterminate sentence, we must assume that law-abiding subjects are so anxious about dangerous offenders (once they have served the sentence that they deserve for the ordinary criminal wrong they have committed) that those subjects' freedom of choice is significantly affected by the knowledge that such prisoners are at liberty. This anxiety must be sufficient to justify the anticipatory force of IPP required to reassure the law-abiding that their rights will be protected.

The high degree of anxiety about potential threats from potential attackers, that IPP justified in this way must assume, is a psychological condition that Hobbes described as "diffidence," and it is a condition that for him was characteristic of the subjects of the state of nature (Hobbes 1968, p. 184). In other words, the assumption upon which the security benefits of IPP may justify the practice is that the law-abiding endure the psychological condition of the state of nature. But if that is right, then the sovereign's claims for its penal laws are hollow, for its laws assume that its subjects lack confidence in its authority; and for the true Leviathan this is inconceivable, since his rule is authorized by none other than the subjects. The laws assume that the subjects are not convinced that the sovereign has succeeded in entirely excluding the state of nature.[24]

For the liberal order, the rule of normality in civil society was premised on the exclusion of the permanent emergency that is life in the state of nature. To ensure that exclusion, emergency rule would no doubt be necessitated from time to time by serious internal or external threats. But, as we saw above, the normalization of emergency conditions that is characteristic of IPP implies a more radical merger of the commonwealth and the state of nature, the state of war and the state of peace. When enemy criminal law is incorporated into the normal legal system, it is assumed that the law cannot take for granted that its subjects are either sufficiently loyal to the sovereign or sufficiently cowed by the sovereign's threats for citizens to be confident in the authority of the sovereign's normative order. Hobbes's sovereign might have faced rebellion or emergency from time to time, but the normalization of emergency, once it has been completely accomplished, converts at least some of the conditions of the state of nature into the normal conditions of civil society. Since for the subjects the "finall Cause, End or Designe" of the contract is "getting themselves out from that miserable condition" that is the state of nature (Hobbes 1968, p. 223), the law effectively assumes that its subjects doubt that Leviathan is up to the job, and that the social contract, at least as Hobbes imagined it, has been a failure.

Liberalism's emphasis on the individual subject's civil or human rights is often counterposed to sovereignty. Where the sovereign enjoys a monopoly of legitimate coercion, rights are precisely the limitation on that power of coercion that render it legitimate. But, as Franz Neumann pointed out, the very possibility of liberal theories of the rule of law depends on the state enjoying that unchallenged monopoly of legitimate coercive power that comes with Leviathan's sovereignty. It is only with that unchallenged monopoly that "restraints on sovereignty will no longer lead to [the state's] disintegration" so that civil rights are rendered conceivable (Neumann 1996, p. 213). Sovereignty therefore, though it appears to be the "negation" of the liberal idea of freedom under the rule of law, is in reality "its very presupposition" (Neumann 1996, p. 214).

Enforcing the right to security reduces the state's claim to sovereignty to a hollow formality that complements the hollowness of its claims to be a liberal political order. When the legislature enacts penal laws that protect the right to security, it institutionalizes its own ideological assumption that citizens do not believe in the authority of the state, thereby exposing its own lack of confidence in government's relation with the people. This decline in the vitality of the political sphere tends to confirm the view that sovereignty is not a quality belonging to the formal normative supremacy of some constitutional body or arrangement, nor to any person's capacity to suspend that constitutional supremacy (Schmitt 2005, p. 5), but is rather, as Martin Loughlin has argued, an attribute of the political sphere arising from the reflexive relations of accountability between people and government (Loughlin 2003, pp. 83–86; see also Kirchheimer 1969; Ramsay 2008). Laws such as IPP are a vivid expression of the weakening, in the imagination of political actors at least, of the relationship that constitutes the sovereign power of the political sphere, the relationship that is the essential precondition of a state being a liberal state.[25]

X. DEMORALIZING BECAUSE DEMORALIZED

The law's institutionalization of the psychological condition of the state of nature entails another feature of Hobbes's nightmare scenario: an insatiable need for the control of threats. Hobbes (1968, p. 184) points out that the most rational method of protection for those experiencing the insecurity of the state of nature is "anticipation." In such circumstances there may be no restraint on the control of threats, and those who have committed serious offenses are far from the only people who will be feared for what they might do in the future. Once the prevalence of such fear and anxiety is the assumed basis of lawmaking, why wait for a criminal offense to be committed? Why not intervene earlier? Certainly *once the public's freedom is defined in terms of its vulnerability to crime*, it can be said to have a legitimate expectation that crime will be dealt with at its earliest stage. The positive duty to reassure the public laid on offenders by IPP might be extended to all the law's subjects. All would then be subject to a duty not to do anything that would contribute to the risk of crime. Inchoate and "pre-inchoate" offenses would be the norm in this structure.[26]

Such inchoate and pre-inchoate offenses are increasingly prevalent. Administrative procedures and criminal laws that impose a liability for the failure to reassure, like that found in IPP, have advanced markedly in recent UK legislation (Ramsay 2009, 2010, forthcoming). IPP is perhaps the most severe example of the enemy criminal law, but civil preventive orders have treated not only terrorism suspects, but sex offenders, football hooligans, youthful "troublemakers," the homeless, street prostitutes, street drinkers, and the mentally ill, among others, as akin to enemies of the state by the use of enemy criminal laws.[27] It is very important to understand IPP in this wider context of the criminalization of conduct that fails to reassure others. One recent example of such laws is particularly instructive.

Probably the most extensive deployment of enemy criminal law (also justified by the vulnerability of the population) is to be found in the duties imposed by the Safeguarding Vulnerable Groups Act (SVGA) 2006.[28] In May 2010, faced with increasing criticism of the scheme's scope, the new Coalition government in the UK announced a review of the scheme introduced by the act and promised "to scale it back to common sense levels" (Her Majesty's Government 2010, p. 20). At the time of writing, the government has published a bill that would repeal the more far-reaching aspects of the law.[29] But it is worth thinking about the scheme as it was originally enacted because it passed through parliament in 2006 with very little controversy, and it provides a very clear picture of where the unchecked influence of the ideology of vulnerable autonomy may lead.

The act required anybody who regularly comes into contact with children or "vulnerable adults" in either the course of their employment or organized voluntary activities to be registered with the Independent Safeguarding Authority (ISA).[30] Doing any such work with children or vulnerable adults without being "subject to monitoring" by the ISA was made a criminal offense (SVGA 2006, sect. 8).[31] Restricting our discussion to children for the present (the rules for vulnerable adults are broadly similar), to be "subject to monitoring" meant that the ISA would receive information about any convictions or cautions from the Criminal Records Bureau and could also consider information from *any other source*, including police or members of the public, about the risk of harm that a person may represent to children. The ISA has the power to bar people from working with children not only when the person has been convicted of or cautioned for a criminal offense, but also when "it appears to the [ISA] that the person . . . may (a) harm a child, (b) cause a child to be harmed, (c) put a child at risk of harm" (Safeguarding Vulnerable Groups Act 2006, Sch 3 [5]). A barred person who works with children commits a criminal offense (SVGA 2006, sect. 7).[32]

The act gives to the civil servants and expert specialists who staff the ISA the power to impose a hugely stigmatic bar on people coming into contact with children or vulnerable adults on the basis of an administrative risk assessment. The presumption of good intentions is withdrawn from those who are officially judged to be a risk for harming children, and their rights will be restricted accordingly. The scheme was to be enforced by imposing criminal liability on anyone who failed to reassure the authorities, either by working with children and not making themselves "subject to monitoring" or doing so when the official risk assessment had barred them.[33]

These provisions institutionalized distrust of the nine million people who it was officially estimated would need to register.[34] That is to say, they institutionalized distrust of more than 10 percent of the population, mostly comprised of parents. The law required that the threat that these people might represent must be anticipated by ensuring that they were "subject to monitoring." In order to take part in some of the most everyday of social interactions, the act required these millions of *parents* to subject themselves to the preliminary procedures of the *enemy* criminal law. The Safeguarding Vulnerable Groups Act reduced the ideology of vulnerable autonomy to the absurd. In so doing, it exposed the falsity of Giddens's claims for a new citizenship built on a right to security. Whatever the benefits that might be achieved by requiring millions of ordinary law-abiding citizens to accept the "manufactured uncertainty" constituted by others' anxiety that they might be sex offenders or potential sex offenders, "remoralising our lives" is not going to be among them. On the contrary, a more likely consequence is, as Richard Ericson put it, "the unraveling of civil society" (2007, p. 213).

The Coalition government's proposed reform aims to repeal the registration and monitoring requirements in the original scheme, and with them the criminal offense of working with children while not being registered. Criminal records checks on people doing paid work and the barring of those assessed as a risk will remain. The most extreme aspect of this scheme has been withdrawn. It is a proposal intended to pull back from some of the uglier consequences of the underlying ideology of vulnerable autonomy. But this is an ideology that still informs and legitimates a range of less politically controversial powers and criminal offenses, not least among them IPP.

In one sense, it must be reassuring to imagine that the contemporary penal regime in general, and IPP in particular, are the work of a "neoliberal Leviathan." For the image suggests the return of a familiar authority: the bad old capitalist state, still firmly in charge. The ideology of vulnerable autonomy, however, presents us with a political reality that is both more disturbing and more interesting than the Hobbesian imagery allows for. There is a new penal "order," and it is associated with the triumph of "neoliberal" economic policy. But it is an order with a marked tendency to abandon the presumption of good intentions and to assume that all social interactions are characterized by distrust. The resulting "right to security" is deeply demoralizing and corrosive of the underlying conditions for social order. But if the new ideology is demoralizing, that is because its underlying political assumptions are themselves demoralized. There is a world of possibility in that.

The regime of vulnerable autonomy has devolved gradually from the old liberal order. It is premised on the attenuation of the political relationship between people and government that constituted the sovereignty that was the precondition of the liberal state. Almost two centuries ago, a liberal thinker, Benjamin Constant, supplied an apt description of our current condition, although at the time he was describing the *ancien regime*. The latter was, he said, made up of "vicious governments, which without being strong, were repressive in their effects; absurd in their principles; wretched in action; governments which had as their strength arbitrary power; for their purpose the belittling of mankind" (Constant 1988, p. 317).

ACKNOWLEDGMENT

I am grateful to Nicola Lacey, Jill Peay, and the participants in the Leiden workshops for their comments and corrections. The usual disclaimer applies.

NOTES

1. Hansard, 29th March 2011, Col 151.
2. Though Wacquant is careful to stress the interdependence of these two arms of the state, and that the current period represents a new relation between them rather than the complete replacement of one by the other.
3. Wacquant's argument draws directly on the American experience, but it is widely recognized that what I will here argue is the normative essence of the public protection agenda—the security interests of potential crime victims—is a key commitment in both American and British political life (Ramsay 2010).
4. For a consequentialist defense of incapacitation of the dangerous see Walker (1991). I explore the peculiar relationship of IPP and consequentialism elsewhere (Ramsay 2012).
5. They are governed by CJA 2003, s227. The rules for life and IPP sentences are different for adults and youth offenders, but I will consider below only the rules for adults.
6. CJA 2003, s225(2).
7. CJA 2003, s225(3).
8. CJA 2003, s225(3A) and (3B).

9. A utilitarian justification based on openly actuarial assessment of the offender might be conceivable, but the statutory basis of the dangerousness assessment appears to be clinical. The information that a court may take into account in making the assessment is only information about "the offender," and does not appear to include statistical information about people who share the offender's characteristics (see CJA 2003, sect. 229(2)). Whether or not clinical assessment can ever be independent of actuarial is a question for another day. The present discussion is restricted to investigation of one way in which the law's formal terms are currently justified.

10. The particular case concerned the admissibility of illegally retained DNA evidence, but Lord Steyn repeated it in R (McCann) v. Manchester Crown Court to justify the designation of antisocial behavior order (ASBO) applications as civil proceedings permitting the use of hearsay evidence.

11. Braithwaite and Pettit (1990, p. 204) insist upon its practical advantages.

12. For a discussion of civic virtue in republican theory, see Pettit (1997, chap. 8).

13. I am indebted to Sandra Marshall for the thought that indeterminacy itself might be the punishment in IPP.

14. I am indebted to Antony Duff for this line of thought.

15. Jakobs work on this subject is not translated into English. I am relying here on the critical account of it by Gomez-Jara Diez (2008). See also Dubber (2010) and Ohana (2010).

16. The tension between the free-market liberal and traditionalist aspects of Hayek's theory worked itself out in the tendency of Thatcherite politics to undermine traditional sources of authority and weaken conservatism itself (Gray 1995).

17. American neoconservatism understands this as a critical problem threatening capitalism's long-term survival (Kristol 1995). Kristol proposes a return to religious morals, but there has been little sign of success, especially in Britain.

18. For a Foucauldian account of the systematic relation between neoliberal economic prescriptions and the development of a moral order that is "embedded" in the market, see Shamir (2008). Shamir's discussion focuses on business ethics and he does not theorize the normative content of the rights and duties in the way I have done here, but he observes that in this "responsibilized" order, individuals have to take responsibility for the consequences of their actions and moderate their self-interest through concern for interdependency (Shamir 2008, pp. 7–9).

19. And we might add atrocities such as the July 2005 London bombings to the list.

20. Locke (1990, p. 190) referred to it as the prerogative, the "power to act according to discretion, for the public good, without the prescription of law, and sometimes even against it."

21. Neocleous (2008, pp. 13–27) cites an impressive list of liberal thinkers on the priority of security. But their formulations are not the same. For Locke, Adam Smith, and John Stuart Mill, for example, security is government's first duty. However, for Montesquieu and Bentham, liberty is nothing other than a perception of security or a branch of security.

22. Moreover, Hobbes (1968, pp. 355–56) seems to have no objection in principle to indeterminate sentences, providing subjects are fairly warned. For a detailed account of Hobbes's theory of punishment, see Ristroph (2009).

23. Once again, it might be possible to justify IPP in a more conventionally utilitarian manner by calculating the risks of future criminal harms avoided using openly actuarial methods rather than make the particular offender's causing of insecurity a punishable wrong. But the present analysis proceeds from the law's actual language, which requires a clinical judgment of risk (Ashworth 2004).

24. This is not to say that the subjects are in the state of nature or that the subjects in fact believe that they are. What is being said is that *the law assumes* that subjects endure the psychological condition of the state of nature.

25. See also Ericson (2007, pp. 31–35, 202) and Ramsay (2008).
26. The term "pre-inchoate" is borrowed from Ashworth (2009, p. 90).
27. For a discussion of these powers as enemy criminal laws, see Ohana (2010).
28. The act's provisions began coming into force in October 2009.
29. Protection of Freedoms Bill 2011, Clauses 63–68. Remarkably, the new Conservative Home Secretary Teresa May, when announcing the review of the scheme, criticized it on the grounds of criminal justice principles, observing: "You were assumed to be guilty until you were proven innocent, and told you were able to work with children" (BBC 2010*b*).
30. The Independent Safeguarding Authority is called the Independent Barring Board in SVGA 2006, but was renamed by the Policing and Crime Act 2009, sect. 81 and the new bill, if enacted, will merge it with the Criminal Records Bureau.
31. The maximum sentence is a fine.
32. The maximum penalty is five years' imprisonment.
33. That the purpose of the scheme was to reassure parents was explicitly stated by Meg Hillier, the Labour minister of state responsible for its implementation. Responding to criticism that the scheme would protect agencies rather than prevent child abuse, she said, "No one is ever going to say that this scheme stops all child abuse. That's not what it is about. What it is doing is that it's playing the rightful role of government, drawing a line about how far we go, but I think it is fair to have that line. When you give your children over to people in a professional setting you can have some assurances and quite strong assurances in this case that they are safe to work with your child" (BBC 2010*a*). When the new government announced the review of the scheme, Hillier defended it, saying, "The scheme was designed to ensure that parents could be certain their children were safe when in the care of professionals and regular volunteers who may be unknown to them" (BBC 2010*b*).
34. The nine million figure is based on Home Office estimates (Balls 2009).

REFERENCES

Agamben, G. 2005. *State of Exception*. Chicago: University of Chicago Press.

Ashworth, A. 2004. "Criminal Justice Act 2003: Part 2: Criminal Justice Reform—Principles, Human Rights and Public Protection." *Criminal Law Review* 41:516–32.

———. 2005. *Sentencing and Criminal Justice*. Chicago: University of Chicago Press.

———. 2009. "Criminal Law, Human Rights and Preventative Justice." In *Regulating Deviance: Redirection of Criminalisation and the Futures of Criminal Law*, ed. B. McSherry, A. Norrie, and S. Bronitt. Oxford: Hart.

Ashworth, A., and A. von Hirsch. 1993. "Desert and the Three R's." *Current Issues in Criminal Justice* 5:9–12.

Balls, Ed. 2009. "Ministerial Statement to Parliament" (December 14). http://www.isa–gov.org.uk/Default.aspx?page=24.

BBC. 2010a. "Are You a Danger to Kids" (Feb 8). http://www.bbc.co.uk/programmes/b00qs991.

———. 2010b. "Child Abuse Vetting Scheme Cancelled as Draconian" (May 15). http://news.bbc.co.uk/1/hi/education/10314055.stm.

Braithwaite, J., and P. Pettit. 1990. *Not Just Deserts: A Republican Theory of Criminal Justice*. New York: Oxford University Press.

Constant, B. 1988. "The Liberty of the Ancients Compared with that of the Moderns." In *Benjamin Constant: Political Writings*, ed. B. Fontana. Cambridge: Cambridge University Press.

Crawford, A. 2009. "The Preventive Turn in Europe." In *Crime Prevention Policies in Comparative Perspective*, ed. A. Crawford. Portland, OR: Willan.

Department of Social Security. 1998. *New Ambitions for Our Country: A New Contract for Welfare*. London: HM Stationery Office.

Dubber, M. 2010. "Citizenship and Penal Law." *New Criminal Law Review* 13(2):190–215.

Ericson, R. V. 2007. *Crime in an Insecure World*. Malden, MA: Polity.

Etzioni, A. 1996. *The New Golden Rule: Community and Morality in a Democratic Society*. New York: Basic Books.

Floud, J., and W. Young. 1981. *Dangerousness and Criminal Justice*. London: Heinemann.

Garland, D. 2001. *The Culture of Control*. Chicago: University of Chicago Press.

Garside, R. 2006. "The Politics of Criminal Justice under Labour." University of Oxford Criminology Seminar, October 25. http://www.crimeandjustice.org.uk/opus313.html.

Giddens, A. 1991. *Modernity and Self Identity*. Cambridge: Polity.

———. 1994. *Beyond Left and Right*. Cambridge: Polity.

———. 1998. *The Third Way*. Cambridge: Polity.

———. 2002. *Where Now for New Labour?* Cambridge: Polity.

Gomez-Jara Diez, C. 2008. "Enemy Combatants vs. Enemy Criminal Law." *New Criminal Law Review* 11(4):529–89.

Gray, J. 1995. *Enlightenment's Wake*. London: Routledge.

Hayek, F. A. 1944. *The Road to Serfdom*. London: Routledge.

———. 1960. *The Constitution of Liberty*. London: Routledge.

———. 1979. *Law, Legislation and Liberty*, vol. 3. London: Routledge and Kegan Paul.

Her Majesty's Government. 2010. *The Coalition: Our Programme for Government*. London: Her Majesty's Government.

Hobbes, T. 1968. *Leviathan*. New York: Penguin.

Jacobson, J., and M. Hough. 2010. *Unjust Deserts: Imprisonment for Public Protection*. London: Prison Reform Trust.

Kirchheimer, O. 1969. "In Quest of Sovereignty." In *Politics, Law and Social Change: Selected Essays of Otto Kirchheimer*, ed. F. Burin and K. Shell. New York: Columbia University Press.

Krasmann, S. 2007. "The Enemy on the Border: Critique of a Programme in Favour of a Preventive State." *Punishment and Society* 9(3):301–18.

Kristol, I. 1995. *Neoconservatism: The Autobiography of an Idea*. New York: Free Press.

Loader, I., and N. Walker. 2006. *Civilising Security*. Chicago: Chicago University Press.

Locke, J. 1990. *Two Treatises of Government*. London: J. M. Dent.

Loughlin, M. 2003. *The Idea of Public Law*. New York: Oxford University Press.

McCormick, N., and D. Garland. 1998. "Sovereign States and Vengeful Victims." In *Fundamentals of Sentencing Theory: Essays in Honour of Andrew von Hirsch*, ed. A. Ashworth and M. Wasik. New York: Oxford University Press.

Ministry of Justice. 2010. *Breaking the Cycle: Effective Punishment, Rehabilitation and Sentencing of Offenders*. London: Ministry of Justice.

Neocleous, M. 2008. *Critique of Security*. Edinburgh: Edinburgh University Press.

Neumann, F. 1996. "The Concept of Political Freedom." In *The Rule of Law Under Siege: Selected Essays of Franz L Neumann and Otto Kirchheimer*, ed. W. Scheuerman. Berkeley: University of California Press.

Ohana, D. 2010. "Trust, Distrust and Reassurance: Diversion and Preventive Orders Through the Prism of Feindstrafrecht." *Modern Law Review* 73(5):721–51.

Pettit, P. 1997. *Republicanism: A Theory of Freedom and Government*. New York: Oxford University Press.

Pettit, P., and J. Braithwaite. 1993. "Not Just Deserts, Even in Sentencing." *Current Issues in Criminal Justice* 4:225–39.

Ramsay, P. 2006. "The Responsible Subject as Citizen: Criminal Law Democracy and the Welfare State." *Modern Law Review* 69(1):29–58.

Ramsay, P. 2008. "Sovereignty, Vulnerability and Police Power in the ASBO." In *Police and the Liberal State*, ed. M. Dubber and M. Valverde. Stanford, CA: Stanford University Press.

Ramsay, P. 2009. "The Theory of Vulnerable Autonomy and the Legitimacy of the Civil Preventive Order." In *Regulating Deviance: Redirection of Criminalisation and the Futures of Criminal Law*, ed. B. McSherry, A. Norrie, and S. Bronitt. Portland, OR: Hart.

Ramsay, P. 2010. "Overcriminalization as Vulnerable Citizenship." *New Criminal Law Review* 13(2):262–85.

Ramsay, P. 2012. "Imprisonment Under the Precautionary Principle. " In *Seeking Security,* ed. I. Dennis and R. Sullivan. Portland, OR: Hart.

Ramsay, P. Forthcoming. *The Insecurity State: Criminal Law after the ASBO*. New York: Oxford University Press.

Reece, H. 2003. *Divorcing Responsibly*. Portland, OR: Hart.

Ristroph, A. 2009. "Respect and Resistance in Punishment Theory." *California Law Review* 97:601–32.

Rose, N. 1999. *Powers of Freedom*. New York: Cambridge University Press.

Sandel, M. 1982. *Liberalism and the Limits of Justice*. Cambridge: Cambridge University Press.

Scheppele, K. 2004. "Law in a Time of Emergency: States of Exception and the Temptations of 9/11." *Journal of Constitutional Law* 6:1001–76.

Schmitt, C. 2005. *Political Theology*. Chicago: University of Chicago Press.

Shamir, R. 2008. "The Age of Responsibilization: On Market—Embedded Morality." *Economy and Society* 37(1):1–19.

Skinner, Q. 1998. *Liberty Before Liberalism*. New York: Cambridge University Press.

Tonry, M. 2003. "Evidence, Elections and Ideology in the Making of Criminal Justice Policy." In *Confronting Crime, Crime Control Policy Under New Labour*, ed. Michael Tonry. Portland, OR: Willan.

———. 2004. *Punishment and Politics*. Portland, OR: Willan.

Wacquant, L. 2009a. "Bringing the Penal State Back In." Lecture at the London School of Economics, October 6. http://www.lse.ac.uk/collections/law/events/events–firstpage.htm.

———. 2009b. *Punishing the Poor*. Durham, NC: Duke University Press.

Walker, N. 1991. *Why Punish?* New York: Oxford University Press.

Zedner, L. 2002. "Dangers of Dystopia." *Oxford Journal of Legal Studies* 22:341–66.

8

Terror as a Theory of Punishment

ALICE RISTROPH

Retribution has a history, a history as lengthy, complicated, and colorful as the history of any human practice. It is not just the practice, but also the theory of retribution that has a history, and so a student of the history of political thought could trace the development of retributive ideas across places and times.[1] Suppose, however, we shift our focus from retribution to *desert*, the term favored by many contemporary theorists. Could one write an intellectual history of desert? Although desert is invoked so often in contemporary punishment theory that it has become something of a cliché, one finds few discussions of desert (by that name) in the political theory tradition prior to the latter half of the twentieth century. Perhaps because there is little history to invoke, theorists often present desert as ahistorical, a question of analytic philosophy rather than an evolving and contested concept in the ever-shifting universe of human ideas.[2] Indeed, one of the claimed virtues of desert as a punishment principle is its purported ability to check the impulses and excesses of people living too much in the moment. But the effort to escape history is doomed to fail, and desert is a creature of its time.[3]

I seek to give an account of deserved punishment today, and in so doing, to suggest some limitations to what desert might become. Desert is not an antidote to public sensibilities, but a vehicle for their expression. Of course, public sensibilities vary by place as well as time, and so desert has a geography as well as a (developing) history. Much of the discussion here focuses on the United States, but there is evidence that the analysis describes at least some other developed western democracies. In America in the early twenty-first century, the sensibilities that shape judgments of desert are fear—and in some cases, the more intense reaction better labeled terror—and anger at those who make us afraid. People are afraid of crime, and especially of physical violence directed against them or members of their perceived community. At the same time, we have come to believe strongly in a right not to be afraid, and in the state's obligation to provide substantial physical protection. Accordingly, we expect and demand that the state will use official force against those who we perceive as threats. And importantly, we think of those who are threatening as deserving the official force that is used against them. We are not simply afraid of crime, we are angry about it, and we believe our anger to be morally justified. These sentiments lead to a belief that those who make us afraid deserve the force that is inflicted to restrain them.

The first strand of this argument—the widespread fear of criminal violence, and the resulting demand for incapacitation of threatening persons—has been well documented (Zimring and Hawkins 1995). But most scholarly commentators have viewed demands for incapacitation as departures from principles of desert, and several have called for a reinvigoration of desert as a limiting principle (Lee 2005; Nilsen 2007). Loosed from the conceptual precision of academic theory, however, desert is a capacious notion that can and does accommodate a near-infinite range of desert bases.[4] My aim here is to explore what characteristics or qualities most often serve as desert bases at this particular historical moment. That investigation yields substantial evidence that contemporary preoccupations with the human agents of fear, terror, and danger shape common conceptions of deserved punishment. In the public understanding, to be dangerous or terrifying is itself a basis of desert.

I make these claims descriptively, but as is often the case, descriptive claims carry normative implications. If, as an empirical matter, notions of danger and terror influence determinations of deserved punishment, desert may be somewhat less appealing than its scholarly proponents have claimed. But proponents of desert-based sentencing have a response, one I consider here. Advocates of particular theories of desert may claim that popular conceptions of desert are misguided or ill-theorized. They would urge that their own more sophisticated accounts of deserved punishment be used to inform and improve popular conceptions. I examine desert's promise to discipline today's passions and suggest that we should not be surprised that this promise has remained unfulfilled. This, then, leads to a final normative question—the question whether policy makers or legal decision makers should defer to populist attitudes concerning deserved punishment. I conclude with some reflections on reform strategies that seek neither to bury nor to praise desert, but to scrutinize the underlying components of desert judgments.

I. THE CONCEPT AND CONCEPTIONS OF DESERT

It is hard to argue against the claim that people should get what they deserve. At that level of generality, the claim is tautological, or close to it: in common usage, to say he deserves X is to say he should receive X. In both scholarly commentary and popular discourse, it is typical to claim that wrongdoers should get as much punishment as they deserve and no more. Indeed, the near-ubiquity of desert rhetoric is probably made possible by the capaciousness of the concept. Persons with a wide range of political and philosophical commitments can all endorse desert, because each can define desert in his or her own terms. Desert may become (if it has not done so already) a term like justice.[5] No one argues seriously against justice, but the definitions of justice are almost as numerous as its proponents. Thus arises the familiar philosophical distinction between concept and conception: different thinkers may recognize the concept of justice, but each holds different conceptions of it (Gallie 1956).[6] So too with desert. The frequent appeals to deserved punishment do not themselves establish any consensus on conceptions of desert. A normative theorist who advances a particular account of deserved punishment must contend with, or at least acknowledge, the empirical fact of competing normative theories.

A distinction often made with respect to the term *legitimacy* may be helpful here. There are so many competing conceptions of political legitimacy that scholars distinguish between normative legitimacy and sociological legitimacy. Normative legitimacy is assessed from the perspective of a given moral or political theory. Sociological legitimacy is an empirical question; the term refers to the degree to which a government or other institution is in fact accepted by its constituents. The two types of legitimacy may coincide, but need not—for example, a government could be accepted as legitimate by its subjects but judged by outside observers to be normatively illegitimate.

We could similarly differentiate sociological from normative desert. Sociological desert is a matter of empirical fact: the actual desert judgments that are made by members of a given society at a given time. Normative desert is a matter of normative theory, and like normative legitimacy, it may or may not be satisfied by the actual conditions of a given society. Commentators have already relied on this distinction in the growing literature on "empirical desert," which is equivalent to what I have just called sociological desert. Empirical desert, as described by Paul Robinson, its leading champion, is based on the community's intuitions of justice; we ascertain empirical desert through "empirical research into those factors that drive people's assessments of blameworthiness" (Robinson 2007a, p. 149). Empirical desert is contrasted with "deontological desert," which, like normative legitimacy, depends on "the arguments and analyses of moral philosophy" (Robinson 2007a, p. 148). In the same way that sociological legitimacy is concerned with the fact of acceptance and not the reasons for which a government is accepted, empirical desert is concerned more with the fact of a desert judgment and less with the underlying rationale for such a judgment. The "intuitions of justice" that underlie empirical desert are "simply behavioral phenomena," and "people hold strong intuitions of justice even though the reasons for their holding those intuitions are inaccessible to them" (Robinson 2007b, p. 1842).

To ask what desert is now is to ask an empirical question: What conception or conceptions of desert shape contemporary judgments of deserved punishment? This empirical question leads to a methodological one: How do we know what "the public" thinks? Public opinion is difficult to assess in many contexts, and criminal justice policy is a distinctively challenging area in which to track popular views. Opinions about appropriate punishment vary depending on the level of detail provided about the offender and the crime (Doob and Roberts 1984). Accordingly, some scholars urge that to determine public attitudes about punishment, we need to rely on measures other than opinion polls, or at least dramatically improve our polling methodology (Roberts et al. 2003). Several recent studies of "empirical desert" have eschewed traditional polling altogether and turned instead to social science experiments to assess popular "intuitions of justice" (Robinson and Darley 1995; Robinson and Kurzban 2007). A third avenue of inquiry, which need not exclude the two approaches just mentioned, is the methodology of political theory. Both polling and the social science experiments of the "empirical desert" school rely, to a considerable degree, on what people say about criminal justice policy.

But perhaps shared views on punishment and the use of force are not so easily surfaced. Judith Shklar described "the most obvious task of political theory" as "the elucidation of common experience, the expression of what is inarticulately known to groups of people at any time" (Shklar 1986, p. 28). In the next section, I refer to public opinion and social science research concerning popular desert judgments. But I also try to assess what is inarticulately known, which may not perfectly coincide with what is articulated. My enterprise is speculative, as initial excursions of theory often are; we will have to see whether the story I explore here rings true.

And, as noted at the outset, my inquiry is normative as well as empirical. Whatever the public thinks (and however we determine that), should it matter? For policy makers or for academic observers, what is the relevance of what people think about punishment? The most zealous advocates of direct democracy might argue that criminal justice policy should be wholly determined by majoritarian preferences in order to be (normatively) legitimate. Proponents of empirical desert make the somewhat different argument that criminal laws are more likely to be accepted (i.e., more sociologically legitimate) and more likely to control crime if they reflect widely held conceptions of deserved punishment. I will argue here that shared inarticulate intuitions—and sometimes even our articulated ones—are important but not necessarily dispositive for both normative theory and social policy. Again, Shklar's account of political theory is helpful. She reminded us that political theory often required "the re-examination of inherited ideas, their adaptation, and even their utter rejection. . . . We all carry with us a mixed bag of *idées reçus*, and in order to travel with it through an ever-changing world we must shift it around occasionally—drop something here and add something there" (Shklar 1986, p. 28). I want to explore what is in the bag today, and perhaps suggest some things worth discarding.

II. DESERT IN A TIME OF TERROR

The question at hand is the psychology of desert judgments. How do individuals decide whether a given punishment is deserved? What characteristics of a wrongdoer, or a crime, are seen as relevant to determinations of desert? Do other considerations, unrelated to the wrongdoer or the offense, serve as factors in desert judgments? Legal philosophers have long identified certain broad factors as ingredients (or synonyms) of desert: blameworthiness, culpability, harm (von Hirsch 1985; Hurd and Moore 2004).[7] But even if the philosophical terminology does not change, the ways in which ordinary persons assess harm and culpability may vary with time. Today, there is considerable evidence that high perceptions of danger are leading to public support for measures to incapacitate the dangerous. At the same time, the rhetoric of desert continues to pervade discussions of penal policy. Is the dual emphasis on incapacitation and desert self-contradictory? To many academic commentators, the answer is clearly yes; incapacitation and desert are at odds as principles of punishment (Lee 2005; Robinson and Darley 2007). These commentators might point out that the average person probably gives little thought to the relationship between his or her concerns for public safety and assessments of desert, and so the possibility of self-contradiction arises. Against the claim of incompatibility, I suggest here that for many individuals "what is inarticulately known" is that to be threatening or terrifying is to deserve severe punishment.

First, consider the place of perceived danger, fear, and terror in thinking about crime. Even before the 2001 attacks that prompted a declaration of "war on terror," residents of the United States lived under the shadow of perceived danger. Indeed, scholars in a number of fields have connected the increasingly punitive American crime policies of the late twentieth century to acute perceptions of risk and danger (Tonry 2004). For example, David Garland has traced demands for severe punishments to the perception that "precariousness and insecurity" are "built into the fabric of everyday life" (2001, p. 155). The sense that criminals pose ongoing threats leads to demands that the state act to control these "predators." Most scholarly commentators express doubt that the fear of crime is based on real increases in risk; indeed, crime rates have declined sharply over the past two decades (Zimring 2006). But for public attitudes, it is perceptions that matter, and it seems clear that perceived danger is connected to demands for aggressive policing, long sentences, and other measures that may protect public safety by containing criminal threats.

In short, Americans were living in fear, and demanding policies that would provide greater security, even before the attacks on New York and Washington in September 2001. Still, those attacks obviously increased the salience of the concepts of threat, terror, and security. Of course, terrorism, under most definitions, is distinct from "ordinary" crime. Indeed, American counterterrorism efforts have been explicitly cast in the language of war rather than the language of law enforcement. But as a few scholars have noted, there are important connections between the "war on terror" and the older but still vibrant "war on crime" (Huq and Muller 2008; Forman 2009; Parry 2009; Resnik 2010).[8] The influences run both ways: strategies, policies, and rhetoric from the war on crime inspired many aspects of the war on terror, and the expanded government powers introduced to fight the war on terror have been deployed in the criminal justice context even when terrorism is not at issue. These policy changes enjoyed considerable public support, seemingly motivated by concerns about future violence and a general endorsement of "law and order" measures in a time of perceived vulnerability (Mythen and Walklate 2006).

The pursuit of law and order takes many forms, including policing strategies and broad definitions of crime, but policies of confinement or detention may be the most visible measures to pursue public safety, and they are of particular interest here. The vast scale of incarceration in the United States is well documented, and much criticized by scholarly commentators. The scholarly dismay is not matched in popular political discourse, however. The general public seems to accept, and possibly to demand, these high levels of confinement.[9]

Interestingly, public attitudes toward mass confinement in the criminal justice context may be seen as continuous with attitudes toward detention policy in the national security context. In both arenas, the preferred path to safety and security is long-term confinement of individuals perceived as dangerous. To be sure, American constitutional law distinguishes between punitive and nonpunitive detention and applies different legal standards to each. But it is far from clear that the public draws any such sharp distinction, nor is the jurisprudential distinction necessarily defensible (Ristroph 2008).

As Judith Resnik (2010, p. 663) has recently urged, we may gain conceptual insight by thinking instead of "an integrated . . . jurisprudence of detention" that spans both prison sentences and ostensibly civil confinement. Both contexts concern "the central challenge, faced daily, by governments trying to maintain peace and security and, hence, incapacitating some individuals feared likely to inflict grave harm to the social order" (Resnik 2010, p. 584).

But it would be wrong to frame mass incarceration, or even preventive civil detention, as purely consequentialist policies indifferent to moral judgments of desert. The rhetoric of retribution and just deserts has persisted alongside the public demands for security via incapacitation of the dangerous. Indeed, sociologists and social psychologists report that a nonconsequentialist, retributive demand for punishment seems to be the most prevalent response to intentional wrongdoing (Gromet and Darley 2009). So it is not surprising to see criminal sentencing policies justified in terms of desert. Less expected, perhaps, are defenses of ostensibly *civil* detention policies that appeal to the concept of desert. Discussions of the treatment of suspected terrorists, including detention as well as other policies, have been framed around the question whether suspected terrorists *deserve* various procedural protections (Sullum 2002; Ashenfelter 2010). And while conservative commentators are most likely to conclude that the answer is no, their position is not an extremist one. Members of the Democratic Party, including Barack Obama, have on occasion suggested that suspected terrorists, by virtue of being suspicious, do not deserve the procedural protections afforded to most criminal defendants.[10]

The key point is that many people hold simultaneously the view that threatening persons should be incapacitated *and* the view that persons should get what they deserve. It is likely that for many individuals, these views simply reflect basic intuitions, and they are not subjected to substantial scrutiny or reflection. If that is the case, the views may be indefensible or contradictory. Indeed, as I have already noted, several proponents of desert have claimed that the pursuit of incapacitation is in obvious conflict with principles of desert. Such commentators might argue that the twin endorsements of security and desert are expressions of public opinion but not manifestations of informed, thoughtful public judgment (Yankelovich 1991). Before we draw this conclusion, however, we might recall Shklar's description of the task of political theory—"the elucidation of common experience, the expression of what is inarticulately known to groups of people at any time" (Shklar 1986, p. 28). Even if the ordinary person does not explicitly reconcile her concern with security via incapacitation with her desert intuitions, we should think carefully about whether such a reconciliation is possible.

It could be that the quality of being dangerous—of posing a threat—is itself seen as a wrong that deserves punishment. Indeed, many jurisdictions have criminalized the act of making threats, and the justifications for such laws are easily reconcilable with desert: threats inflict unwarranted fear on their recipients and accordingly are blameworthy.[11] "In brief, the principal legal interest behind a prohibition of a threat is not the violence itself but the fear it generates or the need to protect a person from the disruption that taking a threat seriously generates" (Blakely and Murray 2002, p. 1062). Once we adopt the view that to cause fear is a blameworthy wrong, it is not difficult to judge dangerous or threatening individuals as deserving the confinement we would like the state to impose on them. Even if one adopts the desert champion's strong claim that deserved punishment, properly so called, can be imposed only for a past wrong, the individual adjudged to be dangerous has already committed the wrong of generating fear. That past (and often ongoing) wrong can serve as the desert basis for incapacitative confinement. Arguably such a view is reflected by the majority opinion as well as a separate concurrence in *Graham v. Florida*, the U.S. Supreme Court's decision barring life without parole sentences for certain juvenile offenders. The majority noted that a juvenile offender who poses "an immediate risk" of violence "deserve[s] to be separated from society for some time in order to prevent . . . an escalating pattern of criminal conduct" (*Graham v. Florida*, 130 S.Ct. 2011, 2029 [2010]). Clearly on this account there is no conflict between desert and prevention. A separate opinion concurring in the judgment in *Graham* similarly seemed to find dangerousness a basis for *deserved* punishment (*Graham v. Florida*, 130 S.Ct. 2011, 2040 [2010] [Roberts, J., concurring]).[12]

Of course, on most philosophical accounts, individual desert requires some form of moral agency.[13] The deserving wrongdoer must act in some way; he must possess the capacity for self-control and choose to perpetrate (or at least to risk perpetrating) a wrong or harm. It is arguably a violation of desert to punish someone who is uncontrollably dangerous—someone who has not deliberately chosen to be threatening, but nevertheless just *is* threatening. Perhaps the violent and insane defendant is the best example. He is threatening; he causes fear; but he does not exercise any meaningful agency to make himself threatening. On some accounts of desert, even the insane defendant deserves punishment, but this appears to be a minority view and, in any case, it is not necessary to defend that view here (Ristroph 2006). The offenders under examination here are those who have acted, who have committed some offense without being legally insane, and who are then incapacitated as dangerous threats. For these offenders, it is possible to say both that (a) they must be confined to protect public safety or security *and* (b) they deserve their confinement.

To view dangerousness as a basis for desert provides a way to reconcile a utilitarian concern for social welfare with individualist premises. Perhaps that reconciliation is particularly important to Americans, whose cultural inheritance includes a special emphasis on free will and individual agency. My account of deserved incapacitation has focused on the United States, where there is ample evidence of desert rhetoric in populist discourse. But a similar story might be told for other countries. A few commentators have analyzed the coincidence of claims of desert and public protection in Britain (McCulloch and Pickering 2009; Ramsay 2011). On the European continent, the literature on "enemy criminal law" suggests an alternative theory that could also reconcile deserved punishment and incapacitation. Introduced by the German legal scholar Günther Jakobs, the phrase "enemy criminal law" classifies as enemies dangerous individuals who are deemed to be public threats.[14] As described by one of the few commentators to address the concept in Anglo-American scholarly publications, three features characterize enemy criminal law: punishment may precede an actualized harm; imprisonment sanctions may be disproportionately severe; and the "enemy" may be denied procedural rights (Gomez-Jara Diez 2008). Though enemy criminal law is much criticized by European scholars, it is also recognized as a descriptively accurate account of European and Latin American laws (Gomez-Jara Diez 2008).

Again, to many Anglo-American desert theorists it is simply a category mistake to label as "punishment" severe prison terms imposed on dangerous persons to prevent future harm. But the theory of enemy criminal law does frame such sentences as punishment, even as it recognizes that the sentences are disproportionate to past offenses. Importantly, the theoretical underpinnings of enemy criminal law are not strictly utilitarian principles allegedly indifferent to individual rights. Instead, theorists of enemy criminal law have found its conceptual justification in a number of social contract thinkers, including Immanuel Kant. This intellectual heritage would surely surprise the Anglo-American school that sees Kant as the godfather of retributive punishment theory. The ostensibly neo-Kantian social contract argument for enemy criminal law runs something like this: A stable political society requires a certain degree of mutual trust; it requires that its members assure one another that they will respect and abide by the law. To fail to provide that reassurance is a basis for punishment—for *deserved* punishment. As put by Carlos Gomez-Jara Diez:

> To the extent that individuals do not provide this minimum level of cognitive reassurance, the legal system does not recognize them as persons (law-abiding citizens) but as sources of danger: in a nutshell, as enemies. Therefore, from the enemies' perspective, the penal system does not impose punishment but sheer coercive measures, and yet, from the citizens' perspective, those penalties are indeed deserved by the enemies (2008, p. 543).[15]

Once again, I emphasize that this account relies on what most Anglo-American desert theorists would consider category mistakes or contradictions in terms. But the theory has been influential in parts of Europe (and in Latin America), and it illustrates that it is possible—for sophisticated theorists as much as ordinary persons unburdened by academic philosophy—to reconcile strategies of preventive confinement with the rhetoric of desert.

III. DESERT AS A RETURN TO REASON

Even if support for deserved incapacitation is widespread, and even if such support can be theoretically defended, it is not clear that policy makers should pursue this approach. If in fact fear and terror are shaping attitudes about deserved punishment, the question arises whether we want to pursue policies driven by such emotions or passions. Perhaps we should pursue another theory of desert. Perhaps we could, and should, discipline judgments made in fear with the orderly, dispassionate conceptions of desert advanced by Anglo-American punishment theorists.

For a more rational desert theory to serve this disciplining function, it needs a way to exclude the influence of fear from assessments of deserved punishment. One option might be to specify carefully the factors a decision maker may legitimately consider when determining desert. The problem with this approach is that desert theorists have never been able to specify these factors, or desert bases, in terms very much more specific than desert itself. As noted above, desert is often defined as a function of some combination of several factors: blameworthiness, crime seriousness, harm, culpability, wrongdoing, autonomy (von Hirsch 1985; Pillsbury 1989; Hurd and Moore 2004). Some scholars define these terms with reference to one another (so, for example, crime seriousness may be a function of harm and culpability); additionally, the components of desert are sometimes treated as interchangeable (culpability and blameworthiness). Because terms such as harm and culpability refer to inexact, elastic concepts, they cannot forestall the possibility that an individual's threatening qualities might be seen as relevant to his desert (Harcourt 1999). The act of making a threat can be construed as either a wrong, a harm, or both. The quality of being threatening, especially if traced to some prior acts by the individual, might similarly be construed as a harm. Although the notion of punishing dangerousness is heresy to most Anglo-American desert theorists, the conceptual resources of these theorists do not seem sufficient to forestall the possibility that nonphilosophical decision makers will evaluate dangerousness to assess desert.

Maybe there is more hope in the methodology, as opposed to the terminology, of desert theory. Late twentieth-century desert theorists have urged that we discipline criminal sentences by introducing rankings, ratios, and geometry. Specifically, thinkers such as Andrew von Hirsch propose a system of rank ordering of offenses, one that places all criminal offenses on a single continuum on the basis of their severity (von Hirsch 1985). Under this approach, sanctions are also ordered on the basis of severity, a task made relatively simple when prison sanctions are the primary sanction. The main question with respect to penalties is the endpoints of the scale—that is, what minimum and maximum penalties will anchor the array of possible sentences (von Hirsch 1985). After the rank ordering is complete, offenses are matched to penalties in order, so that a given offense will not carry a more severe penalty than an offense ranked as more serious on the rank order of crimes.

Could this introduction of order curtail the expansion of penal liability that has been wrought by the notion of deserved incapacitation? A few observations are in order. First, ranking offenses by severity and allocating penalties accordingly is not a method intrinsically linked to desert theory. In fact, Cesare Beccaria and Jeremy Bentham proposed similar approaches in the eighteenth century, though they ranked crimes by harm alone rather than by von Hirsch's combination of harm and culpability (Bentham 1988; Beccaria 1996). Second, the rank-order approach assumes commensurability across all offenses. But it is not clear offenses are commensurable even along the single metric of social harm (as Beccaria recognized), and it is still less clear that the contested conceptions of desert could render all crime commensurable (Beccaria 1996).[16] Imagine one offender who has robbed two homes, in one case holding a resident at gunpoint. A second offender has twice unsuccessfully attempted sexual abuse of a child and is believed likely to reoffend. Is it clear how to rank these offenses relative to one another?[17] Finally, if the rank order is based on assessments of "crime seriousness" that are in turn based on factors such as harm and culpability, this approach will not preclude perceived dangerousness from shaping the analysis. As we have seen, dangerousness might be seen as itself harmful, or as the basis of individual culpability.

Today, in the early years of the twenty-first century, it is clear that many punishment theorists (including many desert theorists) aspire to develop conceptual resources to reform and restrain American sentencing practices. One might share that aspiration for reform, as I do, and nonetheless remain skeptical that desert is a likely means to accomplish it. As much as theorists might like to render desert a rational, dispassionate concept that can check punitive passions, they have not offered any explanation of the components of desert that achieves this goal. Instead, the very concept of deserving seems to invite moral judgments that are likely shaped by passions and emotions. It might be better to acknowledge that "retribution asks basic moral questions which often have emotional responses. As long as the question is what does an offender deserve, the answer is likely to be influenced by emotion" (Pillsbury 1989).

IV. CONCLUSION

Desert and incapacitation are not mutually exclusive, I have argued. It appears likely that the apparent public support for policies of incapacitation coincides with judgments that the incapacitation is deserved. Sentencing reform strategies that emphasize the language of desert are unlikely to curtail support for long-term incapacitation, and may only reinforce it. But I do not think this means those who seek sentencing reform must abandon hope. An alternative strategy would not rely primarily on the concept of desert, but would turn a critical eye to the underlying beliefs, values, and passions that inform desert judgments. If fear is an important ingredient of desert judgments today, perhaps fear itself needs critical scrutiny.

A growing literature on risk perception and cultural cognition studies the way individuals make judgments about what is risky, dangerous, or threatening (Douglas and Wildavsky 1982; Douglas 1994; Sunstein 2005). Not surprisingly, the consensus is that risk perceptions are highly culturally contingent, and, to the degree that risk can be empirically assessed, individuals' risk perceptions are often just wrong. In many instances, though, a judgment that someone or something is threatening is not an empirically falsifiable claim. Our understandings of what (or who) is scary are themselves culturally contingent moral judgments. As one recent article put it, in many instances "risk disputes are really disputes over the good life" (Kahan et al. 2006, p. 1073). It would not be surprising to find that contested or contestable value judgments underlie popular conceptions of threat or dangerousness. And it is likely that, much like assessments of desert, assessments of dangerousness are sometimes intertwined with racial, ethnic, or socioeconomic bias (Ristroph 2006). Fear should be taken seriously, but who is responsible for fear? It is possible, I think, that those who are afraid need to take some responsibility for their own fright—to scrutinize it, perhaps to overcome it, and perhaps simply to live with it. In short, we should take public fear seriously, but we need not take it for granted or take it as necessarily determinative of public policy.

NOTES
1. According to one account, the first explicitly retributive theory of punishment was not advanced until the end of the eighteenth century (Michael and Adler 1933). But this is probably incorrect. Although Michael and Adler are correct to point out that Plato and Aristotle did not themselves advance retributive theories of punishment, each of these

ancient philosophers acknowledged and argued against such theories, which suggests that notions of retribution were present even in ancient Greece.

2. For example, one of the leading book-length studies of desert cites few works older than the mid-twentieth century, and the older works it does cite are not discussions of desert per se (Sher 1987).

3. For a general discussion of the purported antagonism between philosophy and history, and an attempt to dissolve it, see Borradori's (2003) *Philosophy in a Time of Terror: Dialogues with Jurgen Habermas and Jacques Derrida*.

4. As I have shown elsewhere, many of the criminal justice policies decried in the academy as the subordination of desert principles to incapacitation are justified outside the academy in the language of desert (Ristroph 2006).

5. Indeed, some commentators already equate desert with justice (Robinson and Darley 2007; Robinson and Kurzban 2007).

6. Note John Rawls' view that "it seems natural to think of the concept of justice as distinct from the various conceptions of justice and as being specified by the role which these different sets of principles, these different conceptions, have in common" (Rawls 1999, p. 5).

7. Von Hirsch describes desert as a function of crime seriousness, which is in turn a function of harm and culpability. Hurd and Moore portray culpability and wrongdoing to be "the only two ingredients of moral desert" (2004, p. 1141).

8. Shortly after the attacks, William Stuntz (2002) predicted (and recommended) changes in Fourth and Fifth Amendment law that would follow the "crime wave" of September 11, 2001.

9. The American public did not necessarily demand severe sentencing policies, but accepted them, and may now be unable to change the policies even if it wants to (Tonry 2004).

10. According to Congressman Jason Altmire (D-PA), "individuals who actively support terrorist organizations dedicated to harming our nation do not deserve to enjoy the privileges of American citizenship" (Office of Senator Joseph Lieberman 2010). Likewise, President Barack Obama said, "Do these folks deserve Miranda rights? Do they deserve to be treated like a shoplifter down the block? Of course not" (*60 Minutes* 2009).

11. In the United States such laws are sometimes challenged on free speech grounds, and courts have limited the substantive criminal law in this area to "true threats" of physical violence.

12. *Id.* at 2040 [separate opinion of Chief Justice Roberts].

13. Some scholars view autonomy, or capacity to make an independent moral choice, as a component of desert (Pillsbury 1989).

14. The notion of enemy criminal law is derived from Carl Schmitt's friend/enemy distinction, but Jakobs is the source of the phrase. I do not believe Jakobs's work on enemy criminal law is available in English translation, though he discusses some related ideas in "Imputation in Criminal Law and the Conditions for Norm Validity" (Jakobs 2004). For an overview of the theory of enemy criminal law and a discussion relating the concept to American sentencing practices, see Fletcher's (2007) *The Grammar of Criminal Law*.

15. The purported Kantian inspiration for this argument comes from a footnote in Kant's *Perpetual Peace*, where Kant appears to contemplate the possibility that a single individual could exit, or refuse to enter, civil society and thus pose a threat to the society and its members. Against such a person, preemptive and preventive coercion is apparently appropriate:

It is usually assumed that one cannot take hostile action against anyone unless one has already been actively injured by them. This is perfectly correct if both parties are living in a legal civil state. For the fact that the one has entered such a state gives the required guarantee to the other.... But man (or an individual people) in a mere state of nature robs me of any such security and injures me by virtue of this very state in which he coexists with me. He may not have injured me actively (*facto*), but he does injure me by the very law-lessness of his state (*statu iniusto*), for he is a permanent threat to me (Kant 1970/1991, p. 98, n*).

16. "The retributive rank ordering of crimes and punishments (á la von Hirsch) appears just as arbitrary as the utilitarian assessment of social gains and losses, requiring highly debatable empirical and theoretical judgments" (Luna 2003, p. 245).

17. I do not argue that a rank-ordering approach will never yield critical leverage, but only that its leverage is likely much less than proponents of desert hope.

REFERENCES

60 Minutes: President Obama (CBS television broadcast, March 23, 2009), http://www. cbsnews.com/video/watch/?id=4883166n=mncol;lst;1.

Ashenfelter, M. 2010. "Do Terrorists Deserve Due Process?" *The Nation Online* (February 9), http://live.thenation.com/doc/20100222/hayes_video.

Beccaria, C. 1996. *Of Crimes and Punishments*, trans. J. Grigson. New York: Marsilio Publishers (originally published 1764).

Bentham, J. 1988. *The Principles of Morals and Legislation.* New York: Prometheus Books (originally published 1781).

Blakely, G. R., and B. J. Murray. 2002. "Threats, Free Speech, and the Jurisprudence of Federal Criminal Law." *Brigham Young University Law Review* 2002:829–1130.

Borradori, G. 2003. *Philosophy in a Time of Terror: Dialogues with Jurgen Habermas and Jacques Derrida.* Chicago: University of Chicago Press.

Doob, A. N., and J. V. Roberts. 1984. "Social Psychology, Social Attitudes, and Attitudes Toward Sentencing." *Canadian Journal of Behavioural Science* 16:269–80.

Douglas, M. 1994. *Risk and Blame: Essays in Cultural Theory.* New York: Routledge.

Douglas, M., and A. Wildavsky. 1982. *Risk and Culture: An Essay on the Selection of Technological and Environmental Dangers.* Berkeley: University of California Press.

Fletcher, G. 2007. *The Grammar of Criminal Law.* New York: Oxford University Press.

Forman, J. 2009. "Exporting Harshness: How the War on Crime Helped Make the War on Terror Possible." *New York University Review of Law and Social Change* 33:331–74.

Gallie, W. B. 1956. "Essentially Contested Concepts." *Proceedings of the Aristotelian Society* 56:167.

Garland, D. 2001. *The Culture of Control: Crime and Social Order in Contemporary Society.* Chicago: University of Chicago Press.

Gomez-Jara Diez, C. 2008. "Enemy Combatants versus Enemy Criminal Law: An Introduction to the European Debate Regarding Enemy Criminal Law and its Relevance to the Anglo-American Discussion on the Legal Status of Enemy Combatants." *New Criminal Law Review* 11:529–62.

Gromet, D. M., and J. M. Darley. 2009. "Punishment and Beyond: Achieving Justice Through the Satisfaction of Multiple Goals." *Law & Society Review* 43:1–37.

Harcourt, B. 1999. "The Collapse of the Harm Principle." *Journal of Criminal Law and Criminology* 90:109–94.

Huq, A., and C. Muller. 2008. "The War on Crime as Precursor to the War on Terror." *International Journal of Law, Crime and Justice* 36:215–29.

Hurd, H. M., and M. S. Moore. 2004. "Punishing Hatred and Prejudice." *Stanford Law Review* 56:1081–146.

Jakobs, G. 2004. "Imputation in Criminal Law and the Conditions for Norm Validity." *Buffalo Criminal Law Review* 7:491–511.

Kahan, D. M., P. Slovic, D. Braman, and J. Gastil. 2006. "Fear of Democracy: A Cultural Evaluation of Sunstein on Risk." *Harvard Law Review* 119:1071–109.

Kant, I. 1991. "Perpetual Peace: A Philosophical Sketch." In *Political Writings*, ed. H. S. Reiss. Cambridge: Cambridge University Press (originally published 1970).

Lee, Y. 2005. "The Constitutional Right Against Excessive Punishment." *Virginia Law Review* 91:677–745.

Luna, E. 2003. "Punishment Theory, Holism, and the Procedural Conception of Restorative Justice." *Utah Law Review* 2003:205–302.

McCulloch, J., and S. Pickering. 2009. "Pre-Crime and Counter-Terrorism." *British Journal of Criminology* 49:628–45.

Michael, J., and M. J. Adler. 1933. *Crime, Law and Social Science*. London: Kegan Paul, Trench, Trübner & Co.

Mythen, G., and S. Walklate. 2006. "Criminology and Terrorism." *British Journal of Criminology* 46:379–98.

Nilsen, E. S. 2007. "Decency, Dignity, and Desert: Restoring Ideals of Humane Discourse to Constitutional Punishment." *University of California Davis Law Review* 41:111–75.

Office of Senator Joseph Lieberman. 2010. "Lieberman, Brown, Altmire, Dent Introduce Terrorist Expatriation Act." Press release, U.S. Senate (May 6), http://www.lieberman. senate.gov/index.cfm/news-events/news/2010/5/lieberman-brown-altmire-dent-introduce-terrorist-expatriation-act.

Parry, J. T. 2009. "Torture Nation, Torture Law." *Georgetown Law Journal* 97:1001–56.

Pillsbury, S. H. 1989. "Emotional Justice: Moralizing the Passions of Criminal Punishment." *Cornell Law Review* 74:655–710.

Ramsay, P. 2011. "A Political Theory of Imprisonment for Public Protection." In *Retributivism Has a Past. Has It a Future?*, ed. Michael Tonry. New York: Oxford University Press.

Rawls, J. 1999. *A Theory of Justice*. Cambridge, MA: Harvard University Press (originally published 1971).

Resnik, J. 2010. "Detention, the War on Terror, and the Federal Courts." *Columbia Law Review* 110: 579–685.

Ristroph, A. 2006. "Desert, Democracy, and Sentencing Reform." *Journal of Criminal Law and Criminology* 96:1293–352.

———. 2008. "State Intentions and the Law of Punishment." *Journal of Criminal Law and Criminology* 98:1353–406.

———. 2009. "The New Desert." In *Criminal Law Conversations*, ed. P. Robinson, S. Garvey, and K. Ferzan. New York: Oxford University Press.

Roberts, J. V., L. J. Stalans, D. Indermaur, and M. Hough. 2003. *Penal Populism and Public Opinion: Lessons from Five Countries*. New York: Oxford University Press.

Robinson, P. H. 2007a. "Competing Conceptions of Modern Desert: Vengeful, Deontological, and Empirical." *Cambridge Law Journal* 67:145–75.

———. 2007b. "The Role of Moral Philosophers in the Competition Between Deontological and Empirical Desert." *William and Mary Law Review* 48:1831–43.

Robinson, P. H., and J. M. Darley. 1995. *Justice, Liability, and Blame: Community Views and the Criminal Law*. Boulder, CO: Westview Press.

———. 2007. "Intuitions of Justice: Implications for Criminal Law and Justice Policy." *Southern California Law Review* 81:1–67.

Robinson, P. H., and R. Kurzban. 2007. "Concordance and Conflict in Intuitions of Justice." *Minnesota Law Review* 91:1829–907.

Sher, G. 1987. *Desert*. Princeton, NJ: Princeton University Press.

Shklar, J. N. 1986. *Legalism: Law, Morals, and Political Trials*, 2nd ed. Cambridge, MA: Harvard University Press.

Stuntz, W. J. 2002. "Local Policing After the Terror." *Yale Law Journal* 111:2137–94.

Sullum, J. 2002. "Trial Run: Accused Terrorists Get Due Process—When the Government Feels Like It." *Reason* (September 20), http://www.reason.com/archives/2002/09/20/trial-run.

Sunstein, C. 2005. *Laws of Fear: Beyond the Precautionary Principle*. New York: Cambridge University Press.

Tonry, M. 2004. *Thinking about Crime: Sense and Sensibility in American Penal Culture*. New York: Oxford University Press.

von Hirsch, A. 1985. *Past or Future Crimes: Deservedness and Dangerousness in the Sentencing of Criminals*. Piscataway, NJ: Rutgers University Press.

Yankelovich, D. 1991. *Coming to Public Judgment: Making Democracy Work in a Complex World*. Syracuse, NY: Syracuse University Press.

Zimring, F. E. 2006. *The Great American Crime Decline*. New York: Oxford University Press.

Zimring, F. E. and G. Hawkins. 1995. *Incapacitation: Penal Confinement and the Restraint of Crime*. New York: Oxford University Press.

9

Can Above-desert Penalties Be Justified by Competing Deontological Theories?

RICHARD S. FRASE

Numerous contemporary sentencing practices violate some or all theories of desert, and it is likely that these practices will continue no matter how strongly I and other desert theorists condemn them. Thus the best response to such practices may be to try to limit and focus them by articulating their strongest normative justifications and their own inherent limiting principles.

My goal is to identify and evaluate several *nonconsequentialist* arguments in favor of severe, above-desert prison sentences—in particular: life without parole (LWOP), three strikes, other severe mandatory minimum prison terms, and various high-risk-offender laws. I will assume that such sentences seek to reduce crime through deterrence or incapacitation (I do not believe that such measures have been or easily could be supported on a treatment theory). I will focus on nonconsequentialist (deontological) arguments because they compete directly with, and thus pose a more direct challenge to, desert-based arguments.

I will further assume for these purposes that real cases do exist in which even a narrowly tailored above-desert penalty would reduce future serious crimes better than a within-desert penalty, and without clearly unacceptable collateral consequences. I therefore set aside and do not defend severe measures (e.g., the California version of three strikes) that appear, even on their own crime-control terms, to be unnecessary, ineffective, and possibly counterproductive. I assume that the premise of most laws imposing such punishment is that the targeted defendants, or people like them, are expected to commit crimes in the future, at least some of which can be prevented by punishing these defendants more severely than they deserve relative to their past crimes. Finally, I will assume, contrary to some skeptics (e.g., Ristroph 2006), that there is sufficient agreement about the meaning of desert that we can posit actual cases of punishment widely viewed as exceeding desert, at least in relative (ordinal-desert) terms (von Hirsch 1985).

On these assumptions, and to make the exercise more concrete, I examine the following illustrative cases displaying the most common elements of these laws (although not necessarily in their most common forms and combinations; as noted, many of those are indefensible). The risk in doing this, of course, is that readers may take issue with the choice of specific cases or with the supposed "reliable" empirical bases for the sentences. But the theoretical issue posed cannot be addressed without assuming that at least some cases like this do or could exist.

Case 1. An incapacitation-based, nonmandatory LWOP sentence is applied to a repeat (adult-victim) rapist with two prior rape convictions who has failed in previous sex offender treatment programs. The sentencing judge has reliably found that the defendant is very likely to offend again, and that no known treatment methods are likely to eliminate the risk he poses.

Case 2. A deterrence-based, 10-year mandatory minimum penalty is applied to a man with no prior record, convicted of possessing with intent to sell a kilogram of heroin. We will assume the legislature has reliably determined that, even though such offenders are very hard to deter (defendant is not a user but could sell such a drug quantity at a considerable profit), they are not totally undeterrable, and that the 10-year mandatory penalty will discourage such crimes somewhat more than a discretionary or lesser term would.

Case 3. A deterrence and incapacitation-based, nonmandatory 40-year prison term (with parole) is applied to an offender convicted of car theft who has four prior convictions—for larceny, burglary, car theft, and robbery. The sentencing judge has reliably determined that the defendant is very likely to commit one or more of these crimes again because he has no regular job and seems to steal for a living (not to support an addiction). The judge has further determined that career offenders like this one, although strongly attached to their criminal lifestyles, can be deterred by such a severe prison term but are not deterred by a less severe sentence.

In the remainder of this essay, I examine two nonconsequentialist theories that might be cited in support of the sentences described above, notwithstanding the competing nonconsequentialist objection that penalties in excess of desert are fundamentally unfair and unjust:

- a modified Rawlsian theory based on what rational, self-interested people would choose behind the veil of ignorance, not knowing whether, in the real world, they will end up as victims, convicted persons, both, or neither; and
- a competing-rights theory, premised on the view that potential future victims have the right to be protected from an offender's foreseeable future crimes, and that these victims' rights should receive substantial weight, or perhaps even equal or greater weight than the offender's right not to be punished in excess of his deserts.

To my knowledge, the Rawlsian theory has thus far only been discussed by academics. The competing-rights theory finds support in some victims' rights laws, and implicit arguments based on this theory seem to often underlie nonacademic (especially political) discussions of penalties like those in our three illustrative cases. In addition, a version of that theory has surfaced in recent scholarship, and the broader problem of "rights conflicts" has received considerable attention in academic writings.

Even if one or both of the above theories is valid, however, I will argue that each must be strictly limited to ensure that the expected benefits of above-desert penalties exceed their costs and that no equally effective, less severe measures are available. These limits are normally associated with utilitarian philosophy, but they are also implicit in both of the deontological theories being examined here.

I. RAWLSIAN THEORY

Several preliminary observations are in order. First, it must be recognized that Rawls never directly addressed these issues. His primary focus was on distributive justice—on principles for determining a just distribution of primary goods and of social arrangements conducive to individual development. For purposes of developing these principles he assumed a world of "strict compliance" in which the principles he derived would be observed, people and institutions would be just, and there would be little crime. It is therefore necessary to substantially modify not only his focus—shifting from distributive justice to punishment severity—but also his assumptions. In particular, we have to assume a world of "partial compliance" in which a substantial amount of crime exists. This is certainly the world as we know it, perhaps in part because of the failure to comply with Rawls's principles for distribution!

Second, any attempt to apply Rawls's theory to criminal punishment must take account of the apparent indeterminacy of the theory, particularly as applied to punishment—scholars who have examined this topic have come to radically different conclusions. I will return to this problem after summarizing the advantages and key elements of Rawls's theory. However, an important proviso needs to be stated at the outset—I do not ask "what would *Rawls himself* say about above-desert punishment?" Instead, I consider whether different versions of his theory might plausibly support above-desert penalties, and if so, under what conditions.

A. Rawls's Theory: How it Works and Why it Can Be Useful

The Rawlsian framework is potentially a very useful approach in deriving principles of just punishment as well as just distribution of liberties and goods because judgments in all of these areas confront a similar problem: one's sense of fairness and justice is strongly influenced by one's personal characteristics and situation. Therefore, principles of justice need to be developed under conditions of impartiality, where no one knows their own characteristics and situation. Rawls created such conditions by imagining social-contracting parties behind a "veil of ignorance." He referred to this as "the original position" (Rawls 1971).

Rawls then asked what principles of justice would unanimously be chosen by social contractors in the original position (hereafter, "the contractors"), assuming that those persons are free and equal, rational, self-interested, and endowed with two moral powers: (a) a "sense of justice" giving them the capacity to understand, apply, and act from "principles of political justice that specify the fair terms of social cooperation;" and (b) "the capacity to have, to revise, and rationally to pursue a conception of the good" (Rawls 2001, pp. 18–19). Using this approach, Rawls arrived at two principles (Rawls 2001, pp. 42–43): first, all persons in society should have "the same indefeasible claim to a fully adequate scheme of equal basic liberties" and should enjoy as much of these liberties as is "compatible with the same scheme of liberties for all;" second, social and economic inequalities are permitted only if two conditions are met: (a) "they are to be attached to offices and positions open to all under conditions of fair equality of opportunity," and (b) such inequalities must be to the greatest benefit of the least-advantaged members of society"—that is, such members must be better off than they would be under any alternate arrangement. The latter is known as the "difference principle," and it reflects an important way in which Rawls's theory differs from utilitarianism, and in particular, from "average" utilitarianism, which Rawls believed the contractors would reject. Rawls concluded that a contractor would not seek to maximize the liberties and material goods of the average person in society, but instead would apply the "maximin" strategy of maximizing that contractor's position even if he or she ended up occupying the least-advantaged position (Rawls 1971).

One explanation for the difference principle and maximin strategy (Dolovich 2004) is that the contractors would lack sufficient information to rationally maximize the average person's position since they face total uncertainty about a number of critical facts: their odds of being above or below that average (or even above or below the median position); the ratio of very well-off to very disadvantaged persons; and the nature of the "worst case" (which could, under average utilitarianism, be abject poverty, slavery, or even death such as by periodic liquidation of very "unproductive" persons). It has also been argued that the maximin strategy can be derived directly from core values such as equal worth, self-esteem, stability, and harmony that are assumed as part of Rawls's theory (Musgrave 1974). A third explanation for the difference principle is that at least some of the contractors would be (or could imagine becoming, once the veil is lifted) risk averse; as persons with such an aversion (or on behalf of them), the contractors would refuse to approve any arrangement unless it would benefit them if they ended up as one of the least-advantaged persons (Sterba 1977). Dolovich (2004, n. 110) argues that Rawls himself saw uncertainty as the best explanation. One problem with the risk-aversion theory is that some people actually *prefer* risk (i.e., they are gamblers, willing to accept the risk of a very bad outcome in return for the chance of getting a very good one); if the contractors also included (or could imagine becoming) persons with that perspective, they would never unanimously agree to the maximin strategy.

B. Rawls on Punishment and Desert

The first step in applying Rawls's theory to punishment is to identify who the possible least-advantaged groups are in this context. Writers seeking to apply Rawls's theory to punishment issues consider two groups as potentially the least advantaged: crime victims and convicted criminals. Some writers separately identify a third group: innocent persons wrongly convicted. One way of posing the central question, in Rawlsian terms, is to ask whether the contractors would approve of above-desert, crime-preventive penalties in order to improve the lot of potential crime victims, in the belief that the corresponding worsening of the position of convicted criminals and the wrongly convicted would still leave those groups better off than their victims would have been if the crimes had not been prevented. A second way to pose the central question is to ask whether the contractors would, independent of their goal of minimizing the risk of being a crime victim, also want to minimize their risk of being unfairly punished—could they, as rational and self-interested persons, value desert-based (or at least, desert-limited) punishment as well as crime control? Of course, one problem with all of these formulations is that for some crimes, such as illegal drug or gun possession, there are usually no direct victims. For these crimes, the contractors would presumably have to imagine how (postveil) they might be indirectly harmed by such crimes, and in particular, the *worst ways* they might be harmed.

As was noted previously, Rawls's theory seems to generate very different answers to these questions: his theory has been interpreted by some as supporting desert limits and by others as indifferent to—or even undermining—desert principles. Writers who have argued that Rawls saw punishment as based on retributive goals, or at least subject to retributive upper limits, have based this view in part on one of the few comments Rawls specifically made about punishment, in which he seemed to imply that it can only be imposed on persons who deserve it (Rawls 1971; see also Rawls 1955). The Rawls-favors-desert view also draws support from several other quarters: from Rawls's (1971) acknowledgment of the relationship between his approach and Kantian philosophy, which is strongly desert-based; from the fact that at least some modern desert theorists cite or seem to draw from Rawls's work (Cavender 1981; Thornburn and Manson 2007); and from some writers' applications of his methods (see, e.g., Card 1973; Morris 1974; Sterba 1977; Hoekema 1980; Reed 1980; Donnelly 1990; Garvey 2004). But arguments of the latter type often do not convincingly show, or even seek to show, exactly how and why the contractors would inevitably and unanimously adopt desert principles. Rather, Rawls-favors-desert advocates (but also those of the opposing view, discussed below) seem to assume that the contractors will, necessarily, share the advocates' own sense of fundamental values.

Other commentators have concluded that Rawls's method or his premises give retribution no role as applied to punishment, and may even undermine a theory of desert. One view is that the contractors, as rational self-interested persons, care only about minimizing the risks of being a victim of crime or a subject of punishment, and do not care about desert or other issues of fairness per se (see, e.g., Narveson 1974). But again, how can we be sure of that? Isn't it possibly "rational and self-interested" to promote fairness, especially fairness to the least-advantaged group that any of the contractors might end up in? Another view is that Rawls's method justifies above-desert punishment, but only under certain conditions (Dolovich 2004).

A further basis for questioning Rawls's support for a desert-based theory of punishment derives, ironically, from Rawls's statement that desert can play no role in issues of distribution of goods, even if it does play a role in distribution of punishment. Rawls explained the first half of this statement by noting that persons do not deserve the differences in ability and circumstances that would help them get a larger share of material goods, even if they do deserve a larger share based on their greater efforts, and when assessing whether a particular distribution of goods is just, it is impossible to identify and disentangle the contribution of these two factors (Rawls 1971, p. 312). Yet Rawls also stated, without elaboration, that no such problem applies to the distribution of punishment based on desert (Rawls 1955, 1971, pp. 314–15). Supporters of the Rawls-favors-desert-in-punishment view (e.g., Sheffler 2000) defend this so-called asymmetry of desert, arguing that distributions of goods and of punishment are fundamentally different. But other writers (e.g., Husak 2000; Morriarity 2003; Mills 2004; Ristroph 2006) question the asymmetry concept, and some of them go on to question the validity of desert as applied to punishment—if people do not deserve the traits that help them get more goods, and thus do not deserve (or fully deserve) the extra goods, then criminals do not deserve their bad characters, and thus do not deserve (or fully deserve) the punishments that bad character leads them to incur.

Finally, quite apart from the asymmetry problem, it can be argued that any decision to apply Rawls, and especially the difference principle, to punishment issues represents at least a partial rejection of free will and blame. The argument against applying Rawls's theory to punishment issues is that a contractor would not fear becoming a criminal and being severely punished once the veil is lifted, since crime is a matter of choice; the argument against that view and in favor of considering criminals as potentially the least-advantaged group is that the contractors know they might be born into circumstances that make it very hard to avoid crime (Morris 1974; Dolovich 2004). But then, how can they be blamed for those crimes?

However, these two desert-skeptical arguments, while relevant to desert theory generally and further documenting the apparent indeterminacy of Rawls's theory, are of less concern to the question being addressed here, as to whether some version of Rawls's theory can justify above-desert penalties. Such desert-skeptical arguments, if accepted, may justify lower penalties based on mitigated desert, but they do not justify enhanced penalties above what fully deserving offenders should receive.

C. Dolovich's Rawlsian Model

Perhaps the most elaborate attempt to apply Rawls's approach to problems of punishment and the limits of desert is found in an article by Professor Sharon Dolovich (2004). This article adopts a middle ground under which disproportionately severe penalties are only permitted under certain conditions. Dolovich assumes that the contractors would consider three groups as potentially the "least advantaged" persons: crime victims, convicted criminals, and innocent persons wrongly convicted. Her analysis of proportionality focuses on the severity of harm to victims. Since this ignores the other important element of retributive proportionality—mens rea and other culpability factors—her approach might suggest a purely utilitarian conception of proportionality (Garvey 2004, n. 17; Frase 2005). But since she does not say this, and because Rawls's model was intended to be, and is commonly seen as, a nonutilitarian theory, in the remainder of the present discussion it will be assumed that she means to address the legitimacy of penalties that are disproportionate in a retributive sense.

Under Dolovich's Rawlsian analysis (2004, pp. 386–90), it is not permissible to impose a penalty of incarceration for "nonserious" crimes (those that do not "credibly and seriously violate or threaten the security and integrity" of victims). The contractors would reject such a penalty because it would make the offender worse off in terms of security and integrity than his future victims would be if those crimes were not prevented. (Dolovich apparently assumes that the primary preventive mechanism is deterrence, and thus the crimes most likely to be prevented are, like the offender's conviction offense, nonserious.)

As for "serious" crimes (such as those at issue in all three of the illustrative cases posed above), Dolovich argues (2004, pp. 390–94) that the contractors would permit incarceration if it would have "an appreciable deterrent effect" on other crimes of the same severity as the offender's crime. However, two important provisos apply: there must be no risk of wrongful conviction, and the adverse effect of incarceration on the offender's security and integrity must be no greater than the improved effect on the security and integrity of at least one potential victim. The offender's wrongful act justifies putting him, not the victim, in the worst position. At the same time, this "trade" maintains proportionality between the harm of the offense and the punishment (again, assuming that crimes prevented are generally similar in severity to the offender's crime).

A different rule applies (Dolovich 2004, pp. 392–93) in cases where the contractors do assume a risk of wrongful conviction (which, it seems, they would have to). In that case, Dolovich says Rawls's theory requires that the punishment must be likely to deter crimes of equal severity against *at least two* future victims. Since an innocent, wrongly convicted person might now occupy the worst position, the contractors would require a greater crime-preventive effect to counterbalance that even worse worst position. The requirement of equal severity means that the punishment's adverse effect on the offender's security and integrity would still be proportional to the harm of each offense prevented (and thus, generally, proportional to the offender's crime).

In limited circumstances, Dolovich (2004, pp. 394–400) says Rawls's theory would permit punishment that is *disproportionately severe* relative to the offender's past crime. One such case is where disproportionately severe punishment could deter (or otherwise prevent, as by incapacitation?) a more serious crime, and Dolovich gives two examples: (a) a severe penalty for an offense of simple assault that may prevent one or more murders; and (b) a disproportionate penalty for a "nonserious" crime (defined above), which would have "an appreciable deterrent effect" on future "serious" crimes. The maximin principle is satisfied provided that the severe penalty still leaves the convicted person in an equal or better position, in terms of security and integrity, than would be occupied by the victim(s) of the unprevented crime(s). In the first example, Dolovich adds that in such cases "the deterrent effect need not be appreciable," and it does not matter whether the contractors assume a risk of wrongful conviction; apparently it is difficult to punish someone (short of the death penalty, at least) so severely or wrongly that their position is worse than that of a murder victim whose life *might* be spared by the severe punishment. As for the second example, "appreciable" deterrent effect is required, which for these purposes means the disproportionate penalty given the offender convicted of a non-serious crime is "reasonably certain to deter at least two future serious crimes."

Thus far, Dolovich's application of Rawls's theory would seem to permit above-desert punishment only in the third illustrative case (the car thief; his varied prior crimes suggest that his future crimes might be more serious). In the first two illustrative cases, the offender's past and likely future crimes are of equal seriousness, but perhaps those two cases are covered by another set of rules Dolovich derives from Rawls's theory. She argues (2004, pp. 396–99) that disproportionate punishment is permitted where the contractors believe it will prevent future crimes of the same severity, but will do so *more effectively* than would proportionate punishment. There are two further provisos: (a) there must be no risk of wrongful conviction, and (b) there must be some (unspecified) limits to the degree of disproportionality imposed. Again, such punishment effects a "trade" between the adverse positions of the future victim and the convicted, noninnocent offender. According to Dolovich, the wrongfulness of the offender's act justifies this trade, even if the disproportionate punishment puts the offender in a worse position than the victim would have been in were the crime not (more effectively) prevented. The trade is not permitted if there is a risk of wrongful conviction, because then a disproportionately punished innocent offender would be put in a worse position than the victim would have been in.

The permitted trade seems to lack practical significance, given the proviso that there be no risk of wrongful conviction—how could the contractors rationally make this assumption about a world of "partial compliance"? However, even if it must be assumed that there will always be such a risk, it could be argued, citing Dolovich's own analysis, that the contractors might rationally choose to approve disproportionate punishment to more effectively prevent crimes of the same seriousness. In most of her analysis, Dolovich compares the harm of a single offender's punishment with a single victim's preventable harm, and argues that the contractors would want to keep these two harms in proportion. However, in some cases she adopts a rule requiring the prevention of *two* future crimes, which suggests that the *number* of future victims is relevant to the proportionality analysis. And at one point, while arguing for disproportionate punishment of a nonserious offense if it will deter at least two future serious crimes, she notes that the contractors will have to imagine becoming one of these potential victims, and that such victims are "necessarily greater in number than the targeted offenders" (Dolovich 2004, p. 400). This comment seems to reflect the reality that offenders often victimize more than one person, sometimes a great many more. The latter view is certainly a reasonable assumption for the contractors to make when considering severe penalties for repeat offenders (at least two of our illustrative above-desert cases fall into this category). In such cases, the contractors could rationally conclude that, once the veil is lifted, they are more likely to end up being a victim of such a person's crimes than being the offender. They might then impose disproportionate penalties on that offender. Even if this puts the offender in a worse position than any individual victim would have been in if that crime were not prevented (and puts the wrongly convicted person in a worse position still), the contractors arguably would accept that outcome because they are more likely to end up being one of this offender's future victims (or a victim of a similar offender sought to be deterred).

Although the argument just suggested could plausibly be based on a modified version of Rawls's theory, it seems inconsistent with the version Rawls himself favored. Having the contractors "play the odds" of becoming a victim or an offender looks a lot like the "average" utilitarianism that Rawls explicitly rejected in favor of the maximin strategy. Under the latter strategy, the contractors ask themselves, what is the worst position I could end up in, under the proposed (punishment) principles, and would that position be any better under an alternative set of principles? The focus is on the conditions of the worst position, not the probability of being in that position. In addition, such speculation about probabilities may violate one of the assumptions underlying the maximin strategy: that the contractors face total uncertainty about the frequency distribution of worst-case and other outcomes (although the idea that some offenders commit multiple crimes, and that under some circumstances severe punishment can prevent some of those crimes, would seem to fall within the "general facts" about human society that persons in the original position are deemed to know; Rawls 1971, pp. 137–38).

D. The Limits of the Rawlsian Model

Assuming that at least some versions of Rawls's theory might sometimes support above-desert punishment, what are the limits of such punishment? As is implicit in several of the rules Dolovich proposes, it can be argued that persons behind the veil would specify that such severe penalties must be shown to be *effective, necessary,* and *harm-proportioned.* To the extent that severe measures are of weak or unknown effectiveness, or their desired effects are likely to be offset by undesirable consequences (e.g., offenders become more crime-prone in prison, and disadvantaged communities get worse due to mass incarceration), the value of these measures to potential victims diminishes and the original contractors would be less willing to tolerate the measures. The contractors would also reject severe measures that are not needed, given the availability of equally effective but less severe alternatives. This preference for the least onerous effective measure—sometimes referred to as the parsimony principle—is most often associated with utilitarian philosophy (Frase 2004, 2005), but it is also strongly implicit in Rawls's theory, and it would appear to invalidate most mandatory minimum penalties (Dolovich 2004). Thus the LWOP sentence in case 1 is invalid, even though not mandatory for the judge, because it prevents parole and correctional authorities from subsequently reappraising the facts and choosing a shorter but equally effective prison term. And although the minimum penalty in illustrative case 2 is stipulated to be based on a reliable legislative determination that a lesser penalty would provide less deterrence, most mandatory minima lack such a determination and thus cannot be justified by Rawlsian analysis because they prevent sentencing judges from choosing a lesser penalty even when that would be equally effective.

Finally, the seriousness of prevented crimes is an important criterion; to the extent that the crimes prevented are minor (e.g., a string of small thefts from stores), the "payoff" in preventing even a large number of them is outweighed by the suffering that an original contractor would anticipate if he or she were to end up being such an offender. The weighing of expected benefits and burdens is a familiar utilitarian exercise (Frase 2005), but it operates differently (and Rawls would say, more justly) when conducted from behind the veil of ignorance (with or without the maximin strategy). In the real world, most punishment policy makers can scarcely imagine being offenders.

In some cases, more than one of these three limiting principles will combine to invalidate an above-desert sentence. For example, the contractors might reject a very long sentence for selling drugs (even if not, as in case 2, a mandatory sentence) due to uncertainty as to the deterrent effectiveness of such a measure, the harms caused solely by the use of that drug (and not by its prohibition), and the available alternative controls—the number of overdoses prevented, the other harms prevented, and the ease of achieving similar levels of control through alternatives such as addict maintenance.

Within these limits, Rawls's theory is arguably capable of justifying at least some above-desert penalties; for example, the nonmandatory 40-year sentence in illustrative case 3, and perhaps some severe penalties similar to those in cases 1 and 2, but lacking their mandatory features. On the other hand, it can be argued that Rawls's theory would not justify any of these sentences. Dolovich (2004) argues that no one behind the veil would ever agree to give up their dignity and humanity, which is what very severe penalties seem to force them to do. In case 3, the 40-year sentence for an adult offender is, in effect, a life sentence, and one with very little prospect of early release following successful treatment, hence it is a de facto LWOP sentence. Similarly, the life sentence in case 1, even if stripped of its mandatory no-release feature, would probably amount to LWOP. The counterargument is that the original contractors would at least permit such a sentence for repeated serious violent crimes like those in case 1, which also strip victims of their dignity and humanity.

Another reason to doubt a Rawlsian defense of above-desert sentences like those in the illustrative cases is that the contractors would know they are designing rules for an imperfect, partial-compliance world. In such a world, there is an inherent risk of overpunishment, due to the familiar problems of law-and-order politics, short-term expediency, and other limitations of criminal law policy making and application. There is also an inherent risk—indeed, a practical certainty—that severe penalties will be imposed unequally due to failures of detection and proof and exercises of discretion, and that such inequalities will often correlate with race, social class, and other invalid criteria. Thus, the original contractors might rationally seek to counter such upward pressures and abhorrent disparities by recognizing desert as an independent limitation on penalty severity in all cases, without exception. The counterargument is that the contractors, behind the veil, have no way to know whether in the world they will find once the veil is lifted, overpunishment and disparity will be bigger problems than rampant, uncontrolled crime.

These arguments and counterarguments, combined with the earlier discussion of the very different conclusions reached by writers seeking to apply Rawls's theory to punishment severity, suggest a fundamental problem: perhaps this theory is simply too indeterminate to provide useful guidance and specific principles that will be convincing to persons, regardless of their values and politics, when deciding whether and when to permit above-desert punishment. Most writers read Rawls's theory as prohibiting above-desert penalties, at least under most circumstances, so it appears that the theory provides, at most, limited support for such penalties. Let us move on, then, to consider another deontological theory that perhaps provides stronger support, in part because it addresses more directly the fundamental issue of the competing rights and interests of offenders and potential victims.

II. COMPETING RIGHTS OF POTENTIAL CRIME VICTIMS

A second theory dispenses with the veil of ignorance thought experiment and simply asserts that, in the world we are already in, potential victims have a reasonable moral claim against the state to be protected from an offender's foreseeable future crimes. The theory posits, in essence, that citizens have a positive right requiring the state to take measures to prevent such crimes. The strongest form of this theory argues that this positive right must receive at least as much weight as the offender's negative right not to be punished more than he deserves.

A. The Right of Potential Crime Victims to Be Protected

Given the massive literature on various aspects and theories of crime victims' rights, it is remarkable how little attention has been paid to the idea of potential victims' positive rights to be protected. Most of the existing literature deals only with the rights of *current* crime victims, in particular, their procedural rights in the criminal process; their rights to obtain compensation from the offender or the state; and their rights (especially in cases of domestic violence) to have the offender's conditions of release reflect the risk of continued victimization. But there does not seem to be any insuperable legal barrier to recognizing and protecting the rights of future victims who are not also current victims; for example, a class action seeking injunctive relief will often be designed to protect persons who have not yet had their rights violated, but who fear this will happen in the future. Although some theorists question whether future victims (especially those not even born yet) can be rights holders, other writers conclude that a future person can qualify (see, e.g., Rainbolt 2006). Andrew von Hirsch and Andrew Ashworth (2005, pp. 51–52) question whether potential victims can be said to have rights against the state, even if they have rights against the offender. But there are substantial grounds, based on social contract theory, natural law, constitutional texts, and the government's punishment monopoly, to conclude that the government has a duty to protect its citizens from crime and that citizens thus have a right—indeed, a constitutional right—to be protected (Aynes 1984).

Moreover, such rights have been expressly recognized in state and proposed federal constitutional victims' rights amendments. For example, the California Constitution (art. I, sect. 28), recognizes both individual and collective victims' rights. The former includes the right "to be reasonably protected from the defendant and persons acting on behalf of the defendant," the right "to have the safety of the victim and the victim's family considered" in determining pretrial release, and the right "to have the safety of the victim, the victim's family, and the general public considered before any parole or other post-judgment release decision is made" (sect. 28(b)(2), (3), and (16)). In addition, "the rights of victims also include broader shared collective rights that are held in common with all of the People of the state," including the right to have offenders "sufficiently punished so that the public safety is protected and encouraged as a goal of highest importance" (sect. 28(a)(4)). The latter provision, which is addressed specifically to sentencing, has no counterpart in the list of individual victim rights. However, such a provision is found in the proposed U.S. Victim's Rights Amendment, which gives victims the right to "adjudicative decisions that duly consider the victim's safety" (Roach 2005, p. 484).

Von Hirsch and Ashworth (2005, p. 52) also argue that any theory allowing potential victims' rights to be "balanced" against the offender's desert-based moral rights is simply a disguised form of cost–benefit analysis. But even though the weighing of defendant versus future-victim interests resembles the balancing of interests typically done by utilitarians, one can still speak of the latter interests in terms of rights—if one of these people subsequently becomes a victim, and if some person or entity (here, the state) had the duty and the ability to prevent the crime, then the victim can plausibly say that his or her "right to be protected" has been violated.

B. Resolving the Conflict Between Victim and Offender Rights

Assuming that victims, individually or collectively, have moral and sometimes legal rights to be protected from foreseeable future victimization, it seems both theoretically possible and practically likely that such victims' rights will conflict with the offender's right not to be punished in excess of what he deserves based on the crimes for which he has already been convicted. There does not seem to have been much scholarly attention given to this problem, although there is considerable writing on other specific rights conflicts, the problem of rights conflicts in general, and the various logical and jurisprudential tools for resolving such conflicts (see, e.g., Kamm 2002; Brems 2008). Some writers deny that a conflict can exist if each right is properly defined, relying on a technique referred to as "specification" (if the redefining is done ex ante) or a theory of "a priori" rights (which cease to conflict once the particular circumstances are taken into account) (Rainbolt 2006). However, the former approach seems unworkable (rights definitions become too unwieldy), and both approaches ultimately beg the question: in determining *how* each right should be narrowed (ex ante, or under the circumstances) to avoid conflict, what sort of normative or analytic framework must be applied (Zalta 2009, sect. 5.2).

One approach defines rights in term of priorities: right A (or the class of rights to which it belongs) outweighs right B (or its class), subject perhaps to certain exceptions. Some have argued that negative rights always outweigh positive rights, but that priority is difficult to justify across the board. The importance of some positive rights (e.g., a starving man's right to food) may be greater than the importance of some negative rights (e.g., the right not to have one's lunch stolen) (Zalta 2009, sect. 2.1.8). Moreover, the distinction collapses if a positive right (e.g., the starving man's right to food) can be restated in negative terms (the starving man's right not to have anyone interfere with his attempt to steal a nonstarving person's lunch).

Rights priorities are sometimes dictated by differences in the sources of the conflicting rights: a defendant's constitutional right would normally be deemed to outweigh the victim's subconstitutional (statutory) right. Yet even when victims' rights are given constitutional stature, as some states have done, courts may give priority to defendant rights. For example, in *State ex rel. Romley v. Superior Court In and For County of Maricopa*, 836 P.2d 445 (Ariz. Ct. App. 1992), the court held that where a defendant's federal and state constitutional rights to present a defense and effectively cross-examine trial witnesses directly conflict with a victim's state constitutional right to refuse pretrial interviews by the defense, the defendant's rights are superior. The same priority arguably applies if the defendant right in question is substantive (the right not to be punished in excess of desert) rather than, as in *Romley*, procedural. (In *Romley*, the victim's right was based on privacy and thus, like the hypothesized right to be protected from foreseeable harm, was essentially a substantive right.) Rights priorities can also be specified by legislative or constitutional text. For example, section 1 of the proposed U.S. Constitutional Victims' Rights Amendment states that the rights of violent crime victims are "capable of protection without denying the [accused's] constitutional rights," and this language seems to indicate that in the case of conflict, the rights of the defendant should prevail (Roach 2005).

The conflicting victim and offender rights being considered lack textual priority and they cannot be fully reconciled based on a source-of-law theory (both may be of equal stature, and despite cases like *Romley*, above, it is not clear that offender rights must always prevail). In the absence of such clear criteria, courts and theorists resort to other means to resolve rights conflicts, either categorically or case by case. One approach is essentially to compromise or balance the rights, seeking to give some effect to both of them, or at least to the "core" values of each. This is the explicit requirement of case law under the Canadian charter (Roach 2005, p. 509, citing a case holding that "when the protected rights of two individuals come into conflict . . . charter principles require a balance to be advanced that fully respects the importance of both sets of rights"). Applying this solution to victim and offender rights would perhaps require limiting each right to minimize the number of conflicts. But what criteria set these limits? Or, if one right is to be given priority (in general, or in certain circumstances), how is that to be done?

In the end, it seems that courts must seek compromise or set priorities according to the importance of the underlying interests protected by each right (perhaps also giving weight to the probability, imminence, and irreparability of harms for each right, in typical cases or under the facts at hand). In one of the few explicit discussions of the competing rights of potential crime victims, Antony Bottoms and Roger Brownsword (1983, pp. 15–20) cite general principles of rights conflicts developed by Ronald Dworkin and conclude that an offender's desert-based rights should only be overridden in cases of "vivid danger." Bottoms and Brownsword argue that factors to be considered should include the seriousness, frequency, immediacy, and certainty of the threatened future harm. To guard against political pressures to overuse preventive detention, they further stipulate that the defendant must have already been convicted of causing or attempting "very serious violence" (Bottoms and Brownsword 1983, pp. 15–20).

Applying these standards, it can be argued that a substantial risk to human life (of a future murder victim) outweighs at least some additional years of freedom for the defendant (even when the value of the latter is augmented by the physical, emotional, and medical hazards of prison life, and the unfairness of above-desert punishment). Conversely, the defendant's lost freedom and other burdens are serious and in some sense irreparable harms that, if severe enough, ought to outweigh even a fairly certain loss of property by future victims. But in some cases the underlying interests will be of approximately equal importance, in which case the rights conflict is insoluble—akin to the classic case where a trolley driver must either stay on one track and violate A's rights by killing him, or switch tracks and kill B (Rainbolt 2006, p. 181). Moreover, under either of the ad hoc approaches above (compromise or priority based on a weighing of interests), the values underlying each right, or the core of each right, may simply be incommensurable (Brems 2008, p. 29). In that case, again, the conflict may be insoluble.

C. The Sunstein–Vermeule Argument Based on Competing Moral Claims

To make these rights trade-offs and their resolution more specific, consider a recent article by Sunstein and Vermeule (2005) that seems to presuppose the existence of positive rights of potential victims that may compete directly against moral arguments in favor of offenders. These authors argue that, despite moral objections to capital punishment (in general, or in particular cases such as when the penalty is undeservedly severe), the state has a moral duty to use this penalty if executions will deter more killings than they inflict. A key assumption of their argument is that, with respect to duties imposed on the state, there is no moral difference between action and inaction (even if there usually is a difference with respect to duties imposed on individuals). Thus Sunstein and Vermeule argue, the state "kills" by inaction when it permits the death of victims whose lives it could have saved by employing the death penalty. Since the state "kills" either way, persons with deontological moral objections to state killing should prefer the option that results in fewer state killings; that option would be capital punishment, assuming it deters and does so more effectively than alternative punishments.

Of course, those are very questionable assumptions (for a recent meta-analysis concluding that the death penalty does not add measurable deterrence, see Dölling et al. [2009]). And the rhetorical strength of the Sunstein–Vermeule argument—claiming that the state "kills" by inaction—may be limited to crimes like homicide that involve an element of causation and impose liability for negligently, recklessly, or knowingly (not purposefully) causing the prohibited result. It is harder to say that the state "steals," "rapes," or "sells illegal drugs" when it fails to prevent those kinds of crimes. Still, to the extent that these authors are making a deontological, victim-centered moral argument in favor of more severe punishment, their argument may have application to crimes other than homicide. In the context of the kinds of severe prison sentences being examined, the broader Sunstein–Vermeule argument holds that negative-rights-based objections to above-desert penalties can be overcome by positive-rights-based objections to the state allowing serious crimes to occur that could have been prevented by such penalties.

As critics of the Sunstein–Vermeule death penalty defense have pointed out (Steiker 2005; Blumenson 2007), one could argue that even if potential murder victims do have positive rights and can exert a substantial moral claim on the state, a victim's positive right to have his life protected by the state is less weighty than the defendant's negative right not to have his life extinguished. This priority need not be based on any general distinction between positive and negative rights (which, as noted above, is questionable); immediately causing death by the deliberate act of execution is prima facie a more serious moral wrong than doing so foreseeably and indirectly (just as, for individuals, purposeful conduct is more culpable than negligent conduct, and liability is more likely to be imposed for acts that cause immediate harm than for those causing less proximate harm). If we analogize the state's responsibility to that of an accomplice who fails to make proper efforts to prevent a crime despite having a legal duty to do so (Model Penal Code, sect. 2.06(3)(a)(iii)), it should be noted that such liability requires that the actor have a *purpose* to promote or facilitate the crime (which the state lacks here).

Blumenson (2007) further argues that deliberate killing through execution violates more than just that offender's right to life, it "abolish[es] the right to life for everyone" by announcing that life is not inviolable. Blumenson admits that these objections may not apply to penalties other than death; they only apply, he suggests, to penalties that violate rights "reflecting the inviolability of a person," which "at least include the rights to life, to bodily integrity, and to one's thoughts" (2007, p. 230). Of the three illustrative cases posed at the outset, only the first involves a sentence (LWOP) severe enough to possibly be subject to Blumenson's death penalty critique.

Yet even for less extreme penalties, Sunstein and Vermeule's implicit competing-victims-rights argument must overcome the objections, noted above, based on the state's lack of purpose to cause harm to the victims and the lack of direct causation. Still, even if these distinctions make the moral claim against the state of a single, foreseeably-harmed future victim less weighty than the claim of a single offender facing a deliberately imposed above-desert prison sentence, what if the former claims are more numerous, as they would be if imposing an above-desert sentence will prevent multiple serious future crimes that this offender would have committed? Sunstein and Vermeule seem to argue that among competing rights of equal stature, the state is morally bound to pursue the course of action that protects the greater number of rights holders. Perhaps similar reasoning could apply even when victim and offender rights are not of equal stature, provided that the holders of the less weighty right (the right of potential victims to be protected from foreseeable crimes by the offender) are more numerous than the holder(s) of the more valued right.

However, at least in some contexts, it does not seem that rights can be compared and traded off in this way. In the law of self-defense, for example, we do not say that a person may kill an attacker in order to put an end to a string of nondeadly assaults, even if (as is often the case in the domestic violence context) those assaults are very likely to continue in the future. The requirements of proportionality and necessity of defensive force are applied by assessing the severity and imminence of the particular attack being repelled, not the aggregate harms reasonably feared in a string of future attacks. Similarly, under state laws and Fourth and Eighth Amendment decisions, a nonviolent car thief cannot be arrested with deadly force, or given the death penalty, no matter how many cars he is likely to steal in the future.

To summarize, if we allow the right of potential crime victims to outweigh the offender's right not to be punished in excess of his desert, in cases where these rights seem to unavoidably conflict, it seems we must adopt one or both of the following propositions:

- A potential victim's right to be protected is more weighty than the offender's right not to be punished in excess of his desert (despite the state "mens rea" and proximate cause problems noted above). This proposition seems especially strong in cases where the offender is very likely to commit a future crime that is *more serious* than the crime for which he is now being punished.

- Even if (or when) one victim's right does not outweigh one offender's right, the rights of several potential crime victims outweigh the offender's right (but, as noted, rights conflicts usually are not resolved in this way).

Returning to our three illustrative cases, case 3 seems to involve the "especially strong" version of the first proposition above—the offender's extensive prior record indicates a high risk for further crime, including some crimes (burglary, robbery) more serious than the current offense (auto theft). The other two illustrative cases involve a risk of future crimes that are similar if not identical to the current offense. The potential-victims'-rights argument seems weak with respect to the drug offender (case 2), given the absence of identifiable victims in such cases. The principal potential victims include future drug users, their families, and the residents of drug-infested neighborhoods. The positive rights of these potential victims seem quite attenuated, since they are based on harms that are indirect as well as unintended (on the state's part); such rights are therefore of much less weight than the defendant's negative right not to suffer immediate, deliberate undeserved punishment. One could argue, along the lines suggested above, that the victims' moral claims would outweigh the defendant's if it could be shown that the potential indirect harms to these victims are highly probable, highly frequent, and very likely to be prevented by an above-desert sentence. However, as was suggested in section I, these conditions may be quite difficult to meet; in the drug offender case it is only stipulated that the legislature found *some* additional deterrence of heroin sales.

D. The Limits of the Competing-Rights Theory

Rights conflicts should be avoided whenever possible, and this can be done by making sure that each right is defined no more broadly than necessary to protect its core values. On the offender-desert side, conflict can be lessened by adopting a more flexible, limiting retributive model permitting a range of "not-undeserved" penalties (Morris 1974). However, such a model must, itself, be kept within limits or it ceases to have any real meaning or value (Frase 2004). The scope of potential-victims' rights must likewise be defined as narrowly as possible; as with the Rawlsian justification discussed in section I, application of the victims' rights theory should be limited to cases where an above-desert penalty is shown to be *effective, necessary,* and *harm-proportioned.* To the extent that such a penalty is of weak or unknown effectiveness to protect potential victims (as may be true in many drug cases; see above), its value to potential victims diminishes, and with it, the weight to be given to their positive-rights claims. The same is true if an above-desert penalty is not needed, given the availability of equally effective but less severe alternatives, or if the crimes prevented are deemed minor compared with the suffering that above-desert punishment imposes on the offender. In case 1 (LWOP to incapacitate an untreatable repeat rapist), such an offender can be civilly committed (although perhaps that merely imposes punishment under another name). Surgical or chemical castration could also be effective alternatives (although some would say the surgical option is as severe as life imprisonment). In any event, the victims'-rights rationale does not seem to justify an LWOP sentence; many sex offenders cease to be dangerous as they grow older, so holding them all until they die is unnecessary to the protection of potential victims.

In many cases, including perhaps some variations of each of the three illustrative cases, it may also be true that a major shift of punishment resources to social or police prevention measures would be as effective (indeed, perhaps much more effective) than the proposed above-desert penalties. Although such a shift is unlikely to occur in most jurisdictions, the state arguably has a moral duty to exhaust all feasible alternatives—intrinsically immoral state action must truly be a last resort (Steiker 2005, pp. 785–86; Blumenson 2007, n. 68).

With these limits, then, what is wrong with the potential-victims'-rights theory? One objection is that such positive rights are exceptional, at least in U.S. law, and thus should not stand on the same footing as negative rights such as the defendant's right not to be punished in excess of desert. For better or worse, U.S. citizens have few legal and moral claims for proactive protection by their governments. But, of course, new rights of any kind can always be created by positive law; indeed, victims' rights laws in the United States have already recognized many positive as well as negative procedural rights, rights to compensation, and rights to be protected. Constitutional and other positive rights against the government are already well established in other foreign countries, including Canada (Roach 2005).

A more fundamental objection to some of the applications of the potential-victims'-rights argument is that it is impermissible to aggregate and quantify competing rights claims. On this view, if victim rights are less weighty than defendant rights on the individual level (due to the positive/negative distinction, lower state "mens rea," or attenuated crime-victimization links), the former can never outweigh the latter, no matter how many potential victims there are.

A third objection is the problem noted above in the discussion of general rights-conflicts principles: unlike the competing rights to life that were at issue in the death penalty context discussed by Sunstein and Vermeule, the harms to defendants and potential victims that the government "imposes" when it uses or avoids severe prison terms are often incommensurable—in the three illustrative cases, we are trying to compare offender rights violated by a severe prison sentence or other above-desert penalty with the victim rights violated by rapes, burglaries, and the various harms caused by drug selling. The difficulty of making such comparisons may counsel against a theory that critically depends on doing this with some precision.

Finally, there is a "slippery slope" problem in recognizing the potential-victims'-rights argument. How far will courts and legislatures extend this principle? Will the requirements of effectiveness, necessity, and proportionality to prevented harms be rigorously applied, and if not, what degree of disproportionality would the victims'-rights theory ultimately *not* justify? Could it, as von Hirsch and Ashworth (2005, p. 52) suggest, even be used to justify exceptions to bedrock fairness requirements such as proof beyond a reasonable doubt?

III. CONCLUSION

I have considered whether, and under what circumstances, above-desert penalties can be justified under two nonconsequentialist theories: a Rawlsian account of what kinds of penalties would be authorized by contractors in the original position; and a competing-rights theory under which the right of potential crime victims to be protected from foreseeable harm may outweigh the right of an offender not to be punished in excess of his deserts. The Rawlsian model provides at most only limited support for above-desert punishment, and may be too indeterminate to provide a workable and convincing approach to this problem. The competing-rights theory, while perhaps more workable, is problematic; the weighing of victim and offender rights is difficult, since the interests underlying these rights are often incommensurable, and which way the balance tips may depend on whether the rights of multiple potential victims may be aggregated. It has been argued that the logic of both the Rawlsian and the competing-rights theory implies several limiting principles normally associated with utilitarian theory: above-desert penalties, if allowed at all, must be shown to be effective in reducing future victimization, necessary (in the sense that a lesser penalty would be less effective), and proportionate to the harm of the future crimes avoided. These principles, if rigorously applied, would minimize the use of above-desert penalties. However, there is reason to fear that they would not be so applied, particularly under the victims' rights theory, given the strong political appeal of such a theory.

REFERENCES

Aynes, Richard L. 1984. "Constitutional Considerations: Government Responsibility and the Right Not to be a Victim." *Pepperdine Law Review* 11:63–116.

Blumenson, Eric. 2007. "Killing in Good Conscience: What's Wrong with Sunstein and Vermeule's Lesser Evil Argument for Capital Punishment and Other Human Rights Violations?" *New Criminal Law Review* 10:210–38.

Bottoms, Anthony E., and Roger Brownsword. 1983. "Dangerousness and Rights." In *Dangerousness: Problems of Assessment and Prediction*, ed. John W. Hinton. London: George Allen & Unwin.

Brems, Eva, ed. 2008. *Conflicts Between Fundamental Rights*. Antwerp: Intersentia.

Card, Claudia. 1973. "Retributive Penal Liability." *American Philosophical Quarterly* 7:17–35.

Cavender, Gray. 1981. "The Philosophical Justifications of Determinate Sentencing." *American Journal of Jurisprudence* 26:159–77.

Dölling, Dieter, Horst Entorf, Dieter Hermann, and Thomas Rupp. 2009. "Is Deterrence Effective? Results of a Meta-analysis of Punishment." *European Journal on Criminal Policy and Research* 15:201–24.

Dolovich, Sharon. 2004. "Legitimate Punishment in Liberal Democracy." *Buffalo Criminal Law Review* 7:307–442.

Donnelly, Samuel J. M. 1990. "The Goals of Criminal Punishment: A Rawlsian Theory (Ultimately Grounded in Multiple Views Concerned with Human Dignity)." *Syracuse Law Review* 41:741–800.

Frase, Richard S. 2004. "Limiting Retributivism." In *The Future of Imprisonment*, ed. Michael Tonry. New York: Oxford University Press.

———. 2005. "Excessive Prison Sentences, Punishment Goals, and the Eighth Amendment: 'Proportionality' Relative To What?" *Minnesota Law Review* 89:571–651.

Garvey, Stephen P. 2004. "Lifting the Veil on Punishment." *Buffalo Criminal Law Review* 7:443–64.

Hoekema, David A. 1980. *The Right to Punish and the Right to be Punished*. Athens: Ohio University Press.

Husak, Douglas. 2000. "Holistic Retributivism." *California Law Review* 88:991–1000.

Kamm, F. M. 2002. "Rights." In *The Oxford Handbook of Jurisprudence and Philosophy of Law*, ed. Jules Coleman and Scott Shapiro. Oxford: Oxford University Press.

Mills, Eugene. 2004. "Scheffler on Rawls, Justice, and Desert." *Law and Philosophy* 23:261–72.

Morriarity, Jeffrey. 2003. "Against the Asymmetry of Desert." *Noûs* 37:518–36.

Morris, Norval. 1974. *The Future of Imprisonment*. Chicago: University of Chicago Press.

Musgrave, Richard A. 1974. "Maximin, Uncertainty, and the Leisure Trade-off." *Quarterly Journal of Economics* 88:625–29.

Narveson, Jan. 1974. "Three *Analysis* Retributivists." *Analysis* 34:185–93.

Rainbolt, George W. 2006. *The Concept of Rights*. Dordrecht, Netherlands: Springer.

Rawls, John. 1955. "Two Concepts of Rules." *Philosophical Review* 64:3–32.

———. 1971. *A Theory of Justice*. Cambridge, MA: Harvard University Press.

———. 2001. *Justice as Fairness: A Restatement*, ed. Erin Kelly. Cambridge, MA: Belknap Press.

Reed, T. M. 1980. "Contractual Retributivism Unveiled." *Political Theory: An International Journal of Political Philosophy* 8:121–22.

Ristroph, Alice. 2006. "Desert, Democracy, and Sentencing Reform." *Journal of Criminal Law and Criminology* 96:1293–352.

Roach, Kent. 2005. "Victims' Rights and the Charter." *Criminal Law Quarterly* 49:474–516.

Sheffler, Samuel. 2000. "Justice and Desert in Liberal Theory." *California Law Review* 88:965–90.

Steiker, Carol S. 2005. "No, Capital Punishment Is not Morally Required: Deterrence, Deontology, and the Death Penalty." *Stanford Law Review* 58:751–89.

Sterba, James P. 1977. "Retributive Justice." *Political Theory: An International Journal of Political Philosophy* 5:349–62.

Sunstein, Cass R., and Adrian Vermeule. 2005. "Is Capital Punishment Morally Required? Acts, Omissions, and Life-Life Tradeoffs." *Stanford Law Review* 58:703–50.

Thornburn, Malcolm, and Allan Manson. 2007. "The Sentencing Theory Debate: Convergence in Outcomes, Divergence in Reasoning." *New Criminal Law Review* 10:278–310 (reviewing von Hirsch and Ashworth, 2005).

von Hirsch, Andrew. 1985. *Past or Future Crimes: Deservedness or Dangerousness in the Sentencing of Criminals*. New Brunswick, NJ: Rutgers University Press.

von Hirsch, Andrew, and Andrew Ashworth. 2005. *Proportionate Sentencing: Exploring the Principles*. Oxford: Oxford University Press.

Zalta, Edward N. 2009. "Stanford Encyclopedia of Philosophy." http://plato.stanford.edu.

10

Never Mind the Pain, It's a Measure! Justifying Measures as Part of the Dutch Bifurcated System of Sanctions

JAN W. DE KEIJSER

Within the context of criminal law, for most people the word sanction is equivalent to punishment. In the Dutch criminal justice system, punishments are indeed sanctions, but there is a distinct second category of sanctions that may (by definition) not be called punishments. The Dutch criminal code has a bifurcated, dual-track system of sanctions consisting of punishments and *measures*. At sentencing in a criminal court, under the umbrella of "sanctions" an imposed measure can (and often does) mean that, for public safety reasons, people are confined beyond what could be justified on grounds of culpability and harm. Punishments have to conform to the proportionality limits that stem from fundamental notions of desert, which are indeed at the heart of the Dutch philosophy of punishment. Measures have no such limitation. How then can the pain that is inflicted on offenders who are sentenced to a measure be justified in the Dutch sanctions system? One common answer to that question stresses the definition of punishment. Some core elements of generally accepted definitions of punishment are absent for measures. These elements address the deliberate infliction of suffering for an offense. The argument is that a measure does not aim to inflict suffering, so the unintended "subjectively felt" pain needs no justification. Before going deeper into possible other justifications, it will be argued that the definitional answer is unsatisfactory from a moral point of view.

The structure of this essay is as follows. First, some attention is paid to the moral justification of punishment as is generally claimed by Dutch jurists and practicing judges in the criminal courts. Subsequently the historical roots and development of the dual-track system of sanctions are discussed. It will be shown that measures are relatively new to the scene and may be conceived of as a (typically Dutch?) compromise between fundamentally contradictory principles and pressures. The statutory provisions for all measures will be briefly touched upon, after which their justification as commonly given will be described. The remainder of the essay will then focus on two measures aimed at the protection of society that most pressingly require moral justification of the (unintended) suffering that they bring about. These are the entrustment order (TBS) and placement in an institution for persistent offenders (ISD). The nature and workings of these protection measures will be described, after which the question of their justification will be posed and examined once again, but without definitional constraints.

I have limited this discussion to analysis of measures in adult criminal law, and to measures that involve the deprivation of liberty and are aimed at protection of society. I have also limited the analysis to the Netherlands. Although other countries, such as Germany and France, have statutory provisions for measures as well, an international comparative perspective is beyond the scope of this essay. Nevertheless, when relevant, reference will be made to laws or practices abroad.

I. MORAL JUSTIFICATION OF PUNISHMENT IN THE NETHERLANDS

A simple and undisputed fact is that because punishment involves a deliberate infliction of suffering by a state authority, a justification is called for. Such a justification provides the general justifying aim of punishment and the goals at sentencing. Although no such general justifying aim, nor particular goals of punishment are specified in Dutch criminal law, the moral problem of punishment has long been recognized and there *has been* a strong tradition in the Netherlands of thinking (and writing) about these issues.[1] The Dutch schools of thought and contradictions between them are closely related to what can be found in the international literature on the subject.[2] They comprise various versions of retributive reasoning (most notably Polak 1947), utilitarian theories (e.g., Muller 1908, 1934; van Veen 1949), and of course hybrid models (Pompe 1930, 1943, 1957). There has also been a radical school of thought in the Netherlands that even gained international momentum in the second half of the twentieth century: abolitionism, with its main protagonists Hulsman and Bianchi (cf. Hulsman et al. 1969; Bianchi and van Swaaningen 1986). While abolitionism has left the scene as a moral theory of responding to wrongdoing,[3] elements of it may still be found in a relatively new addition to moral theory of punishment: restorative justice (van Stokkom 2004; Walgrave 2008).

In the absence of a formalized or encoded model of doing justice, how should or could the Dutch sentencing practice be justified? What underlying set of justifying notions and goals gives Dutch sentencing legitimacy and regularity, and ties it to notions of equality and culpability? Many Dutch jurists claim to adhere to a hybrid justification of punishment. Also Dutch criminal law handbooks explain that the spirit of our penal code reflects this model (e.g., Jörg and Kelk 1994; Remmelink 1996). The particular shape of that Dutch hybrid model is one in which retribution is the essence and general justification of punishment: no punishment without guilt and no punishment that is above desert, that is, no punishment that is disproportional to the seriousness of the offense and culpability of the offender. *Within* desert limits, utilitarian goals at sentencing should then determine the type and severity of punishment in order to promote the common good (Pompe 1930; Kelk 1994a). However, it is important to note that although desert limitations are considered by many as an unwritten dogma, as early as 1959 the Dutch Supreme Court pointed out that "no punishment above degree of guilt" is not a codified limitation in the Dutch criminal code (*Black Horseman* case: Hoge Raad der Nederlanden [HR] [Supreme Court of the Netherlands], September 10, 1957, NJ 1958, 5 (Neth.)).[4] There is, in other words, no formal legal rule prohibiting punishment severity disproportional to degree of guilt.[5]

Moreover, despite jurists' claimed adherence to the mixed justification model, empirical research has shown that Dutch sentencing practice does not reflect a coherent hybrid model, and can best be described as eclectic (cf. de Keijser 2000; see also Schuyt 2005). Nevertheless, one would not easily find a practicing jurist who would argue *for* punishment without guilt and blameworthiness, and *for* punishment that supersedes the upper limits indicated by desert. Strangely, this is exactly what happens with some of the measures that are present in the Dutch sanctions system, and I will return to the justification thereof shortly. First, however, historical and legal development of the Dutch system of sanctions into a two-track system will be sketched and the actual practice of two of the most intervening and "punitive" measures will be reviewed in more detail.

II. PUNISHMENT AND MEASURES: A BIFURCATED SANCTIONS SYSTEM

The Dutch criminal code was implemented in 1886. It replaced the *Code pénal*, a heritage of the French era in the Netherlands (1795–1813). The new code was based on classic notions of desert. Apart from the adage "no punishment without guilt," it was further driven by a strong desire for punishment to be proportional to the culpability of the offender and the seriousness of the offense. The legislature of the 1886 criminal code strived for a relatively simple system of punishments based on proportionality and desert, and deliberately avoided including measures of any kind in the new criminal code (Nieboer 1973). The principal punishments in the new criminal code were imprisonment, detention (custodial sentence of infractions), and fine.[6] Much later, in 1989, community service was added as a principal punishment, and further expanded in 2001 to also include compulsory courses (e.g., social skills training).

In the initial drafts, the minister of justice, who was responsible for the new code (Modderman), did not foresee a special arrangement for the insane. He considered the existing civil legislation for the mentally ill sufficient (Hofstee 1987). By means of an amendment to the original draft, however, and *exclusively* for reasons of process economy (Bleichrodt 2002), next to punishments a measure was included in the criminal code of 1886. This one and only measure concerned *placement in a psychiatric hospital* (37 CC). The introduction was thus borne out of practicality, and at the time there was no dogmatic reason whatsoever underlying the addition of this measure to the criminal code (cf. Mevis 2006). Nevertheless, the foundation had been laid for the dual-track system of punishments and measures.

In the first half of the twentieth century the ideas of the so-called Modern School, or "new direction" took hold in the Netherlands and were advocated by influential jurists and academics.[7] Many ideas so strongly advocated at that time were in direct conflict with the classic, desert-based nature of the criminal code (Bleichrodt 2002). In the new direction of thinking about sanctions, punishment was primarily considered an instrument for protecting society against future offending. This modern school held rather deterministic views of offending. The emphasis was therefore not on offense and guilt, but rather on the person of the offender and his deficiencies (Janse de Jonge 1991). This implied individualization of punishment in order to effectively treat offenders. And in those cases that were considered incorrigible, or when there was a strong connection supposed to faulty general norms, a preference was stated for incapacitation and punishment with a general deterrent function, even beyond what could be justified on grounds of culpability and harm (e.g., Muller 1934).

The pressures exerted by the Modern School have led to a number of changes in the criminal code, which mainly focused on the aim of protecting society against future offending through individual prevention. One of the consequences was the introduction in 1915 of conditional prison sentences, which enabled extensive intervention in the lives of those conditionally sentenced. But perhaps the most dramatic consequence was the introduction of a (new) measure, the entrustment order (TBS), in 1928 for those with a mental illness or psychiatric defect.[8] Previously only those who were, as a consequence of a mental illness, not considered to be responsible for their criminal act could be placed in a psychiatric hospital (i.e., the 1886 measure). With the new TBS, when, despite an offender's mental defect or illness, the court considers the accused (partially) responsible for the criminal act, he may be sentenced to imprisonment as well as TBS. It is a measure that enables the judge to impose a sentence that protects society beyond the limitations of desert. As such, the influence of the Modern School has led to a dogmatic compromise in the Dutch sanctions system. Actually "compromise" is not the correct word here. The sanctions system was simply given two faces: one with the punishment track, justified in general aim and as such limited by desert, and the other, the measures track, justified by pure instrumental notions. I will return to this shortly.

In the 1980s and 1990s the mood in Dutch society and in criminal politics became dominated by an outcry to protect society against habitual (addicted) offenders and dangerous offenders (van Swaaningen 2004).[9] In this "era of insecurity" (Buruma 2004, p. 44), people became dissatisfied with public safety. Moreover, ideas of risk management and actuarial justice became increasingly popular in criminal justice policy (Buruma 2004).[10] The infrastructure of a dual-track sanctions system and the dogmatics underlying the measures track smoothly accommodated this development. Apart from extensive use by the courts of the measure TBS, a new measure was introduced in 2001. It enabled male addicted habitual offenders to be incarcerated and undergo treatment for a period of two years. In 2004 the scope of this measure was extended to encompass the entire group of persistent offenders, irrespective of gender and irrespective of addiction: this is the ISD.[11] It may be considered a fine example of actuarial justice in the Netherlands (Moerings 2005).

What both measures have in common is the fact that their severity is not constrained by notions of desert. ISD and TBS are exclusively focused on the protection of society through individual prevention: incapacitation and treatment. Another measure aimed at the protection of society is *withdrawal from circulation* (art. 36b CC). It is a rather undisputed and uncomplicated measure pertaining to objects seized (by the police) from a defendant. If the possession of such goods or objects is considered by the court to be in conflict with the law or against the public interest they can be withdrawn from circulation, regardless of whether the accused is convicted or not (Tak 2003).

Apart from ISD and TBS, which are instrumental, *prospective* measures aimed at the protection of society, recent developments have also seen two other measures that are *retrospective* and have a financial or material orientation. First, the 1993 "Strip-them Act" (Tak 2003) was implemented (art. 36e CC). It concerns the *confiscation of illegally obtained profits*. Primarily motivated by the fight against organized crime,[12] it involves the confiscation of profits (in whatever form; e.g., houses, cars) as well as sentencing the convicted offender to pay a sum of money to the state equal to the estimated net value of the criminal profits (cf. Groenhuijsen, van der Neut, and Simmelink 1997). Noncompliance could lead to a default detention of up to six years. Second, a development in criminal justice that ran parallel to the increased focus on security, and individual preventive measures, was an increase in attention to the position of the victim and to (financial) reparation of the harm done. Most notably this led to introduction of yet another measure in 1996: the *compensation order* (art. 36f CC). It involves the obligation for a convicted offender to pay a compensatory sum of money to the state, which is subsequently channeled to the victim. Again, noncompliance by the offender can lead to default detention (up to one year).

In summary, measures can be divided into two broad categories: measures directed at the protection of society, and measures directed at financial restitution or compensation. The first category is prospective, instrumental, and involves the physical deprivation of liberty and/or treatment while inside. The second category is retrospective, reparatory, and, if complied with, does not involve the deprivation of liberty. Table 10.1 provides an overview of the Dutch dual-track sanctions system. As this essay is predominantly concerned with the justification of measures that exact pain to an extent that is above desert, the remainder focuses on those two measures that most directly and severely intervene in the lives of convicted persons. These are the protection measures of TBS and ISD.

Table 10.1 System of Sanctions in Dutch Criminal Code

Dutch Sanctions	
Principal Punishments	*Measures*
Imprisonment	Placement in a psychiatric hospital
Detention	Entrustment order—TBS
Community service and compulsory training	Placement in institution for persistent offenders—ISD
Fine	Withdrawal from circulation
*Accessory punishments*a	Confiscation of illegally obtained profits
Deprivation of certain rights and disqualification to practice certain professions	Compensation order
Forfeiture	
Publication of the court's decision	

a Not further discussed in this chapter.

III. THE JUSTIFICATION OF MEASURES AS IS

In Dutch (judicial) literature, much has been written about the dual-track system of sanctions and about the justification of measures adjacent to punishments. The justification of measures boils down to the following. While Dutch punishments are said to be justified within the hybrid model as briefly described above, things get fuzzier when considering the justification of measures. Measures are neither justified nor limited by the harm caused and culpability of the offender. In fact, measures have little relation to the offense other than that the offense caused the offender to stand before the judge. While the offense is the indisputable and fundamental ground for any *punishment*, for a *measure*, the offense is merely the event triggering the intervention (Mevis 2006). The gravity of the offense and the moral culpability of the offender are, strictly speaking, irrelevant. The basic justifying principle underlying measures, as well as their goal or guiding principle of distribution, is thus the protection of society against offenders who, for instance, because of their psychiatric illness or frequency of offending, pose an unacceptable threat to society. The justification of the measure is the protection of society through specific prevention (Hofstee 1987). This rationale is an unbridled instrumental one.

Unlike punishment, a measure is not a deliberate infliction of suffering. Any pain that is felt as a result of a measure is unintentional, subjective, and subordinate to the goal of promoting public safety. The suffering that is subjectively experienced under a measure needs no particular justification (cf. van Kuijck and Vegter 1999). The measures track within the Dutch sanctions system is thus a clean and fundamental break with any type (strict or loose) of desert-based reasoning. Of course, this can be historically understood as the "compromise" between the classic notions underlying the 1886 criminal code and the ideas of the Modern School and developments in the 1980s and later (cf. above). Proportional retribution of harm and blameworthiness, which is essential for punishment, is alien to measures (Jonkers et al. 1998); a measure lacks the "natural boundaries" (Bleichrodt 2002) of relation to guilt and gravity of the offense.[13]

IV. TBS AND ISD IN PRACTICE
A. TBS

The TBS is a measure that was introduced in the criminal code in 1928. It was the typical product of a time when protection of society through individual prevention emerged as a dominant principle. The measure enables both incapacitation and treatment of persons who are considered dangerous to an extent beyond the desert limitations of the principal punishment of imprisonment. It can be imposed whether the offender is held responsible for his act or not.[14] If the offender is considered to be at least partially responsible, the court will combine the TBS measure with a principal punishment, usually imprisonment. The measure will then be stacked upon the prison sentence and will commence *after* that prison sentence has been served.[15]

It is crystal clear that protection of society through incapacitation is the *primary* goal of the TBS (Buruma 2005; de Kogel 2005; Mevis 2006). The deprivation of liberty is called "forced care"[16] in a forensic psychiatric center. While confined, the TBS subject is to be made an offer for treatment (art. 37c(2) CC), which should be tailored to reduce or eliminate the mental illness or deficiencies in mental development. As such, the treatment aims to reduce dangerousness and promote reentry into society.

It is important to note that the TBS subject is free to decline the treatment offer. Forced care does not imply forced treatment. The measure does not legitimize forced treatment (Mevis 2006). However, the treatment offer does carry with it a lot of indirect force. If the subject declines the offer, his dangerousness to society will be considered to remain unaltered, resulting in (repeated) prolongation of the TBS after the initial period. In this respect de Ruiter and Hildebrand (2009) stress a painful catch-22 situation for a subject who is wrongfully convicted. He will likely refuse treatment, resulting in (indefinite) prolongation of the order. The only hope for getting out is to lie about having committed the offense and undergo treatment by a forensic psychiatrist.

The use of TBS is statutorily (art. 37a(1)) limited to relatively serious crimes, that is, cases for which the *maximum* statutory punishment is at least four years imprisonment.[17] It is imposed for a duration of two years. After two years the order can be extended once for yet another two years if such is considered necessary by a court for further protection of society. While this measure thus appears to have a four-year upper limit,[18] there is an exception for those cases that involve violent offenders. For them, the order may be extended indefinitely in two-year increments, each decided upon by a court that reviews the case. It should be noted that this "exception" encompasses the vast majority of TBS subjects (Vegter 1991; Mevis 2006). All prolongations of TBS orders are requested by the prosecutor. These requests to the court are accompanied by an advisory report of the institution where the patient resides. Once every six years an additional advisory report is required from an independent outsider.

As a result of the limitation of the measure to only serious crimes, and the statutory limitation to a maximum duration of four years, one may be tempted to hint at certain underlying notions of desert that the legislature may have had in mind. If that were the case, however, these limitations are surely poor if not failed operationalizations of a desert principle. The exception of freeing the upper limit when it concerns violent offenders, who make up such a large portion of the clientele, annuls any attempt to tie this measure to any notion of desert. Proportionality considerations can neither be found in practice where one may expect them to play some role. In a recent study on TBSs that were terminated on review by the courts contrary to the advice of the psychiatric center, proportionality concerns were rarely mentioned in the judicial decision or in the following interviews with judges (de Kogel and Hartogh 2005). Furthermore, subjects for whom (despite treatment) there is no hope of eliminating the risk that they pose to society end up in the "long-stay" branch of one of the forensic psychiatric centers. The measure may thus imply a life sentence, quite independent from the offense for which the subject appeared before a court.[19]

The TBS need not always involve the deprivation of liberty. If incapacitation ("coerced care") is not considered an immediate necessity for public safety, conditional TBS may be imposed (art. 38 CC). Conditions will then involve treatment. Conditional TBSs have become relatively rare (cf. Kalidien 2008).

Decisions to impose a TBS, and all subsequent decisions to either extend or terminate the order after the initial two-year period, rely strongly on the clinical advice that behavioral experts and psychiatrists give in forensic psychiatric reports (Buruma 2005; de Kogel and Hartogh 2005; Boone et al. 2008).[20] The psychiatric report necessary for the court to impose the measure provides answers to three core questions: Is there a psychiatric defect or illness? Is there a relation between the defect or illness and the crime at the time it was committed? How large is the risk of recidivism? Increasingly such advice relies on predictions of dangerousness that result from the use of risk assessment tools. Below I will return to such predictions, as they play a crucial role in the justification of measures.

Figure 10.1 shows the number of TBSs imposed and terminated from 1990 to 2008. Obviously the courts are more reluctant to terminate the measure (after each two-year increment) than they are to impose it. As a result, Figure 10.2 shows how the total number of persons subjected to a TBS regime has been growing steadily, from 522 in 1990 to 2,105 in 2008. Moreover, the average TBS length is also increasing. A rough indication thereof is obtained through the average duration of the order by looking at exit or termination cohorts. Figure 10.3 shows that the average duration of the TBS (calculated on termination cohorts) doubled from 4.2 years in 1990 to 8.4 years in 2008.[21]

One of the explanations for the strong increase in the use of TBS measures is that the courts have responded to a societal and political outcry for more public safety.[22] More than 80 percent of all TBSs in 2008 were combinations of this measure stacked upon a prison sentence. The length of those prison sentences was more than three years in 22 percent of the cases (Dienst Justitiële Inrichtingen 2009b).

A detailed study of characteristics of TBS subjects over the period 1995–2000 was carried out by the Ministry of Justice (Emmerik and Brouwers 2001). There are few women TBS subjects: about 5 percent. The average age (in 2007) was 39 years (Kalidien 2008). About 30 percent of TBS subjects are not of Dutch origin (i.e., not born in the Netherlands). Almost the entire TBS population consists of violent offenders (i.e., 98 percent in 2000). In almost 80 percent of the cases the violent offense resulted in physical injury (53 percent) or death (26 percent) of the victim. Sexual (violent) offenders are relatively common within this population, at 28 percent.

B. ISD

Introduced in the Dutch criminal code in 2004, as a follow-up of the measure of incarceration of drug-addicted offenders,[23] the ISD (art. 38m–u CC), placement in an institution for persistent offenders, targets those "habitual" offenders who cause a disproportionate amount of public nuisance through their frequent crimes. The formal rationale reflects an aggregative consequentialist perspective (cf. Duff 1998), based on selective incapacitation.[24] The minister of justice responsible for the introduction of the measure (Donner) wrote in a letter to parliament that the measure fits well within the current strive to put an end to public unsafety. Protection of society against the group of highly frequent persistent offenders by means of incapacitation is the primary goal of this measure (Donner 2004a, 2004b; van Ooyen-Houben and Goderie 2009). The criminal code states: "The measure aims at protection of society and the termination of recidivism of the accused" (art. 38m-2 CC). Secondary to that, the criminal code explains that the measure

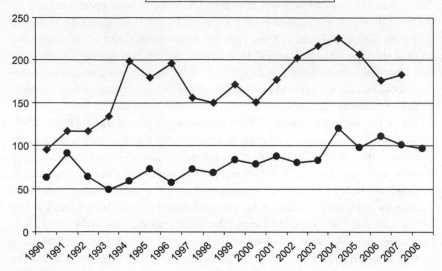

Figure 10.1.
Number of TBS measures imposed and terminated: 1990–2008
Source: Kalidien 2008; Dienst Justitiële Inrichtingen 2009a.

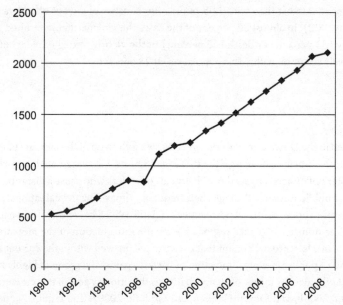

Figure 10.2.
Number of persons in TBS: 1990–2008
Source: Kalidien 2008; Dienst Justitiële Inrichtingen 2009a.

aims to contribute to the resolution of addiction problems that the accused may have or any other problems related to committing offenses (art. 38m-3 CC).

The types of crime involved generally concern offenses that are not very serious, such as shoplifting, vandalism, and theft from cars. It is the frequency of committing these crimes by specific groups of offenders that motivated the measure. For only a single minor offense, only relatively short prison sentences were available to the court. And even when multiple minor offenses were tried simultaneously, the length of possible imprisonment was not considered sufficient by the legislature to protect society from further nuisance. Better protection of the public was deemed necessary by incapacitating high-frequency offenders for a longer stretch of time than admissible on desert grounds (Mevis 2006).

Because ISD is a measure, there need not be a direct connection between the severity of the intervention and the seriousness of the crimes committed. The minister of justice added, however, that the ISD measure *is* proportional to the persistent offending that it is intended to curtail (Donner 2004a). It is that proportionality that is said to legitimize the measure (Donner 2004a). The formal resolution to the tension between desert-based proportionality and pure instrumentalism was thus once again conveniently found in the measures track of the Dutch sanctions system (cf. Struijk 2009). The ISD is imposed for the default duration of two years, although it cannot be extended, as is the case with the TBS. Another important difference with the TBS is that the Dutch Supreme Court ruled that ISD cannot be imposed on top of a prison sentence.[25]

ISD is less complicated than the TBS because imposing it does not depend on diminished responsibility due to psychiatric illness or mental defects. However, it can only be

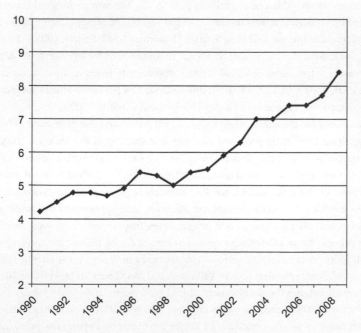

Figure 10.3.
Average length of TBS (in years) by termination cohort: 1990–2008
Source: Kalidien 2008; Dienst Justitiële Inrichtingen 2009b.

imposed at the request of the prosecutor, and not without a behavioral expert's report that, among other things, verifies the willingness of a drug addict to cooperate with addiction treatment. The measure can nevertheless be imposed without a prior behavioral report if the accused refuses to cooperate with such reporting (art. 38m-5 CC). The behavioral report (drawn up by the probation service) includes an estimation of risk of recidivism using a standardized risk assessment tool (i.e., RISc, cf. van der Knaap, Leenarts, and Nijssen 2007).

The target group for ISD appears quite narrowly defined in the criminal code. It nevertheless concerns a substantive group of potential "clients."[26] It concerns very active adult offenders against whom, within the past five years, at least ten written police reports have been registered. The current offense needs to be serious enough to merit remand in custody.[27] Furthermore, within the past five years the offender needs to have had at least three convictions for a crime that resulted in the execution of a sanction. Within the regime of this measure, two categories of offenders are discerned. The first category is offenders who are considered motivated and eligible for behavioral treatment. The second category is those who are unmotivated and not open to treatment. The latter category is placed in a sober incarceration regime, whereas the first is included in treatment and resocialization programs.

Combining the primary goal of incapacitation with treatment and resocialization, but in practice often legitimizing the duration of the sanction with its supposed treatment potential, has proven to be arduous for practitioners. If there appears to be no opportunity or motivation for behavioral change, or when the measure is imposed after refusal of the subject to cooperate in a behavioral report, the bare reality that ISD is a clean removal from society does not equally appeal to all. The straightforward incapacitory nature of ISD is then blatantly revealed (Borgers 2005). At present, many judges appear to be reluctant to impose ISD in such cases (Moerings 2005; Struijk 2005; Lünnemann 2009). For similar reasons, judges do appear to make use of their power to terminate an ISD measure if treatment potential seems insufficient to them in a particular case (cf. Boone et al. 2008). In 2007–8 about one-quarter (24 percent) of ISD subjects were detained in a sober regime (van Ooyen-Houben and Goderie 2009).

The council for the administration of criminal justice and the protection of juveniles has diagnosed three main problems after the introduction of the measure (Raad voor Strafrechtstoepassing en Jeugdbescherming 2007; see also van Ooyen-Houben and Goderie 2009). First, it was introduced too hastily.[28] As a result, the staffs of the institutions were ill-prepared for the task. Second, the ISD clientele required more (psychological) care than was foreseen. And third, the measure offers too little opportunity for realizing structural behavioral changes (behavioral programs are fragmented). Although very little is known at present about the effectiveness of treatment during ISD, economists report that ISD fulfills its crime reduction goal as an incapacitory measure for the clientele of highly persistent addicted offenders (cf. van Velthoven and Moolenaar 2009; Vollaard 2010).

Figure 10.4 shows the development of ISD (and before 2004, SOV) measures from 2001 through 2008. It shows a steady increase. The year 2008 appears to end the trend, but such can only be concluded after a longer time interval beyond the year 2008. The ISD population is a heterogeneous one. Nevertheless, some general characterizations can be made (from Goderie and Lünneman 2008). The average age (in 2007) is 40 years.

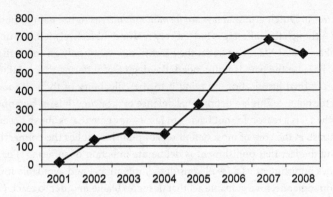

Figure 10.4.
Sentenced to SOV (2001–2003) and ISD (2004–2008).
Source: Kalidien 2008; van Ooyen-Houben and Goderie 2009.

More than 90 percent of those in institutions for persistent offenders are male. Almost three-quarters of the anteceding offenses of those in ISD in 2007 involved theft and breaking and entering. The largest portion of ISD subjects ($n = 200$ in 2007) has a criminal record of between 30 and 60 preceding offenses (average = 80). Almost all subjects are addicted to drugs or have been addicted in the past. About half of them are said to suffer from psychiatric illnesses (not necessarily diagnosed as such).

V. A DEFINITIONAL STOP

Because desert is not a concern when imposing TBS or ISD, there are no upper limits set by notions of proportionality to the offense. While there are differences in severity, in practice, there does not even appear to be an underlying commonsense scale (Hart 1968) linking severity of the measure to gravity of the offense. However, this is not to say that upper limits are absent. For ISD, there is one fixed absolute limit of two years. For TBS, there is a ceiling that is reconsidered every two years. But once you are in, the clinical advice of a forensic psychiatrist is the most important factor underlying the court's decision to continue the measure or to end it.

While the justification of protection measures such as TBS and ISD does, at first glance, not appear to be very complicated from an instrumental perspective, there remains the deeply rooted and uneasy tension between the measures track and the punishments track. The ISD measure, for instance, has put judges in an uncomfortable position, as the legislation directs them to impose the measure even when there is no treatment perspective (for instance, because the accused refuses to cooperate). The supposed (but unproven) rehabilitative effect of such a measure can thus no longer be used for its justification at sentencing. The core of incapacitation remains, but is above desert. The fact that this is an uneasy situation is of course due to the disproportionate amount of suffering that is inflicted on those who are subjected to the measure. It is disproportionate to the culpability of the offender and the seriousness of the offense that made him stand before a judge.

Measures in Dutch criminal law are *formally indifferent* to the pain inflicted on offenders.[29] Although the suffering is indeed very real and subjectively felt, it is unintended pain (Jonkers et al. 1998). This lies at the heart of one commonly given justification for measures. Because the pain is unintended, the degree of suffering that is inflicted does not require formal justification by tying it to the culpability of the offender and the gravity of the offense. This is a definitional defense of measures. It is, in fact, not a justification; rather, it is a reason for not having to justify any pain that is above desert.

In contrast, at the core of most definitions of punishment lies the connection to the offense and the fact that punishment is deliberate infliction of suffering. For instance, Kelk defines punishment as a "well-considered, intentional and avoidable infliction of suffering on someone, for a culpable act that deserves blame in order to reach (a) certain goal(s)" (1994b, p. 16). Definitions of legal punishment abound. However, all authoritative definitions include the intended infliction of suffering for an offense.[30]

All agree that punishment needs a sound moral justification of the suffering inflicted, and the Dutch hybrid model of justifying punishment provides that general justification through desert (cf. above). The question of justifying the pain that measures inflict requires no answer, because measures are not, by definition, punishment.[31] They do not intend to inflict suffering. This is what Hart calls the *definitional stop* in discussions of punishment (Hart 1968). According to Hart, this is an abuse of definition and "it would prevent us from investigating the very thing which modern scepticism most calls in question: namely the rational and moral status of our preference for a system of punishment under which measures painful to individuals are to be taken against them only when they have committed an offense" (1968, p. 6).[32] Here, Hart was arguing against the definitional stop used to prevent giving an answer to the question of why the innocent should not be punished if that would promote the common good.[33]

In the case of Dutch protection measures, the fact that the suffering inflicted is unintentional sets measures apart from punishment.[34] Van der Landen (1992), who was a strong critic of the dual-track sanctions system in the Netherlands, did not question this definitional division based on the intentionality of inflicted suffering (Geeraets 2006). Analogous to Hart's argument, and from the Dutch philosophical perspective, one may reason that the definitional stop prevents us from examining the rational and moral status of deliberately inflicting pain above commonly accepted notions of desert. Using the definitional stop, the deeper issue is sidestepped (Corrado 1996).

Although the pain may be said to be unintentional, it is nevertheless the result of a deliberate action by the court: imposing a measure. Moreover, the pain is not at all accidental or unforeseen. The suffering as a result of the deprivation of liberty by ISD and TBS is both known and foreseen, *at least* to the level of pain associated with ordinary imprisonment (cf. van der Landen [1993], who argues that the TBS exacts more pain than ordinary imprisonment; de Kogel 2005). And if one agrees that deprivation of liberty causes suffering, and this deprivation is imposed intentionally, albeit for a purpose other than suffering (or retribution), the infliction of suffering is then intentional (cf. Geeraets 2006).

Although one may insist on hiding behind the definitional stop, the suffering inflicted by protection measures is so clear, so foreseen, and, as just argued, so intentional that it is embarrassing to remain silent when the question is posed: How can we morally justify measures that inflict suffering beyond desert? Posing this question is not the outcome of some word game. Rather, the current practice of *not* having to pose that question *is*!

VI. AVAILABLE ALTERNATIVES

Measures do not merely coexist with punishments, the protection measures are, in practice, extensions of the punishment system. As such the TBS is commonly *stacked upon* the prison sentence (van der Landen 1993), and ISD is the *next step* if punishments have "failed" (Donner 2004a, p. 9).[35] It is cumbersome to regard measures as extensions when realizing that the punishment track and the measures track are irreconcilable from a dogmatic point of view. Nevertheless, in daily practice the transition of an individual case (person) from one track to the other is a smooth one.

Being serious about moral limitations of state action toward its citizens, it is very peculiar to allow those limitations to be released if, from a consequentialist point of view, those actions fall short of reaching certain goals. If one insists on maintaining the Dutch hybrid model underlying punishments, and on maintaining the scope of current protection measures, whilst rejecting the definitional stop used to sidestep the issue of unintended suffering, few solutions come to mind. With somewhat fewer restrictions, some general justification alternatives appear available.

A. Extend the Hybrid Model to Encompass Measures

One alternative is to extend the existing desert-based proportionality limitations for punishments to measures, thus including measures in the model with desert as general justification *and* limiting principle. This would of course cripple the protection measures as we now know them. In fact, it would render them redundant vis-à-vis punishments options. The result of this solution is de facto abolition of the protection measures as they are currently available in the Dutch criminal code.

For the TBS, the situation will revert to that before its introduction in 1928, meaning that persons who are considered completely irresponsible for their criminal act(s) because of mental illness and insanity cannot be punished. Instead, it remains possible to place them in an institution for the insane using the existing original measure of the 1886 criminal code (37 CC). That measure can be maintained or, perhaps better, abolished. After all, there is currently thorough civil legislation for hospitalization of the insane.[36] There is, however, some danger here of applying yet another definitional stop of sorts. If the "civil" is merely a different mode for imposing interventions that are as—or even more—repressive than criminal sanctions, and subjectively experienced as punitive, than the principled issue remains unaltered (Ashworth 2004), and worse, even better hidden. Examples abroad can be found in sexual violent predator (SVP) laws. In at least twenty states in the United States, such laws allow for indefinite civil commitment of sexually violent offenders *after* they have served their prison sentences (cf. La Fond 2003; Wilson 2004). Regarding the principled issue at stake, Harris (2009) describes the *fig leaf* argument: under the guise of treatment and nominally civil intervention, commitment of SVPs is actually a form of criminal sanction that would be unconstitutional when labeled as such.

Persons whom the court considers at least partially accountable for their actions are available for conventional punishment, and can be offered psychiatric treatment during execution of the sanction. Of course, within the hybrid justification model, that should now occur within the boundaries defined by the harm they have done and their culpability. Any desire for incapacitation and treatment would at a certain point be curtailed by desert (cf. de Hullu 2003).

Moerings (2005) provides a straightforward solution for the specific case of the ISD measure, fitting it within a desert-based model. He argues that one of the main reasons courts have only short prison sentences available to them when considering the cases of persistent offenders is the Dutch custom to put no more than four offenses on the indictment.[37] This is done merely for process economic reasons. When such a restriction or habit is released, more crimes can be tried simultaneously and longer prison sentences can be imposed. The central role that risk assessment has in the court's decision to impose ISD will vanish, or at least become peripheral, in the conventional punishment mode.

B. Deal with the Unintended Suffering

There is, however, another way of retaining protection measures with their current scope, while staying within the principled boundaries of the hybrid model. For persistent offenders, this option actually existed in the UK in the first half of the twentieth century, and is discussed in detail by Morris (1951). It was based on the 1908 Prevention of Crime Act, and involved a two-stage system for dealing with habitual offenders.[38] The first stage was *punishment* of the habitual offender for the substantive crime committed. Called *penal servitude*, this took the form of imprisonment for a period of at least three years. The second stage, after completion of the penal servitude, was *preventive detention* for 5 to 10 years. As the single aim of that preventive detention was segregation, and not punishment, conditions in preventive detention were deliberately very different from conditions in prison. Preventive detainees were subjected to as little official interference as possible. Furthermore, remuneration, better food and clothing, better accommodations, and more association with others led preventive detainees to be seen as the aristocracy of the penal community.[39] These differences were explicitly intended to alleviate the burdens of detention. Ideally, Morris states, preventive detention "will have none of the individual and selective quality of a 'poena', but will express only the collective quality of an act of humane social defence" (1951, p. 243).

Although the specific form and the (mandatory minimum) lengths of penal servitude and preventive detention for habitual criminals in the 1908 Prevention of Crime Act seem rather absurd, the basic underlying idea is attractive. This type of solution requires an *explicit* recognition as a moral problem of the unintended suffering that protection measures exact. Then, something very specific is required during the execution of protection measures. The suffering that incapacitation by deprivation of liberty involves should be counterbalanced as much as possible. In theory, one may aim to counterbalance or compensate that suffering to a degree such that no more subjectively felt pain remains. It seems difficult, however, to believe that the pain resulting from loss of liberty can, through manipulation of living circumstances and material compensation, ever be counterbalanced to a degree that there is no more suffering. Nevertheless, the pain experienced by those who are incapacitated for protective purposes can at least be reduced or compensated to a very substantive degree. Living conditions in ISD, for instance, are currently quite similar to conditions in prison, especially for the group undergoing the sober regime without treatment (cf. above). Furthermore, living conditions in TBS vary between TBS clinics, but can certainly be improved a great deal. The explicit recognition that as much as possible should be done to alleviate or compensate for the pain that these measures cause would make a world of difference. But another grave problem remains: even if the subjectively felt pain is "taken away," how can we know that we are detaining the right people?[40] I will address this problem below.

C. Abandon Desert as a Limiting Principle

The other option is to maintain the measures without insisting on retributive notions to limit their reach. Although this option boils down to maintaining the status quo, there is a bit more to it. After all, the moral and theoretical underpinnings of the two tracks have been argued to be irreconcilable. Insisting on the continuation of the current protection measures does imply commitment to a strict utilitarian outlook on punishment. The bifurcated approach simply carries no credibility in terms of legitimizing the sanctions system. It would therefore be necessary to abandon the oft-avowed commitment by Dutch jurists to the hybrid philosophy of punishment, limited by desert. In fact, from a legal perspective, as first stressed by the Dutch Supreme Court in 1957 (cf. above), a formal limitation of "no punishment above *degree* of guilt" has never existed in codified Dutch criminal law.

By abandoning desert as a limiting principle, the normative theoretical foundation of Dutch sanctions can at least be coherent, and there is no longer a need to embarrass oneself with definitional stops when questions are asked about the amount of suffering that is inflicted. Now, as a *committed* consequentialist, a straightforward answer is readily available to the question of how to justify the pain that ISD or TBS exact. It is because the amount of suffering exacted is outweighed by the protection of society, that is, the common good. Of course, many things can be done to alleviate the suffering of those who are incapacitated, but if that pain is outweighed by the benefits for society, there is no direct (instrumental) need for it.

However, for such a utilitarian justification to hold its ground it has to at least be shown that these measures do promote the common good to a degree that society considers sufficient. That common good is promoted by protection measures in two ways. First, they are supposed to be effective. Of course, the individual prevention by means of incapacitation is, by definition, effective for the duration of the measure, that is, two years for ISD and, in principle, unlimited for TBS. But both measures boast treatment. Although recidivism rates among offenders released from TBS are lower than among those released from prison (Wartna, Harbachi, and van der Knaap 2005), next to nothing is known about the effectiveness of treatment in TBS (Tijdelijke Commissie Onderzoek TBS [Commissie Visser] 2006; Hildebrand and de Ruiter 2009). Effective evaluation of TBS treatment according to current academic standards is simply not available as of yet (Drieschner, Hesper, and Marozzos 2010). The same is true for the ISD measure. So justification in terms of effectiveness may be based on incapacitation, but at present, not on treatment effectiveness. It is certainly questionable whether the incapacitation can be considered a sufficient legitimation for these stark measures.

The second manner in which protection measures may promote the common good is the extent to which they are administered to the *right* persons. Failing to do that seriously subtracts from the common good. The key issue here concerns the quality of the advice given by external rapporteurs to the courts to impose or prolong a measure. This advice is given by the probation service for the ISD measure and by a psychiatrist in the case of TBS. Increasingly outcomes of risk assessment tools are becoming central to such advice and to the subsequent decisions of courts to impose or extend the measures. The structured risk assessment outcome is, of course, not the exclusive factor determining the expert's advice. The content of his report to the court is a combination of clinical assessment and structured assessment.[41]

The scientific and quantitative aura that surrounds risk assessment outcomes appears to stand in the way of their critical evaluation by the courts in daily practice (de Ruiter 2009; Harte 2009). The problem is that individual predictions of future offenses are far from perfect. In fact, a recent study showed that the risk assessment tool (RISc) used by the probation service for advising the courts regarding the ISD measure has no predictive validity for persistent offenders (van der Knaap and Alberda 2009). Interesting data are also available for an important risk prediction tool used in the TBS setting: the HCR-20.[42] In a Dutch study, the HCR-20 risk score was calculated using the dossiers of almost 200 TBS subjects whose TBS had been terminated on the basis of advice that did not use a structured risk assessment tool (de Vogel et al. 2004). In Table 10.2 subjects who actually recidivated within the observation period and those who did not recidivate are compared regarding their calculated risk. Of the actual recidivists, 84 percent did indeed have a high risk score using the HCR-20. These are correct predictions. Not bad. However, 29 percent of those who did *not* recidivate also received a high risk score. These are false positives, and they tend to be overlooked (cf. von Hirsch 1992). If the risk score was used as the exclusive basis for deciding on prolonging the TBS, then for almost one-third of those who would actually desist from crime the prolongation is unjustified.

Table 10.2 HCR-20 Score, Actual Recidivism, and Diagnostic Values (Original Data from de Vogel et al. 2004; de Ruiter 2009)

		In reality...				
		Recidivist		Nonrecidivist		Diagnostic value
HCR-20	High	36	84%	22	29%	2.9
score	Low/moderate	7	16%	54	71%	4.4
		43	100%	76	100%	

Another way of looking at such percentages is by calculating a diagnostic value (cf. Table 10.2, final column). The diagnostic value of a high risk score is the percentage of correct predictions divided by the percentage of false positives. In this case, because the percentage of false positives is large, the diagnostic value of a high risk score (i.e., 2.9) is not particularly impressive.[43] Compare, for instance, the diagnostic value of a witness recognizing the suspect from a correctly performed police lineup: 15 (i.e., 75 percent correct versus 5 percent false positives) (cf. Crombag, van Koppen, and Wagenaar 1994), or more than one billion for a full DNA match (Nederlands Forensisch Instituut 2008). Nevertheless, these scores and the expert advice based on them carry a lot of weight in judges' decision making on measures. Can that be justified?

Yes it can. Low diagnostic value of a high risk score need not necessarily thwart the legitimacy of imposing and prolonging measures. Here we arrive in the area of criminal politics. Using diagnostic values, criminal politics can, and must, become explicit and transparent to continue legitimizing measures from an instrumental point of view.[44] As a consequentialist, one may thus defend the position that, once within the reach of criminal justice, in order to protect society against more than four out of five dangerous persons, it is necessary to accept that almost one out of three persons who are not (anymore) dangerous will also be incapacitated. To me this seems a difficult position to defend. At what point does punishment based on such factors cause more mischief than it prevents (cf. Bentham 1982; see also Tonry 2004)? Moreover, it abandons the "obligation of society to do *individual* justice" (von Hirsch 1992). But apart from a principled rejection, the current level of accuracy of predictions could further qualify as what Duff has called "intolerably inefficient inaccuracy" (1998, p. 143).[45]

But where, then, lies the acceptable threshold in society? At a diagnostic value of 10? Or 1,000? Or should it be maintained that only infinite diagnostic values are enough to morally justify incapacitation based on predicted dangerousness?[46] One should bear in mind that in order to justify protective measures that at least partially rely on risk assessment, the diagnostic value of such assessment needs to be known, and one needs to know the diagnostic value that society would consider acceptable (thus also the proportion of false positives). But even if risk assessment reaches diagnostic values that are considered to be beyond a minimum established threshold, and if the legislature is willing to commit itself to such a measure justification, a couple of problems remain. Most important, and apart from the issues associated with effectiveness, there is the uneasy fact that despite an explicit and accepted diagnostic value of risk assessment, a proportion of people are committed to the state's care who do not belong there. This group, however small it may be or become, will always remain the Achilles' heel and their suffering will require justification time and again.

VII. CONCLUSION

I have roughly sketched some ways of attempting to justify protection measures in the Dutch sanctions system. The first solution could, in its basic shape, serve not to justify current practice, but entails the abolition of protection measures that are above desert. However, by explicit recognition of and attention to the unintended suffering that is exacted by protection measures, the pain can be alleviated or compensated to a high degree. The idea is to maintain the preventive function of measures, while taking the pain out of the equation. Although I doubt that pain resulting from loss of liberty can be completely taken out of the equation, this way of dealing with the measures at least does not sidestep the issue of disproportionate suffering. It takes the issue seriously and addresses it.

The other solution attempted to maintain the current measures practice unaltered. It relied on a strict utilitarian account of punishment.[47] Apart from the fact that all Western jurisdictions consider the implications of unbridled utilitarianism unacceptable for legal, moral, humanitarian, and practical reasons, when push comes to shove it seems a very good candidate if one tries to justify current Dutch protection measures without the necessity of substantive change.

However, the key ingredients for such an instrumental justification are unknown or not known well enough. These involve the effectiveness of treatment in TBS and ISD and the diagnostic value of risk assessments. But even if these key variables were known, and their values considered above established thresholds, this particular utilitarian model reopens the discussion on a number of issues that consequentialism in its barest form has been struggling with. For instance, if this is the justification for measures, surely it must be justified in order to punish or impose a measure[48] on someone innocent of any crime? I am confident that in the Netherlands, as in most Western societies, desert and proportionality may be considered fundamental and universal principles (cf. von Hirsch 1993; Tonry 1996; Roberts 2008).[49] I do not see a future for a strict teleological model for the Dutch sanctions system without desert as a limiting principle. Doing justice to individuals treated as morally responsible agents is too deeply engrained in Dutch legal culture. It was exactly for that reason that the two-track system of punishments and measures has been a handy moral escape.

In summary, in order to eliminate the fundamental tension within the Dutch sanctions system, we are left with either an abolitionist approach concerning measures or a desert-based hybrid approach in which the pain resulting from protection measures is carefully taken out of the equation. But one may even wonder whether there is a political desire to eliminate that fundamental tension. Moreover, who could or would be willing to explain to the public that there is a moral obligation apart from the punishments toward those who are undergoing protection measures to make life as comfortable as possible?

On a final note, many justification issues connected to protection measures in the Netherlands are not uniquely Dutch. For instance, many principled and fundamental objections can be raised against sex offender laws in the United States (cf. Wright 2009), and dangerous and persistent offender laws in the United Kingdom. The English 2003 Criminal Justice Act, so heavily founded on notions of public protection (cf. Ashworth 2004), and, in 2005 in the United Kingdom, the introduction of indeterminate sentencing for public protection (IPP) carry similar moral issues. For such policies, Ashworth has aptly stated that "the growing emphasis on risk assessment and risk-based penal policies not only tends to underplay the problems of effectively identifying and dealing with risk but also led to a neglect of discussions of values and principles"(2004, p. 516). Apart from such obvious similarities, the explicit bifurcated criminal sanctions system of punishments and measures remains the typically Dutch characteristic. For a casual observer, at first glance the Dutch discussion of values and principles appears to be pacified effectively by the differential dogmatics underlying the two tracks. I have argued above that this is insufficient and unsatisfactory. Rather, side-stepping principled issues related to proportionality and guilt only further highlights parallels with policies such as those in the United Kingdom and the United States. These may well portray what lies ahead for the Netherlands.

ACKNOWLEDGMENT

Most work on this essay was done at the Netherlands Institute for the Study of Crime and Law Enforcement (NSCR), Amsterdam, the Netherlands. I would like to thank the editor and other contributors to this volume for their comments on an earlier draft of this contribution, given at a joint meeting in Oegstgeest, the Netherlands. I also thank Ybo Buruma and Pauline Schuyt for their critical reading of the manuscript and suggestions.

NOTES

1. It appears that this vibrant and fruitful tradition in the Netherlands has died out.
2. See Kelk (1994a, in Dutch), Remmelink (1986, in Dutch), and de Keijser (2000) for concise reviews of Dutch schools of thought on the subject.
3. Or, rather, a theory of how not to respond to offending.
4. See van der Landen (1993) for references to subsequent other decisions of the Dutch Supreme Court reiterating this point.
5. Not to be confused with the limitation in the Dutch criminal code that a person who cannot be held responsible for a criminal act (due to defective development or mental illness) cannot be punished (art. 39 CC).
6. There are also accessory punishments specified in the criminal code (cf. Table 10.1, below). These, however, play a minor role in Dutch sentencing and are irrelevant for current purposes.
7. See, e.g., van Hamel (1999) or Muller (1908). For an overview of the Modern School, see Groenhuijsen and van der Landen (1990), and also van der Landen (1992).
8. TBS is used as an abbreviation of the Dutch word *Terbeschikkingstelling* (art. 37a CC). Originally in 1928, it was named TBR: *Terbeschikking van de Regering*. When the law was changed in 1988, TBS became the common phrase.
9. Most clearly the dominant focus in politics on public safety can be found in the policy statement paper from the ministries of justice and internal affairs (Ministerie van Justitie and Ministerie van Binnenlandse Zaken en Koninkrijksrelaties 2002).
10. See Feeley and Simon (1994), who first introduced the term actuarial justice. See also Garland (2001).
11. This is the Dutch abbreviation for *Instelling Stelselmatige Daders*.
12. In Dutch, the popular name for this act is *Plukze*. See Vruggink (2001) for an evaluation of *Plukze*, not only for cases of organized crime, but also for other criminal cases.
13. In the case of punishments, the "why?" question is first answered with "for an offense." In the case of a measure, the answer to that question is "for the protection of society."
14. Those undergoing a TBS are referred to in various ways. Most common denominations are TBS subject, client, and patient.
15. Usually after two-thirds of the prison term has been served, as this is the common proportion that any convict has to serve. The Netherlands and Germany are the only Western

jurisdictions where a TBS can be imposed on top of a prison sentence. In other countries a judge is forced to make a choice between the two (van der Landen 1992; Hildebrand and de Ruiter 2009).

16. *Dwangverpleging* (art. 37d CC).
17. Dutch criminal law has specific maximum punishments per crime codified in the law. A maximum prison sentence of at least four years includes crimes with a vast range of seriousness. For instance, a maximum prison sentence of four years is specified for simple theft in the Dutch criminal code (cf. art. 310 CC).
18. This limitation was added to the 1928 provision as late as 1988.
19. It is for this reason that some defense lawyers have started to advise their clients not to cooperate with a psychiatric report, which is absolutely necessary for the imposition of TBS (cf. Mevis 2009).
20. These reports are drafted by psychiatrists of the Forensic Psychiatric Services (FPD), or in the most serious cases by psychiatrists who have observed the "client" in one of the institutions (e.g., the Pieter Baan Centrum).
21. A different way of looking at development in duration of the measure is to look at entry cohorts. Of those who entered TBS in 1990, the median duration of the order until termination was 7.28 years. This increased to 9.70 years in 1995 (Dienst Justitiële Inrichtingen 2009b).
22. For this and other possible explanations for the increase in the use of TBS by the courts, see van Kuijck and Vegter (1999), and more recently Dienst Justitiële Inrichtingen (2009b).
23. In Dutch, *Strafrechtelijke Opvang Verslaafden* (SOV).
24. For discussions of the penal strategy of selective incapacitation, see Greenwood and Abrahamse (1982), Wilson (1983), Duff (1998), and von Hirsch and Kazemian (2009).
25. Supreme Court, 21 March 2006, LJN: AV1161.
26. Estimated at between 5,500 and 6,000 very active persistent offenders in 2003–2006 (Tollenaar, van Dijk, and Alblas 2009).
27. This, however, cannot be seriously considered as a restraint because even a simple shoplifting merits remand in custody by Dutch law (Mevis 2006).
28. ISD was implemented even before the new measure of incarceration of drug-addicted offenders (SOV) had been properly evaluated as planned (cf. Struijk 2009).
29. Similar to the role of inflicted suffering from a restorative justice point of view. In the case of restorative justice, the reference is the harm done to the victim and the goal is to repair that harm. A restorative intervention is considered successful when that goal has been achieved, in principle regardless of the suffering it involves for the offender and regardless of the fact that the same offense may produce differential levels of objective and subjective harm to victims (e.g., Walgrave 2004). This is against (horizontal) requirements of proportionality (cf. de Keijser 2000).
30. See, e.g., Hart (1968), Honderich (1970), Kleinig (1973), Strijards (1987), and Walker (1991).
31. For examples of more or less explicit versions of the definitional stop in Dutch politics, see, e.g., Donner (2004a) and van Kuijck and Vegter (1999).
32. Please note that despite his choice of wording, Hart did not intend to make a distinction between punishments and measures.
33. The definitional stop reply would of course be that this is not an issue because punishment is only for an offense.
34. See Kooijmans (2002) for an overview of eight definitional and other reasons to set measures apart from punishments.
35. See also the preconditions for imposing the ISD measure described above.

36. In Dutch, bijzondere opnemingen in psychiatrische ziekenhuizen (*BOPZ*).
37. If there are more offenses that the accused has admitted to, the prosecutor will put these *ad informandum* on the indictment.
38. See Morris (1951, p. 39, n. 2) on the use of the terms "dual track" and "two stage."
39. See Morris (1951, pp. 70–77) for description of conditions in preventive detention at the time.
40. Of course, the very same question remains when interventions are labeled as civil commitment (cf. Harris 2009).
41. See Harte (2009) for a critical discussion of the value of such risk assessment tools.
42. Historical, Clinical, Risk Management-20 is an assessment tool that helps mental health professionals estimate a person's probability of violence.
43. Note that the diagnostic value of *not* recidivating is higher for a low risk score (4.4). See Hart, Michie, and Cooke (2007), who considered the use of some risk assessment tools unethical based on their poor precision.
44. See also Moerings (2005).
45. Duff (1998) does, however, describe the argument that perhaps higher rates of false positives may be tolerated because it concerns people who have been found guilty of a crime to begin with. Nevertheless, the question of what rate of false positives as compared with true positives is acceptable remains unanswered. But Duff further presents an argument that a false positive does still concern a person who is considered to be dangerous by his present condition, and it is his present condition that is used as justification (Duff 1998, p. 152). See also Tonry (1992) for a critical discussion of that conception of predicted dangerousness.
46. See Corrado (1996) for an interesting elaboration on the hypothetical situation where predictions of dangerousness are perfect. He discusses retributive opposition against acting on such predictions, but also an interesting solution to retributive objections. The solution is to present the subject with overwhelming evidence of his predicted dangerousness. Subsequently he is given the opportunity to decide to detain himself. If the person refuses, that would then be a crime of reckless endangerment resulting in justified imprisonment (Corrado 1996, pp. 806–7).
47. The type of utilitarianism that Tonry labeled "a mythological beast" (1992, p. 171).
48. The distinction has lost its meaning in this example.
49. See, however, Tonry's (2004) analysis of American penal culture.

REFERENCES

Ashworth, A. 2004. "Criminal Justice Act 2003: Part 2: Criminal Justice Reform—Principles, Human Rights and Public Protection." *Criminal Law Review* 2004:516–32.

Bentham, J. 1982. *An Introduction to the Principles and Morals of Legislation*, ed. J. H. Burns and H. L. A. Hart. London: Menhuen and Co.

Bianchi, H., and R. van Swaaningen, eds. 1986. *Abolitionism: Towards a Non-Repressive Approach to Crime*. Amsterdam: Free University Press.

Bleichrodt, F. W. 2002. "Het strafrechtelijk sanctiestelsel in de revisie." In *Handelingen Nederlandse Juristen-Vereniging: Herziening van het sanctiestelsel*, vol. 132, ed. J. de Hullu, F. W. Bleichrodt, and O. J. D. M. L. Jansen. Deventer, the Netherlands: Kluwer.

Boone, M., A. Beijer, A. A. Franken, and C. Kelk. 2008. *De tenuitvoerlegging van sancties: Maatwerk door de rechter?* The Hague: WODC.

Borgers, M. J. 2005. De ISD-maatregel in handen van de rechterlijke macht. *Delikt en Delinkwent* 35:467–89.

Buruma, Y. 2004. "Risk Assessment and Criminal Law: Closing the Gap between Criminal Law and Criminology." In *Punishment, Places and Perpetrators: Developments in Criminology and Criminal Justice Research*, ed. G. J. N. Bruinsma, H. Elffers, and J. de Keijser. Cullompton, Devon, UK: Willan.

———. 2005. *De dreigingsspiraal: Onbedoelde neveneffecten van de Misdaadbestrijding.* The Hague: Boom Juridische Uitgevers.

Corrado, M. L. 1996. "Punishment and the Wild Beast of Prey: The Problem of Preventive Detention." *Journal of Criminal Law & Criminology* 86(3):778–814.

Crombag, H. F. M., P. J. van Koppen, and W. A. Wagenaar. 1994. *Dubieuze zaken: De psychologie van strafrechtelijk bewijs.* Amsterdam: Contact.

de Hullu, J. 2003. "Naar een afschaffing op termijn van de terbeschikkingstelling?" In *Actuele ontwikkelingen in de forensische psychiatrie*, ed. T. I. Oei and M. S. Groenhuijsen. Deventer, the Netherlands: Kluwer.

de Keijser, J. W. 2000. *Punishment and Purpose: From Moral Theory to Punishment in Action.* Amsterdam: Thela Thesis.

de Kogel, C. H. 2005. "The Netherlands." In *Placement and Treatment of Mentally Disordered Offenders: Legislation and Practice in the European Union*, ed. H. J. Salize and H. Dressing. Lengerich, Germany: Pabst.

de Kogel, C. H., and V. E. Hartogh. 2005. "Contraire beëindiging van de TBS-maatregel: Aantal, aard en verband met recidive." In *Onderzoek & Beleid 236.* The Hague: WODC.

de Ruiter, C. 2009. "Risicotaxatie van gewelddadig gedrag: empirie en praktijk." In *Reizen met mijn rechter*, ed. P. J. van Koppen, H. Merckelbach, J. W. de Keijser, and M. Jelicic. Deventer, the Netherlands: Kluwer.

de Ruiter, C., and M. Hildebrand. 2009. "Over toerekeningsvatbaarheid." In *Reizen met mijn rechter*, ed. P. J. van Koppen, H. Merckelbach, J. W. de Keijser, and M. Jelicic. Deventer, the Netherlands: Kluwer.

de Vogel, V., C. de Ruiter, M. Hildebrand, B. Bos, and P. van de Ven. 2004. "Type of Discharge and Risk of Recidivism Measured by the HCR-20: A Retrospective Study in a Dutch Sample of Treated Forensic Psychiatric Patients." *International Journal of Forensic Mental Health* 3:149–65.

Dienst Justitiële Inrichtingen. 2009a. *TBS in getal: 2008.* The Hague: Ministerie van Justitie.

———. 2009b. *Toenemende verblijfsduur in de TBS.* The Hague: Ministerie van Justitie.

Donner, J. P. H. 2004a. "Wijziging van het Wetboek van Strafrecht, het Wetboek van Strafvordering en de Penitentiaire beginselenwet." Memorie van antwoord, plaatsing in een inrichting voor stelselmatige daders, Eerste Kamer, vergaderjaar 2003–2004, 28 980, D. The Hague: SDU.

———. 2004b. "Wijziging van het Wetboek van Strafrecht, het Wetboek van Strafvordering en de Penitentiaire beginselenwet." Memorie van toelichting, plaatsing in een inrichting voor stelselmatige daders, Tweede Kamer, vergaderjaar 2002–2003, 28 980, nr. 3. The Hague: SDU.

Drieschner, K. H., B. Hesper, and I. Marozzos. 2010. Effectonderzoek in de tbs-sector: theoretische overwegingen en praktische uitvoering bij trajectum Hoeve Boschoord. *De Psycholoog* 45:38–48.

Duff, R. A. 1998. "Dangerousness and Citizenship." In *Fundamentals of Sentencing Theory: Essays in Honour of Andrew von Hirsch*, ed. A. Ashworth and M. Wasik. Oxford: Clarendon Press.

Emmerik, J. L., and M. Brouwers. 2001. *De terbeschikkingstelling in maat en getal: Een beschrijving van de tbs-populatie in de periode 1995–2000.* The Hague: Dienst Justitiële Inrichtingen, Ministerie van Justitie.

Feeley, M. M., and J. Simon. 1994. "Actuarial Justice: The Emerging New Criminal Law." In *The Futures of Criminology*, ed. D. Nelken. London: Sage.

Garland, D. 2001. *The Culture of Control: Crime and Social Order in Contemporary Society.* Oxford: Oxford University Press.

Geeraets, V. 2006. "Ook TBS is bedoelde leedtoevoeging." *Nederlands Tijdschrift voor Rechtsfilosofie en Rechtstheorie* 1:19–28.

Goderie, M., and K. D. Lünneman. 2008. "De maatregel Inrichting voor Stelselmatige Daders, procesevaluatie." Unpublished manuscript, Utrecht.

Greenwood, P., and A. Abrahamse. 1982. *Selective Incapacitation.* Santa Monica, CA: RAND.

Groenhuijsen, M. S., and D. van der Landen, eds. 1990. *De Moderne Richting in het strafrecht.* Arnhem, the Netherlands: Gouda Quint.

Groenhuijsen, M. S., J. L. van der Neut, and J. Simmelink, eds. 1997. *Ontneming van voordeel in het strafrecht: De nieuwe wetgeving in theorie en praktijk.* Deventer, the Netherlands: Gouda Quint.

Harris, A. J. 2009. "The Civil Commitment of Sexual Predators: A Policy Review." In *Sex Offender Laws: Failed Policies, New Directions,* ed. M. G. Wright. New York: Springer.

Hart, H. L. A. 1968. *Punishment and Responsibility: Essays in the Philosophy of Law.* Oxford: Clarendon Press.

Hart, S. D., C. Michie, and D. J. Cooke. 2007. "Precision of Actuarial Risk Assessment Instruments." *British Journal of Psychiatry* 190(Suppl. 49):S60–S65.

Harte, J. 2009. "Een beoordeling ter beoordeling: Opbrengsten en beperkingen van instrumenten voor risicotaxatie in de forensische psychiatrie en mogelijkheden voor wetenschappelijk onderzoek." In *Vrijheid en Verlangen: Liber Amicorum prof.dr. Antoine Mooij,* ed. F. Koenraadt and I. Weijers. The Hague: Boom Juridische Uitgevers.

Hildebrand, M., and C. de Ruiter. 2009. "De strafrechtelijke maatregel terbeschikkingstelling." In *Reizen met mijn rechter,* ed. P. J. van Koppen, H. Merckelbach, J. W. de Keijser, and M. Jelicic. Deventer, the Netherlands: Kluwer.

Hofstee, E. J. 1987. "Monisme of dualisme?" In *Straffen in gerechtigheid,* ed. G. J. M. Corstens, G. E. Mulder, H. Singer-Dekker, and P. C. Vegter. Arnhem, the Netherlands: Gouda Quint.

Honderich, T. 1970. *Punishment: The Supposed Justifications,* 2nd ed. London: Hutchinson & Co.

Hulsman, L. H. C., T. W. van Veen, P. Allewijn, J. Kloek, W. M. E. Noach, and G. E. Langemeijer, eds. 1969. *Heeft het Strafrecht nog Zin?* Nijmegen, the Netherlands: Criminologisch Dispuut Dr. Nico Muller.

Janse de Jonge, J. A. 1991. *Om de persoon van de dader: Over strafrechttheorieën en voorlichting door de reclassering.* Arnhem, the Netherlands: Gouda Quint.

Jonkers, W. H. A., J. P. Balkema, Y. Buruma, J. P. S. Fiselier, and P. C. Vegter. 1998. "De strafrechtelijke maatregel." In *Het penitentiair recht,* vol. 48, ed. W. H. A. Jonkers, J. P. Balkema, Y. Buruma, J. P. S. Fiselier, and P. C. Vegter. Deventer, the Netherlands: Gouda Quint.

Jörg, N., and C. Kelk. 1994. *Strafrecht met mate.* Arnhem, the Netherlands: Gouda Quint.

Kalidien, S. N. 2008. "Tenuitvoerlegging van sancties." In *Criminaliteit en Rechtshandhaving 2007: Ontwikkelingen en samenhangen,* ed. A. T. J. Eggen and S. N. Kalidien. The Hague: WODC.

Kelk, C. 1994a. *De Menselijke verantwoordelijkheid in het strafrecht.* Arnhem, the Netherlands: Gouda Quint.

———. 1994b. Verbreding van het punitieve spectrum. In *Hoe punitief is Nederland,* ed. M. Moerings. Arnhem, the Netherlands: Gouda Quint.

Kleinig, J. 1973. *Punishment and Desert.* The Hague: Martinus Nijhoff.

Kooijmans, T. 2002. *Op maat geregeld?* Erasmus Universiteit, Rotterdam.

La Fond, J. Q. 2003. "Outpatient Commitment's Next Frontier: Sexual Predators." *Psychology, Public Policy, and Law* 9:159–82.

Lünnemann, K. D. 2009. "Met de blik van de rechter: Juridische overwegingen aangaande de ISD-maatregel." *Justitiële verkenningen* 2:106–17.

Mevis, P. A. M. 2006. *Capita Strafrecht: Een Thematische Inleiding.* Nijmegen, the Netherlands: Ars Aequi Libri.

————. 2009. "Spitsroeden Lopen Bij de Tenuitvoerlegging van de Maatregel van TBS." *Delikt en Delinkwent* 1/2:19–31.

Ministerie van Justitie and Ministerie van Binnenlandse Zaken en Koninkrijksrelaties. 2002. *Naar een Veiliger Samenleving.* The Hague.

Moerings, M. 2005. *Het risico van de stelselmatige dader. In Terugkeer in de samenleving: Opstellen voor Jan Fiselier,* ed. Y. Buruma and P. C. Vegter. Deventer, the Netherlands: Kluwer.

Morris, N. 1951. *The Habitual Criminal.* London: Longmans, Green and Co.

Muller, N. 1908. *Biografisch-aetiologisch onderzoek over recidive bij misdrijven tegen den eigendom.* Utrecht: Kemink & Zoon.

————. 1934. "De straf in het strafrecht (Taak en schoonheid van de onvoorwaardelijke straf)." *Tijdschrift voor Strafrecht* 44:15–72.

Nederlands Forensisch Instituut. 2008. *Vakbijlage: De reeks waarschijnlijkheidstermen van het NFI en het Bayesiaanse model voor interpretatie van bewijs.* The Hague: Nederlands Forensisch Instituut.

Nieboer, W. 1973. *Straf en maatregel.* Arnhem, the Netherlands: Gouda Quint.

Polak, L. 1947. *De Zin der Vergelding: Een strafrechts-philosophisch onderzoek,* vol. 2. Amsterdam: Van Oorschot.

Pompe, W. P. J. 1930. "De (zedelijke) rechtvaardiging van de straf in de rechtsorde." *Tijdschrift voor Strafrecht XL* 2:109–19.

————. 1943. "De rechtvaardiging van de straf." In *Praeadviezen over de rechtvaardiging van de straf,* ed. W. J. A. Duynstee and W. P. J. Pompe. 's-Gravenhage: Ten Hagen.

————. 1957. "De mens in het strafrecht." *Themis* 2:88–109.

Raad voor Strafrechtstoepassing en Jeugdbescherming. 2007. *Advies: De Inrichting voor Stelselmatige Daders.* The Hague: RJS.

Remmelink, J. 1986. "Theoretische stromingen in het materiële strafrecht." *Gedenkboek honderd jaar Wetboek van Strafrecht.* Arnhem, the Netherlands: Gouda Quint.

————. 1996. *Mr. D. Hazewinkel-Suringa's Inleiding tot de studie van het Nederlandse strafrecht,* 15th ed. Arnhem, the Netherlands: Gouda Quint.

Roberts, J. V. 2008. *Punishing Persistent Offenders: Exploring Community and Offender Perspectives.* Oxford: Oxford University Press.

Schuyt, P. M. 2005. "Terug naar een veiliger samenleving." In *Terugkeer in de samenleving: Opstellen voor Jan Fiselier,* ed. Y. Buruma and P. C. Vegter. Deventer, the Netherlands: Kluwer.

Strijards, G. A. M. 1987. "De noodzaak van een protolegale strafdefinitie." In *Straffen in gerechtigheid,* ed. G. J. M. Corstens, G. E. Mulder, H. Singer-Dekker, and P. C. Vegter. Arnhem, the Netherlands: Gouda Quint.

Struijk, S. 2005. "Het eerste bestaansjaar van de ISD-maatregel bekeken; een gretig gebruik door de rechterlijke macht of een zekere terughoudendheid?" *Delikt en Delinkwent* 67:933–52.

————. 2009. "De ISD-maatregel in wetshistorisch perspectief." *Justitiële verkenningen* 2:54–74.

Tak, P. J. P. 2003. *The Dutch Criminal Justice System: Organization and Operation.* The Hague: Boom Juridische Uitgevers.

Tijdelijke Commissie Onderzoek TBS (Commissie Visser). 2006. *TBS, vandaag over gisteren en morgen. Parlementair onderzoek TBS.* The Hague: SDU.

Tollenaar, N., J. van Dijk, and J. W. Alblas. 2009. *Monitor veelplegers 2003–2006: Cijfermatige ontwikkelingen (Factsheet 2009-1).* The Hague: WODC.

Tonry, M. 1992. "Selective Incapacitation: Its Ethics." In *Principled Sentencing,* ed. A. V. Hirsch and A. Ashworth. Edinburgh: Edinburgh University Press.

————. 1996. *Sentencing Matters.* New York: Oxford University Press.

————. 2004. *Thinking about Crime: Sense and Sensibility in American Penal Culture.* Oxford: Oxford University Press.

van der Knaap, L. M., and D. L. Alberda. 2009. De predictieve validiteit van de recidive inschattingsschalen (RISc). The Hague: WODC.

van der Knaap, L. M., L. E. W. Leenarts, and L. T. J. Nijssen. 2007. *Psychometrische kwaliteiten van de Recidive Inschattingsschalen (RISc): Interbeoordelaarsbetrouwbaarheid, interne consistentie en congruente validiteit.* The Hague: WODC.

van der Landen, D. 1992. *Straf en maatregel.* Arnhem, the Netherlands: Gouda Quint.

————. 1993. Een pleidooi voor de afschaffing an tbs. *Justitiële verkenningen* 19(3):56–73.

van Hamel, G. A. 1999. "De Internationale Vereeniging voor Strafrecht." In *100 jaar strafrecht: Klassieke teksten van de twintigste eeuw,* ed. Y. Buruma. Amsterdam: Amsterdam University Press (originally published 1889).

van Kuijck, Y. A. J. M., and P. C. Vegter. 1999. "De TBS in de rechtspraktijk." *Justitiële verkenningen* 4:54–66.

van Ooyen-Houben, M., and M. Goderie. 2009. "Veelplegers terug bij af? De ISD in retrospectief." *Justitiële Overkenningen* 2:10–30.

van Stokkom, B., ed. 2004. *Straf en herstel: Ethische reflecties over sanctiedoeleinden.* The Hague: Boom Juridische Uitgevers.

van Swaaningen, R. 2004. "De nieuwe veiligheidscultuur." *Justitiële verkenningen* 7:9–23.

van Veen, T. W. 1949. *Generale preventie.* 's-Gravenhage: D. A. Daamen.

van Velthoven, B. C. J., and D. E. G. Moolenaar. 2009. "Loont de SOV/ISD-maatregel? Een eerste verkenning." *Justitiële verkenningen* 2:31–53.

Vegter, P. C. 1991. "Naar een enkel spoor?" *Sancties* 3:143–145.

Vollaard, B. A. 2010. *Het effect van langdurige opsluiting van veelplegers op de maatschappelijke veiligheid: Lessen van een natuurlijk experiment in twaalf stedelijke gebieden.* Tilburg, the Netherlands: TILEC.

von Hirsch, A. 1992. "Prediction and False Positives." In *Principled Sentencing,* ed. A. V. Hirsch and A. Ashworth. Edinburgh: Edinburgh University Press.

————. 1993. *Censure and Sanctions.* Oxford: Oxford University Press.

von Hirsch, A., and L. Kazemian. 2009. "Predictive Sentencing and Selective Incapacitation." In *Principled Sentencing: Readings on Theory and Policy,* 3rd ed., ed. A. V. Hirsch, A. Ashworth, and J. Roberts. Portland, OR: Hart.

Vruggink, J. 2001. *Gepakt en gezakt: Invloed van de ontnemingsmaatregel op daders.* Leiden: Universiteit Leiden.

Walgrave, L. 2004. "Herstelrecht en de wet." In *Straf en herstel: Ethische reflecties over sanctiedoeleinden,* ed. B. van Stokkom. The Hague: Boom Juridische Uitgevers.

————. 2008. *Restorative Justice, Self-Interest and Responsible Citizenship.* Cullompton, Devon, UK: Willan.

Walker, N. 1991. *Why Punish?* Oxford: Oxford University Press.

Wartna, B. S. J., S. E. Harbachi, and L. M. van der Knaap. 2005. *Buiten behandeling: Een cijfermatig overzicht van de strafrechtelijke recidive van ex-terbeschikkinggestelden.* The Hague: WODC.

Wilson, F. T. 2004. "Out of Sight, Out of Mind: An Analysis of *Kansas v. Crane* and the Fine Line Between Civil and Criminal Sanctions." *Prison Journal* 84:379–94.

Wilson, J. Q. 1983. *Thinking about Crime.* New York: Basic Books.

Wright, M. G., ed. 2009. *Sex Offender Laws: Failed Policies, New Directions.* New York: Springer.

11

Retributivism, Proportionality, and the Challenge of the Drug Court Movement

DOUGLAS HUSAK

Retributive theories of punishment and sentencing differ from nonretributive theories in a variety of respects. Among these is the centrality retributivists afford to the principle of proportionality. Although competing versions of this principle have been offered,[1] I construe proportionality to require that the severity of the punishment should be a function of the seriousness of the crime (von Hirsch and Ashworth 2005, p. 143). If punishment and sentencing are designed to promote future goods, it is less obvious why the state should be so concerned to ensure that the quantum of punishment is proportionate to the seriousness of the offense. At the very least, nonretributivists presumably assign only instrumental value to conformity with the principle of proportionality.

Thus the practical application of any retributive theory of punishment and sentencing depends largely on our ability to implement the principle of proportionality. This task is notoriously problematic, requiring three difficult determinations. First, we need a ranking of crime seriousness; second, a ranking of punishment severity; and finally, some means to establish a correspondence between one ranking and the other. Of these three problems, the last is typically regarded as the most troublesome and has received the most attention. Much of this attention has come from critics of retributivism, many of whom allege that no nonarbitrary correspondence between the two rankings can be defended (Dolinko 1992; Christopher 2002).[2] The first of these problems is probably the easiest. With a few noteworthy exceptions, respondents display a surprising degree of consensus about how to rank the relative seriousness of criminal offenses (von Hirsch and Jareborg 1991). Although I will have more to say about this first problem, I direct most of my focus toward some aspects of the second—the problem of punishment severity.

The principle of proportionality requires *parity* in sentencing severity. But how do we decide if two sentence tokens are disparate? As long as the state imprisons persons who commit serious crimes, the answer to this question is generally regarded as relatively simple. Two terms of imprisonment are equally severe when they are equal in duration. To be sure, given defendants respond differently to equal terms of imprisonment (Bronsteen, Buccafusco, and Masur 2009; Kolber 2009),[3] and factors other than duration affect the severity of imprisonment (Morris and Tonry 1990, pp. 94–95). In light of the epistemological obstacles in considering such factors, however, few theorists regard these difficulties as insuperable. Matters changed radically, however, when states began to make wider use of various alternative sanctions—punishments other than imprisonment (Wasik and von Hirsch 1988). These problems are compounded when jurisdictions levy sanctions pursuant to "dual-track" systems that try defendants either in traditional courts or in alternative courts for the very same offense. It should not be surprising that these dual-track systems make disparity all but inevitable. When two tracks exist side by side, the question arises: *Which* track treats defendants as they deserve? On many occasions, dual-track systems present questions of parity that are nearly insoluble.

I will explore this issue in the context of what has been called "therapeutic jurisprudence" generally and the "drug court movement" in particular. Few developments in contemporary penal policy are as profound as the proliferation of specialty courts designed to deal with given kinds of disputes. Commentators from all sides of the political spectrum—including many of those who subscribe to some version of retributivism—have tended to applaud these developments. In particular, praise has been heaped on the drug court movement; in its first several years of operation it "received almost uniformly positive media coverage and overwhelming public support at both the national and local levels" (Nolan 2001, p. 5).[4] As I will indicate, however, the drug court movement poses a profound challenge to the principle of parity, and thus to retributivism more generally.

Retributivism has a bad name in many circles. A "just deserts" approach has been faulted for fueling the unprecedented growth in incarceration and increase in sentence severity throughout the United States.[5] Although many commentators have sought to refute this allegation, I have little doubt that the mode of therapeutic justice dispensed by drug courts is attractive largely because it is perceived as more humane, compassionate, and potentially beneficial to defendants than the modes of punishment typically inflicted on drug offenders under a retributivist banner. The foregoing sentiments have been conspicuously lacking in contemporary drug policy. Critics of the decades-long "war on drugs" have reached a near-consensus that we punish drug offenders too much and treat them too little. It is easy to understand why liberal opponents of our repressive drug policies tend to be enthusiastic about the drug court movement.

I hope to show that this enthusiasm should be muted, for the mode of justice dispensed by specialty courts generally and by drug courts in particular almost inevitably requires jurisdictions to impose disparate punishments and violate the principle of proportionality. Several measures might help to make violations of proportionality less worrisome, but the most plausible such measure necessitates a fundamental rethinking of our current drug policy. The fundamental rethinking I will urge, however, turns out to jeopardize the very existence of drug courts. As long as we retain a dual-track system and allow drug courts to exist alongside traditional courts for the very same offense, I am pessimistic that we can solve the problems I will identify. If I am correct, the drug court movement can be salvaged within a penal philosophy that takes proportionality seriously only if dual-track models are scrapped. Thus, retributivists should view these courts with suspicion.

Although I believe that the dual-track model in which drug courts are embedded poses special problems for retributivists, it should be noted that it raises a challenge to *any* penal philosophy that takes proportionality seriously.[6] Despite its centrality to retributive thought, other theories of punishment are and ought to be interested in proportionality as well (Ristroph 2005). The intuitive appeal of proportionality is so powerful that nonretributivists struggle mightily to explain how their theories of punishment can accommodate it.[7] After all, the instrumental value assigned to proportionality within consequentialist frameworks still is *value*, even if it is not intrinsic. These heroic efforts suggest that proportionality might be regarded as a deeply shared intuition about penal justice that is essential to any respectable justification of punishment (Farrell, 2010). If I am correct, the drug court movement is hard to reconcile with nearly all penal philosophies.

My central claim should not be construed to suppose that parity is typically preserved elsewhere in the criminal justice system. In fact, sentencing disparities are ubiquitous as long as we continue to rely so heavily on plea bargains.[8] In order to induce guilty pleas, defendants who insist that the state prove their guilt risk a severe "trial tax" or (what is more charitably called) a "plea discount." As a result, two defendants who commit the same crime receive drastically disparate sentences depending on their pleas. Still, I have reason to highlight the respects in which dual-track systems produce disparity and disregard proportionality. No one has proposed a realistic solution to the enormous problems posed by our excessive use of plea bargains, but the means to reduce the disparities created by drug courts are well within our grasp. Or so I will argue.

The structure of this essay is as follows. After this introduction, section I is largely descriptive. I will briefly describe the phenomenon of therapeutic jurisprudence generally and the drug court movement in particular. Section II raises normative concerns. I will argue that we have overwhelming evidence that the dual-track system in which drug courts are embedded imposes punishments that violate the principle of proportionality. Section III indicates how existing practices might be reconciled with the normative worries I claim to have uncovered. I will suggest that these difficulties are best resolved by a drastic change in contemporary drug policy. Although the public can continue to ignore the problems I examine, penal theorists who take proportionality seriously can support drug courts only as a second-best alternative to the more radical solution of drug decriminalization.

I. DRUG COURTS

Therapeutic jurisprudence is among the most important developments in American criminal justice in the past quarter century.[9] Although the term means different things to different people,[10] this broad movement is credited with inspiring the creation of at least 14 "dual-track" systems in which persons who commit specified kinds of offenses may proceed in regular court or be diverted into a specialty court. The types of specialized courts that exist at present include domestic violence, community, mental health, alcohol abuse, homeless, and a host of others. Some commentators describe these as "problem-solving courts;" they "try to alter the behavior of offenders, give support to victims, and improve public safety in high crime neighborhoods, rather than temporarily impede the acts of offenders or simply process their cases" (Sammon 2008, p. 929). Each such court shares the general goal of achieving positive outcomes for defendants. Judges are active participants in this process; some bluntly admit that they aspire to change the behavior of the offender. The hope is not simply that traditional punishments will educate or rehabilitate; the initiative to enhance the welfare of the defendant is taken directly by the court itself.

Drug courts are the crowning achievement of therapeutic jurisprudence. They are said to represent "a significant step in the evolution of therapeutic jurisprudence—the evolutionary step from theory to application" (Hora, Schma, and Rosenthal 1999, p. 448). As a result, drug courts have been called "the most significant penal innovation in the last twenty years" (Miller 2004, p. 1481). In the United States in 2010, approximately 2,400 drug courts each served about 120,000 drug offenders throughout all 50 states (National Drug Court Institute 2010). Among the most notable individuals to pass through these courts are Noelle Bush, niece of former President George W. Bush, and Rush Limbaugh, the prominent conservative talk-radio pundit. Although I suspect that their popularity may no longer be growing—a few municipalities that introduced drug courts have subsequently abolished them—these courts represent a remarkable development in contemporary criminal justice. No one predicts that these courts will vanish anytime soon.

Drug courts differ so much that generalizations are perilous. Some are far more impressive than others and make strenuous efforts to deal with problems beyond those that involve simple drug abuse. Nonetheless, I will paint them with a broad brush. In all cases, eligible offenders are given the option of subjecting themselves to normal adjudication or undergoing a treatment regime designed and overseen by the specialty court. From this point, two procedural differences are noteworthy. First, courts differ about the point at which they assume jurisdiction. Some are *deferred prosecution*, requiring the defendant to waive many of his rights, such as his right to a speedy trial. A greater number are *postconviction*, requiring the defendant to plead guilty and deferring his sentence pending a determination of whether he completes the treatment regime mandated by the court. Second, courts differ radically in their criteria of eligibility and the degree to which these criteria are enforced. Although the federal government imposes a handful of conditions that need to be satisfied in order to obtain funding, the details of the eligibility criteria are not uniform from one court to another. Some require the defendant to be an addict, although what this means and how it is ascertained is not always clear. Others require the defendant to have no prior offenses, not be a gang member, or not be engaged in violence. Once again, the meaning of these necessary conditions is not straightforward or easily verified. All courts, however, require defendants to complete a treatment regime overseen and supervised by the judge. Failure to complete this regime results in prosecution or (when courts are postconviction) the imposition of the deferred sentence for the underlying offense.

Perhaps the best way to gain insight into the drug court movement is to identify the broad trends that have caused the relatively sudden emergence of therapeutic justice generally and that can be expected to contribute to its popularity in the foreseeable future. Five distinct but related factors merit brief emphasis. First, it is a truism that the problem of crime has transformed American democracy and continues to resist a simple solution (Simon 2007). No social response to antisocial behavior has ever proven easy to justify according to the normative principles political and legal philosophers favor. Our current approach of massive incarceration survives mainly by default; few commentators are enthusiastic about it. Frustration with the status quo makes both scholars and professionals receptive to novel proposals. Despite a highly publicized decrease in crime in the United States throughout the past two decades, dissatisfaction among participants in the criminal justice system may be near an all-time high. Judges in particular see a revolving-door system in which defendants are continually arrested, incarcerated, and rearrested. They long to "make a difference" in the lives of those they sentence. One need not subscribe to the "nothing works" mentality to sympathize with the pessimism of professionals. Surely it is no exaggeration to conclude that *little* works, even if states have made some progress in designing more effective rehabilitative programs. Against the background of disappointment with current policy, it is easy to understand why a significant subset of criminal justice practitioners would be eager to take matters into their own hands and adopt measures they believe to be preferable.

Second, our society has failed to develop and fund social programs that might be helpful in preventing crime before it occurs or is repeated. Liberal ideals have been so discredited in the United States that few politicians dare to call for the adoption of measures to combat the root causes of crime.[11] Although everyone knows that criminal behavior is strongly correlated with socioeconomic status, no one proposes to rectify this situation and instead hope that a rising tide of prosperity will lift all boats. If the state had made preventive programs more widely available, it is unlikely that therapeutic ideologies would have gathered so much inertia within our criminal justice system. Therapeutic jurisprudence fills a lacuna; its specialty courts are designed to "adapt their processes to suit the sources of the problems which are driving the actions that bring the wrongdoer to court in the first place" (Sammon 2008, p. 924).

Third, institutions in a capitalist economy are under increasing pressure to be economically efficient. This pressure has been applied to political institutions generally, and it is somewhat surprising that criminal justice policies have not always been subject to the same cost–benefit scrutiny. Mass incarceration is extraordinarily expensive, and it is hard to see what benefits citizens reap that can justify the enormous allocation of tax resources. Even skeptics are willing to experiment with therapeutic justice because they hope that crime can be managed at a lower cost. One of the recurrent themes among proponents of therapeutic jurisprudence is that their programs save money (National Drug Court Institute 2010). The economic recession that emerged in 2008 gives this factor a special salience.

Fourth, perhaps no society in human history embraces therapy as a remedy for social ills more fully than the United States in the twenty-first century. We seek professional therapists and medicines for ourselves and our children to an unprecedented (and alarming) degree (Conrad 2007). Aging, menopause, obesity, social anxiety, erectile dysfunction, and adult attention deficit hyperactivity disorder (ADHD) are among the many conditions said to be amenable to quasi-medical interventions. If society were less receptive to tales of how personal problems could be overcome by hard work and treatment, it is hard to imagine that therapeutic rationales would have found such a comfortable home in our criminal justice system.

Fifth, our legislatures have brought about rampant overcriminalization (Husak 2008). Many behaviors that are problematic but do not seem to merit retribution have been proscribed by our legal system because of an eagerness to *do something* to combat them. All too often, this "something" consists of the enactment and enforcement of a penal statute. According to one commentator, criminal offenses are defined so broadly that members of professional classes typically perpetrate three felonies each day (Silverglate 2009). Once a given mode of conduct becomes eligible for punitive sanctions, the criminal justice system must respond in some way or another to the behavior that has been proscribed. If our penal law focused more narrowly on core offenses that involve culpability and harm, it is doubtful that our criminal justice system would have been tempted to adopt a therapeutic posture to so many defendants.

The above five factors explain the popularity not only of therapeutic jurisprudence generally, but also of drug courts in particular. First, frustration with virtually every aspect of contemporary drug policy is voiced from all points along the political spectrum. Even while crime is dropping generally, levels of drug abuse have remained relatively stable in the United States throughout the past decade (Substance Abuse and Mental Health Services Administration 2010). Moreover, while treatment facilities for drug users may be available to affluent offenders, many of whom can be counted on to check into rehabilitation centers when their drug problems attract negative publicity, poor users are more likely to be arrested and sentenced to prison (Tonry 1995). In addition, the therapy dispensed by drug courts thrives on the supposition that excessive drug abuse is not a voluntary choice, but rather a disease that responds to treatment. Liberals disapprove of punishments for this alleged disease; conservatives disapprove of being soft on crime, but are impatient with the ineffectiveness and costs of our present policy. The persistent claim that drug courts save money has already been mentioned. The final factor is the most crucial, but is most likely to be overlooked. Courts would have no opportunity to dispense therapeutic justice to offenders unless drug use (or, more technically, drug possession) were proscribed throughout the United States. The jurisdiction of these courts presupposes the commission of a crime. Hence, the deepest question—rarely mentioned in the literature about the drug court movement—is that of criminalization. If drug use were not a criminal offense, drug courts would not exist.

Despite their general popularity, serious questions about drug courts have recently been raised. Two points have been discussed extensively. First, the most astounding factor is the untested and unproven empirical assumptions on which these institutions depend. Despite constant assurances that "drug courts work,"[12] almost no reliable data support the truth of this allegation. Drug treatment specialists have struggled for generations to find viable solutions to the complex problems of substance abuse; it would be surprising if untrained judges have managed to identify an effective strategy when experts have failed to devise a viable approach. In much of the literature on drug courts, anecdote substitutes for evidence of effectiveness; this area is dominated by testimonials rather than by sound data.[13] Admittedly, generalizations about effectiveness are nearly meaningless inasmuch as different courts implement very different therapeutic strategies—and some may not dispense anything that qualifies as genuine "therapy" at all. Participants are not *entitled* to treatment if a particular court declines to provide it. Most importantly, putative success rates must be assessed relative to the fact that *most* users quit in their late 20s or early 30s—even without receiving treatment.[14] Thus the fact that a given defendant stops using drugs should not automatically be counted as evidence of the effectiveness of the therapeutic regime. In any event, careful research indicates that "drug courts are by no means the panacea that some had suggested and that caution should be the order of the day when characterizing results" (Marlowe, Dematteo, and Festinger 2003, p. 156).

A second criticism is equally common. Like the rehabilitative ideal that preceded it, therapeutic jurisprudence cares less than adversarial models about the due process rights of defendants. Rehabilitative and therapeutic approaches allow active intervention in the private lives of defendants. Both require indeterminate sentences rather than the fixed penalties imposed under sentencing guidelines. The traditional jobs of many participants in the criminal justice system—especially those of defense lawyers—are altered radically by these courts. Zealous advocacy is easily misconstrued as denial and a counterproductive unwillingness to provide one's client with the help he allegedly needs. Defense council must be wary that defendants are not perceived as uncooperative when they are reluctant to offer candid answers to questions from the bench that might implicate them or their associates in further criminal activity (Boldt 1998).

These two reservations are both forceful and familiar. Commentators are less likely to notice, however, that the very existence of drug courts poses special problems for retributivists. I will argue that the sanctions these courts impose are almost certainly incompatible with the central tenets of a penal philosophy that affords a prominent place to the principle of proportionality. I now support this allegation.

II. PARITY

As I have indicated, proportionality is the bedrock of retributivism. Among the least controversial implications of proportionality is the requirement of *parity*: offenders who perpetrate equally serious crimes should receive equally severe punishments (von Hirsch 1985, p. 40).[15] In principle, it is easy to describe a test to decide whether the dual-track system established by drug courts is capable of satisfying the demands of parity. Suppose that Smith and Jones commit the same drug offense. Smith's case is diverted to a drug court, and Jones's case is adjudicated in a regular court. Both plead guilty and are sentenced. Jones serves a traditional sentence, whereas Smith's sentence is deferred pending the determination of whether he succeeds or fails to complete the treatment regime mandated by the judge. What are the prospects that the demands of parity are met in this scenario? I will conclude that the answer almost certainly is negative.[16] Since Smith and Jones are treated so very differently, disparity is all but inevitable; one court or the other (and possibly both) fails to treat them according to their deserts. If my arguments are sound, retributivists are faced with a limited set of options in trying to salvage the mode of therapeutic jurisprudence dispensed by drug courts.

To decide whether proportionality can possibly be preserved between Smith and Jones, we might begin by determining how some defendants but not others wind up in drug court in the first place. Perhaps the desert basis for any subsequent disparity can be identified before the proceedings take place. In other words, maybe Smith is likely to be diverted to drug court precisely *because* he has not committed "the same offense" as Jones; his crime is different and less serious. But this possibility is remote. No morally relevant criteria differentiated Smith from Jones at the time of their arrest. Prosecutors rather than police play the crucial role in selecting the type of court in which Smith and Jones will be made to appear. In the majority of jurisdictions, the prosecutor possesses the sole power to recommend that a defendant be diverted (Miller 2004, p. 1540), and in some cases "participation in the adult drug court is permitted at the sole discretion of the prosecutor" (Rockwell 2008, p. 13).

I do not mean to suggest that formal criteria for diversion do not exist; here, as elsewhere, meaningful generalizations about the eligibility conditions for entry into drug court cannot be constructed. To cite one example, most courts explicitly preclude offenders who sell rather than merely consume drugs (Miller 2004, p. 1539). In other courts, however, the opposite is true; drug dealers comprise the overwhelming majority of participants—an astounding 95 percent in the Bronx drug court, for example (Bowers 2008, p. 794). To cite a second example, some jurisdictions make efforts to ensure that drug courts are available to addicts. Others, however, take steps to exclude them (Bowers 2008, p. 798). Despite the existence of these diverse formal criteria, it is hard to know how rigorously they are enforced in practice. Moreover, a given defendant typically has no recourse and must proceed through the criminal justice system in the normal manner if the prosecutor decides not to divert his case (Miller 2004, p. 1540). Thus, as with many other specialty courts in a dual-track system, it is only a slight exaggeration to say that drug courts operate at the whim of the prosecutor (Quinn 2000–2001, p. 57). Even when formal eligibility criteria are rigorously observed, it is hard to see how the applicable conditions could justify any subsequent disparity in the sentences of Smith and Jones—as long as the standards for what counts as a *justification* for a disparity must bear on desert and thus be compatible with retributivism. Henceforth I will assume that Smith could appear in drug court and Jones could appear in a regular court even though both committed the same offense.

As I have stipulated, Smith receives a deferred sentence contingent on his completion of the treatment mandated by the drug court, while Jones receives a more traditional punishment—fine or imprisonment. Can their respective sentences possibly be equally severe? If the treatment mandated by the drug court and a more conventional punishment were equal in severity, no violation of proportionality would occur. In order to determine whether these sentences are disparate, the first task is to decide whether the treatment regimes mandated by drug courts qualify as *punishment* at all. This question is surprisingly difficult. Many drug court judges tend to conceptualize the treatment they dispense as an *alternative* to punishment rather than as a *mode* of punishment. If a therapeutic response to drug offenders is not punitive, desert considerations seem totally inapplicable to the entire drug court movement. According to this train of thought, real *punishments* are held in reserve in case defendants fail to complete their treatment. Clearly, a given punishment is unlikely to be equal in severity to a sanction that is not a punishment. It is hard enough to establish that two very different modes of punishment are equally harsh, but nearly impossible to determine that a mode of punishment is equal in severity to a sanction that is not a punishment in the first place. In what follows, I will assume that the coerced treatment mandated by drug courts *is* a mode of punishment rather than an alternative to it. Although the nature of punishment is notoriously controversial, this assumption seems compatible with fairly standard definitions. If punishment is understood as the intentional infliction of a stigmatizing hardship or deprivation imposed on an offender for his offense, the treatment dispensed by drug courts seemingly qualifies as punitive.[17] Defendants probably are stigmatized when they are ordered to undergo treatment, and they unquestionably are made to suffer deprivations.

Assuming that drug courts inflict real punishments on defendants (like Smith), the next question is whether these punishments are equal in severity to those imposed on defendants (like Jones) who commit the same offense but are not diverted from regular courts. However unlikely this possibility may appear at first, it should not be dismissed out of hand. Drug court judges frequently emphasize the difficulty of conforming to their treatment regime. According to Judge Diane Strickland, for example, the demands of her drug court in Roanoke, Virginia, may "seem to be a soft on crime approach," but the "realities are that it's actually much tougher" (Nolan 2001, p. 55). Judge Strickland's perspective is not unusual. James Nolan, author of the most comprehensive monograph on the drug court movement, writes that "judge after judge with whom I spoke made the same point" (Nolan 2001, p. 55). Conservatives in particular would not have been so enthusiastic in supporting the drug court movement if they believed the treatment regimes offered an easy way out for substance abusers. In order to placate the concerns of those who insist we must remain tough on crime, the therapy drug courts dispense is deliberately structured so that compliance is relatively difficult (Nolan 2001).[18]

Despite the rhetoric of many drug court judges, can it possibly be true that drug offenders who are coerced into treatment are typically punished with the same degree of severity as those who are sentenced in regular court? Although my arguments fall short of a conclusive demonstration, it seems intuitively clear that Jones *must* be punished more harshly than Smith. If the sentences imposed on the persons not diverted were not at least *believed* to be more severe, it is hard to see how the threat of traditional punishment could provide a meaningful incentive to comply with the treatment regime mandated by a judge. Rational persons are rarely persuaded to endure a greater hardship when threatened with a lesser hardship. Therefore, it is plausible to suppose that the offender who is sentenced in drug court and is forced to complete a treatment program must *think* his punishment is more lenient than the defendant who is not sentenced in regular court.[19] But how can we tell whether this belief is true? The problem of answering this question is exacerbated because attempts to assess the relative severity of two very different modes of punishment founder when one but not the other is administered pursuant to a form of therapeutic jurisprudence. According to some commentators, the severity of a given punishment "is a matter of how much [it] intrudes upon the interests a person typically needs to live a good life" (von Hirsch and Ashworth 2005, p.157). If we take this suggestion seriously, the sanctions imposed by therapeutic jurisprudence—designed to *restore* rather than *intrude* upon the conditions of a good life—*cannot* be equivalent to those imposed by more traditional modes of punishment. Commentators who apparently believe otherwise—such as the many drug court judges interviewed by

Nolan—should be pressed to explain the metric they presuppose in deciding that two sentences are equally severe.

Moreover, the means by which drug court offenders manage to evade the imposition of their suspended sentence—namely, success with the treatment mandated by the judge—cannot justify the disparate treatment they receive. Retributivists are reluctant to allow *any* event that occurs *after* the commission of the crime—displays of remorse, for example—to be taken into consideration in assessing the seriousness of the offense or the severity of the punishment that is deserved. No one should argue with a straight face that Smith's crime of using drugs is less serious than Jones's identical offense because Smith stops using drugs after he is caught. After all, some offenders tried in regular court also stop using drugs, but this fact does not make their earlier crime any less serious. If I am correct, the very premise of drug courts—that the full force of punishment can be avoided by compliance with a treatment regime—is inconsistent with principles central to a retributivist philosophy.

But the evidence for disparity has only begun. In addition, we must understand what counts as *success* in completing treatment. It might appear that this question is easy. The regimes mandated by a drug court seem no less determinate than the sentences handed down in regular court: drug court judges typically specify, sometimes in writing, exactly what the offender is required to do in order to avoid the deferred sentence. Relapse, however, is painfully common among drug court defendants, even among those who eventually graduate from the program (Rempel et al. 2003). According to some surveys, at least half of all graduates had at least one positive drug test, and many participants had several positive tests (Rempel et al. 2003). Judges have the authority to label these defendants as failures and to dismiss them from the program; defendants are not *entitled* to relapse. Thus, there is enormous flexibility and uncertainty about the conditions under which drug court offenders are deemed to have failed so that a traditional punishment will be levied. At the very least, discretion is exercised in determining whether given participants are complying with the terms of their agreements.

Despite the foregoing difficulties, let us make the heroic assumption that the treatment required of Smith in drug court is just as severe as the traditional punishment imposed on Jones. If so, violations of parity need not occur—as long as Smith is deemed to be successful in conforming to the regime. But we should not generalize about drug courts solely from their successes.[20] Although results vary enormously from one court to another, somewhere between 34 percent and 73 percent of all participants *fail* to graduate from drug court (U.S. Government Accountability Office 2005). What *does* actually happen to Smith if he does not complete the treatment regime to the satisfaction of the judge? It is typically assumed that he simply becomes subject to the punishment that would have been imposed had his case not been diverted in the first place. If Jones is treated in accordance with his desert and Smith receives the same punishment as Jones when he is held to be noncompliant, no violation of proportionality need occur. Any disparity would take place only for those defendants who graduate.

The truth, however, is more complex. First, note that Smith has *already* endured a great part of the treatment regime mandated by the court, albeit unsuccessfully. If his deferred sentence is now imposed, it is arguable that he is punished twice for the same crime. Moreover, the scant data that are available indicate that the sentences of those who fail in drug court tend to be considerably higher than those imposed on defendants who are charged with the same crime but did not enter drug court. According to one study, the sentences for failing participants in New York City drug courts were typically two to five times longer than the sentences for conventionally adjudicated defendants (Bowers 2008, p. 792). This finding all but guarantees violations of proportionality. Disparity occurs when drug court participants succeed, and disparity also occurs when they fail. The rationale for the increased sentence in the latter case is not the seriousness of the underlying offense, but the inability to pass the treatment regime mandated by the court.[21] But this failure, occurring after the crime itself, can no more affect desert than success.

To make matters worse, the distinction between those who succeed and those who fail in drug court is anything but random. The more heavily addicted the user, the less likely he is to graduate from the program (Bowers 2008). Again, it is hard to see how the extent of a given defendant's addiction has anything to do with the seriousness of his crime or the severity of the punishment he deserves for committing it. If addiction bears on desert at all, it undermines voluntariness and thus *decreases* desert. Whether addicted or not, defendants from historically disadvantaged groups are far less likely to graduate from drug court. Although some commentators have expressed hope that drug courts would reduce the notorious racial disparities in sentencing produced by the war on drugs, recent evidence suggests that such courts may actually exacerbate these disparities (O'Hear 2009). Socioeconomic factors partly explain why some participants but not others are kicked out of drug court after failing a single test (O'Hear 2009, p.803). In any event, it is clear that the variables that predict for success in drug court play no justificatory role in a retributive penal philosophy.

Finally, the disparities caused by dual-track systems do not end with formal punishments. Retributivists should not ignore the devastating collateral consequences of drug convictions (Brand-Ballard 2009). The sentences imposed on drug offenders exact an enormous toll, extending to the friends and families of the persons who are punished (Demleitner 2002). These consequences may include the loss of employment opportunities in licensed and unlicensed occupations; the capacity to serve as a juror or a court-appointed fiduciary; the privilege to vote, hold public office, carry a firearm, receive benefits such as public housing and student loans; and a host of others. Defendants who are given the opportunity to avoid these collateral consequences by participating in drug court enjoy a huge advantage over those who commit the same crime but are tried in traditional court. Perhaps retributivists can ignore this disparity by supposing that these hardships are not a part of punishment itself. But they cannot deny that these disparities are an inevitable product of a dual-track system in which some but not all offenders are allowed to participate. In short, these disparities cry out for justification.

For each of the foregoing several reasons, it strains credibility to believe that parity is preserved when Smith and Jones are arrested for the same offense and the former, but not the latter, is diverted to a drug court. Can the several problems I have identified be solved by improving the quality of therapeutic jurisprudence? I think not. According to Josh Bowers, retributive injustice derives from a theoretical inconsistency at the heart of the drug court ideology. These institutions adopt a medical perspective when welcoming participants to drug court, but shift to a penal mentality when dealing with persons who fail the treatment regime. They view the addict as only partly rational and responsible when assessing his original crime, but wholly rational and responsible when evaluating his capacity to respond to the carrots and sticks utilized by the court. On the one hand, drug court defendants are told that they have diseases that drive them to use drugs, then on the other hand, that they are wholly to blame when they do not respond to treatment. Although many drug court judges claim to understand that relapse is an inevitable step in recovery from the affliction of addiction, their tolerance extends only so far. If indeed drug offenders differ from other criminals in being incapable of rational action, it seems misguided to hope that the offer of additional reasons to behave rationally can remedy their condition.

To my mind, Bowers is persuasive in demonstrating the theoretical incoherence in the drug court movement. Our dual-track system betrays our deep "national schizophrenia about drugs" (Hoffman 2000, p. 1477). Some commentators allege that substance addiction is unique; it is "the only psychiatric syndrome whose symptoms are illegal and automatically trigger costly punishments, which sometimes include time behind bars" (Heyman 2009, p. 11). Drug courts owe their existence to the philosophy that addiction is a compulsive disease, even though they expect addicts to be receptive to external coercion. According to the view that users suffer from a "brain disease," addiction is unresponsive to traditional punishments because jails and prisons lack the tools to help addicts quit. Thus, diversion is regarded as justified. But drug courts do not wholly abandon the traditional criminal justice paradigm in which substance abuse is understood as a willful choice. They simply retain this old paradigm as the incentive to respond to treatment.[22] Accordingly, drug courts conceptualize addicts as sick and their crimes as symptomatic of illness only as long as they modify their behavior. When treatment is unsuccessful, however, these courts revert to traditional explanations of drug use and resort to conventional punishment.

If the foregoing arguments are sound, violations of parity, and thus of proportionality, are inevitable when drug courts exist alongside traditional courts. One may think that this conclusion is all that is needed to warrant hostility to the drug court movement among retributivists. This inference, however, would be premature. I will suggest that the proper retributivist verdict on therapeutic jurisprudence generally and the drug court movement in particular is somewhat more complex.

III. DO DRUG COURTS OR TRADITIONAL COURTS PRESERVE PARITY?

Suppose I am correct that Smith (who is punished in drug court) and Jones (who is punished in a traditional court) receive disparate punishments. Hence, their punishments violate the principle of proportionality and should be unacceptable to retributivists as well as to any penal theorist who takes parity seriously. Thus, we need to inquire: *Which* of these two defendants is punished in excess of his desert? Only three alternatives are available:

1. Smith is punished in proportion to the seriousness of his offense, while Jones is punished excessively.

2. Smith is punished leniently, while Jones is punished in proportion to the seriousness of his offense.
3. Neither Smith nor Jones is punished in proportion to the seriousness of his offense.

If these three possibilities indeed exhaust the logical terrain, which of them should we accept? Clearly the answer is crucial in determining the attitude retributivists should adopt toward drug courts. They should be enthusiastic about these courts only if (1) is true and the sentences they impose are proportionate to desert. If (2) or (3) is true, retributivists should oppose these courts. Still, the *depth* of retributive dissatisfaction with these courts depends on which of these latter options is more credible. Moreover, if (3) is true, retributive attitudes about drug courts depend on whether

3a. both Smith and Jones are punished more severely than they deserve; or
3b. both Smith and Jones are punished less severely than they deserve.

If (3a) is correct, as I believe it to be, retributivist hostility toward drug courts is likely to be muted. Although both Smith and Jones are punished with undeserved severity, the punishments imposed in drug courts are a closer approximation of what drug users deserve than those inflicted in regular courts. These courts serve as a mechanism to reduce injustice and lessen the amount of undeserved punishments overall. But even though retributivists should welcome drug courts as an improvement of the status quo, they should not confuse second-best alternatives with an ideal solution. They should reserve their most vehement criticisms not for drug courts, but for the system of drug prohibitions that authorizes extremely harsh sentences in regular courts. In any event, the genuine appeal of drug courts should not distract retributivists from the more fundamental problems that infect contemporary drug policy.

The only way to decide whether (1), (2), (3a), or (3b) is true is to assess the seriousness of drug offenses. "Drug offenses," of course, are of many kinds, and a significant percentage of drug courts deal with a host of other behaviors, including drug trafficking and the commission of violent crimes under the influence of an intoxicating substance. Still, I believe our attention should be restricted to the most basic and fundamental kind of drug offense: the offense of drug *possession* (and/or *use*).[23] This focus is appropriate; the crime of drug possession is sufficient to land a defendant either in regular court or in (most) drug court(s). Thus, we must ask: What punishment *does* a person deserve simply for using drugs? Without an answer, I doubt that we can take sensible positions on the related issues of drug production and distribution. In posing this question, we no longer are interested in parity, but rather in the even more controversial issue of *cardinal* proportionality.[24] If we have any hope of answering it, we need to determine the extent to which the offense of drug use is *serious*. I assume that the seriousness of given crimes is a complex function of wrongdoing, culpability, and harm. Unfortunately there is no straightforward means to balance or weigh these three variables in an all-things-considered judgment of seriousness. Consider harm and culpability, for example. If one offense is more harmful than another, but offenders who commit it are less culpable, which offense is more serious overall? Is a negligent homicide more or less serious, and deserving of more or less punishment, than an armed robbery perpetrated intentionally? This general problem plagues attempts to identify the cardinal seriousness of given crimes.

However formidable it may be in other contexts, this general difficulty is more manageable when assessing the seriousness of the offense of drug possession. Liability for the use and/or possession of drugs does not involve several different kinds of culpability, ranging from negligence to purpose. Instead, liability for drug possession requires (and ought to require) that offenders act *knowingly*. That is, the mens rea of acting knowingly attaches to all material elements of this offense. If a defendant does not know that he is in possession of something, or does not know that what he possesses is an illegal drug, criminal liability should not be imposed (Husak 2007, p. 189). If I am correct, assessments of the seriousness of the offense of drug possession need be less concerned about the difficulty of balancing culpability with other factors. All persons who commit this crime act with the same degree of culpability. By keeping culpability constant, wrongfulness and harm will represent the sole variables that determine the seriousness of the offense of drug use. Admittedly we still need to determine what is *wrongful* about drug possession and/or use. Wrongdoing and harm are conceptually distinct; clearly it is possible to act wrongfully without causing harm, and to cause harm without acting wrongfully (Gardner 2007). Here again, I try to avoid this difficulty by offering a simplifying hypothesis. Many acts are wrong partly or solely *because* of the harm they cause. Drug possession and/or use, I submit, is such an offense. If so, identifying the harm(s) caused by drug use will allow us to assess the seriousness of this offense. Or so I will assume.[25]

What, then, *is* (or *are*) the harm(s) of drug use and/or possession? Why, in other words, is drug use prohibited? This question is surprisingly difficult to answer. Since criminal laws that subject offenders to punishment must always be justified, the burden of proof should be allocated on those who favor criminalization (Husak 2008). The harm of most offenses is obvious. Everyone can identify the interests that are violated by victimizing crimes such as murder, armed robbery, and rape. But the harm caused by drug use is less evident. Of course, it would be unfair to include in an answer the harm that would not be caused were drug use legal. As theorists who favor the decriminalization of drug use keep reminding us, many of the harms associated with drugs are actually the products of drug prohibitions. No one denies this point; debate centers on the extent to which it is true.[26] Once the harm of drug use is identified, the next difficulty is to decide whether it is the *kind* of harm the criminal law may prohibit. In other words, we need to decide whether these harms are *public* harms. This issue too is far from trivial. It is harmful to breach a contract or to commit a tort, but our legal system responds by awarding money damages to the victims rather than by punishing the perpetrators. The criminal law should be used only to proscribe *public* harms.[27]

Does the enactment of drug offenses prevent public harm(s)? Since I have discussed this matter in detail elsewhere, my answer will be brief and conclusory.[28] Relatively few instances of drug use cause harm. Thus drug offenses, I contend, are not designed to prevent persons from causing harm, but rather to prevent persons from creating a *risk* of harm. These prohibitions might be designed to prevent users from risking harm to themselves, or to prevent users from risking harm to others. Neither answer, I have argued, is ultimately persuasive. Drug proscriptions fail to satisfy the conditions that must be met if a criminal offense is justified in order to prevent the risk of harm (Husak 2008). If I am correct, *no* amount of punishment is deserved when persons simply use drugs.[29] It follows that (3a) is the most plausible of the foregoing alternatives: When Smith is punished in drug court and Jones is punished in regular court, *both* are punished in excess of the seriousness of their offense. The basic problem for just deserts theorists is not the acceptability of therapeutic jurisprudence, but rather the regime of drug prohibitions itself.

To be sure, some theorists seek to defend proscriptions of drug use by a very different rationale than I have discussed. The existence of such offenses, it might be said, creates opportunities to coerce defendants into treatment that can be beneficial both to defendants and to society alike. Controversy surrounds the issue of whether and to what extent treatment is effective when it is coerced rather than voluntary.[30] But the more fundamental question about this rationale is normative rather than empirical. The criminal justice system is misused when it forces persons into beneficial regimes. Whatever one may think of perfectionist political agendas generally, they are especially worrisome when pursued through the criminal justice system. The state should not create offenses as a pretext for improving the persons who commit them. This principle would expand the function of criminal justice beyond recognition—an expansion that has no obvious limits and should alarm not only retributivists, but everyone. Why not enact a crime of obesity and use it as an opportunity to coerce offenders to lose weight? Moreover, as we have seen, not everyone successfully completes the treatment regime mandated by the court. Sooner or later, some individuals will have to be punished as the inevitable price for achieving beneficial outcomes for others. This trade-off is unacceptable to a penal philosophy based on just deserts. I conclude that it is crucial not to be blinded by the allure of therapeutic rationales generally. We must preserve the principle that *criminal* offenses are justified only if they proscribe wrongful conduct that renders defendants deserving of punishment.

Although the alternative of drug decriminalization should appeal to retributivists, it is important to add that it should also be attractive to consequentialists. Inter alia, this alternative casts a new light on the oft-repeated claim that drug courts save money for taxpayers (National Drug Court Institute 2010). It is likely that these alleged savings have always been exaggerated. As we have seen, many defendants who quit using drugs would have become abstinent even without the supervision of the court. Moreover, many participants fail the rigorous therapeutic regimes they are required to undergo and their sentences are longer than would have been imposed had they not been admitted to drug court in the first place. In addition, therapeutic justice tends to cause a "net-widening" effect. The existence of drug courts may lead police and prosecutors to proceed in cases in which they would not have bothered previously. Drug arrests have soared since the inception of drug courts, with the annual figure hovering around 1.8 million (King 2008, p. 6). Despite these reservations, I concede that drug courts almost certainly *are* cost effective relative to the status quo. This conclusion, however, amounts to faint praise; almost *any* alterative would fare better than the drug war and its preferred weapon of mass incarceration (Miron 2004). It is hard to believe that drug courts save taxpayer money relative to the option of simply leaving users alone. Even though many drug users cause social harms, many others do not (Sullum 2003). Since persons may wind up in drug court simply by committing the crime of possession or use, these courts do not discriminate between these categories of users. Users who cause social harms are best addressed by invoking statutes that proscribe the social harms they cause. A strategy that uses the penal law to try to improve the behavior of all users is wildly overinclusive. Drug courts do not save money relative to the option of leaving alone those many users who have not caused social harms.

Notice that the conclusion I have defended to remedy the incompatibility between drug courts and retributivism is not readily available for many of the other specialty courts in the therapeutic jurisprudence movement. My preferred option is for the criminal justice system to leave drug users alone, but no reasonable person would propose a similar solution for the matters adjudicated in most other specialty courts—domestic violence or drunk driving, for example. Thus the retributive verdict on drug courts is more negative than on therapeutic justice more generally. Although drug courts are at best a second-best solution, many of the other specialty courts in the therapeutic jurisprudence movement may represent the best we can do in our efforts to combat relatively minor forms of criminality. An honest assessment of therapeutic jurisprudence must proceed court by court.

Drug courts pose an additional worry even if I am correct to characterize them as a second-best solution. The impetus for more meaningful and profound reforms tends to be lost in jurisdictions that have created drug courts. The energy to remove casual drug use from the ambit of the criminal justice system is drained by efforts to make drug courts better than the status quo. If the state lacks sufficient reasons to punish drug use per se, the fact that we do so in the hope of benefiting defendants may lend our punitive regime an aura of defensibility.

Despite the several reservations I have expressed, I anticipate that therapeutic justice will continue to thrive throughout the United States—even with respect to drug offenders. Consider the five factors that explain their popularity. As long as criminal justice officials remain dissatisfied with their careers, nonlegal services that promote therapeutic outcomes are inadequately funded, political institutions are fixated on saving money, society continues to be receptive to therapy generally, and our substantive penal law is prone to overcriminalization, drug courts are unlikely to disappear anytime soon. How should we assess the fact that they are destined to survive? Once again, generalizations about the entire drug court movement are perilous, and my predictive powers are meager. Perhaps scholarly and public support for retributivism will erode; foes of a just deserts model may misconstrue my arguments as yet another reason to embrace a consequentialist theory of punishment that affords only instrumental value to the principle of proportionality. Or maybe commentators will continue to be satisfied with suboptimal alternatives. Or perhaps the tensions I have identified will remain largely unnoticed, the protests of legal philosophers notwithstanding. I do not believe, however, that theorists should be content with the second-best solution that drug courts represent. We should continue to insist that our criminal justice system treat drug users as they deserve, and it is hard to see why they deserve any punishment at all—even when their punishments are imposed under the banner of therapeutic jurisprudence.

ACKNOWLEDGMENT

Special thanks to Eric Luna, Michael Tonry, and members of the Future of Punishment Workshops in Leiden for helpful comments.

NOTES

1. See, e.g., the formulation proposed in Gardner (2007, pp. 221–25). For a nice survey of proportionality analyses, see Sullivan and Frase (2009).
2. More recently, this problem is said to raise issues of incommensurability. See, e.g., Kaplow and Shavell (2002, p. 307, n. 27).
3. To my mind, the difficulties of incorporating these variables in a retributive theory of punishment are practical rather than principled. In a world of perfect knowledge, the quantum of punishment that is deserved by a given offender for a given offense would take into account the "subjective" reactions of the defendant.
4. I see little in the media since the publication of Nolan's book to change this verdict about the level of public support for the drug court movement.
5. This allegation is made forcefully by Whitman (2003).
6. Justice Antonin Scalia goes so far as to say that the principle of proportionality "is inherently a concept tied to the penological goal of retribution" and cannot be applied intelligibly if competing theories of punishment are presupposed. See *Harmelin v. Michigan*, 501 U.S. 957, 989 (1991). I see no reason to accept Scalia's contention.
7. See, e.g., Bentham's tortured explication of "the proportion between punishment and offenses" (1996, pp. 165–74).
8. Although jurisdictions differ, approximately 97 percent of all cases are resolved through plea bargains rather than trial.
9. The popularity of the term "therapeutic jurisprudence" is due almost entirely to the efforts of two theorists—David Wexler, a professor of law and psychology at the University of Arizona, and Bruce Winick, a professor of law at the University of Miami. In the past 20 years, these two authors have written or edited at least seven books on the issue (all with Carolina Academic Press) and deserve credit (or blame) for turning the topic into something of a cottage industry.
10. The website of the International Network on Therapeutic Jurisprudence indicates that therapeutic jurisprudence "is a perspective that regards the law (rules of law, legal procedures, and roles of legal actors) itself as a social force that often produces therapeutic or anti-therapeutic consequences" (International Network on Therapeutic Jurisprudence 2010).
11. See the recommendations in Farrington and Welsh (2007).
12. "We know that drug courts outperform virtually all other strategies that have been attempted for drug-involved offenders" (Marlowe, Dematteo, and Festinger 2003, p. 153).
13. Since drug courts have existed for about two decades, one might expect that they would begin to affect the national rate of addiction. The incidence of addiction in the United States, however, appears to be largely unchanged despite the growth of the drug court movement.
14. See the discussion in Heyman (2009, chap. 4).
15. Here I ignore the complexities posed by the possibility that offenders have different criminal histories.
16. Perhaps my arguments amount to overkill; few theorists would be inclined to think that parity is preserved by a dual-track system in which some but not all defendants are diverted to drug courts. Nonetheless, it is instructive to show that the deviations from proportionality are even greater than they first appear. Moreover, few retributivists have been outspoken

critics of the drug court movement, although some commentators have observed that drug courts "go against the broader retributive trends in drug policy" (Broxmeyer 2008, p. 18).

17. Reasons to adopt this definition are given in Husak (2008). It might be thought that the sanctions imposed by drug courts do not involve the *intention* to inflict a stigmatizing hardship. But I am inclined to think that these courts *do* punish intentionally as a means to improve the welfare of defendants.

18. It is an open question whether these treatment regimes are *unnecessarily* difficult and thus increase failure rates.

19. This perception is reinforced by the high numbers of eligible defendants who elect to participate in drug courts (Bowers 2008, pp. 823–24).

20. Even the earliest empirical studies showed that only *graduates* of drug courts were less likely to exhibit the characteristics that make these courts so popular—such as lower rates of recidivism (Hora, Schma, and Rosenthal 1999, p. 484).

21. For this reason, Bowers (2008) concludes that drug courts resemble early medieval trials by ordeal.

22. What I call the "old paradigm" has plenty of political support. As former President George H. W. Bush cautioned in his 1992 National Drug Control Strategy, we should not "'victimize' drug users. . . . The drug problem reflects bad decisions by individuals with free wills" (The White House 1992, p. 2).

23. Many jurisdictions punish possession *instead* of use, others punish both possession and use. I attach no deep significance to this distinction. It is nearly impossible to use a drug without possessing it, and possession frequently is punished rather than use simply because it is easier to prove.

24. See the discussion in von Hirsch (1985).

25. Here I draw on comments made in Husak (1998, p. 187).

26. See the useful estimates in MacCoun and Reuter (2001).

27. Unfortunately, almost no one has developed a coherent theory to distinguish public from private harms. For an initial attempt to draw the distinction, see Marshall and Duff (1998).

28. I discuss a more detailed examination of the possible rationales of drug prohibitions in Husak (2002).

29. At the very least, these offenses are not *sufficiently* serious to merit criminal liability (Husak, 2010).

30. For example, see Farabee, Prendergast, and Anglin (1998).

REFERENCES

Bentham, Jeremy. 1996. *An Introduction to the Principles of Morals and Legislation*, ed. J. H. Burns and H. L. A. Hart. Oxford: Clarendon Press (originally published 1789).

Boldt, Richard C. 1998. "Rehabilitative Punishment and the Drug Treatment Court Movement." *Washington University Law Quarterly* 76:1206–306.

Bowers, Josh. 2008. "Contraindicated Drug Courts." *UCLA Law Review* 55:783–835.

Brand-Ballard, Jeffrey. 2009. "Innocents Lost: Proportional Sentencing and the Paradox of Collateral Damage." *Legal Theory* 15:67–105.

Bronsteen, John, Christopher Buccafusco, and Jonathan Masur. 2009. "Happiness and Punishment." *University of Chicago Law Review* 76:1037–81.

Broxmeyer, Jennifer. 2008. "Prisoners of Their Own War: Can Policymakers Look Beyond the 'War on Drugs' to Treatment Courts?" *Yale Law Journal Pocket Part* 118:17–21.

Christopher, Russell L. 2002. "Deterring Retributivism: The Injustice of 'Just' Punishment." *Northwestern University Law Review* 96:843–976.

Conrad, Peter. 2007. *The Medicalization of Society: On the Transformation of Human Conditions into Treatable Disorders*. Baltimore: John Hopkins University Press.

Demleitner, Nora V. 2002. "'Collateral Damage': No Re-Entry for Drug Offenders." *Villanova Law Review* 47:1027–54.

Dolinko, David. 1992. "Three Mistakes about Retributivism." *UCLA Law Review* 39: 1623–57.

Farabee, David, Michael Prendergast, and M. Douglas Anglin. 1998. "The Effectiveness of Coerced Treatment for Drug Abusing Offenders." *Federal Probation* 62:3–10.

Farrell, Ian. 2010. "Gilbert & Sullivan and Scalia: Philosophy, Proportionality, and the Eighth Amendment." *Villanova Law Review* 55:321–68.

Farrington, David P., and Brandon C. Welsh. 2007. *Saving Children from a Life of Crime*. Oxford: Oxford University Press.

Gardner, John. 2007. *Offences and Defences*. Oxford: Oxford University Press.

Heyman, Gene M. 2009. *Addiction: A Disorder of Choice*. Cambridge, MA: Harvard University Press.

Hoffman, Morris B. 2000. "The Drug Court Scandal." *North Carolina Law Review* 78:1437–534.

Hora, Peggy Fulton, William G. Schma, and John A. Rosenthal. 1999. "Therapeutic Jurisprudence and the Drug Treatment Court Movement: Revolutionizing the Criminal Justice System's Response to Drug Abuse and Crime in America." *Notre Dame Law Review* 74:439–537.

Husak, Douglas. 1998. "Desert, Proportionality, and the Seriousness of Drug Offences." In *Fundamentals of Sentencing Theory*, ed. Andrew Ashworth and Martin Wasik. Oxford: Clarendon Press.

———. 2002. *Legalize This! The Case for Decriminalizing Drugs*. London: Verso.

———. 2007. "Do Marijuana Offenders Deserve Punishment?" In *Pot Politics*, ed. Mitch Earleywine. New York: Oxford University Press.

———. 2008. *Overcriminalization: The Limits of the Criminal Law*. New York: Oxford University Press.

———. 2010. "The De Minimis 'Defense' to Criminal Liability." In *The Oxford Handbook to the Philosophy of Criminal Law*, ed. Antony Duff and Stuart Green. New York: Oxford University Press.

International Network on Therapeutic Jurisprudence. "Welcome." http://www.law.arizona.edu/depts/upr-intj (accessed October 6, 2010).

Kaplow, Louis, and Steven Shavell. 2002. *Fairness Versus Welfare*. Cambridge, MA: Harvard University Press.

King, Ryan S. 2008. *Disparity by Geography: The War on Drugs in America's Cities*. Washington, DC: Sentencing Project.

Kolber, Adam J. 2009. "The Subjective Experience of Punishment." *Columbia Law Review* 109:182–236.

MacCoun, Robert J., and Peter Reuter. 2001. *Drug War Heresies: Learning from Other Vices, Times, & Places*. Cambridge: Cambridge University Press.

Marlowe, Douglas B., David S. Dematteo, and David S. Festinger. 2003. "A Sober Assessment of Drug Courts." *Federal Sentencing Reporter* 16(2):153–57.

Marshall, S. E., and R. A. Duff. 1998. "Criminalization and Sharing Wrongs." *Canadian Journal of Law & Jurisprudence* 11:7–22.

Miller, Eric J. 2004. "Embracing Addiction: Drug Courts and the False Problem of Judicial Interventionism." *Ohio State Law Journal* 65:1479–576.

Miron, Jeffrey A. 2004. *Drug War Crimes: The Consequences of Prohibition*. Oakland, CA: Independent Institute.

Morris, Norval, and Michael Tonry. 1990. *Between Prison and Probation: Intermediate Punishments in a Rational Sentencing System*. New York: Oxford University Press.

National Drug Court Institute. "Research Findings." http://www.ndci.org/research (accessed October 6, 2010).

Nolan, James L. 2001. *Reinventing Justice: The American Drug Court Movement*. Princeton, NJ: Princeton University Press.

O'Hear, Michael M. 2009. "Rethinking Drug Courts: Restorative Justice as a Response to Racial Injustice." *Stanford Law & Policy Review* 20:463–99.

Quinn, Mae C. 2000–2001. "Whose Team Am I On Anyway? Musings of a Public Defender About Drug Treatment Court Practice." *New York University Review of Law and Social Change* 26:37–75.

Rempel, Michael, Dana Fox-Kralstein, Amanda Cissner, Robyn Cohen, Melissa Labriola, Donald Farole, Ann Bader, and Michael Magnani. 2003. "The New York State Adult Drug Court Evaluation: Policies, Participants and Impacts." New York: Center for Court Innovation. http://www.courtinnovation.org/_uploads/documents/drug_court_eval_exec_sum.pdf.

Ristroph, Alice. 2005. "Proportionality as a Principle of Limited Government." *Duke Law Journal* 55:263–331.

Rockwell, Frederick G., III. 2008. "The Chesterfield/Colonial Heights Drug Court: A Partnership Between the Criminal Justice System and the Treatment Community." *University of Richmond Law Review* 43:5–17.

Sammon, Kathryn C. 2008. "Therapeutic Jurisprudence: An Examination of Problem-Solving Justice in New York." *St. John's Journal of Legal Commentary* 23:923–69.

Silverglate, Harvey A. 2009. *Three Felonies A Day: How the Feds Target the Innocent*. New York: Encounter Books.

Simon, Jonathan. 2007. *Governing Through Crime*. New York: Oxford University Press.

Substance Abuse and Mental Health Services Administration, Office of Applied Studies. "National Survey on Drug Use & Health." Accessed October 6, 2010. http://www.oas.samhsa.gov/nhsda.htm.

Sullivan, E. Thomas, and Richard S. Frase. 2009. *Proportionality Principles in American Law: Controlling Excessive Government Actions*. Oxford: Oxford University Press.

Sullum, Jacob. 2003. *Saying Yes: In Defense of Drug Use*. New York: Jeremy P. Tarcher/Putnam.

Tonry, Michael. 1995. *Malign Neglect: Race, Crime, and Punishment in America*. New York: Oxford University Press.

U.S. Government Accountability Office. 2005. *Adult Drug Courts: Evidence Indicates Recidivism Reductions and Mixed Results for Other Outcomes*. Report to Congressional Committees. Washington, DC: U.S. Government Accountability Office. http://www.gao.gov/new.items/d05219.pdf.

von Hirsch, Andrew. 1985. *Past or Future Crimes?* New Brunswick, NJ: Rutgers University Press.

von Hirsch, Andrew, and Andrew Ashworth. 2005. *Proportionate Sentencing*. Oxford: Oxford University Press.

von Hirsch, Andrew, and Nils Jareborg. 1991. "Gauging Criminal Harm: A Living-Standard Analysis." *Oxford Journal of Legal Studies* 11(1):1–38.

Wasik, Martin, and Andrew von Hirsch. 1988. "Non-Custodial Penalties and the Principles of Desert." *Criminal Law Review* 1988:555–72.

The White House. 1992. *National Drug Control Strategy: January 1992*. Washington, DC: U.S. Government Printing Office.

Whitman, James Q. 2003. "A Plea Against Retributivism," *Buffalo Criminal Law Review* 7:85–107.

12

Drug Treatment Courts as Communicative Punishment

MICHAEL M. O'HEAR

Since their first appearance in Miami in 1989, specialized drug treatment courts have grown phenomenally popular. With more than 2,000 now in existence, drug courts have been implemented in all 50 U.S. states (Huddleston, Marlowe, and Casebolt 2008), as well as at least a handful of other nations (Nolan 2002). Drug courts offer treatment, instead of just incarceration, for offenders, and they purport to be quite successful as a means of structuring the delivery of social services (Marlowe, DeMatteo, and Festinger 2003). Even assuming such instrumental efficacy, however, questions remain as to whether it is appropriate for drug courts to use the forms and coercive power of the criminal justice system. Offenders enter drug court and comply with treatment requirements in order to avoid or minimize punishment in a conventional criminal court. Drug courts themselves routinely impose incarceration and other sanctions for noncompliance. Indeed, quite apart from the sanctions, the treatment regimen is not merely a social service that confers an unqualified benefit on the offender, but itself has something of a penal character: offenders typically must endure close supervision by public officials; comply with intrusive and inconvenient program requirements, including frequent drug tests and court appearances; and admit to legal wrongdoing as a condition of entry. It is thus a mistake to think of drug courts as purely an *alternative* to punishment.[1]

To the extent that drug courts are themselves a type of punishment, it is fair to ask whether they conform to the norms of justice for criminal sanctions. Douglas Husak (2011) pursues this question elsewhere in this volume, considering whether drug courts satisfy proportionality norms. I take up the question somewhat differently. My interest is not in proportionality per se (although I give some consideration to proportionality along the way), but in the communicative qualities of drug courts. The framework of my analysis is derived from Antony Duff's (2001) communicative theory of punishment. Duff's understanding of what makes punishment communicatively appropriate reflects a desire both to condemn public wrongs and to treat offenders with due respect as fellow citizens. Duff's approach is, I think, a quite attractive one for a liberal political community that takes seriously both individual autonomy and shared moral values.

I show how drug court seems in some respects a more communicatively appropriate response to drug offenses than the conventional penal alternatives (simple incarceration and straight probation). Drug court seems a more communicatively attractive punishment insofar as it speaks more directly and forcefully to the particularities of the offense and what the offender must do to reconcile himself with the community. Indeed, even though drug court is typically defended in utilitarian, forward-looking terms, its communicative qualities suggest the possibility of justification on retributive, backward-looking grounds.

I also identify aspects of drug court that seem quite communicatively problematic. Although many of the basic design features of drug court permit and facilitate communicatively appropriate punishment—that is, punishment that focuses the offender's attention on what was wrongful about his or her conduct and what he or she ought to do in order to achieve reform and reconciliation—other aspects of the drug court experience may shift the offender's attention in less suitable directions for penal purposes (such as toward the disease model of drug addiction, which deemphasizes the volitional aspect of drug use). Moreover, drug courts may be administered in ways that give rise to unacceptable levels of penal disproportionality and coercion. Taking these concerns into account, it is uncertain whether, on balance, drug courts represent an advance on the conventional processing of drug cases.

My exploration of these issues proceeds as follows. Section I summarizes key elements of Duff's communicative theory of punishment. Section II lays out some common design features of drug courts. Section III considers whether and to what extent drug courts respond to crime in a communicatively attractive fashion. Initially I assume that the crime is one of simple drug possession. Then I consider the suitability of drug court for drug-trafficking offenders and drug-dependent nondrug offenders.

To the extent that drug courts are communicatively richer than conventional dispositions, they may be seen as part of a broader trend in criminal justice connected to restorative justice and other increasingly popular innovations. I close with a brief consideration of whether the apparent public interest in communicatively richer punishment may bode well for diminished reliance on incarceration, which seems a communicatively impoverished and inappropriate response to most crime.

I. AIMS OF COMMUNICATIVE PUNISHMENT

Broadly speaking, a polity that punishes in a communicative fashion aims to censure its criminal offenders in a way that treats the offenders as both responsible moral agents and members of the polity. Communicative punishment has a backward-looking and a forward-looking character. It is backward-looking because "it takes the primary communicative purpose of punishment to be the communication to offenders of the condemnation they deserve for the wrongs they have committed, and explains that purpose in backward-looking terms of what we, as a polity, owe to victims, to offenders, and to ourselves as a political community . . . as a response to such wrongs" (Duff 2005, p. 1182).

Yet, communicative punishment is also forward-looking because it is hoped that censuring the offender will cause the offender "to understand, and so to repent, [her] wrong as a wrong both against the individual victim (when there was one) and against the wider political community to which they both belong" (Duff 2005, p. 1182). This understanding is intended to accomplish a sort of "moral rehabilitation" of the offender and lead to the performance of reparative actions, even if only in the articulation of an apology, and to reconciliation with the victim and the community.

Despite this forward-looking character, communicative punishment still differs from consequentialist approaches to punishment because its orientation is more to persuasion of the offender and not brute coercion. A hope that the offender will repent and reform is internal to the practice of censuring; such a hope does not imply that censuring is being thought of in purely instrumental terms. Indeed, the communicative approach recognizes important ethical constraints on the pursuit of efficient crime control:

> If I try to persuade another person to do what (I think) she morally ought to do, my aim is of course that she should come to do right. But if am to treat her as a moral agent, as a member of the moral community to which we both belong, my aim cannot be simply to find some efficient means of bringing it about that her conduct conforms to what morality requires. . . . Such an aim could in principle be achieved by deceiving her or bullying her or manipulating her emotions or beliefs—methods that fail to respect her as a moral agent. (Duff 2001, p. 81)

For present purposes, five (overlapping) aspects of communicatively appropriate punishment bear particular emphasis. First, punishment of this sort responds to *public wrongs*, that is, "wrongs in which 'the public,' the community as a whole, is properly interested" (Duff 2005, p. 61). What satisfies this criterion is to some extent culturally contingent, but in a liberal political community (one that is structured around values of individual autonomy, freedom, privacy, and pluralism) the criminal law will concern itself only with "conduct that attacks or injures or threatens important individual rights or interests or social goods and interests that cannot otherwise be adequately protected" (Duff 2005, p. 67).

Second, punishment ought to function as a form of *secular penance*: "It is a burden imposed on an offender for his crime, through which, it is hoped, he will come to repent his crime, to begin to reform himself, and thus reconcile himself with those he has wronged" (Duff 2005, p. 106). Punishment should focus the offender's attention on his wrong in a sustained fashion. It should also help the offender to see what he must do to reform himself in order to avoid such wrongs in the future. Finally, it should offer the offender an opportunity to seek reconciliation with those he has wronged through a process of apologetic reparation.

Third, there should be a *substantive fit* between the punishment and the crime. Different modes of punishment (say, a fine or community service) carry different meanings;

sentencers ought to select a mode in each case based on the suitability of its meaning as a response to the specific offense. We must ask "not just how different modes of punishment can serve the general aim of communicating censure to offenders, but also how they can help to communicate a more substantive understanding of the wrongfulness and the implications of particular kinds of offense" (Duff 2005, p. 145).

Fourth, there must be *proportionality* between the severity of the offense and the severity of the punishment. In light of fit considerations, however, "negative proportionality" is a more suitable objective than "positive." Positive proportionality demands greater rigor in ensuring that "the" proportionate quantum of punishment is imposed, while negative proportionality seeks a range of possible sentences, any of which would be "good enough." The negative approach is preferable because it "gives sentencers more room to attend to the concrete particularities of the crime, without worrying about rendering it commensurable with all other crimes in terms of its seriousness, and to choose between a wider range of penalties, without worrying about rendering them all commensurable in terms of their severity" (Duff 2005, p. 139).

Finally, punishment should aim to persuade offenders in a way that leaves them the *freedom to remain unpersuaded*. This follows from the requirement that "punishment must address the offender as a member of the liberal polity whose autonomy must, like that of any citizen, be respected" (Duff 2005, p. 122). Thus, while "offenders are forced to *hear* the message that punishment aims to communicate and to undergo a penal process intended to persuade them to accept it, they are not forced to *listen* to that message or to be persuaded by it" (Duff 2005, p. 126).

II. DRUG TREATMENT COURTS: BASIC DESIGN FEATURES

Although drug courts differ substantially from one another in the specifics of their operation, many share certain basic design features (National Association of Criminal Defense Lawyers 2009; O'Hear 2009). Some of the more common (if not necessarily universal) characteristics of drug courts include the following:

- Restricted eligibility: defendants facing serious present charges (such as drug trafficking or nondrug felonies) or who have prior convictions for crimes of violence are excluded.
- Entrance is doubly discretionary: both prosecutor and defendant must agree to the defendant's assignment to a drug court.
- Guilty plea is the price of admission: drug court process is structured as either part of the sentence or as a presentencing diversion.
- Close supervision: court appearances and drug screens are much more frequent than in traditional probation.
- Mandatory participation in a drug treatment program: treatment providers are expected to collaborate with the judge in monitoring and enforcing compliance with the treatment plan.

- Graduated sanctions: failed drug tests and other program violations are met with sanctions, which are expected to start small (e.g., a verbal reprimand from the judge or a requirement for a written apology) and increase in severity (e.g., community service, a short jail term, or termination from the drug court).
- Nonadversarial process: defense lawyers (if involved at all) are expected to act as members of the treatment "team," and normal criminal trial rights are not observed in finding and sanctioning violations.
- Indefinite duration: defendants move through distinct phases of treatment and supervision at their own pace, culminating eventually either in successful graduation (which normally relieves the defendant from further incarceration on the underlying charges) or a decision to terminate the defendant from the program for insufficient progress (which normally results in a traditional sentencing or resentencing process on the underlying charges that may result in an even longer sentence of incarceration than would have been imposed had the defendant declined to participate in the drug court at the outset).

My aim in the next section is to assess whether and to what extent a drug court having these typical characteristics may be regarded as a communicatively appropriate punishment. My primary interest is thus in the drug court as a set of formal institutional arrangements and procedures (and not, for instance, as an ideology).

III. ASSESSING DRUG COURT AS COMMUNICATIVE PUNISHMENT

Some may regard it as perverse to evaluate drug court as punishment, for drug court is often discussed as a social service that is an *alternative* to punishment. Yet, drug court is obviously quite different from a voluntary treatment program offered by a traditional mental health agency. Particularly in the postplea and postadjudication models that predominate and that are my focus here, drug court is premised on the defendant's established violation of a criminal statute, relies on the threat of conventional criminal sanctions in order to induce offenders to enter and remain in the treatment program, and involves a sort of state-administered hard treatment and close supervision that is rare outside the penal context. It is thus natural and appropriate for us to ask whether the coercive and stigmatizing aspects of drug court are morally justified, whether drug court instantiates values that reinforce or undercut the values of the criminal justice system more broadly, and (as Husak considers elsewhere in this volume) whether drug court creates intolerable disparities in the treatment of similarly situated offenders. A consideration of the communicative quality of drug court may help us begin to answer such questions.[2]

In order to identify the communicative strengths and weaknesses of drug court, I focus on the five characteristics of communicatively appropriate punishment highlighted in section I. In light of the tendency for drug courts to exclude offenders facing more serious charges, I initially frame the question as whether drug court constitutes a communicatively appropriate punishment for simple drug possession. In the final section I broaden the analysis to consider additional offenses.

A. Do Drug Courts Respond to Public Wrongs?

An important threshold question is whether simple possession is even properly thought of as a public wrong. The offense is plainly outside what Duff refers to as the "central core" of what the criminal law appropriately addresses, that is, the familiar *mala in se* (2001, p. 63). Of course, if drug court is not a response to a public wrong, then it cannot be considered communicatively appropriate punishment: to whatever extent drug courts are purported to communicate a message of censure on behalf of the polity, there would be something false and illegitimate about that message. (On the other hand, if we take drug criminalization as a given, drug court might still be preferred as a less pernicious response to drug possession than the conventional penal responses.)

Although the category of public wrongs extends beyond the core *mala*, it is difficult to say whether the category is so broad as to encompass drug possession. For one thing, what may be considered a legitimate matter of concern to the "public" depends on the particularities on the "public" at issue, and is thus subject to cultural and historical contingencies (Duff 2007, p. 142). There is no good reason, moreover, why public wrongs must be strictly limited to seriously harmful offenses; even minor public nuisances or inconveniences may sometimes fall within the proper scope of the public's concern and condemnation (provided, of course, that punishment is of proportionately modest severity). Yet, our concern is not whether drug possession could constitute a public wrong in *some* polity, but whether it ought to be regarded as a public wrong in *our* polity, which I will take to be a liberal political community whose core values include individual autonomy and privacy. In our polity, the criminalization of some act is surely unwarranted based merely on the fact that a majority of the community finds the act mildly distasteful. It seems unlikely that penal censure can be justified without reference to some type of threatened or actual injury to some more substantial individual or collective interest.[3]

Husak (1998) has critically examined the leading theories of the harmfulness of drug possession, and his analysis casts doubt on whether the offense can properly be considered a public wrong in our political community. For instance, in light of the "miniscule" injury to the possessor associated with the standard drug possession offense, a paternalistic regard for the possessor's own welfare probably cannot justify criminalizing drug possession (if, indeed, purely paternalistic considerations can ever justify criminalization in a liberal polity).

As Husak indicates, an adequate justification is less likely to be found in paternalism than in concerns that *others* will be victimized as a result of drug possession. Because of the well-known link between drug use and more clearly victimizing crime (e.g., assault and robbery), Husak suggests that drug possession might be conceptualized as a form of inchoate offense. Thinking of drug possession in this way shows how the offense might fall within the category of public wrongs that Duff (2007) labels "hybrid offenses." Such offenses have the form of *mala prohibita* because the conduct they criminalize does not intrinsically have the character of a prelegal wrong, but the offenses may nonetheless be morally justified because the criminalized conduct in practice tends to be dangerous (even though danger is not formally an element of these offenses). Hybrid offenses are thus in the nature of *mala in se* structured in the form of rules rather than standards. Although such a structure assures a measure of over- and/ or underinclusiveness, the creation of hybrid offenses is nonetheless justifiable on a variety of prudential grounds, and (once created) the violation of such an offense may constitute a public wrong.[4]

Applying this reasoning, we might think of drug possession as an appropriate hybrid offense to the extent that many drug possessors use drugs, and many drug users become more dangerous as a result—that is, more likely to commit violence, more likely to drive unsafely, more likely to steal or damage the property of others, and so forth. This is not to say that *all* drug possessors are dangerous, but it is to recognize the administrative burdens of sorting out the truly dangerous from the not dangerous, the unreliability of drug possessors' own estimation of their ability to use drugs safely, and the duty of citizens to obey even overinclusive rules that aim to serve the common good and to provide reassurance of public safety.

To be sure, a liberal polity ought to demand more than just a remote risk of harm in order to criminalize conduct, and the possibility remains that the empirical association between drug possession and conventional victimization is too weak to justify criminalization. There must be some limits to the tolerability of overinclusion. Husak, for one, would likely find drug possession unacceptably overinclusive,[5] and he would almost surely be correct for at least some types of drugs.[6] For present purposes, though, I will accept that the criminalization of drug possession may be justified on a hybrid-offense theory, and that drug possession constitutes a public wrong in the same sense that other hybrid offenses (such as driving over the speed limit) constitute public wrongs. Of course, the marginal nature of the public wrong may affect our consideration of whether drug courts live up to the proportionality ideals of communicative punishment.[7]

As to wrongfulness, though, one final issue ought to be addressed: addiction. If drug court is reserved for offenders who are highly drug dependent, and if such offenders are unable to control their desire to obtain and use drugs, then drug court probably cannot be characterized as a response to a public wrong; the participants' lack of volition seemingly removes the wrongfulness of their conduct. However, the meaning of addiction and the extent to which it impairs volition are complex and controversial questions (Hoffman 2000). Suffice it to say that, even assuming the existence of a reliably diagnosable condition of addiction that results in profoundly impaired volition, drug courts do not screen rigorously for this condition. Indeed, drug courts may have budgetary incentives not to reject potential participants based on weak evidence of addiction (Bowers 2008, p. 800). I will assume, then, that drug courts include many participants who are not so volitionally impaired as to preclude wrongfulness, and it is with these participants that I will concern myself in the remainder of the discussion.

B. Can Undergoing the Drug Court Process Function as a Type of Secular Penance?

Communicative punishment should aim to promote repentance, reform, and reconciliation. With those purposes in mind, punishment ought to focus the offender's attention in a sustained way on the wrongfulness of her conduct and what must be done in order to avoid such wrongs in the future. Punishment ought also to provide opportunities for the offender to express "her repentant recognition of the wrong she has done" (Duff 2001, p. 109).

At first blush, drug courts would seem to fare quite well as a form of secular penance. Through a demanding regimen of court appearances, drug tests, and treatment sessions, the drug court process focuses the offender's attention for at least several months on the need to avoid possessing and using drugs and on the changes that the offender can make in her patterns of thought and behavior in order to achieve and maintain a state of abstinence. For many, complying with the regimen and remaining abstinent requires sufficient effort so as to constitute a potentially quite powerful expression of repentance.

There may be some question, though, as to whether drug courts adequately emphasize the "public wrong" aspect of drug possession; if the offender's attention is not drawn to the wrongfulness of her conduct, her efforts at self-reform—however burdensome—seem unlikely to have a genuinely penitential character. The root difficulty lies in the extent to which drug courts buy into the disease model of drug addiction. In this regard, Nolan (2001) has described a set of beliefs that seem to be common among those working in the drug court system—legal and therapeutic professionals alike. These beliefs include the following: drug addiction is a treatable disease, addicts have little ability to control their drug use, the cause of addiction is low self-esteem, and drug courts should thus focus on raising the self-esteem of program participants. To the extent that such premises frame the participants' drug court experience, the communicative nature of the enterprise may be directed away from a message of wrongfulness and civic obligation and toward the pursuit of enhanced self-esteem and individual betterment. Indeed, it would be quite inconsistent for drug courts to condemn conduct over which participants are believed to have little control. Thus it should not be surprising that drug courts tend to treat initial relapses as normal, expected occurrences that warrant only minimal sanctioning (McColl 2002, p. 19).[8]

On the other hand, empirical researchers have also observed harsh, morally charged blaming of participants by drug court judges for repeated failures (Miethe, Lu, and Reese 2000). Indeed, the drug courts' use of both therapeutic and moralistic rhetoric has been characterized by some commentators as reflecting "counter-logical reasoning and theoretical incoherence" (Bowers 2008, p. 829).

It is possible that moralistic blaming may be justified within the disease model if it is characterized not as blaming for drug use per se, but as blaming for a failure to take advantage of the treatment opportunities that are offered to drug court participants. Rosenthal (2002, p. 162) observes that this is precisely the position taken by many drug court officials. Moreover, there may be a personal edge to the blaming insofar as the failure to take advantage of treatment is perceived as a rebuff of the judge's own efforts to help the recalcitrant addict, which may help to explain the harsh tone that the blaming sometimes takes.

If this is the nature of the wrong that drug courts ask participants to contemplate and address, however, we still seem to be somewhere short of a *public* wrong. It is not a crime in the United States to be an addict who fails to take advantage of treatment,[9] and the passive, status-based nature of the "offense" casts considerable doubt on whether it *could* properly be criminalized in a liberal polity. Moreover, even if the failure to take advantage of treatment could in theory be characterized as a public wrong (presumably on the view that addicts are especially prone to commit victimizing offenses as long as they are addicted), drug courts in practice might instead condemn the wrong in purely paternalistic terms or as a personal insult to the judge.[10] Indeed, in light of the screening issues noted earlier, it cannot be assumed that most drug court participants even suffer serious dependency problems, which casts further doubt on claims that drug court sanctioning can be legitimately framed in moral terms as a response to wrongful failures to take advantage of treatment.

The concern thus remains that drug court judges do not adequately emphasize wrongfulness as to the underlying offenses that result in drug court placement and do not emphasize the correct sort of wrongfulness as to subsequent violations. To be sure, there is nothing intrinsic to the drug court, as I have identified its basic design features, that requires a therapeutic, instead of a moralistic, emphasis. But nor is there anything that precludes such an emphasis. Indeed, the close collaboration between therapeutic and legal professionals (which *is* a defining institutional feature) offers reasons to think that the legal professionals working in drug courts may tend to take on therapeutic perspectives over time, at least to a greater extent than they would working in a more conventional criminal court.[11]

C. Is There Substantive Fit Between Drug Court Punishment and the Offense to Which It Responds?

Consistent with the secular penance ideal, the mode of punishment ought to fit the offense. In this regard, the basic drug court impositions (frequent court appearances, drug tests, and meetings with treatment providers) seem quite appropriate. Assuming they are properly framed—perhaps a heroic assumption, in light of the prevalence of disease-model rhetoric—these impositions seem well suited to the communicative task at hand. Indeed, Duff (2001, p. 102) has commented favorably on mandatory treatment as an aspect of traditional probation, assuming that such a requirement is appropriately justified by reference to the underlying offense.

More difficult questions arise in connection with the system of graduated sanctions for program violations. (In order to focus the discussion, I will treat a failed drug test as the prototypical violation.) Although sanctions at the modest end of the scale seem unproblematic, incarceration presents special communicative difficulties. Short jail terms are common responses to violations in many drug courts, with some studies finding average periods of incarceration per participant of 50 days or more (O'Hear 2009, p. 481).[12] Additional incarceration may result from program termination and resentencing. Although the new sentence is formally imposed for the underlying offense and might not be thought to have anything to do with the drug court process, nothing precludes the sentencing judge from increasing the sentence length based on drug court violations, and evidence suggests that this may be a common practice (O'Hear 2009, p. 481). Aggravated sentences in conventional court may thus be conceptualized as part of the graduated-sanctions system.

The communicative approach disfavors incarceration because its message is generally that the offender "has made it impossible for us to live with him in the ordinary community of fellow citizenship" (Duff 2001, p. 150). Such a message would seem inappropriate in light of the marginal nature of the public wrong in possessing or using drugs. On the other hand, Duff recognizes that incarceration may properly be used as a "backup sanction" for failure to comply with the requirements of a noncustodial sentence. Even if incarceration would be inappropriate for the underlying offense, "a persistent refusal to comply with what is penally required becomes a serious enough breach of the conditions of community to warrant imprisonment" (Duff 2001, p. 152). Duff cautions, though, that the failure to comply must be willful, and not due, for instance, to the fact that the penal requirements were unrealistic or infeasible.

The drug court concept of *graduated* sanctions may provide some reassurance in this regard. Incarceration should not result from inadvertent or isolated violations, but should be reserved for persistent violators. It is not clear, though, whether in practice drug court judges uniformly exercise adequate restraint in their use of incarceration. Indeed, evidence of wide interjudge disparities might suggest the contrary.[13]

D. Does Drug Court Punishment Satisfy Proportionality Requirements?

Proportionality may be considered in either absolute (cardinal) or relative (ordinal) terms. In absolute terms, we might question drug court proportionality to the extent that drug possession is itself only a marginal public wrong. Perhaps the imposition of indefinite court supervision, treatment, and testing ought to be seen as excessive, without even getting into the system of graduated sanctions. It is hard to rule out such a conclusion, although defenders of drug courts might well point out that drug courts would still be an attractive innovation if they come closer to hitting the proportionality mark than conventional dispositions. Assuming that drug courts operate so as to divert only prison-bound drug offenders into a system of lesser sanctions, then we might feel comfortable that drug courts at least represent progress on the cardinal proportionality front.

Unfortunately drug courts are not necessarily limited to offenders who are otherwise bound for prison. Quite the contrary, the tendency of drug courts to screen out offenders with serious criminal histories or serious present charges, especially in light of empirical evidence of net widening at the arrest and charging stage following the implementation of a drug court, gives us reason to think that drug courts "are less a diversion from prison than a diversion from other alternatives to prison" (O'Hear 2009, p. 480). Moreover, the use of incarceration as a sanction, the high frequency of drug testing, and the risk of enhanced sentences for those who are terminated mean that there is a very real possibility of *longer* incarceration for drug court participants than nonparticipants.

To be sure, there is something of a "market" check on drug court harshness: if drug courts are generally known to be much harsher for most offenders than conventional case processing, few offenders will opt into drug court.[14] But, as Bowers (2008) has argued, some types of offenders, particularly those who are most drug dependent, are apt to make poor decisions about drug court.[15] The market check, in short, cannot be assumed to be perfect, but rather is subject to many of the normal sources of market failure: cognitive bias, information deficits, duress, and the like. Thus, if we assume that conventional sentences for drug possession often violate the principle of cardinal proportionality, we have little assurance that drug courts actually do much to mitigate the disproportionality.

Ordinal proportionality also seems problematic. Husak addresses this issue at length elsewhere in this volume, so I will only briefly sketch the basic concern. Offenders who commit the same crime may receive wildly different outcomes based on whether or not they enter drug court.[16] Recall that criminal history will often play an important role in disqualifying offenders from drug court, either as a matter of formal eligibility criteria or through discretionary exclusion decisions. Although criminal history may arguably play a modest role in the penal calculus without violating proportionality (Duff 2001, pp. 168–69; Roberts 2008, pp. 217–19), the drug court eligibility determination may effectively give far more weight to criminal history than would be accepted in most standard (retributive) accounts of proportionality. Eligibility determinations may also give considerable weight to other offender characteristics (e.g., those bearing on the likelihood of success in treatment) that likewise have little or no relevance to the seriousness of the offense.

It is hard to assess the scope of the ordinal proportionality difficulties, for the offenders permitted to enter drug court will not necessarily receive more lenient treatment than those who are processed conventionally. Indeed, it is conceivable that most drug court participants experience a roughly similar level of hard treatment compared with what is normally imposed on others convicted of the same offense. Proportionality—properly understood in line with Duff's formulation of *negative* proportionality—may demand no more than this. Moreover, even to the extent that some drug court participants receive unwarranted lenience relative to nonparticipants, it is not clear that the resulting disparities are any worse than if all drug offenders were processed in the conventional way: the personal characteristics that make one likely to be admitted to and succeed in drug court, such as limited criminal history and a strong social support network, may also tend to result in more lenient sentences outside drug court.

E. Do Drug Courts Leave Offenders with Freedom to Remain Unpersuaded?

Communicative punishment seeks to persuade, not coerce. Although the line between persuasion and coercion is not altogether clear, there are reasons to be concerned that drug courts may be overly coercive. Perhaps most troubling, assignment to a drug court has no set end date; participants are expected to remain in drug court for however long it takes to advance through the various phases of treatment. For some participants, the process may take four or five years (National Association of Criminal Defense Lawyers 2009, p. 17). Because the length of time in drug court is determined in large measure by compliance with program conditions, drug courts might be viewed as extending punishment for offenders who remain unrepentant, which, as Duff (2001, p. 122) suggests, may cross the line into excessive coercion.

Other aspects of drug courts also warrant concern. Some studies (e.g., Miethe, Lu, and Reese 2000, p. 537) report drug court judges using bullying language with participants, while others (e.g., Bean 2002, pp. 236–37) suggest that the role of drug court judge is prone to disingenuousness and emotional manipulation. Although not intrinsic to the drug court structure, these aspects of the judicial role may be facilitated by the rejection of a formal, adversarial process and the embrace of broad judicial discretion.

Of course, if a drug court is too oppressive, offenders can either decline to enter the program or remove themselves before completion. The availability of conventional processing as an alternative for the offender may help to mitigate the coerciveness of drug court. But the optional character of drug court may be of limited practical value for many offenders. For instance, drug court critics charge that offenders are pressured to make quick, uninformed decisions about whether to enter drug court (Bowers 2008; National Association of Criminal Defense Lawyers 2009). Moreover, once in, leaving may not be easy. Paternalistic drug court personnel may pressure recalcitrant participants to remain in the program. And, of course, exiting means facing resentencing and the prospect of an even longer sentence than would have been imposed had the offender never entered drug court.

F. Recapitulation: Drug Court for Drug Possession

Can drug court be thought of as a communicatively appropriate punishment for simple drug possession? The answer may depend in part on whether one is focusing on the basic design features of drug courts or on their culture, ideology, and practice.

With respect to design, drug courts seem reasonably compatible with the ideals of communicative punishment. Close supervision, regular testing, and mandatory treatment punish drug possession in substantively fitting ways, communicating to offenders the community's expectation that they desist from drug use, offering meaningful assistance in achieving desistance, and presenting offenders with a burdensome undertaking whose accomplishment may effectively communicate their desire to be reconciled with the community.

From a design standpoint, the most communicatively troubling aspect of drug court may be the availability of incarceration within the system of graduated sanctions. To the extent that drug possession and use are only marginal public wrongs, the harsh exclusionary message of incarceration is arguably never a fitting and proportionate response. Although the notion of *graduated* sanctions implies that incarceration will be reserved as a backup sanction for repeat violators, the near-absence of formal constraints on the use of incarceration raises concerns about whether it is imposed in a sufficiently restrained and consistent fashion. In addition to the risk of disproportionality (both cardinal and ordinal), the use of incarceration also raises questions about whether drug courts are moving beyond what can fairly be characterized as persuasion. The latter concern is heightened by a second troubling design feature: the indefinite duration of the drug court process. Once in a program, offenders remain subject to the system of close monitoring and graduated sanctions until the judge either determines that they have adequately addressed their drug use or terminates them for excessive violations. Although the availability of conventional sentencing (or resentencing) as an alternative to drug court may provide a check on excessive sanctioning and coercion, the "market" does not operate perfectly, and many drug court participants end up receiving harsher treatment and more incarceration than nonparticipants. These considerations suggest a few design changes that would substantially enhance the communicative appeal of drug courts: strict constraints on the use of incarceration for program violations; limits on the amount of time that an offender must remain in the program; allowance of adequate time and counsel for offenders to make careful, informed decisions about entering drug court; and assurances that those who exit the program early in favor of conventional sentencing will not be penalized for poor drug court performance.

If some common design features seem communicatively problematic, drug court culture, ideology, and practice likely present much greater difficulties (although it is harder to know for certain what takes place below the surface of formal institutional arrangements). Of particular concern are manifestations of the disease model of addiction. Although design is my primary concern, an assessment of design cannot wholly disregard culture, ideology, and practice, for within particular contexts, aspects of design may implicitly or indirectly encourage (or at least not satisfactorily discourage) beliefs and patterns of interaction that are communicatively inappropriate. Thus, for instance, I have suggested that if therapeutic professionals tend to see drug use primarily as a manifestation of low self-esteem and not as a violation of civic duty, then drug court design features that encourage legal professionals to step outside their normal roles and engage in extensive, informal collaboration with therapeutic professionals may make it less likely that legal professionals will think and talk about drug offenses as public wrongs.

G. Drug Court for Other Offenses

Although I have assumed up to this point a drug court that admits only offenders who have been charged with simple possession, not all drug courts are so restrictive. Does the analysis change if we assume different offenses? First, consider the possibility of sentencing drug *dealers* to drug court. Although they are currently excluded on a categorical basis from many drug courts, they actually predominate in others (Bowers 2008, p. 794). Criminal codes generally treat trafficking-type offenses as more serious than simple possession, which helps to explain why trafficking defendants find the drug court alternative to conventional sentencing so attractive when they are eligible to participate.

Yet, despite the different legal classification of the offenses, it is not entirely clear that selling drugs is any more serious a public wrong than consuming drugs. Indeed, if we assume that the wrongfulness of consumption lies in the heightened risk that the consumer will engage in more conventionally victimizing conduct, the act of selling seems even further removed from the real harm that is of concern, which may further mitigate the wrongfulness of the seller's conduct (Alldridge 1996).[17] The relative remoteness of harm may be counterbalanced, though, to the extent that drug-trafficking offenses typically involve a greater number of doses than simple possession offenses—more doses means more opportunities for resulting harm to third parties.

What may more clearly serve to justify treating dealers more harshly than simple users is a different category of harms, that is, the harms that are potentially experienced by the users themselves, which might include physical injuries suffered as a result of risky, intoxication-induced behavior; withdrawal symptoms; and the development of dependency. Although (as suggested above) it may be unacceptably paternalistic to say that such harms justify treating drug *use* as a public wrong, drug *trafficking* may be a different matter, at least as to some of the riskier controlled substances. To be sure, the purchaser's consent to the drug transaction might imply consent to the risk of resulting harms, which could mitigate the seller's moral responsibility for those harms. Yet, the "consent" may be of little significance if it is uninformed or offered by a purchaser with an immature or impaired capacity to deliberate and choose. We might thus regard trafficking as an especially wrongful offense to the extent that purchasers are minors, the seriously mentally ill, or the highly drug dependent.[18] And a great deal of selling plainly involves these sorts of customers.[19]

Assuming that trafficking offenses have the character of public wrong that justifies punishment, is drug court the right sort of punishment? In one sense, the fit may seem poor: drug dealers are not necessarily drug users. A regimen of supervision and therapy designed for *users* may seem unlikely to focus the *nonuser's* attention on the wrongfulness of his conduct, to help him see how to reform, or to express his repentant recognition of the wrong.

Yet, the mismatch may not be so great as first appears. Although a drug seller need not necessarily be a user, many sellers do consume. In one survey, 70 percent of state prison inmates serving time for drug trafficking reported drug use in the month prior to their offense (Bureau of Justice Statistics 2007). Indeed, the need to feed a habit may supply an underlying motivation for many offenders to engage in trafficking (Bowers 2008). This would make it especially apt (in a penitential sense) to require such offenders to undergo a treatment regimen. For those trafficking defendants who truly show no signs of dependence, we might rely on screening criteria to keep them out of drug court (although, as noted above, there may be disincentives for drug court officials to enforce such criteria rigorously). On the other hand, drug court might be a fitting punishment even for sellers who do not regularly use drugs to the extent that mandatory attendance at drug court and group therapy sessions could serve to focus sellers' attention on the harmful effects of trafficking on the lives of customers. Indeed, the disease-model rhetoric often used in drug court may be less communicatively problematic with respect to sellers than simple users because this rhetoric might highlight the vulnerability of many users and the predatory character of selling to them.

Proportionality, too, may be less of a concern as to traffickers in drug court than as to simple users, at least to the extent that we view trafficking as a clearer and more serious public wrong. On the other hand, because penalties in the conventional sentencing system tend to be harsher for trafficking offenses, we might be *more* concerned about the coerciveness of drug courts as to sellers than as to users—tougher sentencing laws for trafficking offenses likely cause sellers to feel greater pressure to enter and remain in drug court in order to avoid long prison terms. Still, on balance, drug court does not seem significantly less communicatively appropriate—and in some instances may be more appropriate—as a response to trafficking than to simple possession.

What about drug court for nondrug offenses? I assume here a defendant charged with a property or violent offense that has been linked to an underlying drug dependency, either in that the offense was motivated by a desire to obtain drugs or was driven by the psychopharmacological effects of drug use or withdrawal. Such drug–crime linkages seem common, especially among property offenders.[20] While offenders facing serious nondrug charges would be excluded categorically from many drug courts today, some jurisdictions do employ more inclusive eligibility criteria that welcome even violent offenders (National Association of Criminal Defense Lawyers 2009).

Whether drug court would be an appropriate punishment for drug-dependent property and violent offenders may turn on the specifics of the offense. In general, though, the offenses—burglary, robbery, assault, theft, and other *mala in se*—seem more clearly to be public wrongs than does simple drug possession.[21] Moreover, assuming a close connection between the offense and the drug dependency, undergoing a treatment regimen would appear in many respects an appropriate penance. Yet, at least with respect to the more serious victimizing offenses, drug court may not adequately draw the offender's attention to what really made his or her conduct wrongful. In this context we might be especially concerned about the prevalence of disease-model rhetoric. We might also be concerned about whether drug court is sufficiently severe to satisfy the proportionality objective.

For these reasons, drug court should probably only be imposed as one aspect of the punishment for more serious offenses. For instance, one might imagine a drug-dependent robber or burglar also being required to provide financial reparations for victims or perform some suitable community service in addition to participating in drug court.

At the same time, there remains a possibility that drug court would be too severe for some nondrug crimes perpetrated by drug-dependent offenders (imagine, for instance, prosecutions for shoplifting or minor altercations with the police). Any concerns regarding excessive severity would be much mitigated if the reforms I suggested in the previous section were adopted (e.g., imposing stricter formal constraints on the use of incarceration as a graduated sanction).

Assuming proportionality constraints are satisfied, drug court has the potential to provide a communicatively attractive response to many drug-related nondrug offenses. In this setting, however, there seems a particular need for drug court to remain integrated within the culture and processes of conventional criminal courtrooms, where the modes and rhetoric of censure are better suited to address the victimizing aspects of nondrug offenses. Indeed, one might imagine the most salient aspects of the drug court regimen—mandatory treatment, frequent drug tests, close court supervision, graduated sanctions—simply being folded into the probation process in suitable nondrug cases in general-purpose criminal courts.

IV. CONCLUSION: A NEW PENAL PARADIGM?

Although drug courts are far from a pure realization of the communicative punishment model, they do seem in some respects a considerable advance in communicative richness in comparison with conventional case processing. As against immediate incarceration, drug court offers a much closer substantive fit as a response to the crime of drug

possession (and perhaps a range of other offenses, too). Although traditional probation might be arranged to achieve a comparable degree of fit on a case-by-case basis,
busy judges in general criminal courtrooms may lack the motivation or resources to
provide offenders with a drug-court-like experience on a routine basis. While standard
probation orders may include a requirement to abstain from illicit drugs, such a requirement may make little impression if unaccompanied by close court supervision,
regular testing, and the like. Specialized drug courts thus seem to provide better prospects than conventional dispositions when it comes to focusing drug offenders' attention on their crimes in a sustained way, helping them to see how to avoid committing
more crimes in the future, and facilitating the expression of a commitment to achieve
reform and reconciliation. It is in this sense that drug courts seem communicatively
richer than conventional dispositions, notwithstanding significant concerns regarding
potential disproportionality and coercion.

If the popularity of drug courts stems at least in part from their communicative qualities, other penal trends also seem to suggest a public embrace of greater communicative richness in punishment. These trends are not limited to the growing numbers and
increasing diversity of specialized "problem-solving courts" (e.g., for drunk driving,
domestic violence, and prisoner reentry) that have been directly inspired by drug
courts (Miller 2007; Huddleston, Marlowe, and Casebolt 2008, pp. 18–19). For
instance, victim–offender mediation, community conferencing, and similar programs
that employ restorative justice processes became nearly as ubiquitous as drug courts in
the 1990s.[22] The number of victim–offender mediation programs (just one form of
restorative justice) increased from 150 to 1,200 worldwide between 1990 and 2000
(Victim Offender Mediation Association 2006), and restorative justice programs are
now believed to be in operation in virtually every state (Umbreit et al. 2005, p. 263).
Duff himself has noted the positive communicative qualities of victim-offender mediation (2001, pp. 93–98).

Shaming sanctions, which are sometimes associated with restorative justice, have
also been the subject of a recent surge of interest. Although objectionable on a number
of grounds, shaming sanctions seem to respond to a widespread view that conventional punishments do not adequately express social condemnation of wrongdoing
(Markel 2001).

Finally, growth in the use of victim-impact evidence (Logan 2006) and increased recognition of the rights of victims to participate in the sentencing process (Butler 2006)
may also be seen, at least in part, as reflecting a desire to communicate to offenders the
consequences of their offenses in a more vivid and effective manner. We might thus conceptualize victim–offender confrontation not merely as part of the sentencing process,
but as a substantive, communicative aspect of the offender's punishment.

Observing common communicative threads among these diverse phenomena—
none of which, to be sure, fully embody the ideals of communicative punishment—we
might well wonder if a deeper paradigm shift is afoot. Perhaps, most hopefully, we might
wonder if there will be some movement from overreliance on incarceration to an emphasis on more inclusionary, substantively fitting sentences. The drug court experience,
though, offers at least two important reasons to be skeptical of the prospects for a fundamental shift along these lines.

First, drug courts commonly restrict eligibility to low-level offenders who would not likely face substantial sentences of incarceration in the conventional system. Within the overall picture of drug enforcement, the communicatively richer punishment of drug court seems effectively layered on top of a crude system of incapacitation and deterrence for drug traffickers and drug users with histories of violence. This highlights a broader limitation on the trend toward greater communicative richness: a great many offenders seem to be regarded as dangerous outsiders who do not merit respectful, restrained penal treatment as fellow citizens, but are instead appropriately addressed in the language of naked threats and coercion.[23] This perspective may help to explain an apparent paradox: the era of explosive growth of drug courts and restorative justice programs has also been an era of dramatic growth in the number and severity of mandatory minimum sentencing laws, such as the infamous California three-strikes law,[24] and widespread adoption of indefinite civil confinement statutes for "sexually violent predators."[25] It has also been an era of unprecedented peaks in the American prison population (Bureau of Justice Statistics 2003). Whatever their importance in other respects, drug courts and restorative justice do not appear to have made any appreciable dent in the realities of mass incarceration, and there is no apparent reason to think that such innovations will soon start to play an important role in channeling otherwise prison-bound offenders into more communicatively appropriate modes of punishment.

Second, drug courts are not truly an alternative to incarceration, but a restructuring of the use of incarceration. Instead of an initial sentence, incarceration becomes part of the system of graduated sanctions; in that context, the amount of incarceration may actually match or exceed what would have been imposed normally in the first instance. To be sure, as Duff concludes, the use of incarceration as a backup sanction may not be communicatively inappropriate, but nor is it automatically fitting and proportionate. Earlier I suggested reasons to suppose that these communicative ideals are frequently unmet by drug court sanctioning. This is troubling, for it suggests that even within the narrow class of low-level offenders who are welcomed into drug courts, the emphasis on communicatively richer and more appropriate punishment may be more apparent than real.

This problem with drug courts may point to a deeper challenge for communicatively rich punishment, particularly if it is unaccompanied by a strong commitment to Duff's ideal of leaving the offender free to remain unpersuaded by the message being communicated. Punishment as secular penance is morally more demanding of both the offender and the sentencer than punishment as deterrence and incapacitation, asking both offender and sentencer to recognize their fellowship with, and duties to, the other. Where the sentencer exerts greater moral effort, it seems perfectly natural that an offender's failure to reciprocate would create a sense of personal betrayal and elicit penal responses that might otherwise seem excessive. As I suggested above, such a dynamic does seem present in at least some drug courts and doubtlessly contributes to harshness in the use of graduated sanctions. We might well wonder whether the supervision of penitential punishment is more generally subject to such tendencies toward excessive and communicatively inappropriate use of backup sanctions.

On the other hand, it may be that there are ways of structuring alternative sentencing schemes that mitigate these risks. Elsewhere I have described the use of community conferencing, a restorative justice process, as a response to drug offenses in Milwaukee (O'Hear 2009). This response effectively outsources the selection and supervision of penitential punishment to an ad hoc group of facilitators, community representatives, and other stakeholders. In contrast to drug courts, the judge has no continuous role, but instead only becomes involved in a sentencing capacity after the offender has complied with the conditions she has agreed to in the conferencing process or the process has otherwise been terminated. If conditions are violated, the conferencing group can reconvene to set new conditions in response to violations, but the group has no authority to impose incarceration. If the conferencing process fails and is terminated, the judge is free to impose incarceration, but presumably makes the decision without the background sense of personal betrayal that sometimes manifests itself in drug court.

To be sure, the outsourcing aspect of the community-conferencing model raises a number of concerns itself, particularly relating to transparency and public accountability. Such difficulties may prevent the model from winning as widespread public support as have drug courts.

In any event, even without a personal edge, the use of incarceration as the ultimate backup sanction in communicatively rich alternative sentencing schemes presents a risk that such schemes will produce more, not less, incarceration than would the conventional sentencing system—especially if the schemes are limited to low-level offenders who would not likely receive long sentences in the conventional system. Of course, the incarceration, even if of no less duration, may be more communicatively appropriate because of the context in which it is imposed (i.e., as a backup sanction for willful failures to comply with conditions, rather than as an initial sentence). Still, reformers who embrace more communicatively rich punishment primarily in the hope of diminishing incarceration or general penal severity may find themselves disappointed by the results of their efforts.

NOTES

1. Some drug courts are designed to function as a preplea prosecutorial diversion, but the trend is toward drug courts that admit defendants only postplea or postadjudication (National Association of Criminal Defense Lawyers 2009, p. 17). Although preplea drug courts lack a formal prerequisite to punishment (conviction), we might nonetheless regard them as having a punitive character insofar as they involve state-administered hard treatment premised on the recipient's commission of a crime.

2. The question of whether drug court is attractive *as punishment* may be all the more pressing to the extent that drug court does not succeed *as social service*. Although a number of studies support the conclusion that drug courts may offer (modest) benefits in the area of recidivism reduction (U.S. Government Accountability Office 2005; King and Pasquarella 2009), it is far from clear that the criteria and selection processes used to govern admittance to most drug courts result in anything close to the socially optimal allocation of scarce treatment resources (Caulkins and Kleiman, 2011).

3. Some confirmation of this view might be found, for instance, in the cases that generally protect from criminal punishment private sexual activity between consenting adults, even if such activity is of a sort that is distasteful to many members of the community. See, e.g., *Lawrence v. Texas*, 539 U.S. 558 (2003).

4. Duff uses driving rules as an example. "Driving along a particular road at 80 mph might well not be wrong, because it might not be unreasonably dangerous, prior to the legal specification of a 70 mph speed limit; but once that regulation is in place, breaking it does

constitute a public wrong—if not because drivers should not trust their own judgment about safe speeds, then because it is a matter of civic duty to accept this modest burden." (2007, p. 172).

5. Husak notes, "Many criminals may be drug users, but few drug users are criminals" (1998, p. 206). For purposes of assessing the harms that are prevented by criminalizing drug possession, Husak also cautions that we ought not include "the harms that would not have been caused were possession of that drug not illegal," such as the thefts committed by addicts who might otherwise be able to afford drugs were they legal (1998, p. 201).

6. It is doubtful, for instance, that marijuana use contributes much to victimizing, nondrug crime, except perhaps indirectly to the (highly uncertain) extent to which it serves as a "gateway" to other drugs that are much more clearly associated with nondrug crime, that is, heroin, cocaine, and methamphetamine (Caulkins and Kleiman, 2011).

7. Another harm theory for drug possession, not considered by Husak, is that drugs are often possessed for trafficking purposes, and trafficking (as discussed in the final part of this section) is associated with a distinct and arguably more compelling set of harms than simple possession for personal use. Although the analysis here assumes a defendant charged with simple possession, it is not implausible that many simple possession defendants actually had an intent to distribute but received a lesser charge because of evidentiary difficulties in proving the requisite intent or because a police officer or prosecutor decided that the greater punishment associated with trafficking charges was unwarranted. I would not ascribe much weight to trafficking harms here, though, because it is not clear how often cases charged as simple possession do involve trafficking intentions, and because those trafficking cases involving serious harms seem least likely to be charged as simple possession.

8. Drug court practice also reflects the disease model in other respects, such as labeling participants "clients," instead of "offenders" (McColl 2002, p. 78).

9. *Robinson v. California*, 370 U.S. 660 (1962).

10. Miethe, Lu, and Reese (2000, p. 537), for instance, found that drug court judges commonly used phrases like, "Don't you know what this stuff does to your brain!," "I'm tired of your excuses," and "I'm through with you." In a similar vein, Steen (2002, p. 62) quotes a drug court judge admonishing a sanctioned "client": "Don't do this to you or me ever again." As to paternalism, Nolan (2001, p. 78) observes the tendency among drug court lawyers and judges to characterize sanctions as in "the client's best interests."

11. Thus, as Nolan (2001, pp. 15–38) observes, new drug court judges sometimes go through a period of "cognitive reorientation" that involves a fundamental rethinking of the nature of drug offenses and addiction.

12. In his discussion of drug courts in Cumberland, Maine, and Washington, D.C., Bean (2002, pp. 239–40) notes that 31 percent of participants spent time in jail in one (Cumberland) and 50 percent spent at least three days in jail in the other.

13. For instance, Bean (2002, p. 241) notes that one Denver drug court judge sent only 14 percent of program participants to jail, while his successor incarcerated 40 percent.

14. Despite lay perceptions that incarceration is a categorically tougher punishment than community-based supervision, empirical research indicates that offenders have more nuanced views and sometimes prefer an initial term of imprisonment over "intermediate" sanctions, especially when the intermediate option involves difficult conditions and close supervision (May and Wood 2010, pp. 26–29).

15. This is not to say that all or most drug court participants are highly dependent, but that offenders who are highly dependent are especially prone to make ill-advised decisions to enter a drug court.

16. There may also be disparity concerns in the treatment of those who are admitted to drug court. For instance, Nolan (2001, pp. 102–4) suggests that many drug court judges seem indifferent to disparities in the use of sanctions.

17. One type of third-party harm from which dealers are *not* further removed than buyers is the neighborhood demoralization and disorder associated especially with open-air markets and other forms of flagrant drug dealing (O'Hear 2009; Caulkins and Kleiman 2011). Although not all traffickers operate in this manner, flagrant dealing seems to give rise to a disproportionate share of drug arrests (Beckett, Nyrop, and Pfingst 2006), which may help to justify taking the particular harms of flagrant dealing into account when assessing the wrongfulness of trafficking offenses. On the other hand, it may be more appropriate to characterize these as harms of *criminalization* rather than as harms attributable to drug dealing itself.

18. In his discussion of the wrongfulness of drug dealing, Alldridge (1996) similarly identifies the exploitation of vulnerable users as the heart of the matter, although he focuses more narrowly on the problem of sales to addicts, which he analogizes to extortion—the implicit threat that drugs will be withheld when the addict experiences withdrawal provides the seller with a dominant position that is subject to exploitation.

19. In the most recent available survey of past-month usage of illicit drugs, more than 11 percent of the reported drug users were 17 years of age or younger, and nearly 44 percent were 25 or younger. Drug use was most prevalent in the 18- to 20-year-old range. Moreover, nearly 14 percent of those under 18 indicated that they had been approached by someone selling drugs in the past month. Mental illness also seems disproportionately associated with drug consumption: the rate of illicit drug use was more than twice as high among adults with serious mental illness as in the general population (Substance Abuse and Mental Health Services Administration 2009). Likewise, studies indicate that a relatively small number of "hardcore" users account for the vast majority of spending on illicit drugs (Caulkins and Kleiman 2011), which is suggestive of a high volume of sales to addicts.

20. In one study, about one-third of property offenders in state prison reported that obtaining drug money was a motive for them to commit their offenses, while more than 38 percent reported drug use at the time of their offenses (Bureau of Justice Statistics 2007). In all, more than 63 percent of the property offenders met criteria for drug dependence or abuse—an even slightly higher percentage than among those imprisoned for drug offenses. The corresponding numbers among violent offenders were approximately 10 percent motivated by drugs, 28 percent using drugs at the time of offense, and 47 percent meeting criteria for drug dependence or abuse. Thus, although the numbers are a little lower, there would appear to be no shortage of violent offenders experiencing criminogenic forms of drug dependence.

21. I assume that the offender's drug use has not so impaired his volition or cognitive functioning as to mitigate or eliminate his moral responsibility for the offense.

22. For a description of these and other variations of restorative justice, see Umbreit et al. (2005). When I refer here to "restorative justice," I have in mind what Luna (2009) refers to as the procedural, not the substantive, conception of restorative justice.

23. Not only drug courts, but also restorative justice processes have generally been limited to the least serious sorts of offenses and offenders (Robinson 2006, p. 428).

24. Zimring, Hawkins, and Kamin (2001) describe the rise of "three-strikes" laws in the 1990s, culminating in the adoption of the most extreme version in California.

25. Janus and Prentky (2008) describe the history of these laws.

REFERENCES

Alldridge, Peter. 1996. "Dealing with Drug Dealing." In *Harm and Culpability*, ed. A. P. Simester and A. T. H. Smith. Oxford: Clarendon Press.

Bean, Philip. 2002. "Drug Courts, the Judge, and the Rehabilitative Ideal." In *Drug Courts in Theory and in Practice*, ed. James L. Nolan, Jr. New York: Aldine de Gruyter.

Beckett, Katherine, Kris Nyrop, and Lori Pfingst. 2006. "Race, Drugs, and Policing: Understanding Disparities in Drug Delivery Arrests." *Criminology* 44:105–37.

Bureau of Justice Statistics. 2003. *Prevalence of Imprisonment in the U.S. Population, 1974–2001.* Washington, DC: Bureau of Justice Statistics.

————. 2007. *Drug Use and Dependence, State and Federal Prisoners, 2004.* Washington, DC: Bureau of Justice Statistics.

Bowers, Josh. 2008. "Contraindicated Drug Courts." *UCLA Law Review* 55:783–835.

Butler, Russell P. 2006. "What Practitioners and Judges Need to Know Regarding Crime Victims' Participatory Rights in Federal Sentencing Proceedings." *Federal Sentencing Reporter* 19(1):21–28.

Caulkins, Jonathan, and Mark A. R. Kleiman. 2011. "Drugs and Crime." In *The Oxford Handbook of Crime and Criminal Justice,* ed. Michael Tonry. New York: Oxford University Press.

Duff, R. A. 2001. *Punishment, Communication, and Community.* New York: Oxford University Press.

————. 2005. "Guidance and Guidelines." *Columbia Law Review* 105:1162–89.

————. 2007. *Answering for Crime: Responsibility and Liability in the Criminal Law.* Portland, OR: Hart.

Hoffman, Morris B. 2000. "The Drug Court Scandal." *North Carolina Law Review* 78:1437–534.

Huddleston, C. West, III, Douglas B. Marlowe, and Rachel Casebolt. 2008. *Painting the Picture: A National Report Card on Drug Courts and Other Problem Solving Court Programs in the United States.* Washington, DC: National Drug Court Institute.

Husak, Douglas N. 1998. "Desert, Proportionality, and the Seriousness of Drug Offences." In *Fundamentals of Sentencing Theory: Essays in Honor of Andrew von Hirsch,* ed. Andrew Ashworth and Martin Wasik. New York: Oxford University Press.

————. 2011. "Retributivism, Proportionality, and the Challenge of the Drug Court Movement." In *Retributivism Has a Past. Has It a Future?,* ed. Michael Tonry. New York: Oxford University Press.

Janus, Eric S., and Robert A. Prentky. 2008. "Sexual Predator Laws: A Two-Decade Retrospective." *Federal Sentencing Reporter* 21:90–97.

King, Ryan S., and Jill Pasquarella. 2009. *Drug Courts: A Review of the Evidence.* Washington, DC: Sentencing Project.

Logan, Wayne A. 2006. "Victim Impact Evidence in Federal Capital Trials." *Federal Sentencing Reporter* 19:5–12.

Luna, Erik. 2009. "In Support of Restorative Justice." In *Criminal Law Conversations,* ed. Paul H. Robinson, Stephen P. Garvey, and Kimberly Kessler Ferzan. New York: Oxford University Press.

Markel, Dan. 2001. "Are Shaming Sanctions Beautifully Retributive? Retributivism and the Implications for the Alternative Sanctions Debate." *Vanderbilt Law Review* 54:2157–215.

Marlowe, Douglas B., David S. DeMatteo, and David S. Festinger. 2003. "A Sober Assessment of Drug Courts." *Federal Sentencing Reporter* 16:153–57.

May, David C., and Peter B. Wood. 2010. *Ranking Correctional Punishments: Views from Offenders, Practitioners, and the Public.* Durham, NC: Carolina Academic Press.

McColl, William D. 2002. "Theory and Practice in the Baltimore City Drug Treatment Court." In *Drug Courts in Theory and Practice,* ed. James L. Nolan, Jr. New York: Aldine de Gruyter.

Miethe, Terance D., Hong Lu, and Erin Reese. 2000. "Reintegrative Shaming and Recidivism Risks in Drug Court: Explanations for Some Unexpected Findings." *Crime & Delinquency* 46:522–41.

Miller, Eric J. 2007. "The Therapeutic Effects of Managerial Reentry Courts." *Federal Sentencing Reporter* 20:127–35.

National Association of Criminal Defense Lawyers. 2009. *America's Problem-Solving Courts: The Criminal Costs of Treatment and the Case for Reform*. Washington, DC: National Association of Criminal Defense Lawyers.

Nolan, James L., Jr. 2001. *Reinventing Justice: The American Drug Court Movement*. Princeton, NJ: Princeton University Press.

————. 2002. "Separated by Uncommon Law: Drug Courts in Great Britain and America." In *Drug Courts in Theory and in Practice*, ed. James L. Nolan, Jr. New York: Aldine de Gruyter.

O'Hear, Michael M. 2009. "Rethinking Drug Courts: Restorative Justice as a Response to Racial Injustice." *Stanford Law & Policy Review* 20:463–500.

Roberts, Julian V. 2008. *Punishing Persistent Offenders: Exploring Community and Offender Perspectives*. Oxford: Oxford University Press.

Robinson, Paul H. 2006. "Restorative Processes and Doing Justice." *University of St. Thomas Law Review* 3:421–29.

Rosenthal, John Terrence A. 2002. "Therapeutic Jurisprudence and Drug Treatment Courts: Integrating Law and Science." In *Drug Courts in Theory and in Practice*, ed. James L. Nolan, Jr. New York: Aldine de Gruyter.

Steen, Sara. 2002. "West Coast Drug Courts: Getting Offenders Morally Involved in the Criminal Justice Process." In *Drug Courts in Theory and in Practice*, ed. James L. Nolan, Jr. New York: Aldine de Gruyter.

Substance Abuse and Mental Health Services Administration. 2009. *Results from the 2008 National Survey on Drug Use and Health: National Findings*. Rockville, MD: Substance Abuse and Mental Health Services Administration.

Umbreit, Mark S., Betty Vos, Robert B. Coates, and Elizabeth Lightfoot. 2005. "Restorative Justice in the Twenty-First Century: A Social Movement Full of Opportunities and Pitfalls." *Marquette Law Review* 89:251–304.

U.S. Government Accountability Office. 2005. *Adult Drug Courts: Evidence Indicates Recidivism Reduction and Mixed Results for Other Outcomes*. Washington, DC: U.S. Government Accountability Office.

Victim Offender Mediation Association. 2006. "Restorative Justice FAQ." http://voma.org/rjfaq.shtml.

Zimring, Franklin E., Gordon Hawkins, and Sam Kamin. 2001. *Punishment and Democracy: Three Strikes and You're Out in California*. New York: Oxford University Press.

13

Punishment Futures

The Desert-model Debate and the Importance of the Criminal Law Context

ANDREAS VON HIRSCH[1]

The contemporary interest in a desert-based model for sentencing dates from the mid-1970s, with publication of several works on punishment theory and sentencing (e.g., Kleinig 1973; von Hirsch 1976). Once broached, the idea quickly became influential in penological thinking in the United States and Europe.[2]

The desert model. This emerging literature on penal desert addressed two common objections to traditional retributivism. One objection was that the notion of deserved punishment is essentially incomprehensible, that it rests on obscure "metaphysical" notions of requital of evil for evil. Modern desert theorists put forward a simpler explanation. Punishment, they asserted, is (and should be) a blaming institution. The difference between a criminal and a civil sanction lies, generally, in that the former involves *censure* of the actor for his criminal conduct.[3] In such a censuring response, fairness requires that penalties be ordered consistently with their blaming implications. The severity of the punishment, and hence its degree of implied censure, should thus comport with the seriousness (i.e., the extent of wrongfulness) of the defendant's criminal conduct. Disparate or disproportionate punishments are unjust, because they impose a degree of penal censure on offenders that is not warranted by the reprehensibleness of their criminal conduct.

The other objection was to the harshness of retributive punishment, to its supposed exaction of an eye for an eye. Desert theorists' response has been that a desert model does not require the visitation of equivalent suffering. What is required, instead, is *proportionate* sanctions, reflecting the (comparative) seriousness of the criminal conduct. Proportionate sanctions may be imposed without increasing (indeed, while substantially *decreasing*) prevailing severity levels, as long as penalties are scaled according to the crime's seriousness, and equally reprehensible criminal acts are penalized with roughly comparable severity.

The central principle of sentencing, according to this view, is the principle of desert proportionality: that sentences should be proportionate in their severity with the gravity of criminal conduct (von Hirsch 1985, chap. 3; Duff 2001, chap. 4). The main criterion for deciding the quantum of punishment should thus be retrospective: the degree of harm and culpability of the offender's criminal conduct. Imprisonment, because of its severity, should be visited only on those found to have committed serious crimes. For less reprehensible criminal acts, penalties less onerous than imprisonment should be employed. The degree of burdensomeness of these noncustodial sanctions should also be determined by the gravity of the criminal conduct (von Hirsch 1993, chap. 7).

After emerging in the mid-1970s, the desert model swiftly gained influence. In the United States, some states having (by American standards) liberal political traditions— for example, Minnesota and Oregon[4]—relied on the desert model in fashioning numerical guidelines for sentencing. In Europe, two countries—Finland in 1976 and Sweden in 1989—adopted statutory guiding principles for sentencing that strongly emphasize norms of desert proportionality (see Jareborg 1995, Lappi-Seppälä 2002). England, in 1991, adopted statutory guiding norms, likewise giving proportionality a central role. Parliament watered down those norms in 2003, but also established a sentencing council to provide guiding principles for judges to apply.[5] The council's recent sentencing standards call upon judges to take the seriousness of the conviction offense substantially into account in their sentences (Ashworth 2010). In addition, Canada and New Zealand each have enacted statements of desert-oriented sentencing aims (Roberts 2003). The desert model continues, moreover, to be influential among academic criminologists, legal scholars and philosophers writing on sentencing theory and policy.[6]

It is important to bear in mind, however, that notwithstanding the desert rationale's influence among academic commentators, it has been implemented in systematic fashion in only a minority of jurisdictions. Most European countries continue to operate discretionary sentencing schemes. In the United States, most states do so also, but such schemes often are modified through adoption of statutory mandatory minimum sentences for selected crime categories.[7] Some of the latter measures are notorious— for example, California's three-strikes law, which imposes draconian prison terms (25 years or more) for a third conviction for any of a variety of common crimes.[8] Mandatory minimums do not derive from a desert rationale—indeed, they are plainly inconsistent with such a rationale, because they yield disparate orderings of penalties and also restrict a court's ability to reduce a sentence to reflect circumstances of diminished culpability.

The attraction of the proportionate sentence. Fashions in penology tend to change quickly—as is evident in the ups and downs in the rehabilitative penal ethic's influence in recent decades. What has been surprising about the desert model for sentencing, now in its fourth decade, has been its durability. There remains an active interest in proportionalist sentencing theory, as just noted. A number of proportionality-oriented sentencing guidance schemes also have shown considerable longevity (e.g., those of Finland, Sweden, and Minnesota), and several jurisdictions have recently supported such approaches.[9] What, then, has been the attraction of proportionalism?

For penologists of a liberal persuasion, an attraction has been the model's emphasis on notions of fairness. Traditional crime-prevention-oriented theories focus on instrumental concerns: how various sentencing strategies can best protect *us* from the depredations of *them*, the criminals. Such an instrumentalist perspective threatens unjust results: given a primary orientation to crime prevention, why not do whatever works for that purpose? With some crime prevention rationales—such as the deterrence-based "law and economics" approach—the potential for unfairness is starkly present (see Donohue 2007). The potential fairness problems of some versions of penal rehabilitationism (e.g., the indeterminate sentence) have also been well documented (see, e.g., Allen 1981). Proportionalism, however, attempts to give notions of justice a central role. The emphasis is on devising sanctions that comport with the degree of reprehensibleness of the offender's conduct, and maintaining a reasonable degree of comparability among sentences for offenders convicted of similarly blameworthy criminal conduct.

Proportionalism has the additional attraction of providing a modicum of policy guidance: it suggests a way of scaling penalties. Traditional crime preventive penal conceptions largely fail in this respect. Consider the aim of deterrence: it would be difficult to array sentences according to their deterrent effect, because so little remains known about the marginal deterrent effects of different levels of sentence severity (for the recent research results, see Bottoms and von Hirsch 2010). With rehabilitation programs, matters are not much better. To the extent that treatment programs do work, they tend to succeed chiefly with carefully selected subgroups of offenders, and mainly in small, well-staffed experimental programs.

A proportionalist approach provides more guidance: sanctions should be scaled in severity to reflect the comparative seriousness of crimes. Although such rankings inevitably are matters of judgment, at least some degree of consensus seems possible (at least, within a given legal culture) on what are more and less serious crimes (see, e.g., Sellin and Wolfgang 1964). Granted, there are important unresolved questions. Explicit norms for assessing crimes' comparative seriousness are only beginning to develop (see von Hirsch and Ashworth 2005, pp. 143–46 and app. 3). Controversial questions remain—for example, on how much weight should be given previous criminal convictions.[10] But at least some guidance can be devised to assist with these grading tasks, as the experience with sentencing guidelines and comparable schemes suggests.[11]

A desert model leaves important options open, however. A jurisdiction has a substantial degree of choice concerning the type and form of sentencing guidance: whether, for example, to rely on numerical sentencing guidelines (as Minnesota does) or on statutory guiding principles and judicial review (as Finland and Sweden do).[12] The anchoring of a penalty scale may also depend, to a considerable extent, on prevailing conventions and ethical norms concerning acceptable severity levels (von Hirsch 1993, chap. 5). While both Minnesota's sentencing guidelines and Sweden's statutory standards are recognizable as proportionality-oriented approaches, there are significant differences in the structure and content of these schemes, reflecting larger differences in these jurisdictions' legal and political traditions.

For some decades after the desert model's initial formulation in the mid-1970s, there was sharp controversy between that model and so-called limiting retributivism. According to the latter view's initial formulation by Norval Morris in the mid-1970s

(Morris 1976), desert can have only a restricted role in the determination of sentence. It can do no more, Morris asserted, than provide wide outer limits (i.e., only broad upper, and possibly some lower, bounds) on the quantum of punishment, within which the sentence should be set on other (especially crime preventive) grounds. In his view, moreover, those outer desert limits would be based on community sentiment: sentences should not exceed what is seen by current popular mores as excessive. He thus vigorously opposed desert-based guideline schemes as unwarrantedly restrictive of judges' sentencing choices.

Recent writings on "limiting retributivism," however, make it apparent that the differences between the two schools of thought are diminishing. Richard Frase (2004) and Michael Tonry (1997) now suggest that, under limiting retributivism, the desert-based ranges of permissible sentences should be considerably narrower than those Morris proposed, and that those ranges' limits should be based not on popular mores, but on notions of penal censure. Both the desert model and Frase's and Tonry's formulations of limiting retributivism thus would markedly increase the emphasis that should be given to crime seriousness, compared with Morris's earlier view. The two approaches, therefore, should no longer be perceived as fundamentally opposed viewpoints, but rather as differing variants of penal retributivism.

I. THE "PUNISHMENT FUTURES" PROJECT

In two recent essays (2005 and 2007), Michael Tonry has posed an interesting challenge to the desert model: it is that desert-oriented sentencing models are becoming increasingly unsustainable in practice (especially in the United States and United Kingdom), in view of the variety of recent penal initiatives that apparently pay little heed to proportionality concerns. These measures often are characterized by reduced emphasis on equal treatment, procedural measures of justice, and emphasis on local norms. He urged a new effort to explore novel penal conceptions going beyond the (now) familiar retributive ideas.

The present project grew out of these suggestions. Tonry assembled a group of penal theorists in two successive conferences in the Netherlands, in 2008 and 2010. He asked members of the group to subject such newer initiatives to careful analytic scrutiny—and to consider their implications for penal theory. The result is the essays in this volume.

I shall not undertake a synthesis of these various essays, for their analyses and conclusions speak for themselves. I shall offer a few observations on the essays' general implications when they are considered together. Do they seek to furnish a novel conception of punishment and sanctioning, or provide reason for the need for one, that would replace the desert model?

What emerges from these essays, in my judgment, is evidence of the surprising continued vitality of retributive conceptions. Some of the essays explicitly advocate versions of retributivism. Others use retributive criteria in evaluating "novel" approaches such as "protection measures," drug courts, and the like. None of the essays provide a systematic case for a nonretributive model aimed at replacing the desert model or its variants. This conclusion becomes apparent from the following thumbnail sketch of some of the contributions.

Two essays, by Antony Duff and John Kleinig, review the arguments and assumptions underlying a retributive conception of punishment. Their analyses show sympathy for restorative responses, but ones that would also reflect or express what offenders deserve.

Two other essays, by Douglas Husak and Michael O'Hear, scrutinize drug courts and their ethos. Those schemes give a central role to therapeutic considerations and seemingly allow little scope to desert considerations. Husak's analysis—which is strongly critical—emphasizes how drug court dispositions infringe on ordinal proportionality constraints. O'Hear's discussion is somewhat more sympathetic to drug courts, but he bases his analysis on Duff's penance model of punishment, which employs retributive assumptions and arguments.

The essay by Jan de Keijser examines the Netherlands' two-track scheme. This permits judges, when sentencing convicted offenders, to choose between a punishment track, which operates with retributive constraints, and a "protective measures" track, which lacks such limits, is not denominated as a penal measure, and determines duration of confinement on the basis of risk. De Keijser is skeptical of this approach, in part because of its disregard for desert constraints.

An analysis by Richard Frase considers the practice, in various jurisdictions, of extending sentences beyond an offender's deserved term. He examines this from the viewpoint of two deontological but nonretributive conceptions. One of these is John Rawls's contractualist model of hypothetical contracting parties that set ground rules while putatively unaware of their own personal interests. The other is the "competing rights" perspective, wherein an offender's rights (including the entitlement to upper retributive limits on punishment) may be "weighed" against the victim's right not to be victimized. Frase concludes that the Rawlsian model provides only limited support for punishments in excess of desert, and "competing rights" is itself too problematic to justify any such measures. Implicit in his entire discussion, however, is the retributive premise that there ordinarily should be significant upper limits on the severity of penalties, based on the seriousness of the offenses involved.

It might be objected that desert theories receive continuing support here because of the selection of the contributors. Duff, Kleinig, and I have been active in the formulation of the desert model, Husak's other writings endorse a retributive conception of punishment, and Frase has been a leading advocate of limiting retributivism. However, other members of the group have had no such identification. Moreover, if the desert model were really becoming obsolete, one would expect at least some former supporters of retributivism to have become skeptics—as happened in the late 1970s, when a number of ex-supporters of the treatment model moved to more critical stances.

If retributive perspectives seem to have some continuing vitality, why so? One reason, perhaps, relates to what precedes the sentence: criminal prohibitions and the doctrines of criminal law. When criminals are punished, it is *for* a crime. What constitutes a crime is determined not by sentencing law, but by the principles of substantive criminal law. Maybe those principles do matter. Maybe their character and rationale might point, at least to a degree, toward retributive criteria in sentencing.

An oddity of debate over sentencing rationale in the last four decades is the extent to which it has proceeded independently of thinking about the criminal law's underlying normative principles. Perhaps this should not be surprising. In England and the United States, sentencing has been deemed to be within the province of criminology, and the empirical emphasis of that discipline strongly influenced the sentencing debate. Before the mid-1970s, that debate was preeminently consequentialist and crime preventive in character; it concerned itself largely with the comparative merits of differing crime prevention models—rehabilitation, deterrence, and incapacitation. The optimum sentence (subject only to vague outer desert constraints) was seen as that which would best carry out the criminal justice system's crime prevention mission. When the desert rationale gained influence in the mid-1970s, the themes cited by its proponents (about blame and censure, choice, responsibility, etc.) seemed—for criminologists accustomed to crime prevention models—to be unfamiliar, "unscientific" imports. (It is no coincidence, therefore, that several of the desert model's original exponents were not typical, empirically orientated criminologists, but philosophers or jurists by background.)

The basic normative principles of the criminal law should matter, however. Taking criminal law theory into account need not be a black letter law exercise, and should be helpful in dealing with some of the questions discussed in this volume. Consider the Netherlands's "protection measures," discussed by Jan de Keijser (2011). This involves permitting sentencing judges to opt for replacing a criminal sentence with a noncriminal type of intervention. The scheme continues, however, to permit a criminal conviction to trigger such an intervention. If a conviction is thus relied upon, however, it becomes worth examining its normative implications—for example, whether it may consistently be followed by a purportedly noncriminal sanction.

To explore this issue, I shall proceed inductively. I shall address two approaches analyzed in this volume that depart most markedly from the retributive thinking of the proportionate-sentencing model. The first of these is the one just mentioned: the Dutch "protection measures" scheme. The second is the "fear-prevention" model, examined by Peter Ramsay. Both of these raise questions about how a criminal conviction, or the criminal law principles that underlie it, should affect the kinds of disposition that would be appropriate to those convicted.

II. NONPENAL INTERVENTIONS AND THE NETHERLANDS'S DUAL-TRACK SCHEME

The constraints imposed by the desert rationale depend on a sanction's character as *punishment*. Punishment, desert theory holds, conveys censure or blame, so that a sanction's severity should reflect the degree of blameworthiness of the criminal conduct. Why, however, must the state's interventions against those convicted of crimes always constitute punishments? Perhaps, a variety of *nonpunitive* interventions are conceivable—ones that would leave the state with additional flexibility to deal with troublesome offenders, free of the constraints of desert proportionality. In this connection, we should consider the Netherlands' dual-track system, analyzed by Jan de Keijser (2011).

A. Extended Sentences under Desert Theory

Among desert theorists, a debate has developed about extending an offender's sentence in exceptional cases, on grounds of risk, beyond his normally deserved term. That discussion has assumed, however, that the extensions are *penal* sanctions—for example, longer prison sentences for dangerous offenders. Anthony Bottoms and Roger Brownsword (1983) have thus proposed that sentence extensions beyond the normal deserved term should be permissible, but only in restricted cases to restrain especially dangerous individuals. Based on these authors' analysis, desert would be presumed to be the chief determinant of the sentence, but that presumption could be overcome in exceptional cases where preventive concerns have a high degree of urgency. Their scheme, therefore, would restrict sentence extensions to defendants who have been convicted of seriously violent offenses, and who continue to represent a "vivid danger" (Bottoms and Brownsword 1983, p. 20). Other desert theorists, including Andrew Ashworth and myself have argued against even this limited exception to proportionality requirements (von Hirsch and Ashworth 2005, chap. 4). However, as long as desert-based proportionality requirements are assumed to be a central feature of an equitable system of penal justice, it will not be easy to sustain an argument for the extensive use of punishments that extend substantially beyond the proportionate sentence.

A possible response to this difficulty would be largely to abandon altogether the desert rationale for sentencing. One could, for example, resort to a sentencing model based chiefly on deterrence and incapacitation, as some conservative criminologists, such as James Q. Wilson (1983, chap. 8), have argued. For many penologists and policy makers, however, this solution would be unappealing. It is desirable, they would feel, to have sentencing norms, at least for ordinary cases, that emphasize that there is something *wrong* with criminal conduct, and to have a penal response that reflects its apparent degree of wrongfulness. But might one, nevertheless, adopt a wholly different approach in certain categories of special cases? For those inclined to think so, the Netherlands' bifurcated scheme might have some appeal.

B. The Dutch Bifurcated Scheme: Punishments and Protective Measures

Under the Netherlands' criminal justice system, as described by de Keijser (2011), most convicted defendants receive a sanction that is expressly conceptualized as punishment. What the defendant deserves in virtue of the seriousness of his crime would thus ordinarily matter. While in Dutch practice the desert constraints are not particularly confining—and mainly constitute rather imprecise upper limits on permissible punishments—they do shape criminal policy significantly, and according to de Keijser, that approach has substantial support among legal scholars and policy makers. A drastic reconceptualization of ordinary criminal sanctions, so as to eliminate or minimize the influence of desert considerations, would appear to have little attraction in the Netherlands.

However, the Netherlands also has a second track. For certain categories of offenders, such as persistent criminals, a protective measure may be imposed after conviction—which is *not* deemed a punishment.[13] The "measure," it is asserted, does not constitute the deliberate infliction of suffering; any deprivation experienced by those restrained is unintended, and subordinate to the goal of promoting public safety. Since such sanctions are deemed noncriminal in character, the criteria for their imposition and for the duration of the intervention is not determined by the seriousness of the offender's crime and may well exceed what could be deemed deserved.

The scheme has its attractions. It permits the maintenance of desert standards with their emphasis on censure for criminal wrongdoing and equitable punishment for most criminal cases. This permits the desert track to operate in its own terms, without substantial intrusion of incapacitative aims. In the more limited class of cases where public protection is the primary aim, this is made explicit by treating the interventions as protective measures, not punishments. A certain gain in transparency is thus achieved. Unlike the extended criminal sentence, there are no primarily incapacitative interventions masquerading as deserved ones. With this apparent advantage, what drawbacks may the Netherlands' protection measures approach have?

C. Why Are the Dutch Protective Measures Not Punishments?

According to Dutch law, protective measures are not punishments. It is their supposed nonpunitive character that purportedly justifies exempting the interventions from desert constraints. The mere assertion of lack of punitive intent, however, should not suffice to justify such exemption. What should matter in determining an intervention's status as punitive or nonpunitive is its actual character and criteria for application. In what respects, then, do these protection measures differ from punishments—apart from how they are officially labeled? And how do measures compare to other forms of nonpenal intervention?

To aid this latter comparison, let us contrast the Dutch measures with a classic form of nonpenal constraint: civil quarantine. Quarantine for carriers of dangerously infectious diseases deprives such persons of their liberty, but in a manner that is understood not to be of a punitive character. Why is quarantine not punitive? A central reason is that quarantine is occasioned by an event that is not deemed to constitute a wrongful action on the quarantined person's part, namely, his having contracted (or become a carrier of) a deadly and highly infectious disease. This usually does not involve a choice on the person's part at all: indeed, his becoming infected occurs contrary to his wishes. Certainly there is no *wrongful* choice involved: it is not an element of having a quarantinable condition that the person contracted his condition purposely or negligently. This absence of a wrongful choice is an important reason for not attributing penal status to the quarantine—because it is a central feature of punishment that it conveys disapproval or censure for wrongdoing.

With Dutch-style protection measures, this important reason for withholding penal status is conspicuously absent. The triggering event for invoking the measure is the same as that for criminal punishments, namely, conviction of a crime. There has been a choice, and a wrongful one, on the person's part; typically, that of having performed an action that inflicts or risks harm upon another person. Rather than being a reason for withholding penal status, the character of the triggering event as a wrongful and prohibited act would warrant treating the interventions as punishments.

If the behavior occasioning the state's intervention is the same both for normal punishments and for these protection measures (viz., criminal conviction), might we point to some other significant difference? One might be tempted to point to the criteria for deciding the duration of confinement. Here, there does seem to be a difference. With normal punishments, a crucial factor is the seriousness of the defendant's criminal conduct. With protection measures, however, the criterion shifts to the purely consequentialist one of the person's likelihood of reoffending. This makes measures seem more like quarantine, where the grounds for imposing custody concern the risk posed.

This argument, however, begs the question. This becomes apparent when one asks *why* should the emphasis shift from the seriousness of the offender's criminal act to the risk he poses? If desert matters for normal cases, why should it cease to matter in cases where protective measures are invoked? In both kinds of cases, the defendant must be deemed capable of choice and responsible for his choices, otherwise convicting him for a crime would be inappropriate. With protection measures, the principal ground for invocation is persistence.[14] But repetitive offending does not in itself show that the person is insufficiently capable of choice. This objection also points to the vacuity of claiming that desert proportionality should not apply to measures, because these do not aim at inflicting deserved suffering. Here, the same question would arise: what makes these cases sufficiently different to make the shift in aims appropriate?

A fundamental difficulty with the Dutch two-step approach lies, then, in the conceptual and moral discontinuity between its criterion for invoking the intervention (viz., a conviction for a crime) and the character of sanction imposed (viz., a supposed nonpenal intervention). Whereas in the example of quarantine the trigger for the intervention is a medical condition not involving choice and responsibility on the person's part, here the event triggering the intervention is a *crime*. This latter event is a chosen act for which the person's fault is explicitly recognized by the state through the conviction and the penal censure it expresses.

D. Replacing the Conviction with a Civil-commitment-style Determination?

If a criminal conviction constitutes an impediment to treating protective measure as a civil intervention, why not take the further step of making the entire proceeding a noncriminal matter? One might replace the criminal conviction with a civil determination that the person has committed a dangerous act and constitutes a risk to the public. A precedent for such a proceeding would be the existing procedure for civil commitment of the mentally ill.

In this approach, two requirements would need to be met in order to warrant the imposition of custody as a protection measure. The first would be one of risk, as with the existing Dutch measures: that the person is a persistent offender and likely to reoffend. The second feature would be that, in a newly established civil proceeding, the person is found to have actually committed one or more criminal acts. This would replace the existing requirement of conviction of a crime. It would, however, serve an important function of the latter requirement, namely, ensuring that the person has actually done harm before he loses his liberty on grounds of risk. Someone could not be confined on the basis of mere surmise that he might do injury in the future, unless he has confirmed that surmise by having actually perpetrated (and been proven to have committed) acts that ordinarily would be criminal. However, the character of this proceeding would be civil: there would be no conviction, and thus no formal censure or other indicia of a criminal trial or conviction. By thus dispensing with the conviction, this approach would obviate the objections raised earlier: because the entire proceeding, including the initial commitment, would be civil, there would be no inconsistency between the grounds for the initial judgment against the person and the character of the sanction imposed upon him.

Would such an approach rescue the measures scheme? I think not. To explain why not, we might begin by pointing to the scheme's continued artificiality. Ordinarily there is a substantive difference between the kinds of cases dealt with by criminal law and by civil commitment. Criminal law deals paradigmatically with prohibited and wrongful acts. Civil commitment deals with behavior that is harmful, but not wrongful. In the case of civil commitment of the mentally disabled, the actor's mental condition precludes responsibility, and hence penal censure. With measures restructured as just suggested, however, there would no longer be such a difference. The acts that give rise to the proposed "civil" commitment procedure are ones that criminal law would be quite capable of addressing; that is, harmful and prohibited acts, culpably committed. That procedure would be resorted to—irrespective of the character of the underlying conduct—simply because it would attract the right labels and hence yield a preferred civil sanction exempt from the constraints of desert proportionality. The "definitional stop," of which de Keijser (2011) speaks, remains with us.

Beyond this matter of inconsistency, there lies a basic substantive objection to depriving a competent person of his liberty on the basis of such a purportedly noncriminal mode of proceeding. That objection is a fundamental one: the approach fails to recognize the person as a moral agent. Through conviction and punishment, the criminal law conveys a censuring message to the actor and to other members of the public that the behavior is wrongful and disapproved. Such a condemnatory sanction thus treats its addressees as *persons*, capable of understanding and of reflecting upon the wrongfulness of their actions (von Hirsch and Ashworth 2005, chap. 2). However, the scheme of which we are speaking here—where there would be a wholly noncriminal commitment proceeding—eliminates this vital element of penal censure. It thus fails to accord the person the status of a moral agent. This would treat him much like a dangerous beast, which must be restrained from doing harm because it lacks the requisite capacities for agency.

There is yet another objection: if the entire proceeding is purportedly civil and non-condemnatory, it could no longer recognize the wrongfulness of the conduct as the criminal law's censuring response can. This means that response could not acknowledge to victims or potential victims the culpable injury that the conduct involves. It also would involve abandoning the aspiration that the sanction provides a public valuation of norm-violating interactions among citizens (see von Hirsch and Ashworth 2005, pp. 27–33).[15]

Responding to these arguments would not be easy. Simply stating a preference for a utilitarian sentencing model based on incapacitative aims—as James Q. Wilson (1983, chap. 8) has advocated—would not succeed, as that could not explain why the normal sentence should observe desert proportionality principles rather than being purely crime preventive in character. Arguing, as Bottoms and Brownsword (1983) have done, that crime prevention is of a greater urgency in cases of serious prospective criminality, would not help because their model would create a much stronger presumption against deviating from desert constraints than this revised version of the Dutch protective measures approach would utilize. It is difficult, in my view at least, to envision a convincing rationale for a model that utilizes desert principles ordinarily, but resorts so easily to a noncriminal mode of intervention.

The foregoing critique of the Netherlands's protection measures approach illustrates a point that I made earlier in this essay: the importance of the criminal law context. The Dutch model treats the dispositional phase in the criminal proceeding—namely, the choice between a criminal sentence and a noncriminal measure—as being wholly separate from its antecedents of the criminal proceeding and conviction. That surely is problematic. If the protection measure is preceded by a criminal conviction, the meaning of the criminal conviction as a censuring judgment must be borne in mind, so that the post-conviction response ought also reflect that prior judgment concerning the wrongfulness of the conduct. This would call seriously into question the appropriateness of having the conviction be followed by a supposed civil remedy, which purportedly involves no censure at all. If, however, the criminal conviction were to be replaced by a civil proceeding, however, then it must be asked whether this treats the defendant properly as a rational agent, capable of evaluating the wrongfulness of his conduct. These phases of the process cannot be separated into watertight compartments.

III. PUBLIC ANXIETY AS GROUNDS FOR PENAL INTERVENTION: THE FEAR PREVENTION THEORY

Let me proceed, next, to another, more unusual conception that I shall term the "fear prevention" theory. It is discussed (and also criticized) by Peter Ramsay (2011). The theory accepts (indeed, embraces) the idea of deserved punishment, but drastically alters notions of what could be deserved. The perspective calls into question our basic normative assumptions about what conduct may properly be prohibited through criminal law.

A. Alleviating Public Anxiety: A Sketch of the Fear Prevention Theory

The fear prevention theory, Ramsay notes, was articulated a decade ago by a senior English judge, Lord Steyn, who asserted that "the aim of the criminal law is to permit everyone to go about their daily lives *without fear* of harm to person or property."[16]

This fear prevention perspective, Ramsay suggests, can be seen as reflecting Anthony Giddens's (1991) view of "ontological security" as a precondition of a good life. The latter conception consists of trust in the predictability and safety of ordinary existence, without which citizens would be beset by enervating anxiety. Fear of crime therefore has the capacity to undermine ontological security by increasing people's sense of vulnerability to the apparent hostility of others; it is corrosive of the conditions maintaining a secure sense of the self. Freedom of fear from crime, the argument continues, becomes a "major citizenship right": each person has an obligation not to cause fear in other citizens, and causing fear is a wrong in itself. Moreover, any person who does instill fear in others has the obligation to provide positive acts of reassurance. The upshot is of this reasoning, as Ramsay describes it, is dramatic:

> From this point of view there is no right to be perceived as dangerous. On the contrary, in so far as it results in the fear of crime, to be perceived as dangerous is a wrong against others' citizenship rights, and this justifies control or punishment. This is a wrong against security interests that is independent of the criminal violation of someone else's protected interest. . . . To avoid liability to punishment for this independent wrong the citizen must maintain an awareness of others' security needs, and reassure them where her own actions might give other citizens cause to fear. In this way they fulfill their responsibility to ensure social cohesion and enjoy the rights of citizenship. (Ramsay 2011)

The grounds for punishment, according to this account, need no longer be the harm the actor does or the risks he creates and can be held responsible for. It could depend, instead, on the anxiety his presence generates, irrespective of the factual basis of those fears or his degree of moral responsibility.

B. Threats versus Causing Fear

Fear is one of a variety of emotional states that may be triggered by others' behavior, by natural events, or by the person's own psychological makeup. Other such emotional responses include anger, loathing, and the like. All can affect the quality of people's lives. Emotions of fear, however, need to be submitted to rational and moral critiques. Such feelings may be a reasonable response to the person's actual situation, but they are not always so. Consider the fear of other persons encountered on the street. This reaction sometimes may be justified by the circumstances, but sometimes not. A person making threatening gestures is someone legitimately to be feared. An apparently well-behaved individual sharing the street, however, does not provide any such reasonable basis for anxiety, and that holds even if he does in fact elicit fear by his presence.

To put the fear prevention theory and its difficulties into perspective, it is instructive to look briefly at how threats traditionally have been treated in criminal law and contrast that with the fear prevention theory. Consider, for this purpose, the offense of robbery. Germany's criminal law succinctly describes the elements of this offense: a person commits robbery if he deprives someone of his personal property through threat of serious physical harm.[17] The victim must be intimidated or he will not hand the property over. However, a number of important limitations are included in the prohibition. First, legally protected interests of the person must be at stake: he must lose an item of his property (e.g., his wallet or her purse), and his physical integrity must also be threatened. He faces, in other words, much more than just being made afraid. Second, the threat must emanate from the perpetrator; it is not enough that *someone* scares the victim. Third, the perpetrator must act with the requisite culpability—for example, he must intend to extort money from the victim.[18] If the victim walks in a bad neighborhood where a large and fierce-looking man politely requests cash from him and he hands it over out of fear, that is not a robbery—and should not be deemed a crime.

The fear prevention theory works differently, and operates without such safeguards. It would seem to suffice for the conduct to generate fear. To illustrate, consider the case of a group of rough-looking young men congregating in a public space. This may well produce anxiety in others wishing also to make use of the space. That could, according to the fear prevention theory, warrant prohibiting these youths from so conducting themselves. Indeed, English "antisocial behavior order" (ASBO) legislation permits the issuance of a civil order restricting access to a public space by persons who cause distress to others—with substantial sentences of imprisonment for violations of such orders.[19] Such legislation could be supported by the fear prevention theory, as Ramsay (2011) has pointed out.

With such a legal response to behavior causing public anxiety, the above-mentioned protections of criminal law would disappear. First, no overt threat by the persons targeted by the prohibition would necessarily be required. The putative fearful victim need not be confronted with any actual or threatened intrusion upon his physical integrity, property, or any resource or interest of his which the law ordinarily would protect. It would suffice that he has been made fearful. Second, the supposed offender's behavior would not have to be reprehensible: for example, he need not have tried to intimidate anyone. His mere presence in the space (if under circumstances that inspire fear in others) seemingly could suffice. Third, and perhaps most troublesome, the person or persons facing the state's sanctions need not have been the source of the putative victim's anxiety. If the victim's sense of the threatening character of young men congregating in public spaces derives not from the behavior of these particular individuals, but from other sources (the behavior of other youths on other occasions, neighborhood gossip, media reports, and the like), that would not matter, so long as the victim has been made to feel apprehensive.[20]

The fear prevention theory, moreover, is manifestly vulnerable to stereotyping. To the extent that a given type of person seems scary to others, it would be the fear that matters—and criminal policy may be guided by it. This is made all the more worrisome by the criminal justice authorities' own contributions to the negative stereotypes. With the ASBO program, for example, the English authorities' own lurid depictions of "neighbours from hell" and their supposed depredations appear to have significantly contributed to public anxieties about so-called antisocial behavior and its perpetrators (Burney 2006).

C. Can Protection from Fear Itself Be an Interest?

An actor's conduct, to be criminally proscribed, ordinarily should involve doing or risking harm to others; it should not suffice that other persons merely fear he might do harm. These risks must be to the victim's interests (e.g., to resources to which he should be entitled).[21] The apprehension generated when those interests are threatened may be considered in deciding the appropriateness of prohibiting the conduct, but not apprehension or fear per se, regardless of the source.

However, might not prevention of fear itself be deemed an interest that criminal law should defend? If "ontological security," including freedom from fear, is essential to a good life, as Giddens suggests, then perhaps this should be deemed a vital interest, just as much as the interests traditionally protected by criminal law, such as health, property, and the like. If taking someone's property is punishable because it infringes an important interest, so arguably should be compromising his sense of security. Although freedom from fear has not traditionally been recognized as within the ambit of the harm principle, proponents of the fear prevention theory might contend that it should be.

The harm principle, however, has among its most important aims that of safeguarding the freedom of the actor himself (Simester and von Hirsch 2011, chaps. 3–4). It ensures that only specified resources of other persons ought ordinarily be protected by the criminal law. The principle permits the punishment of intrusions upon others' personal safety, property, and the like, but this still provides room for the actor's own autonomy because it restricts the scope of punishable conduct. He may be punished if he steals the victim's property or threatens to injure him; but not just *any* way of frustrating the latter's preferences or eliciting his anxieties may be deemed a punishable harm. The harm principle also protects the actor's autonomy because it keeps punishable acts within his control: the harms or risks must be those that derive from his chosen conduct, and not chiefly from the victim's attitudes.

Treating fear prevention as an interest per se, however, could legitimize intervention of a far wider scope. What generates fear may be proscribed. Unlike traditional interests such as property or physical safety that are restricted in nature, fear itself is not limited to the anxiety that wrongful invasion of or threat to someone's legally protected personal resources would generate. Criminalization of wide ambit—what scares people—could be the theory's result.

The fear prevention theory, indeed, seems to presuppose a two-tier social order. There is ourselves, *us* the self-styled decent law-abiding citizens, who should be protected from anxieties that may affect the quality of our lives. And there is *them*, those of whom we are fearful, whose options and choices are to be drastically curtailed in order to alleviate our anxieties. The impact of doing so on *their* lives and liberties is thought to be a matter of little concern.

D. The Obligation to Provide "Reassurance"

Yet another troublesome feature of the fear prevention theory is its notion of "reassurance," that the offender who inspires fear in others has an obligation to try to make them feel less afraid. Under a desert rationale, the offender's future behavior—for example, his likelihood of reoffending—has little or no role to play; what matters is the seriousness of his present conviction offense. Under the traditional predictive-rehabilitative ethic, risk of reoffending is given a somewhat greater role. A convicted offender, if deemed a potential recidivist, may be called upon (often, through probation supervision) to take steps to diminish his likelihood of returning to crime. But what ultimately still matters, however, is his degree of likelihood of endangering others. The criterion is thus a substantive one of risk, not of anxiety per se.

Under the fear prevention theory, however, the focus shifts away from risk to anxiety. Reassurance, therefore, would no longer necessarily involve only the person taking steps to reduce his likelihood of offending, but rather his trying to take steps to reduce others' apprehensions about his behavior. The issue would become whether those who fear the person could subjectively be induced to be less afraid. One might well wonder how criminal defendants and ASBO recipients could go about providing such reassurance. So long as such a person is in custody, he can do very little to change others' attitudes toward him. And even if he is undergoing a noncustodial sentence, there may be little he can he do to make others less fearful—especially because that depends so much on other people's perceptions of what he might do.

What ultimately is so worrisome about this reassurance approach is its dependence on other persons' attitudes rather than on the actor's own choices. In desert theory, the sanction depends on the person's chosen conduct when he offends: on the foreseeable harmfulness of his conduct and on the degree of his culpability when he makes that choice. In the rehabilitative ethic, his subsequent conduct matters also, that is, his decision whether or not to reoffend. But it is still *his* choice that matters, not someone else's attitudes. Under the fear prevention theory, however, the emphasis shifts to the feelings and attitudes of other persons—on how fearful they are, and how reassured they might (or might not) feel by any efforts on the offender's part to make amends.

How does the fear prevention conception compare with the Dutch measures approach discussed earlier? With the Dutch scheme, the intervention would be triggered by a criminal conviction, but disregard the censuring implications; the sanction itself would be a civil and purely crime preventive response. The fear prevention theory is, if anything, still more problematic, notwithstanding that it purports to rely on *punishing* those who inspire fear. It would pay scant heed to the character and degree of blameworthiness of the actor's criminal choices. Instead, the theory emphasizes matters largely outside his control—the emotions and anxieties his presence elicits. This would not only infringe the desert constraints that, I have suggested, derive from the criminal law's role as a censuring institution. It would also violate fundamental rule-of-law concerns that, at least for competent actors, the state's intervention should rest on the person's own wrongful choices, not on other persons' attitudes over which he may have no control.

IV. CONCLUDING OBSERVATIONS

In this essay I have suggested that the criminal law context has a vital bearing on the choice of sanctioning theory. Why so? It is because of the special character of criminal prohibitions.

The criminal law has an important preventive element, in that it seeks to induce potential offenders to desist by threatening them with unfavorable legal consequences. However, our legal system makes use of a variety of other kinds of disincentives (consider higher taxes on alcohol and tobacco). What, then, makes criminal law special? It is that its threats are morally loaded. Because punishment connotes reproof or censure, a criminal prohibition also embodies a public moral appeal, that people ought to desist in *virtue of the conduct's wrongfulness*. The message conveyed through the prohibition is that the behavior is reprehensible, and that the person should consider its wrongfulness (and not just the unpleasant consequences) as a reason to desist. The criminal law expresses blame in its very design.[22]

If reproof is built into the meaning of criminal prohibitions, then it is a plausible inference that their censuring character be borne in mind when the next phase of the criminal process is considered—namely, the sentencing phase. That helps explain why modern accounts of the desert model's rationale have tended to be communicative in character. It is because of the criminal sanction's character of conveying blame, arguably, that penalties should be scaled according to the blameworthiness of the criminal conduct. The desert model thus relies upon a rather simple inference from the character of criminal proscriptions as normative appeals. Perhaps, this may help account for the survival, over the past four decades, of desert-based conceptions of punishment.

What of the alternative models? Some of them (such as the fear prevention theory) seek a shift in the standards of criminal liability, so that they rely less on factors within the actor's control and more on others' attitudes or feelings toward him. That, however, poses the question of how such a watering down of notions of wrongdoing and personal responsibility can square with the criminal prohibitions' central censuring role. Others (such as the Dutch dual-track model) involve a change at the sanctioning stage, toward ostensibly "neutral" sanctions that permit escape from the requirements of proportionality. But can such a shift be consistent with the morally loaded implications of criminal prohibition and conviction of crime? How can it treat offenders as moral agents? How can it testify to the recognition of the wrongfulness of much criminal conduct?

I shall not venture any prediction on how long the desert model may survive as an influential sanctioning conception. And I certainly cannot make any confident prediction of what alternative model or models, if any, might replace it. But I do think such questions as these bear thinking about, and will not be so easy to answer.

ACKNOWLEDGMENT
I am greatly indebted to the critical suggestions of Michael Tonry, Jan de Keijser, Peter Ramsay, Andrew Simester, Vivian Schorscher, and Alexander Hevelke.

NOTES
1. The author has published much of his previous English-language writings under his anglicized name, Andrew von Hirsch.
2. See, e.g., Ashworth (1983), Schünemann (1985), Duff (1986, 2001), von Hirsch (1993), Hörnle (1999), and von Hirsch and Ashworth (2005).
3. See von Hirsch (1993, chap. 2).
4. For analysis and comparison of the Minnesota and Oregon guidelines, see von Hirsch (1995). Some years after Oregon's guidelines were adopted, a conservative governor secured enactment of drastic mandatory minimum sentences that restricted the guidelines' applicability. The Minnesota guidelines, however, continue in operation.

5. Criminal Justice Act 2003; see von Hirsch and Roberts (2004).
6. These scholars include Antony Duff, Andrew Ashworth, John Kleinig, Douglas Husak, Anthony Bottoms, Julian V. Roberts, Martin Wasik, Anthony Doob, Nils Jareborg, Petter Asp, Magnus Ulväng, Bernd Schünemann, Tatjana Hörnle, and Tapio Lappi-Seppälä.
7. For a critique and analysis of mandatory minimum sentences, see Tonry (1996, chap. 5); von Hirsch and Ashworth (2005, chap. 6).
8. For a description and critique of California's three-strikes law, see Zimring, Hawkins, and Kamin (2001).
9. For example, recent Canadian and New Zealand legislation, referred to above.
10. For an extensive debate on this issue, see Roberts and von Hirsch (2010).
11. See, e.g., von Hirsch, Knapp, and Tonry (1987, p. 100).
12. For a discussion of the relative merits of numerical sentencing guidelines versus guidance through statutory general principles, see von Hirsch, Knapp, and Tonry (1987, chap. 3).
13. The Dutch measures to which I refer in the text concern so-called ISD (*Instelling Stelselmatige Daders*) protective measures, authorized in the penal code since 2004. These concern persistent property offenders, those having extensive records for such crimes as shoplifting, vandalism, and theft from cars. Where the offender qualifies under this statute, he would ordinarily be convicted for his most recent offense, but then be committed to custody through the mechanism of a "measure," for a period that may well exceed his deserved punishment for the offense. The commitment may involve treatment if he is considered amenable; but if he is thought untreatable, the intervention could be purely incapacitative.
14. This is the basis for invoking ISD measures.
15. See also, Simester and von Hirsch (2011, chap. 1).
16. The statement was made in a different legal context, concerning the admissibility of illegally obtained evidence. Attorney General's Reference (No. 3 od 1999), [2001] 2 WLR 56 at 63.
17. German penal code §249.
18. Notice, however, that the defendant's personal culpability is not enough, he needs to have committed a wrong. Thus it would not suffice for the actor to know he is scaring the victim—unless he is *threatening* him (in the case of the robbery prohibition, threatening him with bodily harm).
19. For a critique of this kind of legislation, see Simester and von Hirsch (2011, chap. 12).
20. This point is reinforced by recent survey research suggesting that much offensive behavior deemed most threatening by the public does not involve personal confrontation at all—for example, car revving and graffiti (see Bottoms 2006).
21. See Simester and von Hirsch (2011, chaps. 3–5).
22. For a more complete discussion of these two features of criminal prohibitions, see Simester and von Hirsch (2010, chap. 1).

REFERENCES

Allen, Francis A. 1981. *The Decline of the Rehabilitative Ideal: Penal Policy and Social Purpose.* New Haven, CT: Yale University Press.

Ashworth, Andrew. 1983. *Sentencing and Penal Policy.* London: Weidenfeld and Nicholson.

———. 2010. *Sentencing and Criminal Justice*, 5th ed. Cambridge: Cambridge University Press.

Bottoms, Anthony E. 2006. "Incivilities, Offense and Social Order in Residential Communities." In *Incivilities: Regulating Offensive Behavior*, ed. Andrew von Hirsch and Andrew P. Simester. Oxford: Hart.

Bottoms, Anthony E., and R. Brownsword. 1983. "Dangerousness and Rights." In *Dangerousness: Problems of Assessment and Prediction*, ed. J. W. Hinton. London: George Allen and Unwin.

Bottoms, Anthony E., and Andrew von Hirsch. 2010. "The Crime-Preventive Impact of Penal Sanctions." In *The Oxford Handbook of Empirical Legal Research*, ed. Peter Cane and Herbert Kritzer. Oxford: Oxford University Press.

Burney, Elizabeth. 2006. "No Spitting: Regulation of Offensive Behavior in England and Wales." In *Incivilities: Regulating Offensive Behaviour*, ed. Andrew von Hirsch and Andrew P. Simester. Oxford: Hart.

de Keijser, Jan. 2011. "Never Mind the Pain; It's a Measure! Justifying Measures as Part of the Dutch Bifurcated System of Sanctions." In *Retributivism Has a Past. Has It a Future?*, ed. Michael Tonry. New York: Oxford University Press.

Donohue, John J. 2007. "Economic Models of Crime and Punishment." *Social Research* 74(2):379–412.

Duff, R. A. 1986. *Trials and Punishments*. Cambridge: Cambridge University Press.

———. 2001. *Punishment, Communication and Community*. Oxford: Oxford University Press.

Frase, Richard. 2004. "Limiting Retributivism." In *The Future of Imprisonment*, ed. Michael Tonry. New York: Oxford University Press.

Giddens, Anthony. 1991. *Modernity and Self-Identity*. Cambridge: Polity Press.

Hörnle, Tatjana. 1999. *Tatproportionale Strafzumessung*. Berlin: Duncker and Humblot.

Jareborg, Nils. 1995. "The Swedish Sentencing Reform." In *The Politics of Sentencing Reform*, ed. C. M. V. Clarkson and R. Morgan. Oxford: Oxford University Press.

Kleinig, John. 1973. *Punishment and Desert*. The Hague: Martinus Nijhoff.

Lappi-Seppälä, Tapio. 2002. "The Principle of Proportionality in the Finnish Sentencing System." In *Flores Juris et Legum*, ed. P. Asp, C. E. Herlitz, and S. L. Holmqvist. Uppsala: Iustus Förlag.

Morris, Norval. 1976. *Punishment, Desert, and Rehabilitation*. Washington, DC: U.S. Government Printing Office.

Ramsay, Peter. 2011. "A Political Theory of Imprisonment for Public Protection." In *Retributivism Has a Past. Has It a Future?*, ed. Michael Tonry. New York: Oxford University Press.

Roberts, Julian. 2003. "An Analysis of the Statutory Statement of Purposes and Principles of Sentencing in New Zealand." *Australia and New Zealand Journal of Criminology* 363:249–71.

Roberts, Julian, and Andrew von Hirsch, eds. 2010. *Previous Convictions at Sentencing: Theoretical and Applied Perspectives*. Oxford: Hart.

Schünemann, Bernd. 1985. "Pläydoer für eine neue Theorie der Strafzumessung." In *Neue Tendenzen der Kriminalpolitik*, ed. A. Eser and K. Cornils. Freiburg: Max Planck Institut für internationales und ausländisches Strafrecht.

Sellin, Thorsten, and Marvin Wolfgang. 1964. *The Measurement of Delinquency*. New York: John Wiley.

Simester, Andrew P., and Andrew von Hirsch. 2011. *Crimes, Harms and Wrongs: On the Principles of Criminalisation*. Oxford: Hart.

Tonry, Michael. 1996. *Sentencing Matters*. New York: Oxford University Press.

———. 1997. *Intermediate Sanctions in Sentencing Guidelines*. Washington, DC: National Institute of Justice.

———. 2005. "Obsolescence and Immanence in Penal Theory and Policy." *Columbia Law Review* 105:1233–75.

———. 2007. "Looking Back to See the Future of Punishment in America." *Social Research* 74(2):353–78.

von Hirsch, Andrew. 1976. *Doing Justice: The Choice of Punishments*. New York: Hill and Wang (reprinted 1986, Boston, Northeastern University Press).

———. 1985. *Past or Future Crimes: Deservedness and Dangerousness in the Sentencing of Criminals*. New Brunswick, NJ: Rutgers University Press.

———. 1993. *Censure and Sanctions*. Oxford: Oxford University Press.

————. 1995. "Proportionality and Parsimony in American Sentencing Guidelines: The Minnesota and Oregon Standards." In *The Politics of Sentencing Reform*, ed. C. M. V. Clarkson and R. Morgan. Oxford: Oxford University Press.

von Hirsch, Andrew, and Andrew Ashworth. 2005. *Proportionate Sentencing: Exploring the Principles.* Oxford: Oxford University Press.

von Hirsch, Andrew, Kay A. Knapp, and Michael Tonry. 1987. *The Sentencing Commission and its Guidelines.* Boston: Northeastern University Press.

von Hirsch, Andrew, and Julian Roberts. 2004. "Legislating Sentencing Principles: The Provisions of the Criminal Justice Act 2003 Relating to Sentencing Purposes and the Role of Previous Convictions." *Criminal Law Review* 2004:649–52.

Wilson, James Q. 1983. *Thinking About Crime*, rev. ed. New York: Basic Books.

Zimring, Franklin E., Gordon Hawkins, and Sam Kamin. 2001. *Punishment and Democracy: Three Strikes and You're Out in California.* New York: Oxford University Press.

INDEX

abolitionism, 65, 66, 67, 70, 71, 77, 81nn2,
    6, 7, 189, 206
    radical, 68, 69
Adler, Mortimer, 8, 164n1
act and omission, doctrine of, 99n7
Alldridge, Peter, 253n18
Allen, Francis A., 5
Alschuler, Albert, 9
Altmire, Congressman Jason, 165n10
American Law Institute, 7, 8, 23
anchor theory
    See punishment, anchor theory
Anglin, M. Douglas, 231n30
anticonsequentialism, 64
antisocial behavior orders, 24n15
apology
    See reparation
Arneson, Richard J., 61n36
Aristotle, 164n1
Ashworth, Andrew J., 12, 35, 36, 82n27,
    107, 123n10, 130, 132, 133, 139,
    152n26, 179, 180, 185, 206, 262,
    271n2, 272nn6, 7
Asp, Petter, 6, 272n6
Australia, 9, 18, 19
    perception of lenient sentencing in,
        102
    public knowledge of custody issues in,
        108
Australian Law Reform Commission, 23n9

Bagaric, M., 106, 107
bail hearings, 104
Bean, Philip, 252nn12, 13
Beccaria, Cesare, 6, 23n7, 163
Bedau, Hugo Adam, 55
"because it is believed", 81n10
behaviors, blaming, 55, 60n31

Belgium
    perception of lenient sentencing in, 102
benefits-and-burdens theories, 8
Benn, Stanley, 47
Bentham, Jeremy, 3, 4, 6, 20, 22n1, 39, 89,
    91, 125n29, 151n21, 163, 230n7
Bergelson, V., 82n18
Berk, 124n19
Bianchi, H., 81nn7, 9, 189
Blair, Tony, 5, 14, 22n3, 143
blame, 15, 49, 54, 82n17, 110, 112, 113,
    119, 124n20, 143, 174, 199, 225,
    230n9, 241, 256, 261, 271
    See also blameworthiness; guilt and blame
blameworthiness, moral, 15, 19, 103, 107,
    112, 117, 118, 122, 123n10, 157,
    158, 163, 190, 193, 261, 270, 271
Blumenson, Eric, 183
Blunkett, David, 22n3
Boonin, David, 58n3
boot camps, 22n5
Borradori, G.,
    Philosophy in a Time of Terror, 165n3
Bottoms, Anthony, 125n30, 181, 262, 266,
    272n6
Bowers, Josh, 224, 225, 231n21, 243
Braithwaite, John, 14, 131, 137, 138, 139,
    140, 151n11
    Crime, Shame, and Reintegration, 14
    republican penal theory, 131, 137–140
Bronsteen, John, 60n26
Brown, Lord, 134
    See also Secretary of State for Justice v. James
Brownsword, Roger, 181, 262, 266
Buccafusco, Christopher, 60n26
Burgess, Anthony, 5
burglary, domestic, 115, 116, 170, 184, 248
Burke, Edmund, 141

Buruma, Ybo, 206
Bush, President George H. W., 231n22
Bush, President George W., 217
Bush, Noelle, 217

California, 11, 13, 22n4, 23n7, 37, 252n9
  State Constitution, 179
  three-strikes laws, 250, 253n24
calling to account, 72–77
  suffering and, 73
Canada, 9, 21, 108, 181, 185
  desert-oriented sentencing aims, 257
  perception of lenient sentencing in, 102
  proportionate sentencing schemes in,
    272n9
  public knowledge of custody issues in,
    108
Canadian Sentencing Commission, 23n9
capital punishment, 9, 11, 21, 112, 182
censure, 34, 36, 37, 40, 49, 54, 55, 56, 77,
    78, 80, 104, 110, 112, 113–114,
    117, 119, 120, 122, 235, 237, 239,
    248, 256, 259, 261, 263, 264, 265,
    266, 271
  disparity in, 256
  penal, 265
CHANGE program, 82n26
Christie, N., 74, 81n7
Clarke, Charles, 22n3
Coalition government
  See England
coercive treatment
  See treatment, coercive
combatants, unlawful, 67
Common Law jurisdictions, 15
common sense, 58n4
community service, 16, 190, 236, 238, 248
compensation, 56, 60n30, 61n38, 73, 77, 78,
    179, 185, 192, 202
  order, 192
competing rights, 170, 178, 181, 183, 185,
    186, 260
condemnation of crime, 77
confinement, 12
  See also detention; imprisonment; incar-
    ceration
consequentialism, 3, 4, 6–10, 11, 13, 19, 20,
    23nn6, 7, 12, 30, 31, 32, 38, 43n2,
    47, 48, 49, 54, 63, 66, 88, 91, 94, 97,
    98, 99, 99nn1, 7, 105, 110, 111, 112,
    122, 132, 137, 146, 150n4, 160,

    197, 201, 203, 204, 205, 216, 228,
    229, 236, 261, 264
anticonsequentialism, 31
  criticisms of, 31
  decline of, 31, 86
  desert-adjusted, 87
  nonconsequentialist, 64, 65, 160, 169,
    170, 186
  post-consequentialist era, 35
  pure, 65
  "side-constrained" model, 64, 65, 67
consistency in process, 17–18
Constant, Benjamin, 150
constitutional order
  exceptional, 145–146
  normal, 145–146
contributory negligence, 75
  See also responsibility
control of threats, 148
conviction of crime, 11, 12, 67, 68, 76, 77,
    78, 149, 175, 257, 261, 262, 263,
    264, 270, 271
  drug, 224, 251
  prior, 11, 12, 13, 16, 18, 19, 102, 103,
    106, 118–119, 124, 125n22, 170,
    237, 258, 269
  postconviction of drug-related crime, 217
  rates of, 38
  replaced with civil determination,
    264–266
  resulting in a sanction, in the Nether-
    lands, 197
  under three-strikes law, 257
  wrongful, 143, 175, 176
Cooke, D. J., 208
Corrado, M. L., 208n46
correctional treatment programs, 3, 5, 9,
    10, 22
Cottingham, John, 43
courts
  alternative, 215
  appeals, 125n31
  becoming more punitive, 101
  criminal, 18, 68, 82, 165n11
  drug
    See drug courts
  in England and Wales, 124, 134, 145
  in the Netherlands, 188, 191, 194, 196,
    201, 203, 204, 207n22
  inner-city, 17
  juvenile, 7

prioritizing defendant rights, 180
problem-solving, 5, 9, 18, 217, 249
  deferred prosecution, 217
  post-conviction, 217
public criticism of, 102, 103, 107, 111,
  118, 122, 123, 124n21
rights conflicts in, 181, 185
rural, 16, 17
sentencing practices of, 103
specialty, 67, 215–216, 218, 221, 229
traditional, 215, 225–229
urban, 16
crime, 56, 94–97
and calling to account, 72–77
and punishment, 6, 7, 8, 20, 21, 22n2,
  24n18, 34, 35, 36, 49, 63, 65, 66, 80,
  92, 94, 108
  burdensome, 60, 66, 67, 69, 77, 78, 79,
    80, 82n25, 245, 257
anchor problem, 93–94
and responsibility, 72–77, 82n18
as a symptom of mental disorder, 69
censure of, 34, 36, 37,40, 49, 54, 55, 56,
  77, 78, 80, 93, 104, 110, 112–114,
  117, 119, 120, 122, 235, 237, 239,
  248, 256, 259, 261, 263, 264, 265,
  266, 271
committed by minorities, 114
competing rights, 170, 178, 179–186,
  260
control of, 111, 112, 121, 158, 169, 173,
  236
decline in, 159
drug, 11, 248
fear of, 134–143, 148, 155, 156, 159
gang-related, 39
gun, 9
harm and, 6, 10, 15, 38, 39, 61nn34, 38,
  56, 61nn34, 38, 67, 68, 69–77, 78,
  79, 81n12, 82n15, 92, 95, 96, 103,
  109, 113, 115, 116, 117, 123nn5, 7,
  8, 10, 125n23, 131, 134, 138, 144,
  149, 151n23, 158, 160, 161, 162,
  163, 165nn7, 10, 173, 174, 175,
  176, 181, 183, 184, 185, 186, 188,
  191, 192, 193, 202, 208n29, 219,
  226, 227, 228, 229, 231n27, 240,
  246, 247, 252nn5, 7, 253n17, 257,
  263, 265, 266, 267, 268, 269, 270,
  272n18
hate-motivated, 116

LWOP laws in response to, 4, 5, 9, 10,
  11–12, 21, 169, 170, 177, 178, 183,
  184, 185
mixed theory of response to, 34–36, 66
nonserious, 175, 176
obligatory crime objection, 95, 96, 97,
  98, 99n6
offender's response to, 82n26
organized, 5, 192, 207n12
policy makers who are tough on, 5, 22n3,
  37
premeditation of, 119, 124n21
prevention of, 5, 13, 54, 64, 67, 69, 86,
  93, 130–266, 172–173, 175, 183
property, 4, 5, 9, 12, 17, 50, 59n17, 71,
  134, 182, 240, 247, 248, 253n20,
  266, 267, 268, 269, 272n13
protection of potential victims, 179–186
public reaction to, 124nn17, 18
rank order of, 163, 166nn16, 17
reduction of, 36, 64
refraining from, 65
reparation for, 77, 78, 79, 80, 192, 236, 248
rights of victims, 179–186, 249
severe sentencing for, 165n9, 169–186
seriousness of, 7, 11, 13, 104, 105, 114,
  115–117, 121, 122, 124nn17, 18,
  133, 163, 165n7, 169–186, 193
ranking of, 36, 163, 166n16, 214
suffering and, 65, 99n5
terror and, 155–166
three-strikes legislation in response to, 37
using out-dated methods to fight, 5
victims and culpability of crime, 124n20
violent and sexual, 11, 17
vulnerability to, 148
wave, 165n8, 165n8
"war" against, 67, 159
wrongdoing, 57, 58
wrongs and, 69–72, 78
See also imprisonment for public protection (IPP)
Crime, Shame, and Reintegration
  See Braithwaite, John
Criminal Justice Act (CJA), 131, 133, 206,
  272n5
criminals, 58, 87, 90, 99, 139, 159, 172, 173,
  174, 225, 252n5, 258
habitual, 202, 262
rights of, 108
culpability, 15, 38, 92, 103, 104, 112, 115,

culpability (*continued*)
117, 118, 119, 121, 122, 123nn5,
7, 8, 10, 124n20, 158, 163, 165n7,
174, 188, 189, 190, 191, 193, 199,
200, 202, 219, 226, 227, 257, 268,
270, 272n18
mens rea, 174
custody, 132, 198, 208n27, 264, 270,
272n13
as a protection measure, 264
rates, 108

dangerous offender laws
See sentencing laws, dangerous offender
Darley, John, 111
Daube, David, 49
Davis, Kenneth Culp, 5, 90
David, M., 90
death penalty, 11–12, 20, 36, 38, 175, 182,
183, 185
See also sentencing laws
decision making,
concerning wrongdoing, 57
racially biased, 6
Declaration of the Rights of Man, 22
definitional stop, 198–200, 265
See also Hart, H. L. A.
de Keijser, Jan W., 81n8, 105, 123, 188–213,
206n2, 260, 261, 262, 265, 271
Dempsey, M. M., 82n19
deprivation
of liberty, 189, 192, 193, 194, 200, 202,
222, 263
of property rights, 59
or loss, 50
Dershowitz, Alan, 9
de Ruiter, C., 193, 207n15
desert, 34, 35, 36, 37, 40, 42, 43nn1, 2, 46,
47–48, 48–49, 124n19, 57, 58n7,
59n21, 60n23, 81n3, 106, 117,
124n181, 155–168, 220, 221, 223,
224, 225, 226, 228, 256–274
abandoning, 262
above-desert penalties, 169–187
and the Dutch criminal code, 190,
262–263
autonomy as a component of, 165n13
beginning of, 8, 9
citations mentioning, 165n2
deontological, 111, 157
disparity in, 220

empirical, 11, 110–111, 112, 114, 157,
158
hard treatment and, 47, 55
in Dutch law, 188, 189, 190, 191, 192,
193, 194, 197, 199, 200, 201, 202,
203–205, 206
institutional, 51, 52
judgments, 107
just deserts, 9, 23n9, 32–32, 36, 47, 160,
215, 228, 229
justice equated with, 165n5
kinds of, 50–53
model debate, 256–274
modified just deserts, 23
moral, 31, 32, 46, 165n7
negative, 91
normative, 157
penal, 64, 140
personal, 50, 59n20
post-desert, 30–45, 43
preinstitutional, 51, 52, 53–54
prejusticial, 33
punitive, 58n8
raw, 51, 52, 60n23
retributive, 58n4, 64, 66, 81n1
Rawlsian theory and, 31–32, 59n
10, 17
terror and, 158–162
See also, pain and suffering; utilitarianism, desert-adjusted
Desert Thesis, 33, 34, 35, 36, 37, 40, 42,
43n2
aggravation and, 117
mitigation and, 117
detention, 144, 159, 160, 190, 192
as punishment in Dutch law, 190
civil, 160
continued, 132
for reasons of public safety, 67
indefinite, 37, 67
nonpunitive, 159
of suspected terrorists, 160
preventive, 42, 131, 138, 139, 181, 202,
208n39
See also confinement; imprisonment;
incarceration
deterrence, 8, 9, 38, 47, 49, 54, 65, 121,
123n3, 169, 170, 175, 177, 179,
250, 258, 261, 262
measurable, 182
Dobash, R. E., 82n19

Dobash, R. P., 82n19
Doing justice, 65, 189, 205
Dölling, Dieter, 182
Dolovich, Sharon, 172, 174–177, 178
dominion, 137–140
Donner, J. P. H., 208n31
Doob, Anthony, 105, 272n6
Double effect, doctrine of, 99n7
DNA evidence, 151n10, 205
drug courts
    and more serious offenses, 246–248
    and public support, 215, 229, 230n4, 251
    argument against, 228–229, 231n21
    as communicative punishment, 238–248
    as secular penance, 240–242
    cognitive reorientation of new judges,
        252n11
    community-based supervision, 252n14
    decisions to enter, 252n15
    design of, 237–238, 260
    disease model, 252n8
    disparity in treatments, 252n16
    dual-track systems, 215, 216, 220–233
    eligibility for, 243–244, 250, 251
    graduation from, 238
    incarceration imposed by, 234, 242,
        245–246, 252nn12, 13, 14
    lack of data that prove that they work,
        219–220
    lack of care with due process rights, 220
    movement, 215–233, 234–255
    paternalism in, 252n10
    postadjudication, 251n1
    postplea, 251n1
    preplea, 251n1
    sanctions imposed by, 231n17, 234, 237,
        242
        bullying language used in, 244, 252n10
        graduated, 242, 243, 245
        moralistic rhetoric used in, 241,
            252n10
    seriousness of offenses, 226–227
drug laws
    decriminalization of, 228–229, 252n5
drugs, 214–233, 230nn12, 13, 231nn19, 20
    addiction to, 198, 240
    age of users, 253n19
    criminalizing use of, 252n5
    dealers of, 246–248
    harms and, 227
    kinds of, 252

illegal, 182, 249, 253n19
marijuana, use of, 252n6
mental illness and use of, 253n19
possession of, 227, 231n23, 245–246
prohibition of, 231n28
trafficking in, 178, 246–247, 252n7,
    253nn17, 18, 19
use of, 220, 221, 223, 225, 226, 228,
    214–233, 240, 241, 243
    associated with property offenders,
        253n20
    associated with violent offenders,
        253n20
"war on", 215, 224
See also drug courts
Dubber, M., 151n15
Duff, R. A., 4, 9, 33, 34, 43n6, 58, 63–85,
    107, 125n24, 151n14, 205, 208n24,
    209n45, 231n27, 234, 235, 239,
    242, 243, 244, 249, 250, 251n4,
    260, 271n2, 272n6
Dworkin, Ronald, 39, 60, 181

Edney, R., 106, 107
Edwards, Paul
    Encyclopedia of Philosophy, 47
Eliade, Mircea
    Encyclopedia of Religion, 58n5
Elffers, H., 105
England, 9, 12, 13, 18, 19, 31, 65, 123n1,
    150n3
    antisocial behavior order (ASBO),
        24n15, 151n10, 268, 270, 272n19
    bombings of July 2005, 151n19
    Coalition government, 132, 148, 149
    Criminal Justice Act (CJA), 131, 150nn5,
        6, 7, 8, 206, 272n5
    Criminal Records Bureau, 149, 152n30
    Dunblane massacre, 143
    Home Office, 23
    House of Lords, 134
    imprisonment for public protection
        (IPP), 130–154, 161, 206
    Independent Safeguarding Authority,
        149, 152n30
    James Bulger murder, 109, 143
    perception of courts being out of touch,
        102
    perception of lenient sentencing in, 102
    public knowledge of custody issues in,
        107

England (*continued*)
    New Ambitions for Our Country: A New Contract for Welfare, 136
    New Labour, 4, 5, 15, 135, 136, 141, 143
    report of Lord Auld, 124n12
    Safeguarding Vulnerable Groups Act, 148, 149
    Sentencing Advisory Panel, 120, 125nn26, 28
    Sentencing Council for England and Wales, 125nn26
    statutory guiding norms, 257
    tougher penal policies in, 108
    See also Wales
equity
    horizontal, 3, 16
    vertical, 3, 11, 12
Ericson, Richard, 149, 152n25
Etzioni, Amitai, 141
evidence
    clinical, 12
    DNA, 151n10
    illegally-obtained, 272n16
    victim-impact, 249
Ewing v. California, 22
execution
    See death penalty

fair play theory, 32, 33
fairness, 173
    and proportionality, 38–40, 42
    in sentencing, 36, 64, 66, 171, 181, 185, 256, 258
    procedural, 5
Farabee, David, 231n30
Farrington, David P., 230n11
fear, 164
    dominion and, 138, 139, 140
    freedom from, 140, 266–270
    harm and, 71, 134, 160
    instilling, 136, 141, 142, 143, 148, 155, 161
        as punishable, 140, 156, 162, 267, 269
        unintentional, 269
    no right to instill, 267
    of crime, 134, 135, 136, 146, 156, 159, 179, 183
    of detection, 71
    prevention model, 261, 266–270, 271
    reassurance, 269–270
    See also sentencing policies, fear-prevention model; threats

Fedorova, Oxana, 60n22
Feeley, M. M., 207n10
Feinberg, Joel, 8–9, 50, 51, 52, 55, 59n20, 60n31, 81n12, 82nn22, 24
    "Justice and Personal Desert", 50
Felonies, 7, 219, 237
Ferri, Enrico, 6
fines, 59
Finland, 13, 257
    statutory guiding principles for sentencing, 257
first offenders, 121, 125n22
flag burning, 116
Fletcher, G., 118, 165n14
    The Grammar of Criminal Law, 165n14
Floud, Jean, 133
Foot, Philippa, 61n36
forfeiture, 23
    argument, 10, 23
    degree of, 23
    of an immunity, 10
    of the right to proportionate punishment, 140, 141, 144
    theories, 23
France
    and the use of measures, 189
Frase, Richard S., 12, 169–187, 230n1, 259, 260
free speech, 165nn11, 12
free will, 46, 161, 174, 231n22
Freiberg, Arie, 10
French Revolution, 22n1

Gardner, John, 43n5, 124n20, 230n1
Garland, David, 31, 122, 131, 143, 159, 207n10
    The Culture of Control, 31, 130, 143
Garside, Richard, 143
German idealism, 23n7
Germany, 267
    and the use of measures, 189, 207n15
    perception of lenient sentencing in, 102
Geske, Janine, 81n6
Giddens, Anthony, 131, 135, 136, 141, 142, 149, 266, 269
    manufactured uncertainty, 142
    ontological security, 266
    Third Way theory, 131, 135, 136, 141, 142, 143, 144
Golash, D., 104, 106

Gomez-Jara Diez, Carlos, 81n5, 151n15, 162
Graham v. Florida, 161
Greece, ancient, 165n1
Groenhuijsen, M. S., 207n7
Guardian, 22n3
guilt
  accessorial, 11
  assumption of, 152n29
  and blame, 15, 190, 191
  as culpable blameworthiness, 15, 89, 193
  false positives and, 208n45
  mens rea and, 69, 174, 185, 227
  pleading, 18, 76, 104, 122, 216, 217, 220, 237
  proportionality and, 206
  punishment of, 8, 43n5, 47, 61, 64, 65, 66, 69, 79, 81n1, 189, 190, 203
  questioning, 7
Gwin, J., 104

"Hampstead liberals", 22n3
Hampton, Jean, 8–9
Hansard, 150n1
hard labor
  See labor, hard
"hard treatment", 34, 36, 37, 40, 47, 57, 60n31, 77, 78, 82nn22, 25, 93, 238, 244, 251n1
  burdensome, 77, 78
  deserved, 40, 55, 56
  threatened, 38
  See also punishment, burdensome
harm, 6, 10, 15, 38, 39, 61nn34, 38, 56, 61nn34, 38, 67, 68, 69–77, 78, 79, 81n12, 82n15, 92, 95, 96, 103, 109, 113, 115, 116, 117, 123nn5, 7, 8, 10, 158, 160, 161, 162, 163, 165n7, 10, 173, 174, 175, 176, 181, 184, 185, 186, 188, 191, 192, 193, 202, 208n29, 219, 226, 227, 228, 229, 231n27, 240, 246, 247, 252n5, 7, 253n 17, 257, 263, 264, 265, 266, 267, 268, 269, 270, 272n18
  from fear, 269
  intentional, 269
  risk of from drug use, 227–228, 240, 252n5
Harman, Gilbert, 61n36
Harmelin v. Michigan, 230n6
Harris, A. J., 201
Hart, H. L. A, 8, 21, 34–35, 38, 43n5,

59nn13, 15, 60n25, 64, 200, 208n32, 209n43
  definitional stop, 200, 208nn30, 32, 41, 43
  Punishment and Responsibility, 34
Harte, J., 209n41
Hastings, James, 58n5
Hawkins, G., 253n24, 272n8
Hayek, F. A., 141, 142, 151n16
Hegel, G. W. F., 4, 22nn1, 2, 36, 92
Hevelke, Alexander, 271
Heyman, Gene M., 230n14
Hildebrand, M., 193
Hobbes, Thomas, 131, 142, 148, 151n22
  Leviathan, 145, 146, 147, 150
Holland
  See Netherlands
homicide, vehicular, 15, 123n7, 124n20
Honderich, T., 208n30
Hörnle, Tatjana, 271n2, 272n6
Hough, Mike, 105, 123, 123n10
House of Lords
  See England
Hulsman, L. H. C., 81n7, 189
Hurd, H. M, 165n7
Hurka, Thomas, 61n36
Husak, Douglas N., 14, 58, 67, 214–233, 234, 238, 239, 240, 244, 252nn5, 7, 260, 272n6
Hutton, N., 107

imprisonment, 19, 23n14, 50, 51, 93, 159, 161, 190, 191, 193, 194, 197, 200, 202, 209n46, 215, 221, 243, 252n14, 257, 268, 291
  and restorative justice, 55
  for life, 115, 124n16, 185
  for public protection (IPP), 130–154, 260
  rate of, 21
  See also detention; incapacitation; incarceration; rate of imprisonment
incapacitation, 8, 9. 48, 49, 54, 102, 131, 137, 139, 150n4, 156, 158, 160, 161, 162, 163, 164, 165n4, 169, 170, 175, 190, 191, 193, 194, 197, 198, 199, 202, 203, 204, 205, 208n24, 250, 261, 262, 263, 272n13
  selective, 197, 207n24
  See also detention; imprisonment; incarceration

incapacitation (*continued*)
incarceration, 46, 138, 198, 250, 251
  alternatives to, 257
  and drug courts, 234, 235, 238, 242, 243,
    245, 246, 248, 249, 250, 251, 252n14
  as punishment, 93, 198
  Committee for the Study of
    Incarceration, 47
  for nonserious crimes, 175
  mass, 160, 177
  of drug-addicted offenders, 195, 208n28
  period of, 132
  proportionate to preventative necessity, 140
  vast scale of in U. S., 159, 160, 215, 218,
    228
Independent Safeguarding Authority
  See England
injustice, 39, 43, 132, 133
  distributive, 42
  retributive, 224, 226
International Network on Therapeutic
  Jurisprudence, 230n10
interventions, nonpunitive
  See sentencing policies, nonpunitive
    interventions

Jakobs, Gunther, 81n5, 140–141, 144,
    151n15, 161, 165n14
Janus, Eric S., 253n25
Jareborg, Nils, 115, 272n6
jurisprudence, therapeutic
  See justice, therapeutic, International
    Network on Therapeutic Jurispru-
    dence
jury nullification, 82n21
just deserts
  See desert
justice, 37, 89, 156, 206
  actuarial, 191, 207n10
  by geography, 16, 17–18
  community, 3, 22
  concept of, 165n6
  criminal, 5, 7, 14, 23n7, 40, 41, 103, 141,
    191, 192, 198, 205
    limits on, 103
    misused in drug cases, 228
  distributive, 41, 43
  individual, 205
  preventive, 67
  punishment and, 22n2, 33, 36, 38
  Rawls on, 31, 32

restorative, 3, 4, 10, 14, 16, 17, 18, 21,
    46, 47, 50, 55, 56, 57, 58n3, 61n37,
    63, 67, 68, 69, 73, 74, 76, 78, 79, 80,
    189, 208n29, 235, 249, 250, 251,
    253nn22, 23, 260
    community conferencing, 250
    shaming sanctions, 249
  retributive, 43, 67
  system, legitimacy of, 110–111
  therapeutic, 9, 37, 41, 67, 82n26, 215,
    216, 217, 222, 229, 230n9
    as a less expensive option, 218
    See also International Network on
      Therapeutic Jurisprudence
juvenile courts
  See courts, juvenile

Kamin, Sam, 253n24, 272n8
Kansas v. Hendricks, 22n4
Kant, Immanuel, 4, 22nn1, 2, 32, 36, 43, 64,
    65, 91, 162
  Kantian philosophy, 173
  neo-Kantian, 31, 43n2, 162
  Perpetual Peace, 165n15
  "principle of equality", 20
Kaplow, Louis, 230n2
Kelk, C., 199, 200, 206n2
Kleinig, John, 8, 23n6, 46–62, 82nn16, 23,
    88, 89, 208n30, 260, 272n6
Knapp, Kay, 23n9, 272nn11, 12
Knight, D., 105
Kolber, Adam, 20, 21, 24n19, 60n26
Kooijmans, T., 208n34
Kristol, I., 151n17
Ku Klux Klan, 59n21
labor, hard, 59n17
Lacey, Nicola, 150
Lappi-Seppälä, Tapio, 272n6
Latin America, 161, 162
law, 38, 39, 40, 41, 43, 52, 53, 59n15, 61n34,
    64, 105, 112, 136, 151nn9, 20, 23,
    24, 159, 160, 268
  abiding, 64, 65, 108, 146, 147, 162, 269
  and censure, 34
  and order, 22n31, 59, 131, 143, 159, 178
  case, 181
  citizen, 144
  civil preventive orders, 148
  Common, 15
  Constitutional, 165n8, 183
  criminal, 7, 8, 15, 33, 67, 68, 69, 70, 71,

72, 74, 76, 77, 79, 80, 81nn11, 13,
14, 82n18, 109, 111, 114, 119, 134,
140, 141, 144, 148, 158, 161, 178,
165nn11, 14, 15, 178, 227, 236,
239, 251n3, 260, 261, 261, 265,
266, 267, 268, 269, 270–271
Dutch, 188, 189, 192, 200, 201, 203,
207nn8, 17, 19, 208n27
enemy, 145, 147, 152n27, 162
theory of, 261
dangerous offender, 5, 12–13
domestic criminal, 81n14
drug, 4, 9, 11, 48, 178
decriminalization of, 219, 228
enemy criminal, 144, 147, 148, 161,
165n14
gay marriage, 6
imprisonment for public protection
(IPP), 145, 148
international criminal, 81n14
LWOP, 5, 9, 11–12, 169, 170
mandatory minimum, 5, 10, 11–12, 21,
169, 170, 250
martial, 145
moral appeal of, 38
natural, 23n7, 179
of self-defense. 183
penal, 146, 147, 219, 229
persistent offender (United Kingdom),
206
reproof of, 271
rule of, 15, 145, 147 230, 270
sentencing, 9, 18, 21, 22n2, 101, 110,
111, 121, 122, 197, 124n11, 247,
250, 260
sexual violent predator (SVP), 3, 4,
12–13, 206
source-of, 181
three-strikes, 3, 4, 5, 9, 10, 11–12, 18, 37,
108, 169, 170, 250, 253nn24, 25,
257, 272n8
tort, 56
traffic, 38
victims' rights, 185
See also American Law Institute; Australian Law Reform Commission; laws,
drug; Independent Safeguarding
Authority (England); Lord Justice
Laws; New Zealand Law Commission; sentencing laws
Lawrence v. Texas, 251n3

legitimacy, 18, 61n34, 82n29, 110, 114,
117, 205
and compliance, 110–111
lack of, 113
normative, 157
political, 157
of censuring power, 112
of punishment, 110, 113, 117, 141, 174,
189
of justice system, 110–111, 122
of legal defenses, 114
of sentencing, 110, 112, 117, 121,
124n20
political, 157
sociological, 157
Leiden Workshop, 58, 81, 123, 150, 230
Future of Punishment Workshops, 230
Leviathan
See Hobbes, Thomas
Lewis, C. S., 5, 13
Lex talionis, 49
liberalism, 131, 144, 145, 146, 147
advanced liberal, 144
atomistic, 144
neoliberalism, 130, 131, 141, 142, 144
post-liberalism, 144
life without parole laws (LWOP)
See sentencing laws
Limbaugh, Rush, 217
Loader, Ian, 133
Locke, John, 49, 59n14, 60n27, 145,
151nn20, 21
Second Treatise of Civil Government, 49
Lockyer v. Andrade, 22n4
Lord Justice Laws, 134
Lovegrove, A., 125n31
Lu, Hong, 252n10
Luna, Erik, 81, 230, 253n22
LWOP (life without parole)
See sentencing laws
Lynch, J., 104

MacCoun, Robert J., 231n26
Major, John, 141
mandatory minimum law
See sentencing laws
Manson, Allan, 117
Markel, Dan, 21, 82n24
Marshall, Sandra E., 82n15, 151n13,
231n27
Martinson, Robert, 58n6, 59n9

Masur, Jonathan, 60n26
Matravers, Matt, 30–45, 43, 81n8
measures
    as used in Holland, 188–213
merit, 48, 52, 58n5, 197, 208n27, 231n29
    model, 99n3
Michael, Jerome, 8, 164n1
Michie, C., 208n43
Miethe, Terance D., 252n10
Mill, John Stuart, 56, 151n21
Minnesota, 16, 23
    guidelines for sentencing, 23n9, 257, 258,
        271n4
Miranda rights, 165n10
misdemeanors, 7
Miss Universe contest, 52
mixed theories, 32, 34–36
Model Penal Code, 7, 23n7
"modified just deserts"
    See desert
Moerings, M., 201, 208n44
Montesquieu, 151n21
Moore, Michael, 9, 32, 33, 36, 43n6, 165n7
    intuitionist theory, 32, 33
moral responsibility
    See responsibility, moral
morality, 5, 52, 70, 236
    as distinguished from ethics, 60n25
    conventional, 60n25
    critical, 60n25
    of treatment plans, 6
    personal, 119
    traditional, 142
Morgan, R., 5, 107
Morris, Herbert, 8, 9, 58n8
Morris, Norval, 5, 8, 9, 15, 202, 209nn38,
    39, 258, 259
Mother Teresa, 60n23
Muller, N., 207n7
Murphy, Jeffrey, 8

natural law
    See law, natural
National Academy of Sciences, 23n11
National Drug Control Strategy, 231n21
Neocleous, Mark, 145, 151n21
neoliberalism
    See liberalism
Netherlands, 12
    bifurcated system of sanctions (punish-
        ments and measures), 188–213,

207n13, 260, 261, 262–264
    discontinuity of, 264, 266
compensation order, 192
conferences of penal theorists, 259
confiscation of illegally obtained profits,
    192
definitions of punishments and measures,
    208n34
Dutch criminal code, 188, 190, 190, 190
    table 10.1, 192, 195, 201, 207n5,
    208n17
Dutch Supreme Court, 190, 197, 203,
    207n4
entrustment order (TBS), 189, 191,
    192 table 10.1, 193–195, 196 fig.
    10.1, 199, 200, 201, 203, 204, 206,
    207nn8, 14, 15
    and psychiatric reports, 208nn19, 21,
    22
    average length of TBS: 1990–2008,
    197 fig. 10.3, 208n21
    four-year upper limit, 208n18
    number of persons in TBS, 1990–
    2008: 196 fig. 10.2
    number of TBS measures imposed and
    terminated, 1990–2008: 196 fig.
    10.1, 208n22
estimating probability of violence,
    209n42
"forced care", 193, 194
hospitals for the insane, 201, 209n36
hybrid model, 189, 190, 193, 200, 201–2
insane, special arrangements for, 190
maximum punishments, 208n17
Modern School, 190, 191, 193, 207n7
persistent offenders, 202, 208n26
protection measures, 189, 192, 199, 200,
    201, 202, 203, 204, 205, 206, 261,
    262, 263, 264
public safety, 188, 191, 193, 194, 195,
    207n9
punishments, 190, 192 table 10.1, 193,
    199, 201, 201n13, 262
    accessory, 207n6
    and measures, 201, 206, 207n13,
    208nn32, 34
    maximum, 208n17
    related to sanctions, 188
recidivism, 195, 198, 203, 204 table 10.2,
    209n43
risk assessment, 195, 198, 202, 204, 205,

206, 209nn41, 43
sanctions, 188, 190, 190–192, 192 table
    10.1, 193, 197, 200, 201, 203, 205,
    206
selective incapacitation, 195, 208n24
sentencing under Dutch law, 188, 189,
    190, 192, 199, 207n6
  indeterminate sentencing for public
    protection (IPP), 206
  "strip-them act", 292, 207n12
  treatment of habitual addicted offenders
    (ISD), 191, 195, 198, 199, 202, 203,
    204, 206, 207n11, 208nn23, 27, 28,
    35, 272nn13, 14
    cannot be imposed on top of a prison
      sentence, 208n25
    number of SOV, then ISD measures
      imposed: 2001–2008, 199 fig. 10.4,
      208n26
  withdrawal from circulation, 191
Neumann, Franz, 147
New Labour
  See England
New York State
  Bosket case, 109
New Zealand
  desert-oriented sentencing aims, 257
  Law Commission, 125n25
  public opinion and penal policies in,
    108
  proportionate sentencing schemes in,
    272n9
Nolan, James L., 222–223, 230n4, 241,
    252nn10, 11, 16
norms,
  about right and wrong, 23n10
  community behavioral, 10, 111, 259
  ethical, 258
  of criminal law, 144, 258
  of justice, 234
  legal, 144, 191, 257
  macropublic, 56
  proportionality, 234, 257
  republican, 140
  sentencing, 262
  socially sanctioned, 48, 56, 110
  to be observed, 53
  transgression of, 54
Norrie, A. W., 82n17
"nothing works", 23n11, 58n6, 59n9, 64, 86,
    99, 218

Obama, Barack, 160, 165n10
"obligatory crime objection", 95, 96, 97, 98,
    99n6
offenders
  and Dutch law, 200
  and fellowship with sentencer, 250
  and freedom to remain unpersuaded, 244
  and future crimes, 12, 15
  and proportionality, 35, 41, 190, 244
  and rehabilitative programs, 13
  culpability of, 121, 190
  dangerous, 12, 130–154
  deterrence of potential, 121, 170, 183
  drug-dealing, 221
  drug-dependent, 12, 208n28, 222,
    230n12, 234
  eligibility for drug court, 248, 248
  expectations of, 33
  first, 11
  habitual, 12, 202
  outlaw theories, 11
  property, 12, 248, 253
  punishment of, 59n15
  rights of 179–185
  sentencing of, 109, 236
  sex, 9, 163
  violent, 194
Ohana, D., 151n15, 152n27
O'Hear, Michael M., 14, 81, 234–255, 260
Oregon
  guidelines for sentencing, 257, 271n4
Otto, M., 101

pain and suffering, 4, 50, 95, 96, 97, 188,
    202
  from punishment, 59, 66, 68, 69, 94, 95,
    188, 192, 193, 199, 200, 202, 203,
    205, 206
  unintended, 202
parens patrie rationale, 7
Parker, H., 105
parole, 6, 7, 9, 24n14, 105, 170, 177, 179
  board, 7, 23n7, 130, 132, 133, 134
  eligibility for, 130, 132, 133, 134
  grant rates, 108
  hearings, 104
  LWOP sentences, 4, 161, 169, 177
  See also Wells v. Parole Board
parsimony, 3, 4, 5, 7, 14, 93, 137, 141, 177
Pasek, Justine, 52, 60n22
  See also Miss Universe contest

Peay, Jill, 150
penalties
　See punishment; sanctions; sentencing
　　laws; sentencing policies
penalty scale, 35, 36, 258
　desert-based, 58n7
perjury, 24n18, 116
Persson, I., 99n3
Pettit, Philip, 151nn11, 12
　republican penal theory, 131, 137–140
Plato, 164n1
plea bargains, 216, 230n8
pleasure and pain, 88, 89, 90, 92
post-desert
　See desert
Pound, Roscoe, 101
premeditation, 119, 124n21
Prendergast, Michael, 231n30
Prentky, Robert A., 253n25
prevention of crime
　See crime, prevention of
prison, 225
　as sanction, 163
　conditions, 105, 203
　drug users and, 219, 225, 243, 253
　hazards of, 181
　inmates becoming more crime-prone,
　　177
　population, increase in, 123, 130, 132
　release from, 104, 203
　return of, 130, 131
　term, 93, 162, 169, 170, 177, 182, 183,
　　185, 191, 197, 201, 202, 208n17,
　　247, 257, 262
　　conditional, 191
　　followed by a TBS measure, 193, 195,
　　　197, 201, 208n15
　　followed by civil confinement, 201
　U. S., 60, 250
probation, 7, 10, 78, 198, 235, 237, 242,
　　248, 249, 269
　aims of, 78
　as burdensome punishment, 82n25
　behavioral report, 197
　choice of, 203, 204
　case-by-case, 3, 249
　officers, 16, 19
proportional sentencing
　See proportionality
proportionality, 3, 4, 5, 7, 8, 9, 10, 11, 14, 19,
　　23nn10, 12, 13, 37–40, 41, 43, 50,

51, 53, 60, 114, 115, 120, 140, 175,
　176, 183, 194, 206, 207, 214–229,
　230nn1, 3, 234, 237, 256, 257, 258,
　271
　against, 41, 42
　analyses of, 230n1
　and crime seriousness, 114
　and desert, 35, 48, 197, 198, 201, 205,
　　261, 262, 264, 265, 266
　and dual-track systems, 216
　and the drug court movement, 214–233,
　　234, 235, 240, 243–244, 247, 248,
　　249
　and measures, 197, 199
　backward-looking, 67
　cardinal, 35, 36, 39, 226, 243, 245
　components of, 114
　desert-based, 262
　deviations from, 230n16
　future victims and, 176
　in Dutch law, 190, 194, 197, 199, 206,
　　207
　in sentencing, 35, 60nn26, 31, 113, 121,
　　123n10, 188, 190, 197, 257, 259
　linked to retributivism, 21, 23n7, 37, 42,
　　120, 174, 220, 230n6
　negative, 237, 244
　ordinal, 35, 36, 39, 115, 116, 243, 244,
　　245, 260
　positive, 237
　requirements of, 208n29
　severity of harm to victims, 174, 175
　utilitarian conception of, 174
　See also courts, drug; desert
public opinion, 11, 123n2, 157, 158, 160
　and consequentialism, 105
　and response to crime, 73, 118n24
　and retributivism, 105
　and sentencing, 101–122, 125n27
　　as a source of punitiveness, 108–109
　　ensuring effective censure, 112–113
　　legitimacy-compliance link, 110–112
　　public ignorance of, 107–108
　　unprincipled attitudes to, 109
　　volatility of views, 109–110
　at bail or parole hearings, 104
　direct importation model, 104, 118
　exclusionary model, 103–104
　research and polls, 105, 106, 157
　ways of measuring, 103, 10–106, 157
punishment

alternative, 11, 220, 238
anchor theory, 92–93
and freedom to remain unpersuaded,
   237, 244–245
and sanctions, in the Netherlands,
   188–213
as a deterrent, 5, 9, 22n2, 36, 38, 47, 55,
   65, 89, 108, 121, 123n3, 132, 169,
   170, 174, 175, 176, 177, 178, 182,
   190, 191, 250, 258, 262
as expressive, 82n24
as secular penance, 80, 236, 240–242,
   250
burdensome, 60n31, 66, 67, 69, 77, 78,
   79, 80, 82n25, 241, 245, 257
capital, 9, 11, 21, 182
communicative theory of, 34, 54, 78, 79,
   82n25, 119, 234–255, 271
consequentialism and, 6–10, 23n7, 12,
   24n14, 30–43, 43n2, 64, 65, 66, 67,
   86, 87, 88, 99, 150n4
crime-preventative, 5, 13, 64, 86, 93,
   172, 175, 258, 259, 261, 266,
   270
desert considerations and, 8, 30–43,
   47–55, 60n23, 86–101
disparity, 178, 215, 216, 220, 221, 223,
   224, 252n16
   due to geographic location, 17
   in drug courts, 221–233, 238
fair play theory, 32, 33
fitting the offense, 20, 22, 236–237,
   242–243, 261
future of, 21–22, 43, 101–122, 274
imprisonment for public protection
   (IPP), 130–150
in theory, 40–42, 58
incapacitative, 3, 13, 19, 161, 263, 265, 272
leniency in, 96
mixed theory, 34–36
Model Penal Code, 7
non-punitive, 8, 77, 81n8
parsimony, 3–4, 5, 14, 93, 137, 141, 177
policies and practices of, 3, 6, 10, 11, 14,
   16, 22n5
prior offenses and, 11, 18–19, 103, 106,
   118, 119, 163, 170, 184
purpose of, 77–81
Rawlsian theory and, 31, 36, 43nn1, 2,
   171–178, 184, 186, 260
restorative justice and, 14, 15, 16, 46,

   56–57, 61n37
   retributivism and, 3, 4, 7–8, 20, 24n19,
     36–37, 43n5, 58n4, 63–81, 81n1, 87
severity of, 7, 16, 22n4, 68, 92–93
   ranking of, 214, 258
state, future of, 101–129
terror, used as, 155–168
theories of, 19–21, 22nn1, 2, 40–42
utilitarianism and, 8
   desert-adjusted utilitarianism and,
     86–101
See also abolitionism; CHANGE pro-
     gram; consequentialism; desert;
     labor, hard; incapacitation; "nothing
     works"; proportionality; public
     opinion; retributivism

quarantine, civil, 263, 264
   compared to Dutch punishments and
     measures, 263

R (McCann) v. Manchester Crown Court,
   151n10
Ramsay, Peter, 12, 15, 81, 130–154, 261,
   266, 267, 268, 271
rate of imprisonment, 21
Rawls, John, 8, 31, 32, 33, 35, 36, 40, 41,
   43nn1, 2, 48, 59n10, 60n27, 89,
   165n6, 170, 184, 186
   A Theory of Justice, 31
   Rawlsian theory, 31, 171–178, 260
recidivism, 10, 11, 13, 16, 18–19, 23, 118,
   119, 121, 125nn22, 23, 194, 197,
   203, 204 table 10.2, 208,n43,
   231n20, 251n2, 269
   estimate of, 198
   reduction in, 251
Reese, Erin, 252n10
reformatories, 7
Reagan, Ronald, 31, 36
rehabilitation, 4, 8, 13–14, 17, 21, 23n7, 47,
   48, 49, 59n9, 64, 67, 102, 104, 199,
   217, 218, 219, 220, 236, 257, 258,
   261, 269, 270
reintegration, 14, 56
   See also justice, restorative
"relational theory of blame", 82n17
Remmelink, J., 206n2
   See sentencing policies, remorse of offender
     and
   68, 74, 77, 78, 79, 80, 192, 236, 248

reparation *(continued)*
  apology as, 79, 236
  moral, 80
Resnik, Judith, 160
responsibility, 46, 63–81, 82nn17, 18, 136,
     151n18, 164, 247, 253n21, 261,
     265, 271
  moral, 46, 267
  See also contributory negligence
restitution, 50, 55, 56, 58n3, 60n30, 61n38,
     77, 192
  See also justice, restorative
restoration, 57, 63–81
  less radical, 68
  radical, 68
  See also justice, restorative
retributivism, 3, 4, 7, 8, 9, 13, 14, 15, 16, 17,
     19, 20, 21, 22, 23nn6, 7, 24n19, 30,
     31, 32, 33, 34, 35, 36, 37, 43, 43nn1,
     3, 57, 58n4, 63–81, 81n1, 91, 99n1,
     99n7, 102–103, 104, 105, 106–107,
     114, 115, 118, 119, 120, 121,
     123nn4, 5, 124n21, 132, 140, 155,
     160, 162, 164, 166n16, 173, 174,
     189, 203, 208n46, 209n46, 214,
     216, 224, 226, 229, 230n3, 231n16,
     235, 244, 256, 259, 260, 261
  ancient philosophers and, 165n1
  and drug court movement, 214–233, 235
  continued vitality of, 259
  exceptional deviations from, 87
  limiting, 9, 66, 87, 99n1, 184, 258, 259
     260
  negative form of, 64, 87
  objections to, 256
  postretributivism, 86, 99
  rank ordering of crimes and punish-
     ments, 163, 166nn16, 17
  rejection of public input at sentencing,
     106–107
  relaxed theories of, 87, 99n1
  revival of, 33, 36, 37, 41, 42, 43, 63, 64,
     65, 66, 81
  robust, 63, 69, 77, 80
  weaknesses of, 63, 80
  See also sentencing theories
Reuter, Peter, 231n26
"right to punish", 59n14
  See also Locke, John
Ristroph, Alice, 15, 151n22, 155–168
Rivera, Zuleyka, 52

See also Miss Universe contest
Roberts, Chief Justice John, 165n12
Roberts, Julian V., 13, 101–129, 124n17,
     125n27, 272nn5, 6, 10
Robinson, Paul H., 81n3, 110, 111, 112,
     157, 165n5
Robinson v. California, 252n9
Rosenthal, John Terrence, 241
Rossi, P., 124n19
Routledge Encyclopedia of Philosophy, 58
Ryberg, Jesper, 23n6, 58, 86–100, 99n4,
     103, 112, 113, 124n18

Sadurski, Wojciech, 58n8
sanctions, 12, 14, 112, 113, 161, 163, 215,
     220, 222, 231n17, 234, 252nn10,
     15, 16, 258, 263, 268
  backup, 243, 245, 250, 251
  criminal, 114, 201, 206, 234, 238, 262,
     271
  Dutch bifurcated system of, 188–213
  graduated, 238, 242, 243, 245, 248, 250
  "neutral", 271
  noncustodial, 257
  penal, 113, 262
  proportionate, 256
  punitive, 14, 219
  shaming, 249
  See also justice, restorative
sanctuary, compulsory, 81n9
Sandel, Michael, 141
Scalia, Justice Antonin, 230n6
Scandinavia, 18, 19, 21, 23n10
Scanlon, Tim, 32, 43n2
  The Desert Thesis, 32
Scheffler, Samuel, 43n1
Schmitt, Carl, 165n14
Schorscher, Vivian, 271
Schünemann, Bernd, 271n2, 272n6
Schuyt, Pauline M., 207
Scotland
  perception of lenient sentencing in, 102
Secretary of State for Justice v. James, 134
security, 130, 131, 133, 136, 137, 145, 146,
     147, 150n3, 151n21, 159, 160, 161,
     165n15, 175, 191, 192, 267, 269
  medium prison, 19
  of victims, 130
  objective, 133, 137
  ontological, 135, 136, 206, 269
  personal, 14

public, 131–159
right to, 133–135, 141, 142, 144, 149,
    150, 158
subjective, 133, 137, 138, 140
supermaximum prison, 19
threats to, 131
sentencing laws
    dangerous offender, 3, 5, 12–13, 15,
        24n15, 42, 81n3, 131, 133, 134,
        136, 137, 138, 139, 140–141, 143,
        146, 150n4, 151n9, 156, 158, 159,
        160, 161, 162, 163, 164, 185, 191,
        193, 205, 206, 209nn45, 46, 240,
        262, 266, 267
    death penalty, 11, 175, 182, 183, 185
    drug, 4, 9, 48
    incapacitative, 3, 12, 13, 19, 161, 263,
        265, 272n13
    life, 150n5
    LWOP (life without parole), 4, 5, 9, 10,
        11–12, 21, 161, 169, 170, 177, 178,
        183, 184, 185
    mandatory minimum, 3, 4, 5, 9, 10,
        11–12, 21, 42, 169, 170, 177, 202,
        250, 257, 271n4, 272n7
    maximum life imprisonment, 124n16
    sexual predator, 3, 4, 12–13, 22n4, 250
    three-strikes, 3, 4, 5, 9, 10, 11–12, 21, 37,
        108, 169, 250, 257, 250, 253nn24,
        25, 257, 272n8
    truth in sentencing, 9
sentencing policies
    alternative sanctions, 215
    coherence of, 112
    declining public confidence in, 124n11
    desert-based, 156, 173, 191, 193, 201,
        206, 256, 258, 259, 262, 271
    disparity of, 178, 220, 221, 223, 256
        in drug courts, 215, 216, 221, 224,
        225, 230n16, 252n16
    double jeopardy rule, 13, 107
    dual-track, 98, 188–213, 221–233,
        261–266, 271
    fear-prevention model, 261, 266–270,
        271
    geographical differences, 16, 17, 19
    hybrid approaches, 87, 97, 98, 189, 190,
        193, 200, 201, 202, 203, 206
    increase in severity of, 103, 215
    interventions, nonpenal, 26
    legitimacy of, 18, 82n29, 110–111, 112,

113, 117, 121, 122, 124n20, 174,
    189, 205
"legitimate sympathy" and, 117
leniency of, 96, 102, 121
measuring predicted dangerousness, 205,
    209nn45, 46
mitigation and, 118, 123n4
nonretributive, 66, 214, 259, 260
nonpunitive interventions, 261
ordinal rankings of offenses and, 116, 117
prior convictions and, 11, 18–19, 88,
    102–103, 106, 118, 119, 120, 122,
    124n13, 170, 176, 184, 217, 237,
    272n10
public confidence and, 111, 124n12
public education and, 122, 123n9
nonpenal interventions, 261
racial disparities in, 224
rank-order approach to, 163, 166nn16, 17
    numerical, 257, 258, 272n12
    statutory guiding principles and judi-
        cial review, 257, 258
remorse of offender and, 34, 71, 103, 118,
    119, 120, 121, 123n4, 124n13, 223
"tolerance for a lapse" and, 118
See also fear; imprisonment for public
    protection (IPP); proportionality;
    public opinion; retributivism; threats
sexual predator laws
    See sentencing laws
Shamir, R., 151n18
Sharp, F., 101
Shavell, Steven, 230n2
Sher, George, 47, 58n8
Shklar, Judith, 158, 160
Sidgwick, Henry, 58n4
Simester, Andrew P., 271, 272nn15, 19,
    21, 22
Simon, Jonathan, 207n10
Simons, K., 106, 123n6
Slobogin, C., 107
Smith, Adam, 151n21
South Africa
    perception of lenient sentencing in, 102
Stanford Encyclopedia of Philosophy, 58
State ex rel. Romelly v. Superior Court In and
    For County of Maricopa, 180–181
Steyn, Lord, 134, 151n10, 266
    See also sentencing policies, fear-preven-
        tion model
Straw, Jack, 22n3

Strickland, Judge Diane, 222
Strijards, G. A. M., 208n30
Stuntz, William, 165n8
Sweden
    statutory guiding principles for sentenc-
        ing, 257, 258
subjectivity, 19–21, 24
suffering
    See pain and suffering
Sullivan, E. Thomas, 230n1
Sunstein, Cass R., 182, 183, 185
Supreme Court, 5, 58
Sweden, 16

Tasioulas, J., 82n28
Taslitz, A., 111
Teresa, Mother
    See Mother Teresa
terror,
    desert and, 158–162
    used as punishment, 155–168
    war on, 159
terrorism, 67, 148,159
test
    alternate means, 4
    ends-benefit, 4
Thatcher, Margaret, 31, 36, 141, 151n16
therapeutic jurisprudence
    See justice, therapeutic
Third Way
    See Giddens, Anthony
threats, 38, 111, 140, 144, 147, 148, 155,
        159, 160, 161, 165, 250, 267–268,
        272nn17, 20
    See also fear
three-strikes laws
    See sentencing laws
Tonry, Michael, 3–29, 30, 33, 43n3, 123,
        143, 209nn45, 47, 49, 230, 259,
        271, 272nn7, 11, 12
trial, criminal, 76, 81, 82n20
training schools, 6
treatment, 48
    and resocialization, 198, 203
    behavioral, 198, 203
    coercive, 41–42, 234
    drug court, 231n18, 234
    correctional, 9–10
    regimes imposed by drug courts, 231n18,
        234, 237
    therapeutic professionals, 246

See also "hard treatment"
truncation, 20
Tyler, Tom, 111

Ulväng, Magnus, 272n6
United Kingdom
    See England; Wales
United States, 16, 18, 19, 21, 22, 65, 150n3
    desert development in, 155–168
    perception of lenient sentencing in, 102
    public knowledge of custody issues in,
        107
    sentencing policies
        after 2011, 165n9
        in the realm of criminology, 261
    Sentencing Commission, 120, 124n19
    Victim's Rights Amendment, 180, 181
    war on terror, 159
utilitarianism, 8, 99n1, 104, 172, 189, 203
    average, 172
    desert-adjusted, 86–101
    hedonistic, 88
    "mythological beast", 209n47
    unbridled, 206

value, 216
    fit model, 99n3
    intrinsic, 99n2
    merit model, 99n3
    monist, 87
    pluralist, 87
    transvaluation, 95, 99n6
values, 72
    Victorian, 141
van der Landen, D., 200, 207nn4, 7
van Hamel, G. A., 207n7
van Koppen, 105
van Kuijck, Y. A. J. M., 208nn22, 31
Vegter, P. C., 208nn22, 31
vehicular homicide
    See homicide, vehicular
Vermeule, Adrian, 182, 183, 185
"victim impact", 60
victim-offender mediation, 249
victims, 58, 115, 123n5, 124n20, 130, 235,
        268
    impact of crime and, 123n8
    potential future, 170, 179, 182, 185
    responsibility of, 74, 82n18
    rights of, 170, 179–185, 249
    See also evidence, victim-impact

vigilantism, 111
violence, domestic, 75, 115, 217
Virginia, 23
Virginia Criminal Sentencing Commission, 24
von Hirsch, Andreas, 9, 12, 15, 19, 23n9,
  33, 35, 36, 39, 81n3, 82nn24, 27,
  93, 107, 115, 118, 123n10, 125n30,
  139, 163, 165n7, 166n16, 179, 180,
  185, 208n24, 231n24, 256–274
von Hirsch, Andrew
  See von Hirsch, Andreas
Vruggink, J., 207n12
vulnerability, 146
  See also England, Safeguarding Vulnerable Groups Act

Wacquant, Loic, 131, 150nn2, 3
Wales, 19
 Home Office, 23
 imprisonment for the public protection
  (IPP), 130, 148, 150n5, 151n23,
  161, 206
 perception of courts being out of touch,
  102
 perception of lenient sentencing in, 102
 report of Lord Auld, 124n12
 Sentencing Advisory Panel, 120,
  125n126
 Sentencing Council for England and
  Wales, 125nn26, 27

tougher penal policies in, 108
Walker, Neil, 133
Walker, Nigel, 10, 23n12, 43n3, 208n30
Washington (State of), 11, 13, 23
Wasik, Martin, 272n6
Wechsler, Herbert, 7, 8
welfare, 31, 130, 136
 "positive welfare society", 137
Wells v. Parole Board, 134
Welsh, Brandon C., 230n11
Wexler, David, 230n9
Whitman, James Q., 230n5
Williams, B., 81n11
Wilson, James Q., 208n24, 262, 265
Winick, Bruce, 230n9
Winick, C., 123n2
Wisconsin, 81n6
Wong, David B., 61n36
Wootton, Barbara, 35, 69
wrongs, 71, 72, 74, 75, 82n15, 161, 241
 "mala in se", 81n13, 239, 240, 248
 "mala prohibita", 81n13, 239
 public, 75, 76, 236, 239–240, 246251n4
wrongdoing, 48–50, 53–55, 56–58, 59, 60,
  69, 71, 74, 76, 82n16, 163, 240
 moral, 59, 69

Young, Warren, 133
Zimring, Franklin E., 253n24, 272n8